COMPUTATIONAL APPROACHES TO ECONOMIC PROBLEMS

Advances in Computational Economics

VOLUME 6

The titles published in this series are listed at the end of this volume.

Computational Approaches to Economic Problems

edited by

Hans Amman

University of Amsterdam

Berc Rustem

Imperial College of Science, Technology and Medicine

and

Andrew Whinston

University of Texas

KLUWER ACADEMIC PUBLISHERS

DORDRECHT / BOSTON / LONDON

Library of Congress Cataloging-in-Publication Data

Computational approaches to economic problems / edited by Hans Amman, and Berç Rustem, and Andrew Whinston.
p. cm. -- (Advances in computational economics ; v. 6)
Includes index.
ISBN 0-7923-4397-2 (hb : alk. paper)
1. Econometrics--Congresses. I. Amman, Hans M. II. Rustem, Berc. III. Whinston, Andrew B. IV. Series.
HB139.C644 1997
330'.01'5195--dc21 96-54607

ISBN 0-7923-4397-2

Published by Kluwer Academic Publishers,
P.O. Box 17, 3300 AA Dordrecht, The Netherlands

Sold and distributed in the U.S.A. and Canada
by Kluwer Academic Publishers,
101 Philip Drive, Norwell, MA 02061, U.S.A.

In all other countries, sold and distributed
by Kluwer Academic Publishers Group,
P.O. Box 322, 3300 AH Dordrecht, The Netherlands

Printed on acid-free paper

Printed in the Netherlands

Table of Contents

Introduction to ACE Volume ix

List of Contributors xi

Part One:

Factor-GARCH Modeling of the Treasury Term Structure
Christopher F. Baum and Basma Bekdache 3

Analyzing a Small French ECM-Model
Jean-Louis Brillet 17

Wavelet Basis Selection for Regression by Cross-Validation
Seth A. Greenblatt 39

Computational and Inference in Semiparametric Efficient Estimation
Robert M. Adams, Allen N. Berger, and Robin C. Sickles 57

Generating Random Numbers in *Mathematica*
David A. Belsley 71

Linked-Cone Profit Ratio Estimates of U.S. Total Factor Productivity Growth, Using DEA/AR Methods
R. G. Thompson, E. A. Waltz, P. S. Dharmapala, and R. M. Thrall 79

Several Algorithms to Determine Multipliers for Use in Cone-Ratio Envelopment Approaches to Efficiency Evaluations in DEA
Kaoru Tone 91

Part Two:
Computational Methods in Finance

The Estimation of the Heath-Jarrow-Morton Model by Use of Kalman Filtering Techniques
Ramaprasad Bhar and Carl Chiarella 113

Neural Networks for Contingent Claim Pricing via the Galerkin Method
Emilio Barucci, Umberto Cherubini, and Leonardo Landi 127
Asset Liability Management
Diem Ho 143
An Efficient Parallel Implementation of a Lattice Pricing Model
Soren S. Nielsen 161
Projected Dynamical Systems for International Financial Policy Modeling and Computation
Anna Nagurney and Stavros Siokos 175
Monitoring Active Portfolios Using Statistical Process Control
Emmanuel Yashchin, Thomas K. Philips, and David M. Stein 193

Part Three: Computational Methods for a Social Environment

Ordering: Human versus Computer
Alfred Norman, Greg Leonard, Leigh Linden, Kara Meythaler, Kim Murray, Herb Newhouse, Nancy Tantzen, and Michael Ziegler 209
Strategic Uncertainty and the Genetic Algorithm Adaption
Jasmina Arifovic 225
Fluctuating Benefits and Collective Action
Bernardo A. Huberman 237
A Trade Network Game with Endogenous Partner Selection
Leigh Tesfatsion 249
Learning in a Computable Setting. Applications of Gold's Inductive Inference Model
Francesco Luna 271

Part Four: New Computational Methods

The Range Process in Random Walks: Theoretical Results and Applications
Pierre Vallois and Charles S. Tapiero 291
Numerical Analysis of a Monetary Overlapping Generation Model
Jenni X. Li 309
A Numerical Procedure to Estimate Real Business Cycle Models Using Simulated Annealing
Willi Semmler and Gang Gong 327

Part Five: Computational Methods – Networking and Software

The Internet: A Future Tragedy of the Commons?
Alok Gupta, Dale O. Stahl, and Andrew B. Whinston 347
The DUALI/DUALPC Software for Optimal Control Models
Hans M. Amman and David A. Kendrick 363

Introduction to ACE Volume

Computational Approaches to Economic Problems

This volume contains a selection of papers presented at the first conference of the Society for Computational Economics held at ICC Institute, Austin, Texas, May 21–24, 1995.

Twenty-two papers are included in this volume devoted to applications of computational methods for the empirical analysis of economic and financial systems; the development of computing methodology, including software, related to economics and finance; and the overall impact of developments in computing. The wide ranging contributions represented in the volume indicate the growing interest in the topic due to the increased availability of computational concept and tools and the necessity of analyzing complex decision problems.

The papers in this volume indicate the diversity of interest in the subject. It is hoped that this will motivate readers to further investigate the potential of computational methods and their applications.

The editors

List of Contributors

Robert M. Adams, Rice University, Houston, TX 77005, U.S.A.

Jasmina Arifovic, Department of Economics, Simon Fraser University, Burnaby, BC V5A 1S6, Canada

Hans Amman, Center for Applied Research in Economics, The University of Texas, Austin, TX, U.S.A.

Emilio Barucci, DIMADEFAS, Università di Firenze, Via C. Lombroso 6/17, 50134 Firenze, Italy
(E-mail: barucci@stat.ds.unifi.it)

Christopher F. Baum, Department of Economics, Boston College, Chestnut Hill, MA 02167, U.S.A.

Basma Bekdache, Department of Economics, Wayne State University, Detroit, MI 48202, U.S.A.

David A. Belsley, Department of Economics, Boston College, Chestnut Hill, MA 02167, U.S.A.

Allen N. Berger, Board of Governors of the Federal Reserve Systems, Washington, DC 20551, U.S.A.
and
Wharton Financial Institutions Center, Philadelphia, PA 19014, U.S.A.

Ramaprasad Bhar, School of Finance & Economics, University of Technology, Sydney, P.O. Box 123, Broadway, NSW 2007, Australia
(E-mail: r.bhar@uts.edu.au)

Jean-Louis Brillet, Département Etudes Economiques d'Ensemble, Institut National de la Statistique et des Etudes Economiques (INSEE), France

Umberto Cherubini, Ufficio Studi – Banca Commerciale Italiana, Via Borgonuovo 2, 20100 Milano, Italy
(E-mail: cherubini@telnetwork.it)

H. Amman et al. (eds.), Computational Approaches to Economic Problems, xi–xiv.

Carl Chiarella, School of Finance & Economics, University of Technology, Sydney, P.O. Box 123, Broadway, NSW 2007, Australia
(E-mail: c.chiarella@uts.edu.au)

P.S. Dharmapala, College of Commerce, Sultan Qaboos University, Oman

Gang Gong, Department of Economics, Graduate Faculty, New School for Social Research, 65 Fifth Ave., New York, NY 10003, U.S.A.

Seth A. Greenblatt, Chief Scientist, Betac International Corporation, 2001 N. Beauregard St., Alexandria, VA 22311, U.S.A.

Alok Gupta, Graduate School of Business, University of Texas, Austin, TX 78712, U.S.A.

Diem Ho, IBM Management Technologies Consulting Practice, EMEA Banking Finance and Securities, Bâtiment Rives de Seine, 68/76 Quai de la Rapée, 75592 Paris Cédex 12, France

Bernardo A. Huberman, Dynamics of Computation Group, Xerox Palo Alto Research Center, 3333 Coyote Hill Road, Palo Alto, CA 94304, U.S.A.

David A. Kendrick, Department of Economics, University of Texas, Austin, TX 78712, U.S.A.
(E-mail: kendrick@walras.eco.utexas.edu)

Leonardo Landi, Dipartimento di Sistemi e Informatica, Università di Firenze, Via S. Marta 3, 50139 Firenze, Italy
(E-mail: landi@aguirre.ing.unifi.it)

Greg Leonard, Department of Economics, University of Texas, Austin, TX 78712, U.S.A.

Jenny Li, Department of Mathematics, Penn State University, University Park, PA 16801, U.S.A.

Leigh Linden, Department of Economics, University of Texas, Austin, TX 78712, U.S.A.

Francesco Luna, Department of Economics, Università di Venezia "Ca' Foscari", 3246 Dorsoduro, 30123 Venice, Italy

Kara Meythaler, Department of Economics, University of Texas, Austin, TX 78712, U.S.A.

Kim Murray, Department of Economics, University of Texas, Austin, TX 78712, U.S.A.

Anna Nagurney, Department of Finance and Operations Management, University of Massachusetts, Amherst, MA 01003, U.S.A.
and
Department of Mathematics and Department of Infrastructure and Planning,

Royal Institute of Technology (KTH), S-100 44 Stockholm, Sweden

Herb Newhouse, Department of Economics, University of Texas, Austin, TX 78712, U.S.A.

Alfred Norman, Department of Economics, The University of Texas at Austin, Austin, TX 78712-1173, U.S.A.

Thomas K. Phillips, IBM Retirement Fund, 262 Harbor Drive, Stamford, CT 06904, U.S.A.

Willi Semmler, Department of Economics, Graduate Faculty, New School for Social Research, 65 Fifth Ave., New York, NY 10003, U.S.A.

R.C. Sickles, Rice University, Houston, TX 77005, U.S.A.

Stavros Siokos, Department of Industrial Engineering and Operations Research, University of Massachusetts, Amherst, MA 01003, U.S.A.

Dale O. Stahl, Department of Economics, University of Texas, Austin, TX 78712, U.S.A.

David M. Stein, IBM Retirement Fund, 262 Harbor Drive, Stamford, CT 06904, U.S.A.

Nancy Tantzen, Department of Economics, University of Texas, Austin, TX 78712, U.S.A.

Charles S. Tapiero, ESSEC, B.P. 105, 95021 Cergy-Pontoise, France

Leigh Tesfatsion, Department of Economics and Department of Mathematics, Iowa State University, Ames, IA 50011–1070, U.S.A.
(E-mail: tesfatsi@iastate.edu; http://www.econ.iastate.edu/tesfatsi/)

R.G. Thompson, Professor of Decision and Information Sciences (DISC), University of Houston, TX, U.S.A.

Kaoru Tone, Graduate School of Policy Science, Saitama University, Urawa, Saitama 338, Japan
(E-mail: tone@poli-sci.saitama-u.ac.jp)

R.M. Thrall, Professor of Administration and Noah Harding Professor of Mathematical Sciences, Emeritus, Rice University, Houston, TX 77005, U.S.A.

Pierre Valois, Département de Mathématiques, Université de Nanci I, B.P. 239, 54506 Vandoeuvre les Nancy Cédex, France

E.A. Waltz, University of Texas, School of Public Health, Houston, TX, U.S.A.

Andrew B. Whinston, Graduate School of Business, University of Texas, Austin, TX 78712, U.S.A.

Emmanuel Yashchin, Department of Mathematical Sciences, IBM T.J. Watson Research Center, Yorktown Heights, NY 10598, U.S.A.

Michael Ziegler, Department of Economics, University of Texas, Austin, TX 78712, U.S.A.

PART ONE

CHRISTOPHER F. BAUM AND BASMA BEKDACHE

Factor-GARCH Modeling of the Treasury Term Structure *

1. Introduction

In this paper, we test the multivariate model of securities' excess returns formulated by Engle et al. (1990) on an expanded set of maturities. By applying their methodology to the entire Treasury term structure, we consider the applicability of a parsimonious common factor approach to the dynamics of short-, medium-, and long-term interest rates. We extend their methodology to incorporate asymmetric GARCH representations, in which the slope of the yield curve (and its sign) affects the evolution of the conditional variance of excess returns in fixed-income and equity markets. We find this approach quite successful in explaining the comovements of excess returns on the spectrum of Treasury issues for the 1962–1992 period.

The paper is organized as follows. In the first section, we present some stylized facts about the postwar term structure, making use of Coleman et al.'s (1993) estimates of spot yields to construct holding period returns and excess returns *vis-à-vis* the return on a one-month security. We then present similar evidence on the series' second moments. In contrast to many studies which have focused solely on money-market yields, we consider the entire Treasury term structure, so that we may make inferences about the behavior of capital market rates, and the interactions between short- and long-term fixed income returns and equity returns. Section 3 presents an explicit model of the second moments of excess returns, applying the Factor GARCH specification of Engle et al.'s no-arbitrage term structure model (1990) to the entire Treasury term structure and equity returns. In the last section, we make some summary remarks.

* We acknowledge the comments of John Barkoulas and participants at the 1995 Conference of the Society for Computational Economics. The usual disclaimer applies.

H. Amman et al. (eds.), Computational Approaches to Economic Problems, 3–16.

2. Stylized Facts about the Postwar Term Structure of Treasury Rates

A very large proportion of empirical term structure models have been applied to the observable spot yields in the U.S. Treasury bill market – that is, yields for zero to 12 months' tenor discount bills, which are readily available from CRSP as the "Fama files." In this study, we consider the entire Treasury term structure – for bills, notes, and bonds – so that both money market and capital market returns may be modeled. We make use of a set of monthly estimates of Treasury market spot yields constructed from coupon securities' quotations by Coleman et al. (1993, CFI).

Our work is based on the spot yields for the 14 specific tenors analyzed by CFI for their sample period of 1955 through 1992,[1] transforming them into estimated one-month holding period returns.[2] We model excess return series, created by subtracting the annualized holding period return on a one-month Treasury from the holding period return for each longer tenor. Taking the one-month security (the shortest maturity reported by CFI) as the risk-free rate, the resulting excess return series show the compensation that has been earned, ex post, by those who have assumed the risks associated with holding longer maturity bonds. These excess returns are not necessarily increasing in tenor. We also consider the variance in these excess returns series, and how it is changing over time. A moving-window estimate of variance (with a window of 12 months' width) was calculated for each excess returns series. Analysis of these estimates reveals that the variability of excess returns increased dramatically in the 1980s when the Federal Reserve deemphasized interest rate targeting.

The correlations between excess returns on short-term securities and excess returns on longer-term securities vary considerably over the sample. One-, two- and five-year securities' excess returns were quite highly correlated to excess returns on the three-month security until the mid-1980s. Returns on the long-term (20 year tenor) security were much more weakly related to those on three-month bills, but vary from below 0.20 to nearly 0.60 over the period. In Figure 1, we present estimates of correlations between the three-month excess returns series and those of 12 months, 2 years, 5 years, and 20 years.[3] These movements suggest that excess returns are quite strongly interrelated at all tenors, reflecting the comovements of risk premia on the various tenors' yields, and lend further support to the concept of a common-factor-based modelling strategy.

These stylized facts about the postwar Treasury term structure suggest that a workable term structure model should explicitly consider time variation in the second moments of residual series as well as capture the interaction among tenors. The following section presents such a model in which we have implemented time variation in the second moments, as well as asymmetry

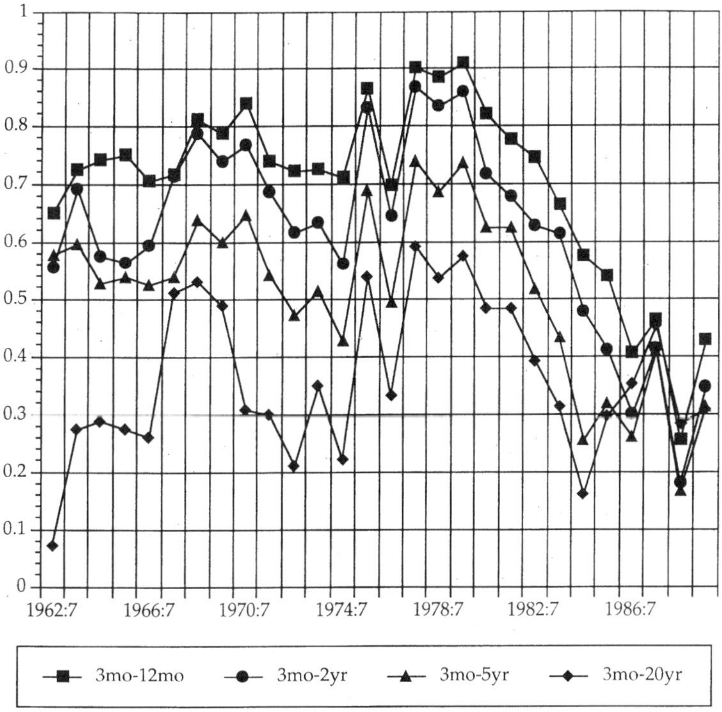

Note: simple correlations computed annually from 36 observations.

Fig. 1. Moving correlations among excess returns on Treasury securities.

in the modelled conditional variances, using the approach of Gourieroux and Monfort (1992).

3. Estimates of Factor-GARCH Models for the Treasury Term Structure

Term structure modelling has followed two broad strands of development: general equilibrium models, such as those pioneered by Cox et al. (1985), and no-arbitrage partial equilibrium models. In this paper, we consider a model of the latter genre, developed by Engle et al. (1990), and extend it to the consideration of the complete Treasury term structure rather than just its short end. In this framework, we consider whether time-varying volatility in asset returns is a meaningful determinant of excess returns in the medium and long-term sectors of the Treasury market. The term structure literature contains scattered evidence that conclusions drawn from Treasury bill data do not readily extend to the medium and long term sectors of the Treasury market.

For instance, Engsted and Tangaard (1994) extend the work of Hall, Anderson and Granger (1992) and study the cointegration properties of the term structure of interest rates, using 2-, 5-, and 10-year yields from McCulloch and Kwon's (1993) data. They find that the breakdown in the cointegrating relationship between short rates that occurs during the 1979–1982 Federal Reserve operating policy shift does not appear in the longer maturity term structure. This suggests that risk premia behave differently over the maturity structure, and that the explanation that term premia become nonstationary with a regime shift may not hold true for longer maturities.

Similar evidence is found in a study by Froot (1989), where survey data on interest rate expectations are used to study the relative importance of time-varying term premia and expectational errors in explaining rejections of the pure expectations theory. He finds that average expected excess holding period returns increase with maturity, and that term premia on long term bonds are more volatile than those of shorter tenors. Canova and Marrinan (1995) study excess returns on five-year securities generated by one- and three-month holding periods, and find that one- and three-month excess returns series have different statistical properties. They conclude that there are "nontrivial differences in the risk characteristics in agents investing at different maturities" (p. 64) and suggest that a segmented markets approach may be warranted.

Engle et al. (1990, henceforth ENR) argue that a multivariate approach to the modelling of asset returns is clearly justified, since even in static asset pricing models, the full covariance matrix of asset returns is required to derive estimates of a single asset's risk premium. The implication for dynamic modeling of the term structure becomes an empirical challenge, as allowing for temporal heteroskedasticity in this covariance matrix will imply, for instance, a very high dimensional multivariate ARCH model. If the number of assets is kept small, the ability to incorporate these cross-market effects is hindered; yet the number of time-varying covariances to be modelled grows rapidly with the number of assets. ENR deal with this dilemma by proposing the use of Engle's (1987) Factor-ARCH specification, which provides a parsimonious structure for the conditional covariance matrix of asset returns, rendering the problem tractable for a sizable number of assets. In this section, we sketch their approach, which we then apply to the full term structure of Treasury returns.

ENR model the N-vector y_t of asset excess returns as dependent on a mean vector μ_t and a time-varying covariance matrix H_t, where H is then expressed (ENR (1)) as

$$H_t = \sum_{k=1}^{K} \beta_k \beta_k' \lambda_{kt} + \Omega, \tag{1}$$

where K, the number of common factors driving the covariance matrix, is presumably much smaller than N, and Ω is an $N \times N$ positive semi-definite matrix. They illustrate that this model may be related to Ross' (1976) arbitrage pricing theory factor model. To implement the model, it is necessary to replace the unobservable factors λ_{kt} with measures of the conditional variances of some "factor-representing" portfolios of the assets, θ_{kt}, which are by construction perfectly correlated with the latent variables λ. In ENR's application to twelve maturities of Treasury bills and a stockmarket index, they choose two factors – an arbitrarily weighted bond portfolio and a pure stock portfolio – as sufficient, and apply a recursive representation where the stockmarket portfolio's excess returns are generated in a univariate model, but the bond portfolio's excess returns depend as well on the stockmarket portfolio's behavior.

3.1. Excess Returns for Treasury and Stockmarket Index Portfolios

We use the Coleman et al. (1993, henceforth CFI) yields to construct estimates of one-month holding period returns. Comparable returns on a diversified stock portfolio are derived from the CRSP value-weighted index for the NYSE/AMEX, which is first available in July 1962. Our sample for this section of the paper thus extends from that date through December 1992, the terminal point of CFI's study.

The one-month tenor in CFI's data is taken as an estimate of the riskless return, and excess return series for all tenors and the stockmarket index are constructed as the difference between their one-month holding period returns and the corresponding "riskless" return. Summary statistics for these one-month excess return series are given in Table 1. Mean excess returns are similar for the short- and medium-term tenors, but fall off sharply for 15 years, becoming negative at 20 years. Excess returns for the stockmarket index are almost four times larger, on average, than for any Treasury security. The variance of excess returns series grows markedly with maturity, surpassing that of the stockmarket index for the 15- and 20-year tenors. Treasury excess returns are positively skewed: sizably for the short-term tenors, but negatively for the stockmarket. All excess return series exhibit excess kurtosis, generally declining with tenor; the stockmarket series' kurtosis is smaller than that of any tenor. Significant serial correlation is found in almost every Treasury series, but is not present in either the stockmarket series or its square.

The last row of the table presents similar statistics for an equally-weighted portfolio of Treasury securities. Given the greater number of shorter maturities in the CFI data, this portfolio has a duration of 65 months, or almost 5.5 years. Mean excess returns for the Treasury portfolio are 8 basis points per month higher than the riskfree rate, which averages 46 basis points per month (5.66% per annum). The equally-weighted bond portfolio would yield, on average, 6.69% per annum, with a variance slightly less than that of a 48-month Treasury. The stock portfolio, by comparison, would yield 11.35% per annum (inclusive of dividends), with a variance more than five times higher than that of the equally-weighted bond portfolio.

TABLE 1

Descriptive statistics of excess returns series

Series	Mean	Variance	Skewness	Kurtosis	Q(12)	QSQR(12)
3 month	0.081	0.016	2.165	11.159	95.512	103.433
6 month	0.091	0.078	1.590	10.733	51.387	144.593
9 month	0.101	0.188	1.188	9.558	45.415	145.273
12 month	0.097	0.350	0.956	9.373	43.431	146.538
18 month	0.119	0.737	0.668	8.954	45.069	132.509
2 year	0.112	1.258	0.589	9.161	40.898	123.192
3 year	0.130	2.296	0.128	7.527	32.807	115.507
4 year	0.115	3.746	0.012	6.741	24.013	110.691
5 year	0.124	4.823	0.010	5.272	22.547	123.290
7 year	0.107	7.720	0.054	3.379	18.064	151.013
10 year	0.073	12.633	0.274	2.954	24.061	174.612
15 year	0.007	26.737	0.476	3.161	28.163	147.441
20 year	–0.103	41.007	0.041	2.969	23.879	107.062
VW stock	0.453	19.793	–0.330	2.269	12.304	14.069
EW bond	0.081	3.697	0.343	3.817	32.316	150.908

Notes: Q(12) is the Ljung-Box statistic for 12th order serial correlation in the excess returns series. QSQR(12) is the equivalent statistic for the squares of the excess return series. VW Stock is the value-weighted index of NYSE/AMEX equities. EWB is an equal-weighted portfolio of the Treasury tenors. Statistics are calculated over the monthly observations 1962:7–1992:12.

A natural question in considering a set of highly correlated assets such as Treasury securities of different tenors is the extent to which a small number of common factors are driving their prices and yields. To gauge this commonality, we followed ENR's approach and performed principal components analysis on the sample covariance matrix of the Treasury and stockmarket excess returns series. The largest eigenvalue explains 77% of the total variance, with the second explaining 14% and the third an additional 5%. Almost 97% of the total variance is explained by the first three principal components. Although the number of significant eigenvalues does not specifically indicate the number of dynamic factors appropriate for our model, it would appear that a two-factor model might be able to capture the behavior of the excess returns series.

3.2. Asymmetric GARCH Models of Portfolio Excess Returns

Following Engle et al. (1990, p. 223), we do not attempt to determine portfolio weights within the model, but rather specify weights for two factor-representing portfolios: an equally-weighted bond portfolio and a portfolio containing only the stockmarket index. As noted above, the set of tenors for Treasuries in our data imply that the equally-weighted bond portfolio will have risk characteristics approximately equal to a 5.5-year tenor security. In fitting a GARCH model to the portfolio excess returns series, we considered various asymmetric forms of the basic GARCH model. Other researchers (cf. Gourieroux and Monfort (1992)) have found support for asymmetries in either the mean equation or the conditional variance equation of the GARCH formulation. In the context of the factor-representing portfolios' excess returns, we might expect the conditional variance to respond differently to increases and decreases in risk. The estimates presented below are the outcome of a specification search over various forms of asymmetry.

In formulating a model for excess returns of the bond and stockmarket portfolios, we did not find support in the data for the GARCH-in-mean formulation used by ENR (p. 223), in which the conditional mean of each portfolio's excess return series depends only on its conditional variance. Specifications of the conditional mean that included (current or lagged) excess returns on the alternate portfolio were more successful. Our results also exhibit the "causality in variance" (ENR, p. 224), but in a different direction: making use of an asymmetric response coefficient, we find that the sign of lagged excess returns in the bond equation plays a significant role in each portfolio's conditional variance equation.

For the stockmarket portfolio, we found greatest support for a specification that includes lagged excess returns on the 20-year maturity "long bond." There appears to be meaningful asymmetry in the variance equation's intercept, depending on the sign of lagged excess returns on the bond portfolio. This asymmetry was captured by a dummy, D_{B240}, which takes on a value of unity when lagged excess returns on the bond portfolio are positive. Implementation of the GARCH(1,1) model for the stockmarket index portfolio via RATS' BHHH algorithm yields (standard errors in parentheses):

$$
\begin{aligned}
R_{\text{Stock}} &= \underset{(0.156)}{0.447} + \underset{(0.021)}{0.116} R_{B240_{t-1}} + u_{\text{Stock}}, \\
\theta_{\text{Stock}} &= \underset{(0.034)}{1.185} + \underset{(0.050)}{1.918} D_{B240_{t-1}} + \underset{(0.002)}{0.129} u^2_{\text{Stock}_{t-1}} + \underset{(0.009)}{0.798} \theta_{\text{Stock}_{t-1}}
\end{aligned} \tag{2}
$$

where R_{Stock} is the excess returns series for the stockmarket portfolio. The asymmetry in the variance equation suggests that the conditional variance, θ_{Stock}, increases markedly when bond excess returns have been positive: that is, when the yield curve is positively sloped. This is appealing, in that it

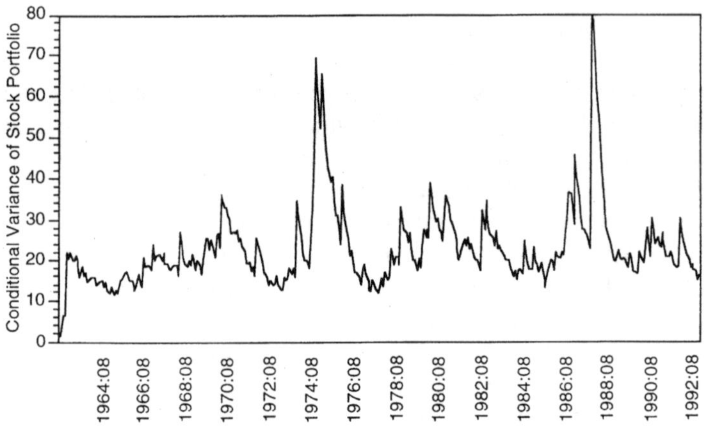

Fig. 2. Estimated conditional variance of stock portfolio.

suggests that a higher (lower) level of risk in the bond market – as reflected in higher (lower) term premia – will increase (decrease) volatility in the stockmarket, as the markets (and their respective derivative markets) act to equalize the "market price of risk" across fixed-income and equity venues.

The estimated model for the stockmarket index exhibits a strong interaction between lagged bond returns and current returns in the stockmarket. The persistence of the ARCH effect is quite strong in the variance equation. Ljung-Box Q statistics for 12 autocorrelations of the residuals and their squares are 9.22 and 19.32, respectively: both insignificant at the 5% level, indicating that the model appears to have captured the time-dependent aspects of the excess returns process. The coefficients of skewness and kurtosis of the residuals of -0.27 and 1.88 are both significant at the 95% level, suggesting that the variance equation exhibits some misspecification. The estimated conditional variance series, presented in Figure 2, illustrates the pattern in market volatility, with sizable increases in the mid-70s and at the time of the crash of 1987. With these two exceptions, the volatility of excess returns appears to have been relatively constant throughout the sample period.

Examination of a number of alternative specifications for the bond portfolio's conditional mean and variance equations led to a model of bond excess returns which included the contemporaneous excess returns of the stockmarket index. With a single lag in the variance equation, this GARCH(1,1) model yielded:

$$
\begin{aligned}
R_{\text{Bond}_t} &= \underset{(0.047)}{-0.037} + \underset{(0.013)}{0.064} R_{\text{Stock}_t} + u_{\text{Bond}}, \\
\theta_{\text{Bond}_t} &= \underset{(0.012)}{0.034} + \underset{(0.100)}{0.332} u^2_{\text{Bond}_{t-1}} - \underset{(0.073)}{0.169} D_{B240_{t-1}} \\
&\quad \cdot\; u^2_{\text{Bond}_{t-1}} + \underset{(0.053)}{0.787} \theta_{\text{Bond}_{t-1}}.
\end{aligned}
\tag{3}
$$

The conditional variance equation for the bond portfolio's excess returns also exhibited asymmetry, but the form of the asymmetry links the magnitude of the ARCH effect to the sign of lagged excess returns on the bond portfolio. The dummy D_{B240} is set to unity when lagged excess returns are positive; given the dummy variable's interaction with the lagged squared error, this suggests that a negative error (excess returns falling short of that predicted by the mean equation) will have a far larger effect on the conditional variance than a positive error (excess returns larger than that predicted by the mean equation). In short, bad news matters, and the arrival of bad news will drive up the conditional variance by almost twice as much as will an element of "good news" of the same algebraic magnitude.

The estimated excess returns of the bond portfolio exhibit a strong interaction effect with contemporaneous stockmarket returns, with sizable persistence in the conditional variance series. The conditional variance of the bond portfolio exhibits a highly asymmetric response to the sign of lagged bond returns. Q statistics for the residuals and for their squares of 32.36 and 144.69 are both highly significant, indicating that unexplained time dependence remains in the series. The residual series exhibits significant skewness (coefficient of 0.36) and kurtosis (coefficient of 4.12). Figure 3 presents the estimated conditional variance series for excess returns of the bond portfolio. In contrast to the stockmarket portfolio, this series reflects a marked shift following the Federal Reserve's move to monetary targeting in October 1979. The conditional variance remains several times higher than its pre-1979 value throughout the 1979–1982 period, and only in recent years does it drift downward to levels previously experienced.

In this model, the interactions between returns in the bond markets and the stockmarket capture investors' portfolio substitution behavior between these sectors of the capital markets. While ENR essentially modelled shifts between stocks and "cash," or very short-term Treasuries, we are able to consider longer-term fixed-income investments which possess substantial market risk.

3.3. A Dynamic Model of Treasury Term Structure Volatility

Estimation of the models presented above for excess returns of the equally-weighted Treasury portfolio and the stockmarket portfolio has yielded two

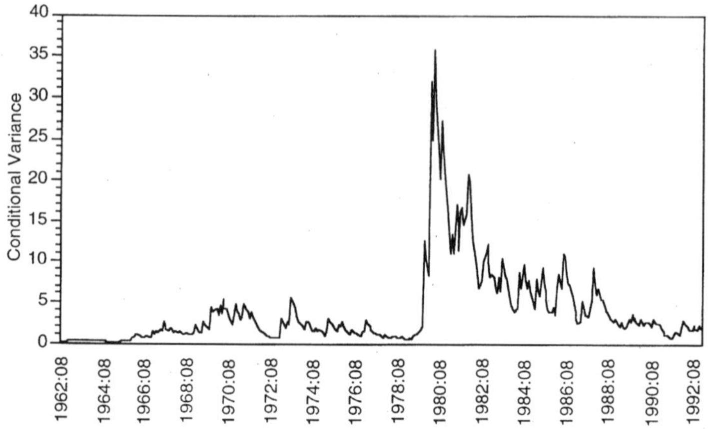

Fig. 3. Estimated conditional variance of equally-weighted Treasury portfolio.

series for each of those portfolios: the predicted excess returns and the estimated conditional variances. Following Engle et al.'s methodology, these estimated series are used as predetermined variables in our models for individual maturities of Treasury securities' excess returns and conditional variances. The structure of the model implies that the individual securities' excess returns should be driven by the returns and conditional variances of a small number of common factors. In a first application, we model the security excess returns as a linear function of the two portfolios' excess return series, with a conditional variance given by a linear function of the two portfolios' conditional variances. This model (analogous to Engle et al., (1990, p. 226)) may be written as:

$$
\begin{aligned}
R_{i,t} &= \lambda_i + \beta_{\text{Bond}_i} \hat{R}_{\text{Bond}_t} + \beta_{\text{Stock}_i} \hat{R}_{\text{Stock}_t} + v_{i,t} \\
v_{i,t} \mid \Im_{t-1} &\sim N(0, h_{i,t}) \\
h_{i,t} &= \sigma_i + \beta^2_{\text{Bond}_i} \hat{\theta}_{\text{Bond}_t} + \beta^2_{\text{Stock}_i} \hat{\theta}_{\text{Stock}_t}.
\end{aligned}
\tag{4}
$$

This model incorporates a constant, λ, in the mean equation, to capture non-time-varying components of the individual security's risk premium (for instance, the "on-the-run" effect that newly auctioned Treasury securities exhibit, in which their yield is driven down by demand for that specific issue). The model is estimated for each of the thirteen maturities. While the β coefficients are highly significant for all tenors, examination of their asymptotic standard errors indicate that the direct effect of the stockmarket portfolio's excess returns and conditional variance is of considerable importance for short-term Treasury returns, but never meaningful for tenors greater than two years. In contrast to Engle et al. (1990, p. 226), we found that the stockmarket index has significant direct effects on the 3–12 month segment of the yield curve.

Since the stockmarket factor does not appear to play a direct role in the individual securities' excess returns and conditional variances for medium or long tenors, we respecify the model as a single-factor model in which the estimated excess return and conditional variance of the equally-weighted bond portfolio is the only direct effect. This still incorporates the movements of the stockmarket portfolio, since the recursive structure of the portfolio models imply that the bond portfolio's excess returns and conditional variance estimates are derived from both the bond and stockmarket portfolios. The single-factor model estimated for individual Treasury maturities is thus:

$$
\begin{aligned}
R_{i,t} &= \lambda_i + \beta_{\mathrm{Bond}_i} \hat{R}_{\mathrm{Bond}_t} + v_{i,t} \\
v_{i,t} \mid \Im_{t-1} &\sim N(0, h_{i,t}) \\
h_{i,t} &= \sigma_i + \beta^2_{\mathrm{Bond}_i} \hat{\theta}^2_{\mathrm{Bond}_t}.
\end{aligned} \tag{5}
$$

Results for this single-factor model, estimated for each of the thirteen maturities via the BHHH algorithm, are presented in Table 2.[4] The constant term, λ, is insignificant for most tenors longer than one year. The constant in the conditional variance equation is insignificant, although a negative point estimate appears for longer tenors. The β coefficient is highly significant for all tenors, which given the structure of the model is an indication that the restrictions embodied in a static model of excess returns as a random series with homoskedastic errors may be rejected by the GARCH alternative. For the 3-, 6-, and 9-month tenors, the restriction that the square of the β coefficient in the mean equation appears in the conditional variance equation can be rejected. For all longer tenors, the specification of the model for individual maturities' excess returns and their conditional variance appears appropriate. It is quite apparent from the magnitude of these coefficient estimates that Treasury securities of longer maturities possess greater sensitivity to the conditional variance of the Treasury portfolio, and, given the recursive nature of the model, to the conditional variance of the stockmarket portfolio.

Simple correlations of the predicted values of our one-factor model are quite high for adjacent tenors, and decline notably as the difference in tenors increases – a quite realistic outcome, given the workings of the Treasury market. For instance, one-year and three-year securities' returns are correlated at 0.91, but the correlation declines to 0.74 for ten year securities and 0.60 for twenty years' tenor. This feature of the model should be contrasted with the general equilibrium models of the term structure, such as that of Cox, Ingersoll and Ross (1985), which generate perfect correlations among rates at all tenors. The correlations of these predicted values are quite consistent with the original excess return series to which they are fit; for instance, the correlations between 3-month securities' excess returns and those of 1-, 2-, 5- and 20-year securities are 0.768, 0.685, 0.550, and 0.381 over the full sample,

TABLE 2

One-factor model for individual Treasury maturities

$$R_{i,t} = \lambda_i + \beta_{\text{Bond}_i} \hat{R}_{\text{Bond}_t} + v_{i,t},\ v_{i,t} \mid \Im_{t-1} \sim N(0, h_{i,t}),\ h_{i,t} = \sigma_i + \beta^2_{\text{Bond}_i} \hat{\theta}_{\text{Bond}_t}$$

Tenor	3 mo	6 mo	9 mo	12 mo	18 mo	2 yr	3 yr	4 yr	5 yr	7 yr	10 yr	15 yr	20 yr
λ	0.040	0.050	0.043	0.033	0.027	0.008	0.008	–0.015	–0.001	–0.021	–0.061	–0.122	–0.309
se(λ)	0.004	0.009	0.013	0.018	0.026	0.035	0.043	0.054	0.063	0.084	0.104	0.150	0.242
β bond	0.067	0.139	0.214	0.292	0.435	0.571	0.808	1.044	1.183	1.505	1.884	2.691	3.692
se(β)	0.002	0.005	0.009	0.012	0.017	0.022	0.028	0.034	0.037	0.047	0.058	0.082	0.141
σ	0.000	0.001	0.005	0.011	0.016	0.032	–0.005	–0.049	–0.066	–0.093	–0.199	–0.453	0.063
se(σ)	0.000	0.002	0.004	0.008	0.015	0.026	0.033	0.041	0.051	0.088	0.114	0.167	0.721
Var	0.016	0.076	0.180	0.334	0.699	1.194	2.174	3.556	4.565	7.303	11.825	24.818	37.948
Skew	2.171	1.661	1.239	0.986	0.679	0.592	0.119	0.003	0.012	0.070	0.279	0.487	0.080
Kurt	11.079	10.931	9.860	9.704	9.363	9.591	7.917	7.061	5.508	3.443	3.026	3.355	3.396
Q(12)	90.11	52.57	47.07	44.88	45.47	41.27	32.45	23.30	21.89	17.47	23.94	27.70	22.51
signif	0.000	0.000	0.000	0.000	0.000	0.000	0.001	0.025	0.039	0.133	0.021	0.006	0.032
QS(12)	93.41	149.22	150.32	149.22	134.13	122.97	113.84	107.39	120.15	148.55	165.88	125.69	93.45
signif	0.000	0.000	0.000	0.000	0.000	0.000	0.000	0.000	0.000	0.000	0.000	0.000	0.000

Notes: asymptotic standard errors are given below the coefficient estimates. Var, Skew and Kurt are the variance, skewness, and kurtosis of the residuals. Q(12) is the Ljung-Box statistic for 12th order serial correlation in the residuals. QS(12) is the equivalent statistic for the squares of the residual series.

whereas the correlations among the respective predicted values are 0.76, 0.67, 0.54 and 0.36. Thus, this aspect of the data – the observed comovements of the excess returns series across tenors – seems to be faithfully reflected in the one-factor model's estimates.

4. Summary Remarks

We have implemented a variation on Engle et al.'s (1990) Factor-ARCH model for the full term structure of Treasury securities over the postwar era. The implications of their model – that a small number of common factors can successfully capture the joint behavior of securities prices over a wide range of tenors – are clearly supported by the data for short-, medium-, and long-term Treasuries. Individual tenors' returns are well explained by the innovations in a bond portfolio's returns, and their conditional variance is successfully represented as a transformation of the portfolio's conditional variance series. The interactions between volatility in the bond markets and the stockmarket are more precisely modelled in our analysis, in which we use an asymmetric GARCH approach to allow "good news" and "bad news" to have differing effects on the evolution of volatility. Despite the massive increase in Treasury rates' variance engendered by the Federal Reserve's 1979 shift in operating policy, the Factor-ARCH model captures the dynamics of the process, and is capable of dealing with the very sizable changes in bond returns generated at the long end of the term structure in response to parallel shifts in the yield curve.

Notes

1. We do not consider their "long" tenor, as it does not correspond to a fixed maturity.
2. The discrete tenors in CFI's study do not allow us to derive holding period returns (as one could from the Fama Treasury bill files). We thus constructed hypothetical spot yields for the missing tenors as linear interpolations of the CFI spot yields.
3. The moving correlations are computed annually from 36 monthly observations; the date on the horizontal axis is the left endpoint of the three-year span.
4. Conceptually, the estimation of this model should take into account the "generated regressor" nature of the predicted expected return series to deal with Pagan's (1984) critique. In our context, this would necessitate maximum likelihood estimation of the full system of 13 single-factor models joint with models (2) and (3). We are investigating the feasibility of this approach, which is computationally burdensome.

References

Canova, Fabio and Jane Marrinan, 1995, 'Predicting excess returns in financial markets', *European Economic Review* 39(1), 35–70.

Coleman, T.S., L. Fisher, and L. Ibbotson, 1993, *Historical U.S. Treasury Yield Curves, 1926–1992*, New York: Moody's Investors Services.
Cox, J., J. Ingersoll, and S. Ross, 1985, 'A theory of the term structure of interest rates', *Econometrica* 53, 385–467.
Engle, R.F., 1987, 'Multivariate ARCH with factor structures: cointegration in variance'. Unpublished working paper, University of California at San Diego.
Engle, R.F., V. Ng, and M. Rothschild, 1990, 'Asset pricing with a Factor-ARCH covariance structure: Empirical estimates for Treasury bills', *Journal of Econometrics* 45, 213–237.
Engsted, T. and C. Tangaard, 1994, 'Cointegration and the U.S. term structure', *Journal of Banking and Finance* 18, 167–181.
Froot, K.A., 1989, 'New hope for the expectations hypothesis', *Journal of Finance* 44, 283–305.
Gourieroux, C. and A. Monfort, 1992, 'Qualitative threshold ARCH models', *Journal of Econometrics* 52, 159–199.
Hall, A.D., H.M. Anderson, and C.W.J. Granger, 1992, 'A cointegration analysis of Treasury bill yields', *Review of Economics and Statistics* 74, 116–126.
McCulloch, J. H. and H. Kwon, 1993, 'U.S. term structure data, 1947–1991'. Unpublished working paper #93-6, Ohio State University.
Pagan, A., 1984, 'Econometric issues in the analysis of regressions with generated regressors', *International Economic Review* 25(1), 221–247.
Ross, S., 1976, 'Arbitrage theory of capital asset pricing', *Journal of Economic Theory* 13, 341–360.

JEAN-LOUIS BRILLET

Analyzing a Small French ECM Model

ABSTRACT. We have used the structure of a preexisting small model of the French economy,and adapted it to an ECM format. The new model should

- present more explicit formulations,
- have better stabilized properties,
- separate the long term formulation and the short term dynamics,
- give results easier to interpret,
- but still be usable for policy analysis.

We start by presenting the properties of the standard model. Then we apply in sequence an ECM format to all econometric equations. This process allows us to introduce interesting improvements, going beyond the scope of this particular model.

We simulate the model over a very long period, observing the existence and specificity of the numerical convergence to a steady state grow path. We analyze the response of the model to shocks, both in the short and long term, associating it to the ECM specifications.

We then build the long term model, analyzing its logical structure, and check the identity of its properties to the normal version. Finally, we analyze the eigenvalues of the linearized dynamic process, associating them to individual dynamics.

INTRODUCTION

The small model we shall describe now uses the global framework of MicroDMS,[1] quite representative of French models. The central innovation will be the presence of clearly established short and long term formulations through an error correction model structure. But the size of the sample will forbid to apply cointegration tests, and maybe speak of error correction, although the formulations in the model work for a sample of 17 OECD countries.

H. Amman et al. (eds.), Computational Approaches to Economic Problems, 17–37.

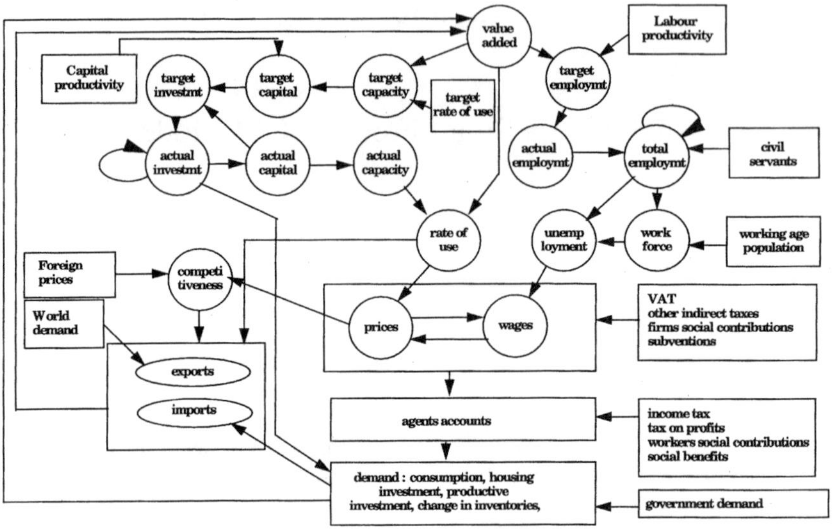

Fig. 1.

The General Formulation

We shall in general try to apply the most restrictive form of an error correction model

$$\Delta(x_t) = a\Delta(x_t^*) + b(x_{t-1}^* - x_{t-1}),$$

where x_t^* represents the desired value[2] of the dependent variable x_t, the a term shows the instantaneous adaptation to a change in the desired value, and b the following equilibrating process, during later periods.

We shall estimate simultaneously (non linear least squares) all coefficients: a, b and the parameters in the target formulation.

The General Logic

Micro DMS can be defined as a neo-keynesian model, with strong supply-oriented features but almost no financial sector. The above graph gives a general view of the model framework. We shall now concentrate on the most important behavorial equations.

Employment of Firms

Actual employment adapts itself partially to a desired value

$$\Delta\text{Log}(le_t) = \lambda\Delta\text{Log}(le_t^*) + \mu\text{Log}(le_{t-1}^*/le_{t-1}),$$

where $LE_t^* = Q_t/\pi_t^*$, and π_t^* a desired (structural) value of labour productivity, supposed to grow at a constant rate (actually we shall introduce a break in 1979).

$$\begin{aligned}\mathrm{Log}(\mathrm{le}^*) = \mathrm{Log}(\mathrm{q}) - (&\underset{(32)}{0.030} * \mathrm{time} - \underset{(-4.5)}{0.0052} * (\mathrm{time} > (-1))\\ &* (\mathrm{time} - (-1)) + 4.828)\end{aligned}$$

$$\Delta\mathrm{Log}(\mathrm{le}) = \underset{(12)}{0.597} * \Delta\mathrm{Log}(\mathrm{le}^*) + \underset{(5.8)}{0.489} * (\mathrm{Log}(\mathrm{le}^*_{-1}) - \mathrm{Log}(\mathrm{le}_{-1}))$$

WORK FORCE

Rather than unemployment, we shall model the work force. The error correction feature can be justified, for economic reasons, concerning in particular long term equilibrium.

If the work force is high compared to employment and working age population, job creation will call more for the unemployed, and the work force will grow less. Individuals who lose their jobs will be more easily discouraged, persons reaching working age will look less actively for a job, and persons reaching the normal age of retirement will be more led (or persuaded) to get out of the work force. Even with equal employment movements (both in and out) the work force will grow less (in algebraic terms).

$$\mathrm{acpop}^* = \underset{(4.3)}{0.751} * \mathrm{l} + \underset{(7.5)}{0.391} * \mathrm{avpop} - \underset{(3.6)}{5634}$$

$$\Delta(\mathrm{acpop}) = \underset{(4.1)}{0.465} * \Delta(\mathrm{acpop}^*) + \underset{(3.1)}{223} * (\mathrm{acpop}^*_{-1} - \mathrm{acpop}_{-1})$$

The yearly changes in unemployment and employement are not proportional, but depend also on levels. The short and long term sensitivities of the work force to employment are in order 0.35 and 0.75.

PRODUCTIVE INVESTMENT

It follows the usual error correcting accelerator framework.

$$\mathrm{Log}((\mathrm{i}^* + \mathrm{k}_{-1})/\mathrm{k}_{-1}) = \underset{(4.4)}{0.223} * \mathrm{Log}(\mathrm{acc}) + \underset{(3.3)}{0.222} * \mathrm{pratio} + 0.0156$$

$$\begin{aligned}\Delta(\mathrm{Log}((\mathrm{i} + \mathrm{k}_{-1})/\mathrm{k}_{-1})) &= \underset{(3.4)}{0.314} * \Delta\mathrm{Log}(((\mathrm{i} + \mathrm{k}_{-1})^*\mathrm{k}_{-1})\\ &+ \underset{(4.3)}{0.228} * (\mathrm{Log}(((\mathrm{i} + \mathrm{k}_{-1})/\mathrm{k}_{-1})^*)_{-1} - \mathrm{Log}((\mathrm{i} + \mathrm{k}_{-1})/\mathrm{k}_{-1})_{-1}),\end{aligned}$$

where $acc = q/q(-1)/(average\ ut)/ut$ and $pratio = marg/(pu * k_{-1})$.

The Wage Rate

We shall use a Phillips-type formulation, violating somewhat our principles on ECM format, but including a long-term stabilization of the share of wages in production.

$$\begin{aligned}
\Delta \mathrm{Log}(w\ hw)) = {} & \underset{(11.1)}{1.040} * (0.710 * \Delta \mathrm{Log}(pu) \\
& + (1 - \underset{(8.8)}{0.710}) * \Delta \mathrm{Log}(pu_{-1}) - \underset{(-2.6)}{0.395} * (\Delta(urate + urate_{-1})) \\
& + \underset{(3.3)}{0.163} * (0.710 * \mathrm{Log}(pu_{-1}) + (1 - 0.710) * \mathrm{Log}(pu_{-2}) \\
& - \underset{(-4.8)}{2.748} * (urate_{-1} + urate_{-2}) - \mathrm{Log}(1 + tcse_{-1}) \\
& + \mathrm{Log}(q_{-1}/le_{-1}) - \mathrm{Log}(w_{-1}hw_{-1}) - \underset{(-1.7)}{0.00843}.
\end{aligned}$$

The Value Added Price

The long term margins ratio will depend on the rate of use of capacities

$$\mathrm{Log}(pva^*) = \mathrm{Log}(w\cos t) + \underset{(2.8)}{0.326} * ut + \underset{(4.1)}{0.0938}$$

$$\begin{aligned}
\Delta \mathrm{Log}(pva) = {} & \underset{(16.8)}{0.595} * \Delta \mathrm{Log}(pva^*) \\
& + \underset{(5.5)}{0.171} * (\mathrm{Log}(pva^*_{-1}) - \mathrm{Log}(pva_{-1}))
\end{aligned}$$

The Trade Prices

$$\mathrm{Log}(pex^*) = \underset{(7.4)}{0.580} * \mathrm{Log}(pp) + (1 - 0.580) * \mathrm{Log}(petxf) - \underset{(-1.8)}{0.0811}$$

$$\Delta\text{Log(pex)} = \underset{(9.6)}{1.191} * \Delta\text{Log(pex}^*)$$
$$+ \underset{(1.5)}{0.251} * (\text{Log(pex}^*_{-1}) - \text{Log(pex}_{-1}))$$

$$\text{Log(pimxe}^*) = \underset{(3.8)}{0.224} * \text{Log(pp)}$$
$$+ (1 - 0.224) * \text{Log(petmxef)} - \underset{(-1.9)}{0.0090}$$

$$\Delta\text{Log(pimxe)} = \underset{(17.2)}{1.108} * \Delta\text{Log(pimxe}^*)$$
$$+ \underset{(2.7)}{0.420} * (\text{Log(pimxe}^*_{-1}) - \text{Log(pimxe)}_{-1}))$$

INTERESTS PAID BY FIRMS

We shall decompose all interests paid into the ones due to previous debts, with a rate **mir** changing with reimbursements, and to the new ones, contracted at the present rate **ir**.

$$\text{cis} = \text{cis}_{-1} * \text{mir}/\text{mir}_{-1} + 1.139 * \text{ir}/100. * \text{bfs}.$$

THE HOUSEHOLDS SAVINGS RATIO

The formulation uses as explanatory elements.

- growth of the real revenue (marginal propensity to consume),
- inflation (real holdings effect),
- growth of unemployment (safety savings),
- the level of the real revenue itself.

$$\Delta * \text{Log(sratio)} = \underset{(2.3)}{0.999}\Delta\text{log(rdip)} + \underset{(3.0)}{1.139} * \Delta\Delta\text{Log(pu)}$$
$$+ \underset{(3.4)}{0.172} * \Delta\Delta\text{Log(unemp)} + \underset{(3.2)}{2.090} * \Delta\text{Log(rdip)} - \underset{(-1.1)}{0.0991}$$

$$\Delta\Delta\text{Log(sratio)} = 1 * \Delta(\Delta\text{Log(sratio)})$$
$$+ \underset{(1.5)}{0.309} * (\Delta * \text{Log(sratio)}_{-1} - \Delta\text{Log(sratio)}_{-1}).$$

External Trade

The formulations are quite traditional.

$$\text{Log}(\text{mxe}^*) = \text{Log}(\text{ddem} - \text{dinv}) + \underset{(15.5)}{1.082} * \text{Log}(\text{opb})$$

$$- \underset{(-3.3)}{0.386} * (0.5 * \text{Log}(\text{compm}) + 0.5 * \text{Log}(\text{compm}_{-1}))$$

$$- \underset{(-3.0)}{0.150} * \text{Log}(1 - \text{ut})) - \underset{(-2.7)}{2.67}$$

$$\Delta\text{Log}(\text{mxe}) = \underset{(6.5)}{0.911} * \Delta(\text{mxe}^*)$$

$$+ \underset{(2.6)}{0.928} * (\text{Log}(\text{mxe}^*_{-1}) - \text{Log}(\text{mxe}_{-1}))$$

$$\text{Log}(\text{x}^*) = 1 * \text{Log}(\text{wd}) - \underset{(-2.6)}{0.395} * (\underset{(2.5)}{0.532} * \text{Log}(\text{compx})$$

$$+ (1 - 0.532) * \text{Log}(\text{compx}_{-1}))$$

$$- \underset{(-4.2)}{0.611} * \text{Log}(\text{utx}) - \underset{(-8.6)}{0.0150} * \text{time} + \underset{(2.3)}{12.57}$$

$$\Delta\text{Log}(\text{x}) = \underset{(7.0)}{1.077} * \Delta\text{Log}(\text{x}^*) + \underset{(2.3)}{0.398} * (\text{Log}(\text{x}^*_{-1}) - \text{Log}(\text{x}_{-1}))$$

The Changes in Inventories

We suppose that firms try to keep as inventories a constant share of their production.

$$(\text{dinv}/\text{q}_{-1})^* = \underset{(4.6)}{0.623} * (\text{q} - \text{q}_{-1})/\text{q}_{-1} - \underset{(-4.9)}{0.0180}$$

$$\Delta(\text{dinv}/\text{q}_{-1}) = \underset{(5.3)}{0.718} * \Delta(\text{dinv}/\text{q}_{-1})^*$$

$$+ \underset{(3.7)}{0.990} * ((\text{dinv}/\text{q}_{-1})^*_{-1} - (\text{dinv}/\text{q}_{-1})_{-1})$$

Model Properties

An Ex-Post Simulation

Results look satisfying, except for household consumption and the savings ratio.

Variable	Percentage error	Variable	Absolute error
GDP	1.31	Savings ratio	2.77
Household consumption	2.10	Profits ratio	0.62
Productive investment	4.32	Change in inventories	17.2
Exports	1.53	Capacity utilization	1.04
Imports	2.67	Rate	
Unemployment	5.83		
Employment	0.93		
Wage rate	1.19		
Production price	1.05		

A Very Long Term Simulation

We shall now analyze the long term properties of the model. For this we need a very long term simulation, with a steady state growth path. No change is needed in the model specifications, except for the elimination of trends, and setting the growth of productivity in the employment equation.

Exogenous Assumptions

We now have to make coherent the evolutions of exogenous variables. In practice only three growth rates have to be set (and can be): q, for quantities, p, for prices, and n, for population.

- State demand, world demand, exogenous production elements grow at rate q.
- Total and working age populations, exogenous levels of jobs and individual workers grow at rate n.
- Foreign prices in foreign currency grow at rate p.
- Pensions and other contributions, measured in purchasing power per head, grow at rate q − n, as well as the labour productivity trend. This ensures that job level grows at rate n.
- The tax rates, the real interest rate, the exchange rate, the various exogenous ratios keep constant.

RESULTS

Numerical Results

The growth rates we shall use are

q, the growth rate of quantities = **0.028**
p, the growth rate of prices = **0.024**
n, the growth rate of population = **0.003**

We shall chose as the horizon the year 2500. This period can look abnormally far away, but the few graphs which follow will prove that this is not the case.

At this horizon, the results are consistent with long term conditions. We can check that

- Global quantities grow at rate q.
- Prices grow at rate p.
- Populations grow at rate n.
- Current values grow at rate $p + q$.
- Undimensioned ratios keep stable.
- Wages grow at rate $p + q - n$ (keeping stable the share of wages in value added).

Comments on the Graphs

The following graphs (generally presented in growth rates) present some cycles in the beginning (2000–2100) then, converge according to a hierarchy which can be (for prices for instance) associated with the one found in he later sensitivity analysis.

One can see that **quantities** (Figure 2) converge rather fast, but if graphically (Figure 2a), convergence appears to be achieved around 2040, Figure 2b shows that there is still in 2300 a slight difference to the target growth rate (0.028), which seems to have completely disappeared in 2500.

In the "short" run, the simulation shows cyclical properties, which can be associated to the investment–capital dynamics. A lower than average capacity utilization level leads to high exports, low imports, and a subsequent investment decrease. This will be confirmed numerically later.

In the final period, the relative convergence of quantities is coherent to what one could expect from a demand shock: investment, consumption, GDP, and imports are higher than average, exports are lower.

Prices (Figure 3) converge numerically a little later (2060?) which we will show to be coherent with the associated dynamics measures (eigenvalues). A monotonous convergence combines with some cyclical short run evolutions, again with a logical hierarchy.

The **ratios** (Figure 4) take much longer to converge, in particular the second one, a balance between heterogenous elements. In the long run, they

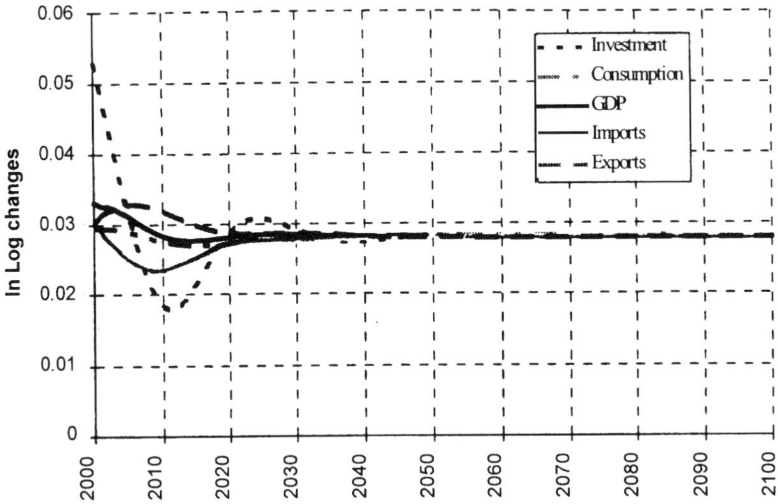

Fig. 2a. Evolution of quantities.

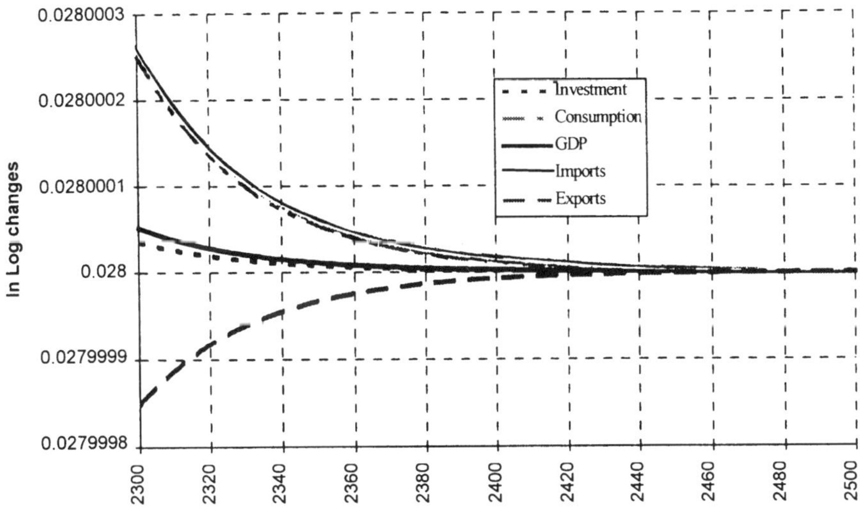

Fig. 2b. Evolution of quantities (long term).

convergence from opposite directions, which could look strange as both have capital as denominator. But we shall show that this is quite logical for our model.

Proceeding now to a sensitivity analysis of our model, we check that its properties conform to those of others of the same kind, with the addition of long term stability. We shall not present the results here, for lack of space,

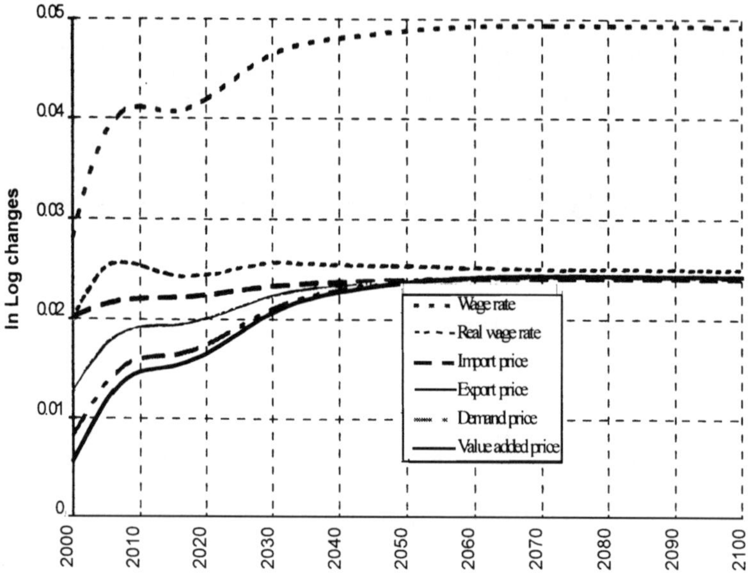

Fig. 3. Evolution of prices ("short" term).

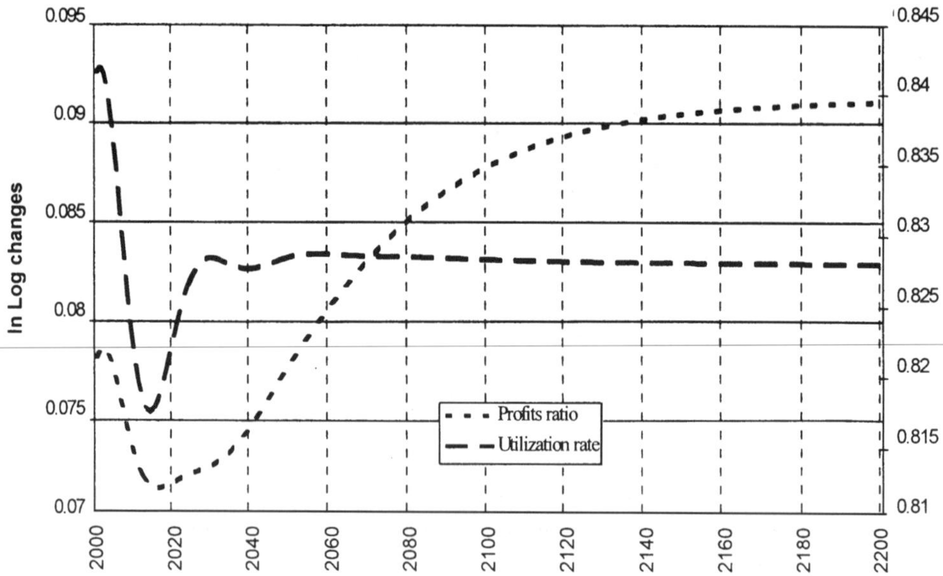

Fig. 4. Evolution of ratios (long term).

and will wait for the production of the long term model to discuss the long term properties.

THE LONG TERM MODEL

We can create a model assigned to the study of the long term. The formulations will have the single purpose of allowing the computation of the long term solution.

For this, we just have to:

- extract the long term formulation,
- move its lags one period forward,
- add the long term difference between variable and target (which depends only on coefficients and growth rates),
- replace the remaining lagged variables by their instantaneous counterpart divided by the appropriate growth rate.

We have now a model without lags, which we can simulate for any given period.[3]

THE STRUCTURE OF THE MODEL

Compared to other studies in the same field, the structure of the model is much less modified. The logical structure will stay roughly the same, the main innovation being the instantaneous character of adaptations.

- Productive capacities, and housing stocks, adapt immediately to demand.
- The interests paid are associated with the long term debt (increasing deficits will have an immediately large effect on interest paid).
- A change in the exogenous exchange rate will produce an identical rise of domestic inflation, eliminating any gain in competitiveness. This introduces one degree of indetermination.

THE PROPERTIES

Long Term Simulations versus Simulating the Long Term Model

This model will prove less costly in getting the long term properties, as it requires the computation of a single period, but it is also more difficult to achieve convergence, as instantaneous capacity adaptation suppresses a precious equilibrating process.

An Application: Expliciting the Interactions of Ratios

We shall study the evolution of the different **ratios**: unemployment rate (urate), utilization of capacities (ut), margins ratio (tmarg), ratio of margins to capital (pratio).

While these elements converge to a long term stable value, this target is the result of an optimization process using several criteria.

A Priori Observations

Using only the equations related to these ratios, we get
(1) $\mathrm{g}(\mathrm{scrap}, q, \mathrm{i}/\mathrm{k}) = \mathrm{f}(\mathrm{ut}, \mathrm{pratio})$
(2) $\mathrm{pratio} = \mathrm{tmarg} * \mathrm{pva}/\mathrm{pu} * \mathrm{ut}/\mathrm{prodk}$
(3) $\mathrm{tmarg} = \mathrm{f}(\mathrm{ut})$
(4) $\mathrm{pva}/\mathrm{pu} = \mathrm{f}(\mathrm{ut}, \mathrm{urate}, \mathrm{roth}, \mathrm{tcse}, \mathrm{hw}, p, q - n, q/\mathrm{ne})$
with four equations and five "unknown" variables.

This fortunately allows variables, in particular pva/pu,[4] to follow the changes in the other elements of the economic equilibrium, in particular demand-oriented variables. What is lacking is actually an equation linking the ratio pva/pu to economic conditions and the ratios themselves, a link too complex to be explicited here. But we can see that pva/pu (or rather pu/pva) can be used as a composite indicator of competitiveness.

We can also eliminate individual influences, and observe how this affects the system.

ut *in (3) (fixed margin ratio)*: The margins ratio remains at the base value. This makes pratio depend on the sole ut and pva/pu. This would fix ut and pratio except for the presence of pva/pu. In other words, eliminating the "price" instrument would forbid any outside[5] change to modify any of the ratios, if not for the different evolutions of prices (for instance in a closed economy).

pratio *in (1) (no profitability in investment)*: The utilization ratio is fixed, as the only determinant of the accumulation rate. The margins ratio is also fixed (from (3)) but not the other elements.

ut *in (1) (no reequilibration in the accelerator)*: The ratio of margins to capital is fixed. (4) expresses a link between the two criteria: the unemployment and utilization rates.

For each of these "models" we shall shock some of the assumptions, concentrating on the ones which affect directly our supply system, and observe how the change in specification affects model properties.

Quantitative Analysis

The two first shocks will be the same as previously, concerning demand and supply:

1. an increase in government demand (by 0.5 GDP points),
2. a decrease in the social security contribution of employers, by one point.

The others (not presented here) will be associated with the the ratio system. We shall

3. increase the productivity of capital by one point,
4. increase the productivity of labour by one point.

For each of these five shocks we can consider:

(a) the normal model,
(b) a model with no Phillips effect, with normal prices,
(c) a model with no Phillips effect, in which prices have the same base value,
(d) a model with capital valued at the added value price,
(e) a model with the margins ratio in the investment equation,
(f) a model with no capacity in value added prices,
(g) a model with no capacity in investment,
(h) a model with no profitability in investment.

A Shock on Domestic Demand

Its results appear in Table 1. All elements are presented in percentage.

The base model

The first column shows the usual consequences of a demand shock: an expansion of demand through other elements (productive investment, consumption, inventories, housing investment), with a degradation of external trade due to inflation. Productivity of labour is unchanged, capacities, capital and investment grow in identical proportions. Ratios show

- a large decrease in the unemployment rate,
- a small decrease in the margins and utilization ratios,
- a large increase in the profits ratios.

This can be interpreted in the following way:

- (1) sets a negative influence of pratio on ut: if pratio increases, more capital will be built.
- (3) sets a positive influence of ut on tmarg: if ut increases, firms will feel allowed to increase margins.
- If we eliminate pratio and tmarg in the accounting equation (2), we get a negative link between ut and pva/pu (we shall call it (2')), while (4) sets a positive one (for the same reasons as (3)).
- Our shock decreases urate, and thus increases the constant term in (4). The curve moves upwards, and the new solution shows an increase in

TABLE 1

First shock: government investment

	Normal model	No Phillips effect	No capacity in VA prices	No capacity in investment	No profits in investment	Normal model, same prices	Same prices,No Phillips effect	K price =PVA or I=(Tmarg)
Quantities								
GDP	0.381	0.620	0.375	0.502	0.357	0.417	0.594	0.389
Added value (real)	0.329	0.596	0.322	0.450	0.305	0.369	0.573	0.340
Imports	1.044	0.688	1.048	1.123	1.029	1.062	0.672	1.044
Energy imports	0.576	0.709	0.571	0.702	0.552	0.597	0.671	0.568
Non-energy imports	1.121	0.685	1.126	1.192	1.107	1.138	0.672	1.121
Exports	-0.417	0.020	-0.425	-0.364	-0.427	-0.410	0	-0.426
Domestic demand	0.576	0.709	0.571	0.702	0.552	0.597	0.671	0.568
Investment	0.373	0.595	0.370	0.704	0.306	0.421	0.573	0.340
Change in inventories	0.329	0.596	0.322	0.450	0.305	0.369	0.573	0.340
Household consumption	0.384	0.324	0.381	0.495	0.363	0.400	0.290	0.376
Housing investment	0.384	0.323	0.381	0.495	0.362	0.400	0.290	0.376
Productive process								
Productive capital	0.371	0.597	0.366	0.706	0.305	0.421	0.573	0.340
Productive capacities	0.371	0.597	0.366	0.706	0.305	0.421	0.573	0.340
Capacity utilization rate	-0.042	0.000	-0.044	-0.254	0	0	0	0.000
Employment								
Firms employment	0.329	0.596	0.322	0.450	0.305	0.369	0.573	0.340
Productivity	0	0	0	0	0	0	0	0
Total employment	0.246	0.445	0.241	0.336	0.228	0.262	0.408	0.242
Work force	0.162	0.293	0.158	0.221	0.150	0.165	0.256	0.152
Unemployment	-0.470	-0.849	-0.460	-0.641	-0.436	-0.356	-0.554	-0.329
Prices								
Added value price	2.123	-0.086	2.167	2.497	2.048	2.135	0	2.056
Production price	1.969	-0.086	2.009	2.315	1.899	1.965	0	1.893
Exports price	1.129	-0.049	1.152	1.326	1.089	1.127	0	1.085
Import price	0.440	-0.019	0.449	0.516	0.424	0.414	0	0.399
Local demand price	1.843	-0.086	1.881	2.167	1.778	1.825	0	1.758
Wage rate	2.135	-0.086	2.167	2.567	2.048	2.149	0.000	2.056
Unitary wage cost	2.135	-0.086	2.167	2.567	2.048	2.149	0	2.056
Ratios								
Savings ratio	0	0	0	0	0	0	0	0
Interest rate	0	0	0	0	0	0	0	0
Margins ratio	-0.011	0.000	0.000	-0.070	0	-0.010	0	0.000
Profits ratio	0.334	0.001	0.366	-0.055	0.412	0.333	0.000	0.412
Margins on capital	0.222	0.000	0.237	-0.002	0.267	0.241	0	0.000
Price ratio: VA to demand	0.280	0.000	0.286	0.330	0.271	0.309	0	0.298
Other elements								
Wages	2.374	0.339	2.401	2.897	2.271	2.403	0.387	2.290
Margins	2.448	0.510	2.496	2.886	2.361	2.501	0.573	2.403
Social security payments	1.831	-0.139	1.869	2.151	1.767	1.822	-0.036	1.755
Added value (current)	2.459	0.510	2.496	2.958	2.360	2.511	0.573	2.403
Household revenue (curre	2.234	0.238	2.269	2.673	2.147	2.232	0.290	2.140
Household revenue (real)	0.384	0.324	0.381	0.495	0.363	0.400	0.290	0.376

pva/pu and a decrease in ut, thus a decrease in tmarg and an increase in tpro.

- In other words, facing a demand shock, firms will have to deal with an increase in the wage cost, affecting *ex-ante* their sole margins. In this context, their optimizing behaviour will lead to a mixed deterioration of criteria, including a loss in competitiveness, a decrease in the rate of use of capacities, and a lower margin ratio, while of course maintaining an increase in real margins (by 2.448–2.123 # 0.325%).

A Model with No Phillips Effect

From the above considerations, it is clearly useful to see what happens in our model if there is no Phillips effect, or in other word if urate does not appear in (4).

The change in the figures is striking: the ratios keep to the base value (except for unemployment), activity increases, with a multiplier almost doubled, and prices decrease, although by a much smaller margin

Indeed, in our four equation-system, there are now only four unknowns, and the shock on demand does not affect directly any of the equations. Firms have no reason to change their behaviour.

The increase in activity can be clearly related to the elimination of the competitivity loss. Suppressing the Phillips effect makes the initial inflationary effect disappear. And if prices do change a little, it is because indexes have not the same base level, and the shocks changes their weights in accounting equations.

We have been able to produce a base simulation in which all deflators are equal (seventh column). Now no price changes,all imports grow like demand, and exports stay stable.

A Shock on the Social Security Rate (Firms)

This time we are dealing with a supply shock. This means that in any of our models the equilibrium should be modified.

Actually there is one exception: we can (through the wage equation) make the charge lay on the wage earners themselves. As this case looks less interesting here (this does not mean it is less realistic) we will concentrate on the alternate assumption. However, we shall present the associated results for one case.

The results are presented in Table 2 (with eight colums).

Let us treat first the case above (seventh column) without the Phillips effect. Not surprisingly, the results are globally proportional to the previous case, except of course for household consumption.

Coming back to the normal model, we observe the usual effects of a supply shock in the long run: amplification of the deflationary effect, increase

TABLE 2

Second shock: social security firms contribution

	Normal model	No Phillips effect, w2	No capacity in VA prices	No capacity in investment	No profits in investment	Normal model, same prices	No Phillips effect, w1	No Phillips effect, w2
Quantities								
GDP	0.510	0.894	0.566	0.539	0.569	0.437	0.256	0.656
Added value (real)	0.524	0.953	0.583	0.555	0.586	0.457	0.247	0.710
Imports	-0.001	-0.562	0.098	0.087	0.103	-0.109	0.289	-0.589
Energy imports	0.455	0.669	0.505	0.485	0.509	0.365	0.289	0.457
Non-energy imports	-0.076	-0.764	0.051	0.040	0.056	-0.187	0.289	-0.759
Exports	0.412	1.117	0.348	0.294	0.352	0.424	0	0.939
Domestic demand	0.455	0.669	0.505	0.485	0.509	0.365	0.289	0.457
Investment	0.485	0.845	0.544	0.394	0.586	0.403	0.247	0.592
Change in inventories	0.524	0.953	0.583	0.555	0.586	0.457	0.247	0.710
Household consumption	0.420	0.326	0.485	0.489	0.485	0.297	0.410	0.161
Housing investment	0.421	0.325	0.485	0.489	0.485	0.297	0.410	0.161
Productive process								
Productive capital	0.485	0.847	0.544	0.394	0.586	0.403	0.247	0.592
Productive capacities	0.485	0.847	0.544	0.394	0.586	0.403	0.247	0.592
Capacity utilization rate	0.039	0.105	0.039	0.160	0	0	0	0.117
Employment								
Firms employment	0.524	0.953	0.583	0.555	0.586	0.457	0.247	0.710
Productivity	0	0	0	0	0	0	0	0
Total employment	0.391	0.711	0.416	0.402	0.417	0.325	0.176	0.505
Work force	0.258	0.468	0.262	0.257	0.262	0.204	0.110	0.317
Unemployment	-0.747	-1.357	-0.573	-0.615	-0.566	-0.441	-0.238	-0.686
Prices								
Added value price	-2.028	-5.398	-1.728	-1.804	-1.642	-2.151	0	-4.687
Production price	-1.892	-5.037	-1.621	-1.705	-1.535	-1.984	0	-4.328
Exports price	-1.093	-2.932	-0.936	-0.985	-0.886	-1.147	0	-2.515
Import price	-0.429	-1.156	-0.375	-0.395	-0.354	-0.424	0	-0.933
Local demand price	-1.781	-4.743	-1.515	-1.606	-1.431	-1.846	0	-4.030
Wage rate	-1.332	-4.743	-1.020	-1.133	-0.933	-1.459	0.721	-4.030
Unitary wage cost	-2.038	-5.425	-1.728	-1.840	-1.642	-2.164	0	-4.717
Ratios								
Savings ratio	0	0	0	0	0	0	0	0
Interest rate	0	0	0	0	0	0	0	0
Margins ratio	0.011	0.029	0.000	0.041	0	0.011	0	0.023
Profits ratio	-0.510	-1.038	-0.445	-0.188	-0.492	-0.492	-0.151	-0.903
Margins on capital	-0.202	-0.554	-0.177	0.000	-0.214	-0.247	0	-0.545
Price ratio: VA to deman	-0.248	-0.655	-0.213	-0.198	-0.211	-0.305	0	-0.657
Other elements								
Wages	-0.964	-4.096	-0.629	-0.754	-0.540	-1.155	0.888	-3.570
Margins	-1.504	-4.469	-1.155	-1.218	-1.065	-1.693	0.247	-3.988
Social security payments	-1.799	-4.824	-1.522	-1.618	-1.436	-1.849	0.031	-4.073
Added value (current)	-1.514	-4.496	-1.155	-1.259	-1.065	-1.704	0.247	-4.010
Household revenue (curr	-1.368	-4.433	-1.038	-1.125	-0.953	-1.554	0.410	-3.876
Household revenue (real)	0.420	0.326	0.485	0.489	0.485	0.297	0.410	0.161

in exports, investment and consumption, decrease of the share of imports in demand(even of imports themselves).

One can be surprised however by the evolution of the ratios: the margins ratio increases a little, but the two profits ratios deteriorate. Again, this is due to the ratio pva/pu: (3) tells us that any change in the wage cost is transmitted entirely into value added prices, leaving the margins ratio linked to the sole ut. As the effect is lower on pu, pratio decreases, leading to a higher utilization rate and margins ratio. In other words, the gain in traded quantities through competitiveness has to be paid by lower unitary profits.

One could also think that without a Phillips effect the ratios would improve. This is not the case, although the other elements: prices, production, exports, imports, employment (apart from household consumption of course) do slightly. The Phillips effect actually limited the deflation in the normal case, and the variation of pva/pu. But this unitary decrease is more than offset by the increase in quantities, and real profits do improve.

This time, starting from equivalent levels for all prices does not modify the image, although the general improvement is somewhat lessened (but the associated solution is more artificial).

A Shock on Capital Productivity (results not shown)

We shall increase capital productivity by 1% percent, supposedly in one step.

This increases the ratio of margins to capital. The main changes appear in the ratio of margins to capital, and the rate of use of capacities. The improved potential profits lead to an increase of capacities, which is however more than offset in by the *ex-ante* reduction in capital level.

A Shock on Labour Productivity (results not shown)

Although the shock applies to structural productivity, apparent productivity will of course present the same change. This change should in principle benefit to the economy.

Production increases by about 0.5%, dividing by two the *ex-ante* job loss. This is mostly due to the gains in competitiveness linked to the decrease of prices. This decrease is not due at all to the increase in labour productivity (as wages are indexed) but from the rise in unemployment, and the Phillips effect. If we suppress the Phillips effect, the prices do not change *ex-ante*, and *ex-post* neither.

The Dynamics

We shall come back to our original model to study the dynamics of convergence to the long term solution.

The Model
We shall eliminate the lags higher than one by piling them up into as many identities. We shall then log-linearize the model, which gives

$$(\Delta x/x) = A(\Delta x_{-1}/x_{-1}) + B(\Delta x/x) + C(\Delta z/z) \quad \text{with}$$
$$A = (\delta f/f)(\delta x_{-1}/x_{-1}), \quad B = (\delta f/f)/(\delta x/x) \quad \text{and}$$
$$C = (\delta f/f)/(\delta z/z).$$

The Method
To study the dynamics of the model, we shall rely essentially on the computation of the eigenvalues of $(I - B)^{-1}A$.

They will describe the convergence process, in terms of actual convergence (modulus lower than one), and cyclicity (real or complex values).

We shall further try to associate eigenvalues with dynamic influences of specified variables, by observing the consequences of the elimination of lagged variables.

- the values do not change: the dynamic variable has no influence,
- one value disappears: the variable explains the associated dynamics,
- one or several values change: the dynamics of the variable is linked with others.

The Results
We get 28 non zero[6] eigenvalues, much less than lagged variables. They all have a modulus lower than one, except for the largest, which we shall be able to associate with the savings ratio itself. But as the explanatory elements are double derivatives, this quasi unitary eigenvalue expands from period to period a null effect.

Some values can be expected to associate with particular variables. In ECM formulations, written as

$$\Delta(x_t) = a\Delta(x_t^*) + b(x_{t-1}^* - x_{t-1})$$

if the target is only composed of exogenous elements, we should obviously get an eigenvalue of $\lambda = 1 - b$.

In practice, the following associations can be made immediately:

rank	real part	1 − b	variable	definition
1	1.003	1.000	SRATIO	Savings ratio
2	0.9712	0.9720	CIG	Interests paid by government
3	0.9680	0.9688	CIX	Interest paid by the rest of the world
12	0.7318	0.7486	PEX	Exports price
14	0.6652	0.6639	EBEM	Margins of households
15	0.5998	0.6049	X	Exports
16	0.5143	0.5805	PIMXE	Imports price
17	0.3864	0.3859	RBEI	Revenue of individual workers
18	0.3684	0.3689	FFCEI	Contribution of ind workers to capital
22	0.07190	0.07240	MXE	Non energy imports

For the other variables, the situation is more complex, as the ECM format has introduced a much larger number of lags. However, we can observe the following associations.

rank	real part	imagin part	variables
4	0.9519		prices
5	0.9294	0.01048	prices
6	0.9294	−0.01048	prices
7	0.8869	0.2063	investment, capital, production
8	0.8869	−0.2063	investment, capital, production
9	0.8540		households: investment, interest, unemployment
10	0.7885	0.06394	households: investment, interest, unemployment
11	0.7885	−0.06394	households: investment, interest, unemployment
13	0.6872		unemployment, employment
19	0.3447	0.07621	unemployment, employment
20	0.3447	−0.07621	unemployment, employment
21	0.1863		?
23	−0.07806	0.4856	investment, capital, production
24	−0.07806	−0.4856	investment, capital, production
25	−0.3677		production, prices ?

CONCLUSION

Our initial goal was to build an error correction model which combined readability in terms of properties and usability fot the usual policy diagnoses. It seems we have reached this target, although some properties could still be improved and the interpretation is not fully complete. In the process, we have been able to make some observations which can be applied in a more general way.

THE LIST OF VARIABLES

Name	Definition
acpop	Active population
avpop	Work force
bfs	Firms deficit
cis	Interests paid by firms
compm	Imports price competitiveness
compx	Exports price competitiveness
ddem	Domestic demand
dinv	Change in inventories
hw	Hours worked per year
i	Productive investment
ir	Current interest rate
k	Capital
l	Employment
le	Firms employment
mir	Average interest rate paid
mxe	Imports (excluding energy)
opb	Opening of borders (trend)
petmxef	Foreign production price (in Francs, import weighted)
petxf	Foreign production price (in Francs, export weighted)
pex	Export price index
pimxe	Import price index (non-energy)
pp	Production deflator
pratio	Profits ratio
prodk	Capital productivity
pu	Demand deflator
pva	Value added deflator
q	Value added
rdip	Read disposable income
roth	Rate of other indirect taxes
scrap	Scrapping ratio
sratio	Household savings ratio
tcse	Social security rate (firms)
time	Time (=0 in 1980)
tmarg	Margins ratio
unemp	Unemployment rate

Name	Definition
urate	Unemployment rate
ut	rate of use of capacities
utx	Corrected rate of use
w	Hourly wage rate
wcost	Unitary wage cost
wd	World demand
x	Exports

NOTES

1. Brillet J.-L., *Le modèle MicroDMS*, INSEE Méthodes No. 44, juin 1994.
2. The notion of "desired value" must be taken here in a wide sense. It can represent actually a long term equilibrium value, resulting from the confrontation of the behaviour of two agents or even of a natural and uncontrolled evolution.
3. It will not give however a constant solution, as the exogenous variables change according to the growth assumptions presented earlier.
4. Which appears only because firms sell at one price, and buy capital at another.
5. By "outside" we mean not affecting directly an equation of the subsystem, as the exogenous assumptions listed above.
6. We have considered as zero eigenvalues not only the truly null ones but also the one with a modulus of less than 10^{-3}.

SETH A. GREENBLATT

Wavelet Basis Selection for Regression by Cross-Validation

ABSTRACT. Much of the attention paid to wavelets in the statistical literature has been in the area of nonparametric regression, smoothing, and denoising. Generally, the wavelet-based techniques involve finding an appropriate threshold level and using that threshold to either shrink or zero out wavelet coefficients, depending upon their sizes. Recently, a new technique for threshold determination based upon cross-validation has been introduced. In this study, we look at several criteria that may be used, in conjunction with cross-validation, to select the most appropriate wavelet basis for the problem at hand and then we apply the resulting technique to financial market data.

1. Introduction

A great deal of attention has been paid in the statistical literature to the use of wavelets for nonparametric regression, smoothing, and denoising. The usual approach (Donoho et al. 1994) is to transform a signal using the discrete wavelet transform, determine a threshold that represents the noise in the series, set to zero all wavelet coefficients smaller in magnitude than the threshold, optionally shrink other coefficients, and inversely transform the wavelet coefficients to recover the estimate of the denoised signal. There are a number of questions that still need to be answered within this framework. We need to know to which levels of the wavelet decomposition we should apply the thresholding procedure. It is also extremely important to set the threshold appropriately. If the threshold is too high, we could remove important information about the underlying signal. If it is too low, we could leave in too much noise. In addition, we want to represent the signal in the most appropriate basis. The selection of threshold and basis are the questions to which this study addresses itself.

The remainder of the paper proceeds as follows. Section 2 provides an introduction to nonparametric regression using wavelets. Section 3 briefly reviews the recently introduced method for threshold determination by cross-validation. The following section discusses various criteria for basis selection. Section 5 presents the results of computer experiments looking at basis selec-

H. Amman et al. (eds.), Computational Approaches to Economic Problems, 39–55.

tion in the context of wavelet regression by cross-validation. The following section applies the techniques discussed in earlier sections to stock market and foreign exchange data. The final section discusses the conclusions indicated by the current study and possible directions for future research.

2. Nonparametric Regression Using Wavelets

In nonparametric regression, the basic model is as follows:

$$g_i = \mathrm{f}(t_i) + \epsilon_i, \tag{1}$$

where g_i is an observed data series; $\mathrm{f}(t_i)$ is the underlying data generating process; ϵ_i is an *iid* $N(0, \sigma^2)$ error process; $t_i = i/n$.

Our goal is to estimate the underlying data generating process or, conversely, to find and remove the noise. To accomplish this task using wavelets, we follow a simple four stage procedure.

1. Decompose our data series using the discrete wavelet transform (DWT),
2. Determine an appropriate threshold from the empirical[1] wavelet components,
3. Apply the threshold to the empirical wavelet components, following a policy of either hard or soft thresholding,
4. Reconstruct the data series using the inverse DWT.

In our procedure above, we refer to policies of hard and soft thresholding. Hard thresholding entails simply setting all empirical wavelet components smaller in magnitude than the threshold to exactly zero. When we apply soft thresholding, we set small empirical wavelet components to zero as we did for hard thresholding, then we shrink the remaining components toward zero by an amount equal to the magnitude of the threshold. Since we shrink the empirical wavelet components, this class of technique is known as a wavelet shrinkage estimator.

The actions of setting some components to zero and shrinking others makes a great deal of intuitive sense if approached in the proper manner.

We may look at hard thresholding as a test of the null hypothesis that each empirical wavelet component is actually zero. We can consider our threshold to be a sort of critical value (at an appropriate significance level) for the hypothesis test. If a particular empirical wavelet component is greater in magnitude than the threshold, we may reject the null hypothesis and assume that the component is not zero. If, however, the component is smaller in magnitude than the threshold, then we cannot distinguish the component's value from zero. Assuming that the component should actually have a value of zero, we set it accordingly.

We can similarly get an intuitive understanding of the reasons why we wish to shrink empirical wavelet components. We may represent the discrete wavelet transform as a matrix or, equivalently, as a linear operator. If we apply this operator, named $\mathcal{W}$, to our data series, then (1) gives us:

$$\mathcal{W}g_i = \mathcal{W}\mathrm{f}(t_i) + \mathcal{W}\epsilon_i. \tag{2}$$

This shows us that each wavelet component ($\mathcal{W}g_i$) is made up of both the underlying data generating process ($\mathcal{W}\mathrm{f}(t_i)$) and the associated errors ($\mathcal{W}\epsilon_i$). When we shrink an empirical wavelet component, we are removing the error part of that particular component, leaving the transformed data generating process.

Threshold selection is another step in the wavelet regression process that seems innocuous enough, but is actually the subject of wide debate in the literature. There have been a number of methods for the selection of thresholds, but due to space constraints we shall only mention a few of the most commonly used methods.

Donoho and Johnstone (1993) propose the Universal Threshold:

$$\hat{\sigma}\sqrt{2\log n}\,,$$

where n is the number of observations in the data series and $\hat{\sigma}$ is an estimate of the noise level. The authors show that, asymptotically, this threshold will remove all the noise and give a estimate at least as smooth as the underlying data generating process. The problem with this approach is that it often underfits the data and gives us an estimate *smoother* than the underlying data generating process.

In another study, the same authors (Donoho and Johnstone 1994a) propose another approach to threshold selection where they derive an estimator based on Stein's method for estimating the quadratic loss unbiasedly for a decision problem with independent Gaussian noise. This method, called *SureShrink*, computes thresholds on a level-by-level basis over each level in the wavelet decomposition. This technique also tends to underfit the data, in practice.

The approach to threshold selection that we wish to concentrate upon in this study is Cross-Validation (Nason 1994). We discuss this technique in some detail in the next section, below.

3. Wavelet Regression by Cross-Validation

In a recent paper, Nason (1994) proposed a new technique for the determination of the threshold level for a wavelet shrinkage estimator. The technique uses a cross-validation score to estimate the integrated square error (ISE) of a soft thresholded estimator. To compute this score, the data series is split into odd- and even-indexed observations. This works well due to the dyadic nature of the "fast" discrete wavelet transform. We then proceed to find the threshold that minimises our estimated ISE. We use this threshold level to soft threshold our data, giving us our cross-validation wavelet regression estimate.

Our cross-validation score estimate of the ISE ($\mathrm{M}(t)$) is:

$$\hat{\mathrm{M}}(t) = \sum_j \left(\hat{f}_{t,j}^{\mathrm{EVEN}} - \bar{g}_j^{\mathrm{ODD}}\right)^2 + \left(\hat{f}_{t,j}^{\mathrm{ODD}} - \bar{g}_j^{\mathrm{EVEN}}\right)^2 \tag{3}$$

where $\hat{f}_{t,j}^{\mathrm{EVEN}}$ is a threshold estimate of f_t at point j computed from the even-indexed observations, $\hat{f}_{t,j}^{\mathrm{ODD}}$ is the corresponding estimate computed from odd-indexed observations, $\bar{g}_j^{\mathrm{ODD}}$ is a version of the even-indexed observations as interpolated from the noisy odd-indexed observations, and $\bar{g}_j^{\mathrm{EVEN}}$ is the corresponding series interpolated from the noisy even-indexed observations. We then minimise $\hat{\mathrm{M}}(t)$ with respect to the threshold (which is implicit in the two $\hat{f}$ estimators). Since this threshold has been found using a series of length $n/2$, we must make adjustments to find a threshold appropriate for a series of length n. The adjustment is:

$$t_n \approx \left(1 - \frac{\log 2}{\log n}\right)^{-1/2} t_{n/2}, \tag{4}$$

where t_n is our cross-validation threshold level that we may use to soft-threshold g_i to compute our estimate of $\mathrm{f}(t_i)$.[2]

4. Criteria for Basis Selection

Most of the literature about basis selection discusses criteria for determining the *best* basis and fast algorithms for searching a tree built from a library of a large number of possible bases. While these search algorithms have been developed to be fast, there is always going to be overhead in conducting a search over a large number of bases. There is also extra complexity involved in the implementation of a search for a large library such as a wavelet packet library[3] that is not present for a small library, such as Daubechies' compactly supported orthonormal wavelets as described in Daubechies (1988, 1992, 1993). In some situations, the extra computational cost of searching a large library is worthwhile, in others, the improvement in fit made by searching a small library may be good enough.

This paper looks at four criteria for basis selection to be used in conjunction with cross-validation for threshold selection. While these criteria may be applied to basis selection from a large library such as a library of wavelet packets, for purposes of exposition we will look at selection from a small library, the Daubechies extremal phase family of compactly supported orthonormal wavelets with order of regularity ranging from 1 to 10.

The four criteria which we minimise to determine best wavelet basis are:[4]

1. Density of representation (after thresholding):[5]

$$\frac{1}{N}\sum I(|w_i| > 0),$$

2. Bit-length norm:

$$\sum \log\left(1 + \frac{|w_i|}{\epsilon}\right),$$

where ϵ is the chosen threshold,
3. Log energy:

$$\sum_{w_i \neq 0} \log\left(\frac{w_i^2}{\|\boldsymbol{w}\|_2^2}\right),$$

4. Shannon entropy:

$$-\sum_{w_i \neq 0}\left(\frac{w_i^2}{\|\boldsymbol{w}\|_2^2}\right)\log\left(\frac{w_i^2}{\|\boldsymbol{w}\|_2^2}\right).$$

These criteria have been widely discussed in the literature.[6] Each of them have advantages and disadvantages for various uses, but that discussion is beyond the scope of this study.

The simplest and least computationally taxing criterion, density of representation, has a great deal of intuitive appeal. It has been shown (Donoho 1993) that the success of a denoising scheme is directly tied to the sparseness of representation in a particular orthonormal basis. Based upon this principle, the best representation should be the one with the lowest density of representation. If this criterion works relatively well, in practice, as compared to the more computationally intensive techniques, then there may be good reason to use it rather than the alternatives.

5. Results of Computer Experiments

In this section we present the results of computer experiments carried out on three test data generating processes to look at the behaviour of the four candidate criteria for the selection of wavelet basis from among the extremal phase family of Daubechies' compactly supported orthonormal wavelets with order of regularity ranging from one to ten.

The test data generating processes are those used in Nason (1994). The first, shown in Figure 1 is a smooth signal sampled 256 times evenly on the interval $[0, 2\pi]$

$$\text{cvf1}(x) = \sin(x) + \sin(3x).$$

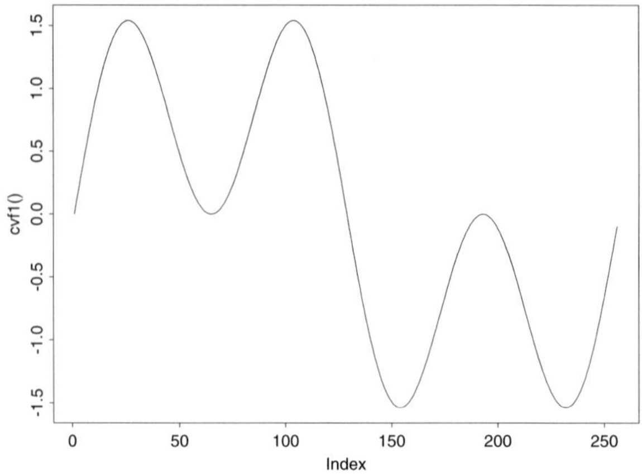

Fig. 1. Test signal 1: smooth signal.

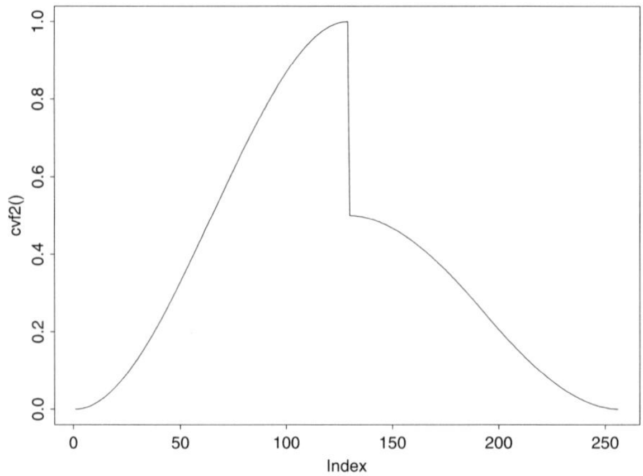

Fig. 2. Test signal 2: piecewise polynomial signal.

The second, shown in Figure 2 is a piecewise polynomial with a discontinuity sampled 256 times evenly on $[0, 1]$

$$\mathrm{cvf2}(x) = \begin{cases} 4x^2(3-4x) & : \quad x \in [0, \frac{1}{2}] \\ \frac{4}{3}x(4x^2-10x+7)-\frac{3}{2} & : \quad x \in (\frac{1}{2}, \frac{3}{4}] \\ \frac{16}{3}x(x-1)^2 & : \quad x \in (\frac{3}{4}, 1] \end{cases}$$

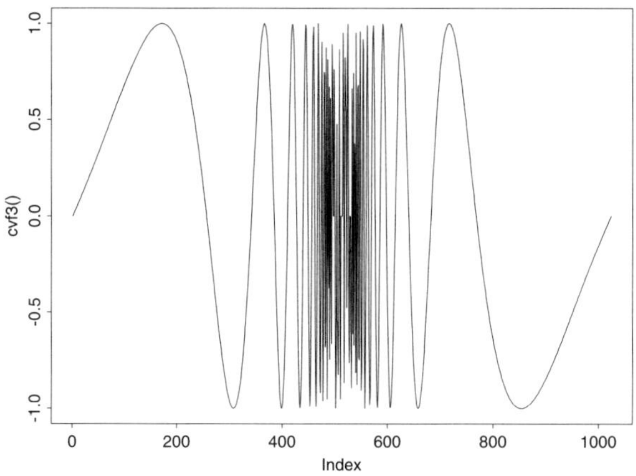

Fig. 3. Test signal 3: chirp signal.

Our third test function, shown in Figure 3 is a chirp signal sampled 1024 times evenly on $[-1, 1]$

$$\text{cvf3}(x) = \sin\left(\frac{\pi}{x}\right).$$

We added Independent Gaussian noise with zero mean to all three signals. The standard deviations for the noise series' were: 1.0 for the smooth signal, 0.1 for the piecewise polynomial, and 0.3 for the chirp.

For each test signal, we ran 100 computer experiments where we generated pseudorandom noise, added it to the signal, computed the values of each of the test criteria for each of the candidate wavelets, and chose the wavelet with the lowest value for each criterion. We also chose, at random, one of the experiments for each of the test signals to show the quality of reconstruction for each of the criteria.

Figures 4, 5, and 6 show the results of the 100 computer experiments. For each plot, the horizontal axis represents the order of regularity for the wavelets and the vertical axis represents the number of times out of 100 that each wavelet was selected.

Since we are choosing bases to represent the underlying processes, we would ideally see these criteria regularly choosing the same basis for a given DGP. This, however, does not appear to be the case. Although there generally are bases that various criteria favour, the only test that chooses the same basis more than half the time is Shannon entropy.

Figures 7, 8, and 9 present examples of the reconstructions that we get by soft thresholding using the thresholds determined by cross-validation and the bases selected by the four test criteria.

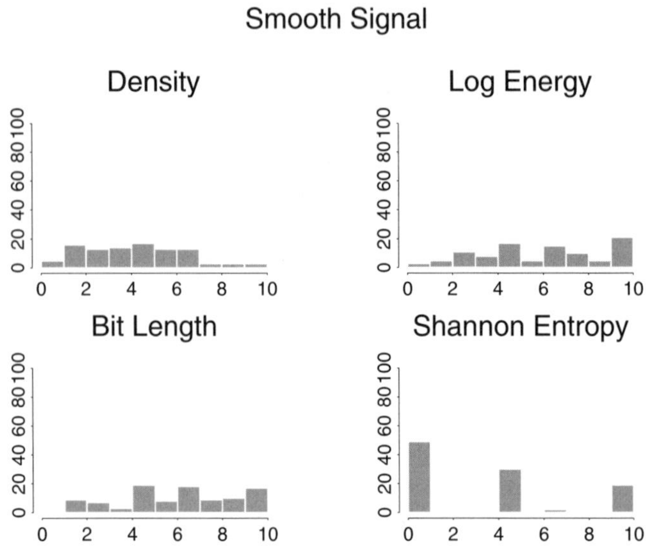

Fig. 4. Histograms showing the results of four criteria choosing best wavelet basis for a smooth signal from library of Daubechies extremal phase compactly supported orthonormal wavelets.

In general, the computationally simple and intuitively appealing density of representation selects a basis that gives us a reconstruction as visually appealing as any of the more complicated criteria. Based upon these limited results, it would appear that we could, for independent Gaussian noise, use the density of representation criterion with little loss of effectiveness.

We ran 100 further computer experiments just as before except that we applied our cross-validation threshold to the coefficients of each basis *before* computing the value of each criterion. In the previous experiments, we only applied the threshold before the density of representation criterion.

The main difference in the results is that the log energy generally chooses the Haar wavelet basis when we apply the threshold before the criterion. Even though the log energy criterion was more consistent in selecting a basis, its selections produced rough, spiky reconstructions. Based upon these preliminary results, there does not seem to be any gain from thresholding the coefficients before applying the selection criteria.[7]

6. Financial Examples

In this section, we apply the technique proposed above to data from financial markets. We look at stock index data over a period containing a stock market

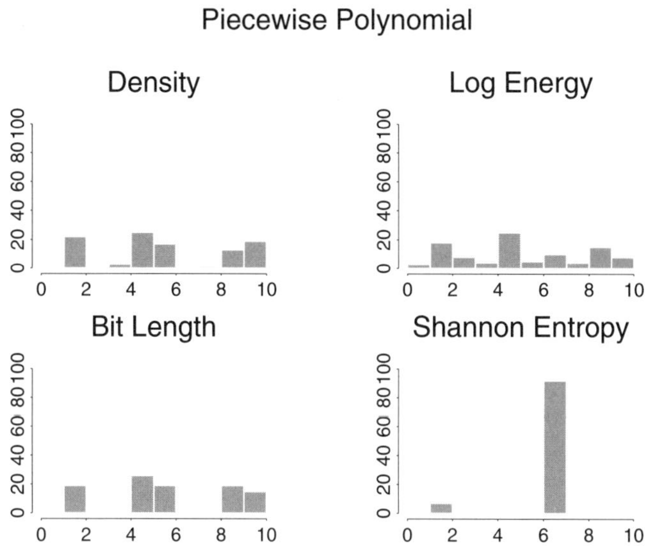

Fig. 5. Histograms showing the results of four criteria choosing best wavelet basis for a piecewise polynomial signal with a discontinuity from library of Daubechies extremal phase compactly supported orthonormal wavelets.

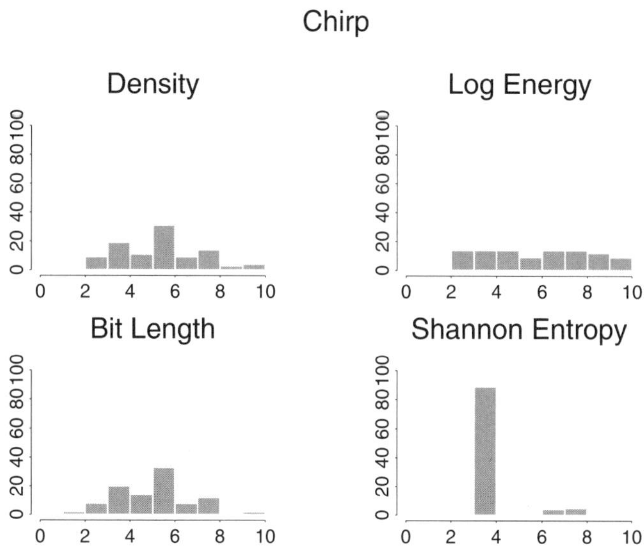

Fig. 6. Histograms showing the results of four criteria choosing best wavelet basis for a chirp signal from library of Daubechies extremal phase compactly supported orthonormal wavelets.

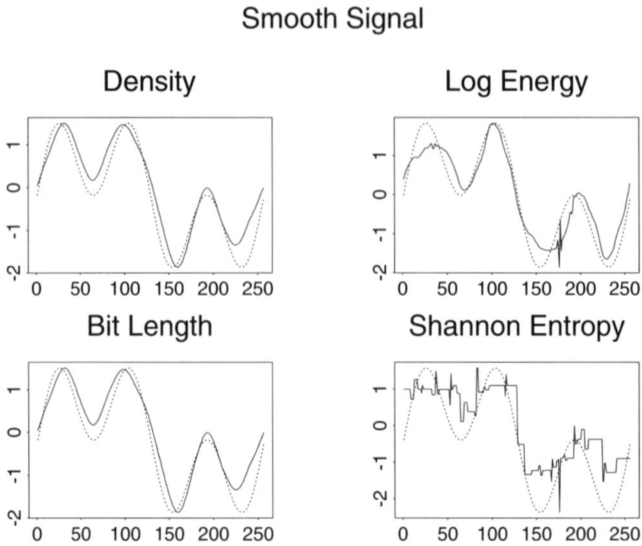

Fig. 7. Best estimate of the smooth signal as selected by four criteria from the library of Daubechies' extremal phase compactly supported orthonormal wavelets. Dotted line shows the true underlying data generating process.

crash. We then look at returns data for two foreign exchange data series. All data were obtained through Datastream and edited to remove all days that the markets were closed such as weekends and holidays.

Our first example comes from the daily FTSE 100 stock index beginning in January 1985 and running for 1024 observations. If we look at the raw data (Figure 10), we can see that it has an obvious discontinuity. This sudden drop in the index is due to the stock market crash of October 1987. Any estimate of the underlying data generating process should maintain this feature.

Figure 11 shows the curve estimated using universal thresholding. We can see that the sharp features, such as the crash, are no longer present. This oversmoothing is a common problem for universal thresholding. We can also see that there is a severe problem with boundary effects[8].

We may contrast this oversmoothed result with Figure 12 where we find the curve as estimated by cross-validation and wavelet basis selection using the density of representation criterion. The detailed features, such as the stock market crash are maintained. We have also avoided much of the boundary effect problem.

Our other two examples are from the exchange rate markets. We may examine the raw log returns data for the French Franc/British Pound exchange rate (Figure 13) and the Deutsch Mark/British Pound exchange rate (Figure 15)

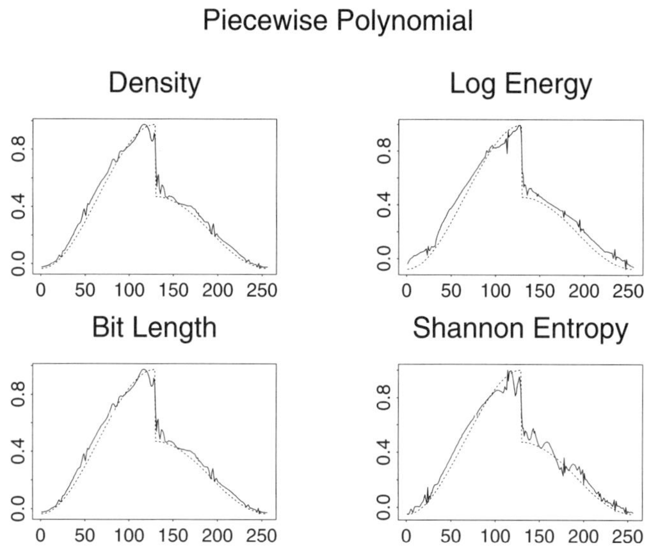

Fig. 8. Best estimate of the piecewise polynomial signal as selected by four criteria from the library of Daubechies' extremal phase compactly supported orthonormal wavelets. Dotted line shows the true underlying data generating process.

and see that they are both primarily noise. There is very little underlying structure to be seen. The curves estimated with cross-validation and wavelet basis estimation in Figures 14 and 16 show somewhat cyclical behaviour. There are also spikes evident in both figures. These should be considered candidates for outlier testing. This testing may be done with either a wavelet-based outlier test (Greenblatt 1994, 1995) or with a more traditional type of outlier test (Barnett and Lewis 1994).

7. Discussion

In this study, we briefly reviewed wavelet regression, threshold determination by cross-validation, and basis selection criteria. We then presented the results of two sets of computer experiments showing the behaviour of four selection criteria in conjunction with cross-validation threshold determination when applied to three test signals and a small library of wavelet bases. Based upon the results of these experiments, we observed that the simple selection criterion of density of representation compared favourably with more complicated, computationally intensive criteria and that the extra computation involved in thresholding *before* applying the selection criteria is unwarranted. Finally, we applied the proposed technique to several financial data series.

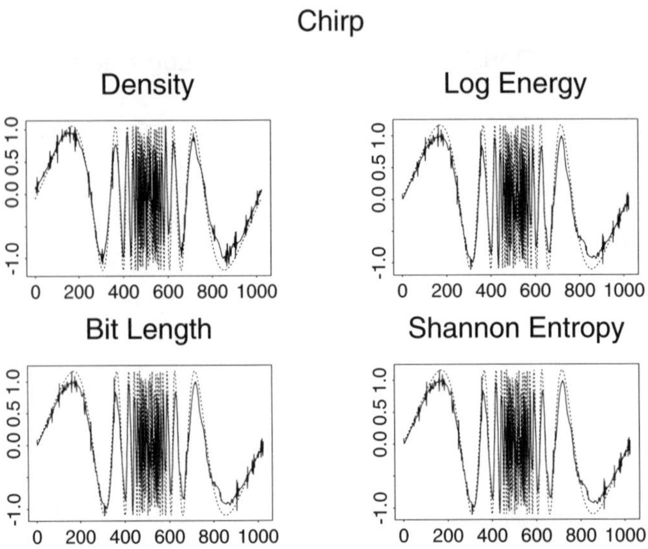

Fig. 9. Best estimate of the chirp signal as selected by four criteria from the library of Daubechies' extremal phase compactly supported orthonormal wavelets. Dotted line shows the true underlying data generating process.

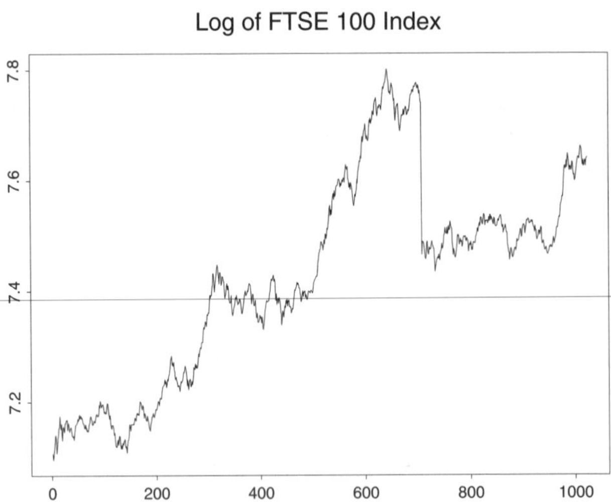

Fig. 10. Log of Daily FTSE 100 Index from January 1985 for 1024 observations.

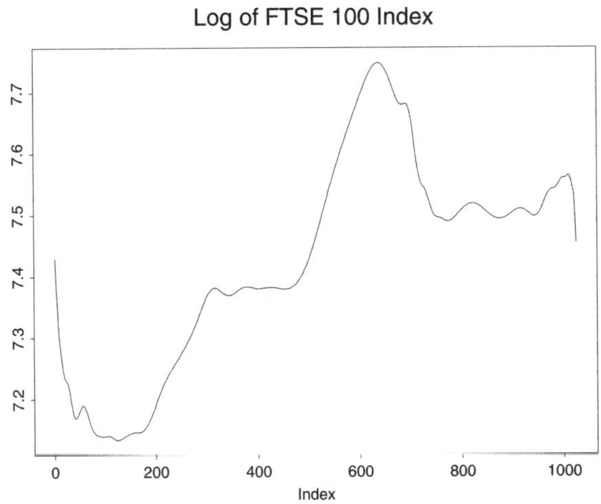

Fig. 11. Log of Daily FTSE 100 Index from January 1985 for 1024 observations denoised by standard wavelet techniques with universal thresholding.

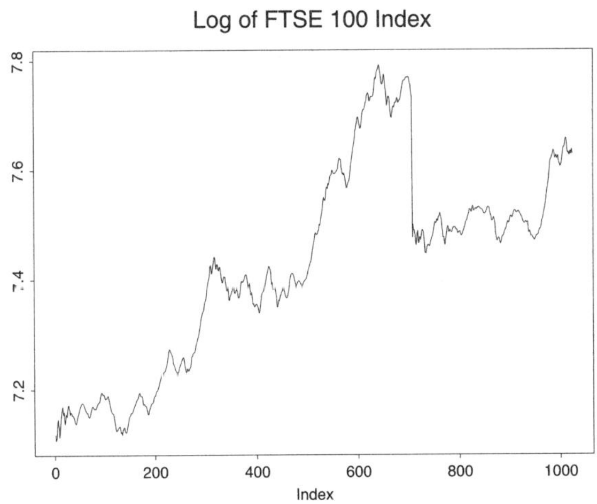

Fig. 12. Log of Daily FTSE 100 Index from January 1985 for 1024 observations denoised by density selected cross-validation wavelet techniques.

The obvious direction in which this work should continue is to look at the behaviour of these selection criteria when we use cross-validation to determine threshold levels on a level-by-level basis, and when we determine threshold levels by cross-validation in conjunction with larger libraries, such as wavelet packet libraries. We would also like to investigate the behaviour, in similar situations, of other selection criteria, such as the non-additive information cost functions of Taswell (1995).

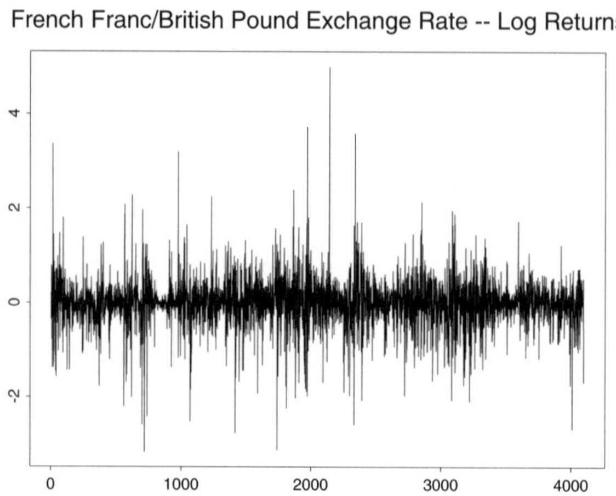

Fig. 13. Daily French Franc/British Pound exchange rate log returns data from January 1974 for 4096 observations.

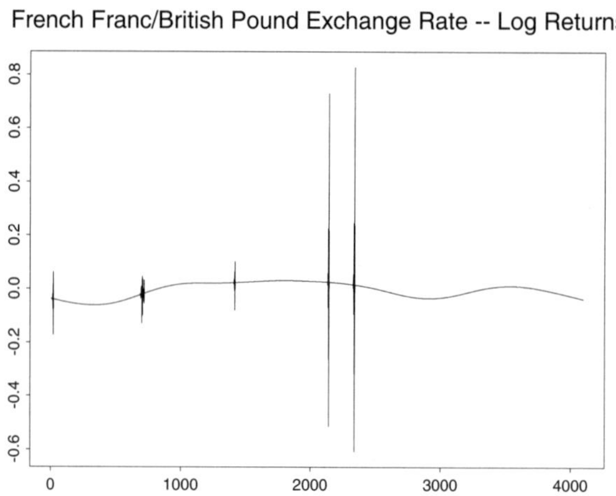

Fig. 14. Daily French Franc/British Pound exchange rate log returns data from January 1974 for 4096 observations denoised by density selected cross-validation wavelet techniques.

Cross-validation appears to be a promising technique for the determination of threshold levels for the nonparametric wavelet regression modeling of noisy signals. Used together with an appropriate basis library and an effective means for selecting from that library, this technique could become an important tool for econometricians and statisticians in the near future.

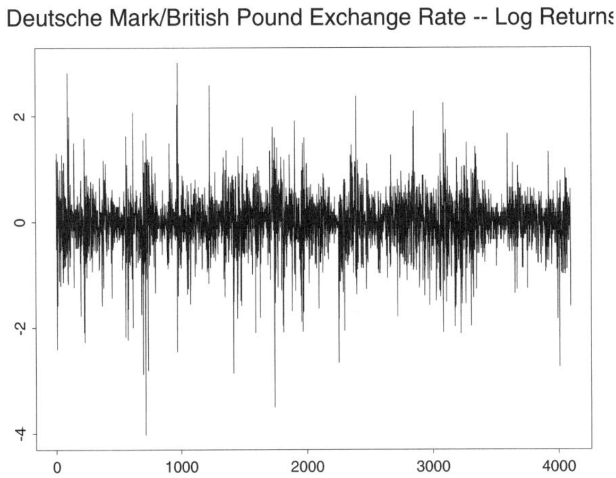

Fig. 15. Daily Deutsche Mark/British Pound exchange rate log returns data from January 1974 for 4096 observations.

Fig. 16. Daily Deutsche Mark/British Pound Exchange Rate Log Returns data from January 1974 for 4096 observations denoised by density selected cross-validation wavelet techniques.

Acknowledgements

I would like to thank Ian Garrett and Chris Brooks for providing the FTSE 100 data and exchange rate data, respectively. I would also like to thank Guy Nason for discussions and the use of his WAVETHRESH package to do the underlying wavelet transforms in this study. The cross-validation and selection code and any errors contained therein are, however, my own.

NOTES

1. We refer to empirical wavelet components because they were estimated from data, rather than a true data generating process.
2. Details regarding the properties and derivation of the cross-validation estimate of ISE may be found in (Nason 1994).
3. See Wickerhauser (1991, 1993) for detailed discussion of wavelet packets.
4. In all that follows, anytime we mention the threshold, we are referring to the threshold chosen by cross-validation as described in Section 3.
5. This criterion is equivalent to the threshold counting norm mentioned in (Wickerhauser 1993).
6. For more in-depth discussion of these and other criteria, see (Wickerhauser 1991; Wickerhauser 1993; Coifman and Wickerhauser 1992; Donoho and Johnstone 1994b; Taswell 1995).
7. Detailed results of these experiments are available from the author upon request.
8. We get these boundary effects because the scaling and wavelet filters wrap around the endpoints of the data. There have been a number of attempts in the literature to rectify this, with mixed success.

REFERENCES

Barnett, V. and T. Lewis, 1994, *Outliers in Statistical Data* (3rd ed.), Wiley Series in Probability and Mathematical Statistics, Chichester: Wiley.

Coifman, R.R. and M.V. Wickerhauser, 1992, 'Entropy based methods for best basis selection', *IEEE Trans. on Inf. Theory* 38(2), 719–746.

Daubechies, I., 1988, 'Orthonormal bases of compactly supported wavelets', *Comm. Pure and Appl. Math.* 41, 909–996.

Daubechies, I., 1992, *Ten Lectures on Wavelets*, Number 61 in CBMS-NSF Series in Applied Mathematics, Philadelphia: SIAM.

Daubechies, I., 1993, 'Wavelet transforms and orthonormal wavelet bases', in I. Daubechies (Ed.), *Different Perspectives on Wavelets*, Volume 47 of *Proceedings of Symposia in Applied Mathematics*, pp. 1–33.

Donoho, D.L., 1993, 'Unconditional bases are optimal bases for data compression and for statistical estimation', *Appl. Comput. Harmon. Anal.* 1, 100–115.

Donoho, D.L. and I.M. Johnstone, 1993, 'Ideal spatial adaptation by wavelet shrinkage', Preprint, Department of Statistics, Stanford University.

Donoho, D.L. and I.M. Johnstone, 1994a, 'Adapting to unknown smoothness by wavelet shrinkage', *Journal of the American Statistical Association*, accepted for publication.

Donoho, D.L. and I.M. Johnstone, 1994b, 'Ideal denoising in an orthonormal basis chosen from a library of bases', Preprint, Department of Statistics, Stanford University.

Donoho, D.L., I.M. Johnstone, G. Kerkyacharian, and D. Picard, 1994, 'Wavelet shrinkage: Asymptopia?', *Journal of the Royal Statistical Society, B*, to appear.

Greenblatt, S.A., 1994, 'Wavelets in econometrics', *Maple Technical Newsletter*.

Greenblatt, S.A., 1995, 'Wavelets in econometrics: An application to outlier testing', in M. Gilli (Ed.), *Computational Economic Systems: Models, Methods, and Econometrics*, Volume 5 of *Advances in Computational Economics*, Dordrecht, Kluwer Academic Publishers, pp. 139–160.

Nason, G.P., 1994, 'Wavelet regression by cross-validation', Preprint, Department of Mathematics, University of Bristol.

Taswell, C., 1995, 'Near-best basis selection algorithms with non-additive information cost functions', in *Proc. IEEE-SP Symposium on TFTSA-94*, IEEE-SP, to appear.

Wickerhauser, M.V., 1991, 'INRIA lectures on wavelet packet algorithms', Lecture Notes, INRIA.

Wickerhauser, M.V., 1993, 'Best-adapted wavelet packet bases', in Volume 47 of *Proceedings of Symposia in Applied Mathematics*, pp. 155–171.

ROBERT M. ADAMS, ALLEN N. BERGER, AND ROBIN C. SICKLES

Computation and Inference in Semiparametric Efficient Estimation *

ABSTRACT. This paper examines computational issues in semiparametric efficient estimation of stochastic panel distance functions. Our basic model is an extension of Hausman and Taylor (1981), Park and Simar (1995), Park et al. (1996), and allows for a subset of the regressors to be correlated with the random effects. We motivate issues of computation and inference by analyzing the productive efficiency of U.S. banks.

1. Introduction

Recently in the efficiency literature, several semiparametric efficient methods have been developed that estimate the slope parameters efficiently while making minimal assumptions on the distribution of the effects and regressors. Park and Simar (1995) introduced a semiparametric efficient estimator which makes minimal assumptions on the distribution of the effects. Park et al. (1996) extend the Park and Simar (1995) semiparametric efficient estimator to allow for different, more complex correlation patterns. Both of these articles center on the derivation of the semiparametric efficient estimator, but they do not discuss the computational methods used in estimation. This article extends the work in Park and Simar (1995) and Park et al. (1996) by allowing for a subgroup of the regressors to be correlated with the effects in the spirit of Hausman and Taylor (1981) and by discussing the computational issues involved. The new estimator is then illustrated by estimating efficiency in the banking industry.

There has been a great deal of research interest in the topic of efficiency in the banking industry over the past several years (see Berger et al. (1993) for a review). Banking represents an interesting topic of research for several reasons. First, banking has historically been a regulated industry with limited

* The opinions expressed do not necessarily reflect those of the Board of Governors or its staff.

H. Amman et al. (eds.), Computational Approaches to Economic Problems, 57–70.

market entry, which might allow inefficiencies to persist over time. Second, the financial services produced by the banking industry create some interesting measurement issues. Specifically, the determination of outputs in the banking industry posses a problem for research. Deposits posess both input and output characteristcs. Finally, a study of the banking industry is of academic interest because all of the major efficiency measurement techniques have been applied to banking data over the last several years. In this study, we use panel data of over 25,000 observations of U.S. banks over a 10-year period.

We discuss the different computational methods available to estimate the semiparametric efficient estimator. We choose kernel-based methods to estimate the joint density between the effects and correlated regressors. Computation of the kernels involves choice of a kernel function as well as binwidth selection, which ultimately affects the convergence of the semiparametric efficient estimator. This paper discusses kernel choice and binwidth selection methods.

We model the stochastic distance frontier by modifying a semiparametric efficient estimator developed by Park et al. (1996). We assume that product mix affects the efficiency of firms causing outputs to be correlated with effects. We then apply a model that makes minimal assumptions about the parametric form of the stochastic structure of firm inefficiencies.

In Section 2, we describe the basic model to be estimated. In Section 3, an efficient estimator in the class of estimators which do not impose distributional assumptions on the model is developed. This is done by deriving the asymptotic lower bound for the parameter estimates of interest in the presence of nuisance parameters, while allowing for dependencies between the random effects and the outputs. The efficient semiparametric estimator attains this lower bound. Section 4 discusses computation of the semiparametric estimator. Section 5 describes the data. Section 6 compares the results of the estimation. Results using a within estimator and Hausman–Taylor estimator are compared to the estimates of our model.

2. The Model

We start with the output distance function as a motivation for our model of a firm with multiple outputs and inputs. The output distance function provides a radial measure of technical efficiency that describes the fraction of aggregated outputs, given chosen inputs. For a particular observation i, the output distance function can be approximated by:

$$D(x, y) = \frac{\prod_1^m y_{ji}^{q_j}}{\prod_1^k x_{ki}^{r_k}} \leq 1, \tag{1}$$

where y_{ji} and x_{ki} are the levels of output j and input k. The q_j and the r_k are the weights which describe the technology of the firm. When a firm is producing efficiently or when the value of the distance function equals one, then it is not possible to increase the value of output without either decreasing another output or increasing inputs.

It is convenient to linearize (1) using logarithms of outputs and inputs and include error terms, which results in the following Cobb–Douglas form:

$$0 = \sum_j \gamma_j \ln y_{j,it} - \sum_k \beta_k \ln x_{k,it} + \alpha_i + \epsilon_{it}. \tag{2}$$

By construction, the output distance function is linearly homogeneous in outputs. Normalizing with respect to one y_j linear homogeneity results in the following transformation:[1]

$$-\ln(y_J) = \sum_j \gamma_j \ln \widehat{y}_{j,it} - \sum_k \beta_k \ln x_{k,it} + \alpha_i + \epsilon_{it}, \tag{3}$$

where $\widehat{y} = (\widehat{y}_j) = (\frac{y_j}{y_J})$, $j = 1, \cdots, J-1$.

This is basically a generic panel data model where we estimate the firm specific efficiency levels in a stochastic panel production frontier model. The model fits into the class of production frontier models (Aigner et al., 1977; Meeusen and van den Broeck, 1977; Sickles and Schmidt, 1984; Cornwell et al., 1990) and gives rise to the analysis of firm efficiencies (heterogeneities). For the basic framework of the model, we consider a panel frontier model with firm specific heterogeneities, derived from the distance function above. Let $X_{it} = -\ln x_{k,it}$, $Y^*_{it} = \ln \widehat{y}_{j,it}$ and $Y_{it} = -\ln(y_J)$:

$$Y_{it} = X'_{it}\beta + Y^{*\prime}_{it}\gamma + \alpha_i + \epsilon_{it}, \tag{4}$$

where we assume N independent observations (X_i, Y^*_i, Y_i) and $X_i = (X'_{i1}, \ldots, X'_{iT})$, $Y^*_i = (Y^*_{i1}, \ldots, Y^*_{iT})$, $Y_i = (Y_{i1}, \ldots, Y_{iT})$. The X_i are i.i.d. $k \times T$ dimensional random vectors with unknown density function g and β is a k dimensional unknown vector. The ϵ_{it} are considered i.i.d. random variables from $N(0, \sigma^2)$ with unknown σ^2 and the $(\alpha_i, Y^{*\prime}_i)$ are i.i.d. from unknown density h. It is important to note that the α's are orthogonal to the X_i, but not to Y^*_i. We assume the support of the marginal density of α is bounded above (below). Let $(\alpha, Y^{*\prime}, X')'$ denote generic observations $(\alpha_i, Y^{*\prime}_i, X'_i)'$ and $\bar{Y}^* = T^{-1}\sum_{t=1}^T Y^*_t$.

Consider the joint distribution of $(\alpha, Y^*)'$. We assume that firm heterogenieties are correlated only with long run movements of Y^*, i.e. only with $\bar{Y}^*$. Thus, the density h can be described in the following manner:

$$h(\alpha, Y^*) = h_M(\alpha, \bar{Y}^*)p(Y^*), \tag{5}$$

where h_M represents the joint distribution of α and $\bar{Y}^*$ and $p(Y^*)$ represents an arbitrary function.

3. Efficient Estimation of the Slope Parameters

We utilize the estimation procedure derived in Park et al. (1996) and allow for multiple regressors to be correlated with the effects. In this estimation method, efficient estimation of the slope coefficients does not depend on the nuisance parameters, i.e. the nonparametric part of the model. In other words, the slope parameters can be efficiently estimated regardless of the nonparametric part of the model. For an excellent discussion on efficient estimation see Bickel et al. (1993) as well as Newey (1990) and Robinson (1988). For expositional purposes, we present the estimator as an extension of Park et al. (1996). The derivation of the estimator follows along the same lines as in Park et al. (1996).

We will now show the information bound and estimator for the model above. Let $X' = (X'_{i1}, \ldots, X'_{iT})', Y^{*\prime} = (Y^{*\prime}_{i1}, \ldots, Y^{*\prime}_{iT})'$ and $Y_i = (Y_{i1}, \ldots, Y_{iT})'$ for the generic observations (X, Y^*, Y). Let $\theta = (\beta\gamma)$. Let $S_t(\theta) = Y_t - X_t\beta - Y_t^*\gamma$ and $U_t = S_t(\theta) - \overline{S_t}(\theta)$ where Y_t is the relative output and $\overline{S_t}(\theta) = T^{-1}\sum_{t=1}^{T} S_t(\theta)$. Let

$$\omega(\bar{s}, \bar{y}^*) = \int \phi_{\overline{\sigma}}(\bar{s} - u)h_M(u, \bar{y}^*)du = \phi^*_{\overline{\sigma}}h_M(., \bar{y}^*)(\bar{s})$$

be the joint density of $(\overline{S}(\theta), \overline{Y}^*)$, where $\overline{\sigma} = \sigma/\sqrt{T}$ and $\overline{Y}^* = T^{-1}\sum_{t=1}^{T} Y_t^*$. Let

$$I_0 = \int \frac{(\omega')^2}{\omega}(\bar{s}, \bar{y}^*)d\bar{s}d\bar{y}^*$$

be the Fischer information for location of ω, where ω' is the derivative with respect to the first component of the vector.

The efficient scores and information bound are obtained (see Theorem 3.5 in Park et al., 1996):[2]

$$\ell^*_\beta = \sigma^{-2}\sum_{t=1}^{T} U_t X_t - (\bar{X} - E(\bar{X}))\left(\frac{\omega'}{\omega}\right)(\bar{S}, \bar{Y}^*)$$

$$\ell^*_\gamma = \sigma^{-2}\sum_{t=1}^{T} U_t Y_t^*$$

$$I = \begin{pmatrix} \sigma^{-2}\Sigma_W(X) + I_0\Sigma_B(X) & 0 \\ 0 & \sigma^{-2}\Sigma_W(Y^*) \end{pmatrix},$$

where $\overline{X} = T^{-1}\sum_{t=1}^{T} X_t$ and where Σ_W and Σ_B denote the within and between covariance operator.

To construct an efficient estimator of θ (Park et al., 1996).[3] First, find a $\sqrt{N}$-consistent estimator $\tilde{\theta}_N$ of θ. In our model, we choose the Hausman–Taylor estimator. Second, consider $\tilde{\ell}$ as $\tilde{\ell}(x, y^*, y, \theta, \sigma^2, h)$ and construct a suitable estimator $\hat{\tilde{\ell}}(.,.,.,\theta; X_1, Y_1^*, Y_1, \ldots, X_N, Y_N^*, Y_N)$ of $\tilde{\ell}(.,.,.,\theta,\sigma^2,h)$ using the computational methods discussed in the next section. The efficient estimator is then formed by including $\hat{\tilde{\ell}}$ in a one step Newton–Raphson iteration:

$$\hat{\theta}_N = \tilde{\theta}_N + N^{-1}\sum_{i=1}^{T}\hat{\tilde{\ell}}(.,.,.,\theta; X_1, Y_1^*, Y_1, \cdots, X_N, Y_N^*, Y_N).$$

Specifically, construction of the nonparametric part of $\hat{\tilde{\ell}}$ follows by estimating ω, the unknown distribution of the random effects and $\bar{Y}_{it}^*$. The efficient estimator of ω is defined as:[4]

$$\omega(\bar{s}, \bar{y}^*, \theta) = N^{-1}\sum_{i=1}^{N} K_{s_N}(\bar{s} - \overline{S}_i)\prod_{j=1}^{J} K_{s_N}(\bar{y}_j^* - \overline{Y}_{ji}) + c_N,$$

where $K_s = K(t/s)/s$. We use a higher order normal kernel defined as: $(1.5 - 0.5z^2)\phi(z)$, where $\phi(z)$ is a typical normal kernel.[5] We assume the same bandwidth and kernel for all variables and simplify the kernel by using a product kernel as opposed to a multivariate kernel.

The semiparametric efficient estimator is then defined by:

$$\begin{aligned}\hat{\theta}_N &= \tilde{\theta}_N + N^{-1}\hat{\mathrm{I}}^{-1} \\ &\times \begin{bmatrix} \sum_{i=1}^{N}\left[\sum_{t=1}^{T}\tilde{\sigma}^{-2}\tilde{U}_{it}X_{it} - (\bar{X}_t - \bar{X})\left(\frac{\hat{\omega}'}{\hat{\omega}}\right)(\tilde{S}_i, \overline{Y}_i^*, \tilde{\theta}_N)\right] \\ \sum_{i=1}^{N}\sum_{t=1}^{T}\tilde{\sigma}^{-2}\tilde{U}_{it}Y_{it}^* \end{bmatrix}\end{aligned}$$

where

$$\widehat{I} = \begin{pmatrix} T\tilde{\sigma}^{-2}\widehat{\Sigma}_W(X) + \widehat{I}_0\widehat{\Sigma}_B(X) & 0 \\ 0 & T\tilde{\sigma}^{-2}\widehat{\Sigma}_W(Y^*) \end{pmatrix}$$

$$\hat{I}_0 = N^{-1}\sum_{i=1}^{N}\left(\frac{\hat{\omega}'}{\hat{\omega}}\right)^2(\tilde{S}_i, \overline{Y}_i, \tilde{\theta}_N),$$

where $\tilde{\theta}_N$ is the Hausman–Taylor estimator, and where $\tilde{\sigma}^2, \tilde{\mathrm{U}}_{it}$ and $\tilde{\mathrm{S}}_i$ are used for $\tilde{\sigma}^2(\hat{\theta}_N), \tilde{U}_{it}(\hat{\theta}_N), \tilde{S}_i(\hat{\theta}_N)$.

Given the efficient estimator $\widehat{\theta}_{N,T}$, α_i are predicted by:

$$\widehat{\alpha}_i = \bar{S}_i(\widehat{\theta}_{N,T}).$$

Relative technical inefficiencies of the i-th firm with respect to the j-th firm can be predicted by: $\widehat{\alpha}_i - \widehat{\alpha}_j$. We normalize with respect to the most efficient firm: $\max_{j=1,\ldots,N}(\widehat{\alpha}_j)$. Relative technical efficiencies are then derived by taking the distance of each firm's α_i from the most efficient firm.

4. Computation and Smoothing

As shown in the previous section, estimates of the joint density of effects and a subgroup of the regressors are embedded in the semiparametric efficient estimator. Computation of this density should involve a nonparametric procedure, so that a large class of densities can be covered and ensure that the true density is included. Several computational methods are available to nonparametrically compute the joint distribution. These methods include smoothing by convolution, orthogonal series approximation, and kernel estimators. We choose kernel estimators because of their generality (Scott, 1992).

When using kernel estimators, two decisions arise: kernel choice and optimal binwidth selection. Kernel choice can be determined by finding any functional form that meets the necessary assumptions (sum to one, nonnegativity, moment restrictions, etc.). Generally speaking, density functions fit these requirements. The literature (see Scott 1992, Silverman 1986) discusses optimal kernels. However, the selection of kernel made in this paper is based on the desire to improve convergence of the density estimator. Higher order kernels allow us to increase the convergence at the cost of violating the nonnegativity of the kernel estimate. The higher order kernel imposes restrictions on the higher moments of the kernel function. These restrictions can be generalized in the following manner:[6]

$$\int K = 1, \quad \int w^i K = 0, \quad i = 1, \ldots, p-1 \quad \text{and} \quad \int w^p K \neq 0,$$

where p is the order of the kernel. It can be shown that these restrictions increase the convergence of the estimates as the order increases. This can be seen by considering the bias for a p-th order kernel in the univariate case:[7]

$$\text{BIAS}\{\hat{f}(x)\} = \frac{1}{p!}\, s^p \mu_p f^{(p)}(x)$$

which is $O(s^p)$. We use a higher order normal kernel ($p = 4$),[8] because the dimensions of the kernel estimates have a direct bearing on the convergence of the semiparametric efficient estimator. Higher order kernels represent one possible method for dealing with the 'curse of dimensionality'.[9]

A more important aspect of computation in the semiparametric efficient estimator is binwidth selection. Binwidth selection is important because the smoothing parameter determines the levels of bias and variance. At the optimal binwidth, the effects of bias and variance are equalized and mean integrated squared error of the estimates is minimized.

Several methods of optimal binwidth selection are available. These methods include plug in methods, biased cross validation, unbiased cross validation, and bootstrapped cross validation, as well as the bootstrap method proposed by Park and Simar (1995). These methods differ in their approaches to approximate the roughness of the density estimate, where Park and Simar's method centers on the estimation of the slope parameters. The roughness of the density estimate is defined as: $R(f) = \int f^2(x)dx$. In this paper, we discuss plug in methods and compare them to the bootstrap method of Park and Simar. We do not consider the other methods because the theory regarding these methods in the multivariate case is incomplete in the literature.[10]

Plug in methods represent a computation free method of binwidth selection. They generally are calculated by making additional assumption about the distribution of the data to find the optimal binwidth. For multivariate product kernels, the binwidth value that minimizes asymptotic mean integrated squared error for the bivariate case is:

$$s_i^* = \sigma_i(1-\rho^2)^{5/12}(1+\frac{\rho^2}{2})^{-1/6}n^{-1/6},$$

where ρ is the correlation between the variables and s differs across variables. One can see that the optimal binwidth depends on the correlation between variables in higher dimensional cases. One plug in method can be derived by assuming independence of the variables and by applying a normal kernel. The 'normal reference rule' is described by the following:

$$s_i^* = \left(\frac{4}{d+2}\right)^{1/(d+4)} \sigma_i n^{-1/(d+4)},$$

where d is the dimension of the kernel and n is the sample size. Silverman (1986) suggests a more simplified version of this plug in method. Simplifying the kernel to have the same binwidth across all variables, we get the following plug in method:

$$s_{\text{opt}} = \left(\frac{4}{(2d+1)}\right)^{1/(d+4)} \sigma n^{-1/(d+4)},$$

where $\sigma = d^{-1}\sum_i \sigma_i$ is the average marginal variance. Even though these methods make additional assumptions on the data to select the optimal binwidth, they do simplify computation of the joint density and can be considered an approximation for the binwidth. We use the plug in method that accounts for the higher order kernel. This plug in method is derived in the similar manner as above:

$$s_{\text{opt}} = \left(\frac{4}{(2d+1)}\right)^{1/(d+2*p)} n^{1/(d+2*p)},$$

where p is the order of the kernel. This method is derived from the Taylor series expansion of the higher order kernel.

Park and Simar (1995) suggest the following binwidth selection method for their semiparametric efficient estimate, $\hat{\theta}$. The bootstrap choice of s is $s^* = \arg_s \min C(s)$:

$$C(s) = \left(\frac{1}{M}\right) \sum_{m=1}^{M} \left[\hat{\theta}_{N,T}^{*(m)}(s) - \hat{\theta}_{N,T}(s)\right]' \left[\hat{\theta}_{N,T}^{*(m)}(s) - \hat{\theta}_{N,T}(s)\right],$$

where $\hat{\theta}_{N,T}^{*(m)}(s)$ denotes the m-th pseudo sample bootstrap version of $\hat{\theta}_{N,T}(s)$ using binwidth s. This binwidth selection criteria is geared towards optimizing the semiparametric efficient estimator. The method centers on computing the most efficient results for the slope parameters. We are interested in the slope parameters, given the fact that the distribution of the effects and a subgroup of the regressors is unknown.

5. Results

As an illustration of the estimator and computational methods, we apply the semiparametric efficient estimator to a banking data set used in Berger (1993) and Akhavein et al. (1996).[11] The data are separated into three groups according to branching regulations: statewide branching (State), limit branching (Limit), and no branching (Unit). We use a Cobb–Douglas stochastic panel distance function (Schmidt and Sickles 1984, Cornwell et al. 1990) for estimation, where $y = \ln(\text{real estate loans})$; $X = \ln(\text{labor}), \ln(\text{capital}), \ln(\text{purchased funds}), \ln(\text{demand deposits}), \ln(\text{retail time and savings deposits}), \text{size}$; $Y^* = \ln(\text{commercial and industrial loans}), \ln(\text{installment loans})$. Along the lines of the asset approach to output determination (assets are outputs), we assume demand and savings deposits are inputs.

A Hausman test for orthogonality, which tests the performance of within estimation relative to random effects and thus the correlation assumptions of the firm heterogeneities, was performed on each of the data sets. In each test, the null hypothesis of no correlation was rejected at the 95% level.

The efficient semiparametric estimator of θ is based on a bandwidth s chosen using a specification defined in Silverman (1986) in the following manner:

$$s_{\text{opt}} = \left(\frac{4}{(2d+1)}\right)^{1/(d+2*p)} n^{1/(d+2*p)},$$

where d is the dimension of the kernel estimates, p is the order of the kernel and n is sample size. We use this specification for optimal bandwidth as opposed to the method in Park and Simar (1995) and Park et al. (1996) for

TABLE 1

Unit banks regressions

	Estimated Slope Coefficients		
	Within	Hausman–Taylor	Semiparametric Efficient
L	–0.2144 (0.0148)	–0.1971 (0.0141)	–0.1987 (0.0107)
K	–0.1335 (0.0081)	–0.1369 (0.0077)	–0.1349 (0.0059)
Purf	–0.0988 (0.0046)	–0.1022 (0.0044)	–0.1008 (0.0033)
DD	–0.2756 (0.0104)	–0.2931 (0.0099)	–0.2861 (0.0076)
OD	–0.3674 (0.0110)	–0.3883 (0.0106)	–0.3873 (0.0082)
ciln	0.3595 (0.0047)	0.3593 (0.0047)	0.3593 (0.0044)
inln	0.2904 (0.0051)	0.2893 (0.0051)	0.2893 (0.0050)
size	–0.0017 (0.0074)	0.0142 (0.0072)	0.0080 (0.0056)
Adjusted R^2	0.9282	0.9272	0.9243
F-Test	17240	16991	16271

TABLE 2

Limit banks regressions

	Estimated Slope Coefficients		
	Within	Hausman–Taylor	Semiparametric Efficient
L	–0.1943 (0.0170)	–0.2009 (0.0161)	–0.1879 (0.0132)
K	–0.2257 (0.076)	–0.2119 (0.0073)	–0.2356 (0.0061)
Purf	0.0703 (0.0046)	0.0753 (0.0043)	0.0678 (0.0035)
DD	–0.2864 (0.0108)	–0.2848 (0.0104)	–0.2920 (0.0088)
OD	–0.3973 (0.0127)	–0.4058 (0.0121)	–0.3948 (0.0099)
ciln	0.3245 (0.0047)	0.3250 (0.0047)	0.3250 (0.0044)
inln	0.3474 (0.0061)	0.3484 (0.0060)	0.3484 (0.0059)
size	–0.0017 (0.0074)	0.0510 (0.0079)	0.0477 (0.0066)
Adjusted R^2	0.9469	0.9461	0.9460
F-Test	20274	19985	19706

its simplicity. The optimal binwidths for Unit, Limit, and State banks are: 0.5104, 0.5178, 5141.[12]

The within, Hausman–Taylor and efficient semiparametric estimates and standard errors for the stochastic panel distance function are presented in Tables 1, 2, and 3 for unit, limit, and state banks.

TABLE 3

State banks regressions

	Estimated Slope Coefficients		
	Within	Hausman–Taylor	Semiparametric Efficient
L	–0.1464 (0.0160)	–0.1561 (0.0149)	–0.1292 (0.011)
K	–0.1383 (0.0097)	–0.1316 (0.0090)	–0.1438 (0.0068)
Purf	–0.1223 (0.0049)	–0.1258 (0.0047)	–0.1226 (0.0034)
DD	–0.3076 (0.0107)	–0.3019 (0.0102)	–0.3211 (0.0081)
OD	–0.4433 (0.0102)	–0.4428 (0.0098)	–0.4548 (0.0074)
ciln	0.3895 (0.0048)	0.3901 (0.0048)	0.3901 (0.0042)
inln	0.2780 (0.0053)	0.2778 (0.0053)	0.2778 (0.0050)
size	0.0581 (0.0071)	0.0605 (0.0067)	0.0650 (0.0051)
Adjusted R^2	0.9600	0.9609	0.9435
F-Test	29554	30236	11126

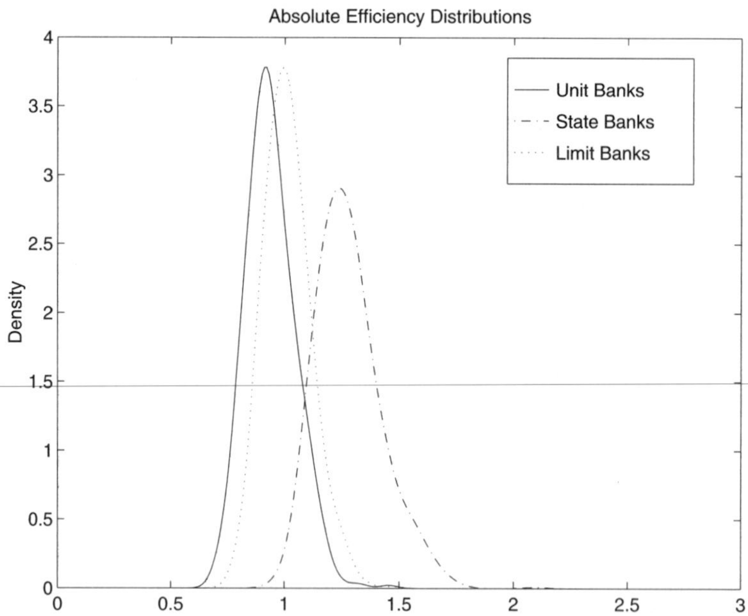

Fig. 1. Absolute efficiencies in semiparametric efficient regression.

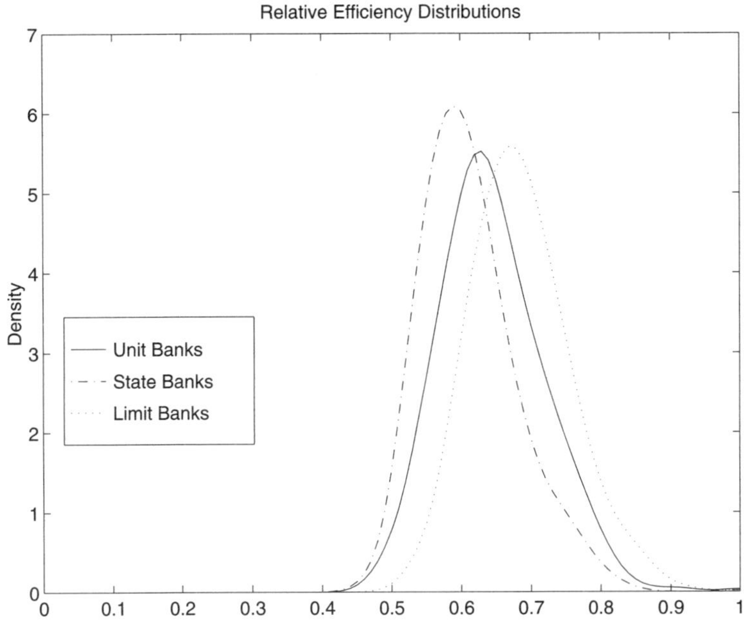

Fig. 2. Relative efficiencies in semiparametric efficient regression.

We now move on to describe our technical efficiency results obtained from the semiparametric efficient estimation. Figure 1 shows absolute technical efficiencies for the three bank types and Figure 2 show relative technical efficiencies. We use a naïve kernel[13] to estimate the density of the relative and absolute efficiencies. A naïve kernel is based on a histogram and is defined for a kernel, $K(t)$, as: $1/2$ for $|t| < 1$, 0 otherwise. Table 4 shows means and variances for absolute and relative technical efficiencies. Kolomogrov–Smirnoff tests against normality indicate that the distributions of the absolute efficiencies are close to normality.

Average relative technical efficiency ranges from 61 to 68.5%, where limit banks are on average more efficient than unit or state banks. Table 4 shows average efficiencies for Unit, Limit and State banks. These results are similar to Berger's, who found that banks in statewide branching states (State) tend to be less efficient than banks in unit branching (Unit) or limited branching (Limit) states, where untruncated average efficiencies[14] are 67.8, 57.6 and 58.6% for the three bank types. These differences can be attributed to the differing correlation structure and coefficient heterogeneity. Furthermore, the rankings of bank types by average efficiency parallels Berger's (1993). According to Berger (1993), these results contradict the usual expectation that greater competition in statewide branching states results in higher efficiencies.

TABLE 4

Average efficiencies for Unit, State and Limit banks

Bank Type	Average Efficiency	
	Relative	Absolute
Unit	0.644 (0.051)	0.940 (0.107)
State	0.611 (0.067)	1.28 (0.140)
Limit	0.685 (0.0695)	1.01 (0.1026)

6. CONCLUSION

In this study, we extend the semiparametric estimator derived in Park et al. (1996) to allow for a subgroup of regressors to be correlated with the effects. We discussed the computational issues involved with estimation using a semiparametric efficient estimator. These issues in the case of kernel estimation involve kernel choice and binwidth selection. Both of which effect the convergence of the estimates. Our study shows that the plug in methods can be effective in estimating the kernels for the semiparametric efficient estimator.

The estimator is illustrated using a stochastic panel distance frontier in the banking industry, which allows for multiple outputs and inputs. Our results on efficiencies were similar to those obtained in Berger (1993).

NOTES

1. See Lovell et al. (1995) for a complete discussion.
2. The proof is the same as in Park et al. (1996), except Y^* is a vector and I is block diagonal.
3. See also Bickel et al. (1993).
4. See next section for a discussion.
5. Higher order kernels are used to insure proper convergence of the multidimensional kernel estimates.
6. The kernel estimator can be described as a minimization problem. One minimizes roughness of the estimates given several constraints. See Scott (1992).
7. We consider the univariate case here for expositional purposes. It is easy to generalize the bias for the multivariate case. See Scott (1992).
8. The $p = 3$ and $p = 4$ higher order normal kernels are equivalent, because the normal kernel is already symmetric.
9. We have applied the normal kernel to the estimator. The higher order kernels improved the results giving evidence to the dimensionality problem. See Scott (1992) for a discussion of other possible methods of handling the 'curse of dimensionality'.
10. See Scott (1992).
11. A detailed description of the data can be found in Berger (1993).

12. Park and Simar's (1995) and Park et al.'s (1996) method was applied to the data with similar end results. The method finds a minimum in the same regions as the plug in method.
13. A naïve kernel estimate is used, because we do not want to oversmooth the bounded relative efficiencies.
14. Berger truncates the efficiencies to allow for extremely lucky or unlucky firms.

REFERENCES

Akhavein, Jalal D., P.A.V.B. Swamy, and Stephen B. Taubman, 1996, 'A general method of deriving the efficiencies of banks from a profit function', *Journal of Productivity Analysis*, forthcoming.

Bauer, Paul W., Allen N. Berger, and David B. Humphrey, 1993, 'Efficiency and productivity growth in U.S. banking', in H.O. Fried, C.A.K. Lovell, and S.S. Schmidt (Eds), *The Measurement of Productive Efficiency: Techniques and Applications*, Oxford: Oxford University Press, pp. 386–413.

Begun, J.M., W.J. Hall, W.M. Huang, and J.A. Wellner, 1983, 'Information and asymptotic efficiency in parametric-nonparametric models', *Annals of Statistics* 11, 432–452.

Berger, Allen N. (1991), 'The profit-concentration relationship in banking', Finance and Economics Discussion Series (FEDS) No. 176, Board of Governors of the Federal Reserve System.

Berger, Allen N. (1993), "Distribution-free' estimates of efficiency in U.S. banking industry and tests of the standard distributional assumptions', *Journal of Productivity Analysis* 4, 261–292.

Berger, Allen N., Diana Hancock, and David Humphrey, 1993, 'Bank efficiency derived from the profit function', *Journal of Banking and Finance* 17, 317–347.

Berger, Allen N., Gerald A. Hanweck, and David Humphrey, 1987, 'Competitive viability in banking: Scale, scope and product mix economies', *Journal of Monetary Economics* 20, 501–520.

Berger, Allen N. and David Humphrey, 1991, 'The dominance of inefficiencies over scale and product mix economies in banking', *Journal of Monetary Economics* 28, 117–148.

Berger, Allen N. and David Humphrey, 1992, 'Measurement and efficiency issues in commercial banking', in Zvi Griliches (Ed.), *Output Measurement in the Service Sectors*, Chicago: National Bureau of Economic Research, University of Chicago Press, pp. 245–279.

Berger, Allen N., William C. Hunter, and Stephen G. Time, 1993, 'The efficiency of financial institutions: A review and preview of research past, present and future', *Journal of Banking and Finance* 17, 221–249.

Bickel, P.J., C.A.J. Klaassen, Y. Ritov, and J.A. Wellner, 1992, *Efficient and Adaptive Estimation in Non- and Semi-Parametric Models*, Baltimore: Johns Hopkins University Press.

Cornwell, C., P. Schmidt, and R.C. Sickles, 1990, 'Production frontiers with cross-sectional and time series variation in efficiency levels', *Journal of Econometrics* 46, 185–200.

Good, D., M.I. Nadiri, Lars-Hendrik Roller, and R.C. Sickles, 1992, 'Some implications for the efficiency and welfare gains in the European airline industry', *Journal of Productivity Analysis*, special issue edited by J. Mairesse and Z. Griliches.

Hausman, J.A. and E.E. Taylor, 1981, 'Panel data and unobservable individual effects', *Econometrica* 49, 1377–1398.

Lovell, C.A. Knox, Sue Richardson, Peter Travers, and Lisa Wood, 1994, 'Resources and functionings: A new view of inequality in Australia', in Wolfgang Eichhorn (Ed.), *Models and Measurement of Welfare and Inequality*, Berlin/Heidelberg: Springer-Verlag.

Newey, W.K., 1990 'Semiparametric efficiency bounds', *Journal of Applied Econometrics* 5, 99–136.

Park, B.U. and L. Simar, 1995, 'Efficient semiparametric estimation in stochastic frontier models', *Journal of the American Statistical Association* 89, 929–936.

Park, B.U., R.C. Sickles, and L. Simar, 1996, 'Stochastic frontiers: A semiparametric approach', *Journal of Econometrics*, forthcoming.

Schmidt, P. and R.C. Sickles, 1984, 'Production frontiers and panel data', *Journal of Business and Economic Statistics* 2, 367–374.

Scott, David W., 1992, *Multivariate Density Estimation: Theory, Practice, and Visualization*, New York: John Wiley and Sons.

Silverman, B.W., 1986, *Density Estimation for Statistics and Data Analysis*, London: Chapman and Hall.

DAVID A. BELSLEY

Generating Random Numbers in *Mathematica*

ABSTRACT. *Mathematica*'s random number generator is described. It is among the "New Class," and, while not perfect, it has massively long periodicity along with many other excellent characteristics. It is shown how this can be combined with *Mathematica*'s other attributes to allow random variables of most distributions to be generated with relative ease.

Having before me the prospect of a large number of Monte Carlo studies examining the small-sample properties of various standard econometric tests, I have been looking closely at today's software to pick a computational environment affording a reasonable compromise between speed of development and production. For speed of development, few packages are as flexible as *Mathematica*. For speed of production, superior alternatives could be found. Development, however, is my immediate concern, so I began examining the random number generation facility in *Mathematica* more closely, for this is clearly the heart of a Monte Carlo study, a spot where mediocrity cannot be tolerated. I was interested with what I found, and it is this that I share with you here.

Random Variables and Random Numbers

A Monte Carlo experiment is a strenuous and systematic exercise of a statistical object, put through its paces under known conditions so often that we can begin to understand its typical (likely) behavior. The driving force behind this exercise is a random number generator. Now, there are several ways of generating a random variable x with a given cumulative distribution $F(x)$: the *inverse transformation* method and the *rejection* method are two commonly employed techniques.

The inverse transformation method is based on the fact that, for any random variable x with CDF $F(x)$, the random variable $y = F(x)$ clearly has the

H. Amman et al. (eds.), Computational Approaches to Economic Problems, 71–77.

property that $\Pr[y \in dy] = dy$, $0 \le y \le 1$, which characterizes the uniform distribution. Thus, y is distributed as the uniform $U(0,1)$. And hence, if we draw a y from $U(0,1)$, the random variable $x = F^{-1}(y)$ will be distributed as $F(x)$. This procedure works well if F^{-1} is easily computed, and in *Mathematica*, the supplied package `Statistics: Inverse Statistical Functions.m` provides these inverse functions for many standard random variables. Unfortunately, they often involve complicated transcendental elements that must be carried out in *Mathematica*'s interpreted mode and therefore tend to be slow – a definite minus, particularly realizing that even a small Monte Carlo experiment can involve the generation of literally millions of random numbers. But they are readily accessible and doable in *Mathematica* – a large plus. Certainly for the purposes of designing an experiment and obtaining provisional results, this situation is hard to beat.

If F^{-1} does not exist, one can use numerical approximations. Such procedures are readily developed in *Mathematica*, but they too are costly in computational time. The inverse does not exist, for example, for the commonly chosen Gaussian random variable. And while numerical approximations exist for this distribution, the more common solution is to use the Box–Muller (1958) transformation

$$y = [-2\ln(x_1)]^{-1/2} \cos 2\pi x_2,$$

which is shown to be $N(0,1)$ when x_1 and x_2 are independent draws from $U(0,1)$. Thus, independent draws on $U(0,1)$ become independent standard Gaussians.

The rejection method provides a generation procedure that is completely general. One simply picks a comparison function $g(x)$ that dominates a known desired probability density $f(x)$ and that has an easily computed indefinite integral $G(x)$ that is readily invertible. Then one draws two uniform variates, one from the range of G, transformed via G^{-1}, to determine a point x_0 in the domain, and a second from $U(0,1)$ to accept (or reject) the draw in proportion to $0 < f(x_0)/g(x_0) < 1$. While completely general, this method can require many sterile draws if g is not a good approximation to f. Thus, the ease with which one can define special functions in *Mathematica*, taking different shapes over different regions of the domain, combines well with *Mathematica*'s excellent facility for both numerical and symbolic integration and its ability to solve for inverses to make *Mathematica* a particularly fertile environment for developing random variable generators of this type.

The preceding brief review of the important means for generating random variables highlights one important point: each requires means for generating uniform random numbers, and thus the quality of the facility for generating such random numbers becomes a major concern in picking a good Monte Carlo experimentational environment. One can, of course, always develop one's own generator, but, for the sake of speed, it is clearly better to be able to rely on a resident procedure running in compiled, rather than interpreted, mode. *Mathematica* possesses the built-in function `Random[]` that has many options for special applications; my concern here, however, is with its basic facility for generating real uniform random numbers.

GENERATING $U(0, 1)$

Random numbers are, ideally, a sequence of numbers displaying no patterns, admitting of no prediction, and admitting of no simple description. But any iterative scheme is clearly a simple description. Thus, less ideally, but more realistically, one deems a sequence of numbers as random if no set of computations on its outcome can reveal the simple description that generated it. There are three common classes of random number generators in currency: *linear congruential*, *shift-register*, and *lagged-Fibonacci* generators.

The linear congruential generator, a staple ingredient in the ROM of some personal computers and many software packages that provide random number facilities, forms a sequence in which the $(n+1)$st element is formed as

$$x_{n+1} = (ax_n + b) \bmod m.$$

The effectiveness of this process in generating reasonable random numbers with reasonable cycling rates (the length of the series before repetition) depends on the choice of the parameters a and b and the modulus m. Large prime numbers for m produce the best cycling rates. Poor choices for a and b can readily produce short cycling rates and/or series displaying patterns.

Shift-register generators form the binary representation of the $(n+1)$st element from the iterative process

$$\mathbf{x}_{n+1} = \mathbf{x}\mathbf{T}^n,$$

i.e., the sequence $\{\mathbf{x}, \mathbf{x}\mathbf{T}, \mathbf{x}\mathbf{T}^2, \mathbf{x}\mathbf{T}^3, \ldots\}$, where $\mathbf{x}$ is a binary k-vector, $\mathbf{T}$ is a $k \times k$ binary matrix, and all arithmetic is done modulo 2.

Lagged-Fibonacci generators begin with r seed values $\{x_1, \ldots, x_r\}$, an operation $*$ (mod m) [typically $+$ or $-$], and a rule

$$x_n = x_{n-r} * x_{n-s}, \qquad s < r.$$

The familiar *Fibonacci numbers* occur with $* = +$, $r = 2$, and $s = 1$.

Each of these generators can work reasonably well in many circumstances, but the best of their practical "tuning" values can give them but moderate cycling periods, and, except for the lagged-Fibonacci numbers, they do not produce sequences that pass the full panoply of tests for random numbers. Actually, one can coax longer cycling periods from these algorithms, but only at the cost of very large storage requirements and high computational effort (low speed). For example, by making k very large, literally in the thousands, the shift-register generator can produce moderately large cycling periods. The increase in storage and computational cost here is obvious. Likewise, one can "extend" the linear congruential generator to include k lagged terms with a modulo p, picked prime, which can be shown to have a cycling period of p^k. And the lagged-Fibonacci generator can achieve very large cycling periods if one uses sufficiently long lags. Thus, the scheme $x_n = x_{n-607} * x_{n-243} \bmod 2^{32}$ has period of roughly 2^{607+32}, albeit it at the cost of hanging onto massive numbers of lags.

A New Class of Random Number Generators

Now, the last figure is written as 2^{607+32} instead of 2^{639} to highlight a comparison, for it turns out that a slight modification of the lagged-Fibonacci procedure can change the plus to times and produce a cycling period of $2^{607*32} = 2^{19,424}$ at low cost and modest storage. This is the so-called New Class of random number generators introduced by Marsaglia and Zaman (1991), which come in two flavors: add-with-carry (AWC) and subtract-with-borrow (SWB).

Each of these related procedures begins with a number base b, a pair of lags r and s ($< r$), a set of r nonnegative "digits" or seeds $\{x_1, \ldots, x_r\}$ in base b, and a carry bit $c = 0$ or 1. The AWC generator follows the iterative scheme: if $x_{n-r} + x_{n-s} + c < b$,

$$x_n = x_{n-r} + x_{x-s} + c,$$

and the carry bit is set to $c = 0$. And if $x_{n-r} + x_{n-s} + c \geq b$,

$$x_n = x_{n-r} + x_{n-s} + c - b,$$

and the carry bit is set to $c = 1$. It is clear that x_n must always lie between 0 and b, so $x_n/b \in [0, 1)$. With appropriately chosen base b and lag-length r, the storage is minimal and the arithmetic can be very efficient, using only additions and register shifts and avoiding multiplications.

The SWB generator has a similar scheme that follows: if $x_{n-r} - x_{n-s} - c \geq 0$,

$$x_n = x_{n-r} - x_{n-s} - c,$$

and the carry (borrow) bit is set to $c = 0$. And if $x_{n-r} - x_{n-s} - c < 0$,

$$x_n = x_{n-r} - x_{n-s} - c + b,$$

and the carry (borrow) bit is set to $c = 1$.

According to Marsaglia and Zaman, both of these generators pass all "randomness" tests with flying colors and have excellent periodicity, which can be shown to be $b^r \pm b^s \pm 1$, where the $+$ refers to AWC and the $-$ to SWB. This figure is clearly dominated by the first term if $r \gg s$.

Mathematica's `Random[]`

The built-in *Mathematica* routine `Random[]` uses the subtract-with-borrow procedure with tuning parameters $r = 48$, $s = 8$, and $b = 2^{31}$. Each call to `Random[]` calls this process twice to fill a machine double, and, depending on the seed, this configuration can produce 2^{10} separate cycles, each with a period of 10^{445}. This is impressive indeed. The facility in practice is very fast and very effective, and it certainly lends to *Mathematica* true legitimacy as an environment in which to conduct Monte Carlo studies. Now if we could only compile the run-time code for the rest of the study . . .

Given the preceding, the recent research of Tazuka et al. (1993, 1994) is quite interesting. For they have shown that this New Class is not really all that new. Indeed, they show that the series produced by AWC and SWB can be approximated very closely by a standard linear congruential generator with a very large prime modulus. The approximation is within b^{-L}, where L is the number of elements of the AWC/SWB series joined to create each uniform random number. In the configuration used in *Mathematica*, we have seen that b is 2^{31} and $L = 2$. The series produced there, then, matches a series from a corresponding linear congruential generator within the first 62 bits of representation.

Furthermore, these generators should be subject to the same latticing problems known to plague the linear congruential generator; that is, the points will line up in equi-spaced parallel hyperplanes. And Tazuka et al. show this to be the case for AWC/SWB generators for dimensions exceeding the largest lag (48) for the situation in *Mathematica*. This is somewhat disappointing, for it now appears that the real advance with AWC/SWB generators is not that they are really a whole new class of random number generator with thoroughly desirable properties, but that they are just a computationally efficient means for producing series from linear congruential techniques with massively large prime moduli, configurations that would otherwise be either very expensive or completely impractical to implement. This is certainly an important step forward, and it certainly means that the procedure given in *Mathematica* is among the best currently available. But there are likely to be advances, possibly combining the output from such generators with others, that can avoid the latticing problem.

It is an interesting question of just how important the latticing problem actually is to any particular Monte Carlo study. If the purpose of the generation mechanism is merely to spread out the conditions under which the statistical object of interest is to be investigated, such regularity may be of no consequence whatsoever. This is often the case for Monte Carlo type experiments conducted in econometrics. If, however, the studies are comparing large numbers of objects, greater in number than the dimensionality above which latticing occurs, the latticing could indeed impose structure in the results that is unwarranted and possibly unfortunate. But, for the small-sample studies upon which I am about to embark, I foresee no problems arising from such latticing and am grateful to have available an otherwise very fast and decent random number generator possessing astronomically large cycling periods.

SOME PRACTICAL CONSIDERATIONS

As noted above, the built-in function `Random[]` has many options. It has been my experience, however, that, if possible, it is best to eschew the options and "roll one's own" transformation. Thus, the function

```
Table[Random[Real,0.,12^.5],100]
```

will produce 100 uniforms with a unitary variance. The same series (if seeded with the same `SeedRandom[]`) can be produced in one-third the time with

```
Table[Sqrt[12.]*Random[], 100].
```

Similarly, the expression

```
Table[Random[NormalDistribution[0,1], 100]
```

will produce 100 independent standard Gaussians using the option provided by the packages that accompany *Mathematica*, but, using the same seed, exactly the same series can be produced in roughly one-half the time using `Gaussian[]`:

```
Gaussian[mean_:0 ,variance_:1] := N[mean +
    Sqrt[variance] Sqrt[-2 Log[Random[]]]
    Cos[2Pi Random[]]]
```

Indeed, even greater efficiencies are available if one needs to generate numerous independent standard Gaussians, as would be required in Monte Carlo work. I am endebted to Robert Stine for showing how such repetitive generation can be given yet another roughly four-fold computational supercharge using the *Mathematica* `Compile[]` function as follows: first define a basic standard Gaussian with

```
pi2 = N[2 Pi];
gauss = Compile[{},Sqrt[-2 Log[Random[]]]
    Cos[pi2 Random[]]];
```

then, to create a `seriesLength` by `size` matrix of independent standard Gaussians (or a `seriesLength` set of independent `size`-multivariate

Gaussians), use

```
SphericalStandardGaussian[size_,seriesLength_:1]:=
    If[seriesLength>1,
    Return[Table[gauss[],size,seriesLength]],
    Return[Table[gauss[],size]]
]
```

These functions are provided with my package `StatUtilities.m`.

REFERENCES

Box, G.E.P. and M.E. Muller, 1958, 'A note on the generation of random normal deviates', *Annals of Mathematical Statistics* 29, 610–611.

Couture, R. and P. L'Ecuyer, 1994, 'On the lattice structure of certain linear congruential sequences related to AWC/SWB generators', *Mathematics of Computation* 62, 799–808.

Marsaglia, G. and A. Zaman, 1991, 'A new class of random number generators', *The Annals of Applied Probability* 1, 462–480.

Tezuka, S., P. L'Ecuyer, and R. Couture, 1993, 'On the lattice structure of the add-with-carry and subtract-with-borrow random number generators', *ACM Transactions on Modeling and Computer Simulation* 3, 315–331.

R.G. THOMPSON, E.A. WALTZ, P.S. DHARMAPALA, AND R.M. THRALL*

Linked-Cone Profit Ratio Estimates of U.S. Total Factor Productivity Growth, Using DEA/AR Methods**

One of the most important steps that a country can make to become competitive is to achieve economic efficiency

Nobel Laureate L. Klein [12]

ABSTRACT. Solow's total factor productivity (TFP) equation is revisit ed in a Data Envelopment Analysis (DEA) context. Linked-cone (LC) profit ratios were used to measure the capital share and, in turn, TFP growth for the United States. Market imperfections are allowed for, and the role of slacks is evaluated. For the years 1980, 1985, and 1990, DEA methods were applied to Organization for Economic Cooperation and Development (OECD) data for ten leading industrialized nations, namely, Canada, United States (U.S.), Japan, Australia, Belgium, France, Germany, Italy, Sweden and United Kingdom. For the U.S., the LC estimates of TFP growth were noticeably greater than the TFP estimates using the standard growth accounting approach; and similarly, the LC estimates of TFP growth were greater than the TFP estimates using Malmquist indexes. Unfortunately, ignoring slacks in Malmquist indexes may well bias the efficiency measures and, in turn, the TFP growth estimates.

1. INTRODUCTION

In 1957, Solow [19] developed a total factor productivity (TFP) equation to segregate shifts of the aggregate production function from movements along it. Autonomous technical change was measured by the equation

$$\frac{\dot{A}}{A} = \frac{\dot{q}}{q} - w_k \frac{\dot{k}}{k}\,, \tag{1}$$

* Russell G. Thompson is Professor of Decision and Information Sciences (DISC), University of Houston; E.A. Waltz is a Graduate Research Assistant, University of Texas School of Public Health, Houston; P.S. Dharmapala is Assistant Professor of the College of Commerce, Sultan Qaboos University, Oman; and R.M. Thrall is Professor of Administration and Noah Harding Professor of Mathematical Sciences, Emeritus, Rice University. Computations were made by the OPCON Corporation, 5 Noontide Circle, The Woodlands, Texas 77380.

** DEA is an advanced operations research (OR)/management science (MS) method called Data Envelopment Analysis; and AR is an assurance region method used to bound the modeled prices (multipliers) in the DEA model. Linked-cones (LCs) provide a linkage of the input and output multiplier bounds.

H. Amman et al. (eds.), Computational Approaches to Economic Problems, 79–90.

where q is product, k is capital, w_k is capital share, and A is the accumulated effects of shifts over time. Constant returns-to-scale (CRTS) were assumed. Solow highlighted (i) the role of slacks, "something must be done about idle capacity," and (ii) the role of market imperfections, "monopolistic factor markets."

In 1994, following Caves et al. [3], Fare et al. [8] used distance functions (see, e.g., [9]) and Malmquist indexes to measure TFP growth.[1] Distance functions provide radial measures of efficiency; possible positive primal slacks are ignored.

DEA efficiency measures include radial efficiency; possible positive primal slacks are not necessarily ignored (see, e.g., [5]).

As well-known, *a priori* weight choices are not required in either distance function or DEA analysis, in contrast to fixed weights in econometric analysis (see, e.g., Lovell [15]). This added flexibility permits weight choices limited by only bounds on the multiplier ratios, called assurance regions (ARs). Linked-cone (LC) ARs link the input and output multiplier bounds; whereas, cone-ratio (CR) ARs do not link these bounds.

In a 1994 LC-AR (LC) analysis, Thompson and Thrall [24] showed maximizing relative efficiency did not necessarily maximize the profit ratio (and vice-versa); see also [20]. Notably, LC profit ratios allow for positive profits; and hence, imperfect competition may be allowed for. If unique, the LC multipliers provide unique estimates of the capital share and, in turn, TFP growth rates.

1.1. Objectives and Procedures

The major objective of this paper was to apply LC profit ratio methods to OECD data for the 10 nations identified in the Abstract in the years 1980, 1985 and 1990. Ranges of value data were used to develop AR bounds for the multiplier ratios. The LC model gave unique optimal multipliers for both the maximum (MPR) and minimum (mPR) profit ratios for the U.S.; these multipliers were used to estimate the capital share and, in turn, TFP growth rates for the U.S.

1.2. Highlights of the Study

The LC estimates of U.S. TFP growth (LC Approach) were noticeably greater than those found by use of standard growth accounting procedures (Standard Approach); and also, they were greater than those found by use of Malmquist indexes. Allowance for market imperfections in the LC multipliers seems to explain the difference. Ignoring slacks in Malmquist indexes may bias these indexes and the corresponding estimates of TFP growth.[2]

1.3. Related Macro Analyses

Economic. Numerous economists have studied the international productivity and competitiveness of the U.S. economy and its leading industrial counterparts. In 1988, a Palo Alto Conference focused on the determinants of productivity growth and competitiveness. The basic concepts [11] included the production function

$$q = f(k, L) \tag{2}$$

underlying (1). Many other prominent economists have also been involved in the productivity and competitiveness debate (see, e.g. [14]). Apparently, econometric methods have been primarily used.

OR/MS. Macroeconomic efficiency and productivity studies include those by Golany and Thore [10], Lovell and Pastor [16], Waltz and Thompson [25], Melyn and Moesen [17], and Cooper et al. [7]. Heretofore, LC profit ratios have not been used to estimate the capital share and, in turn, TFP growth.

1.4. Outline for Paper

An aggregate production possibility set, as in (2), is analyzed by DEA/AR methods. A brief description is provided of the methodology. An example is used to show the presence of slacks and their relevance for Malmquist indexes. Some key DEA/AR measures are summarized. For the U.S., LC Approach estimates of TFP growth are compared to Standard Approach estimates and also to Malmquist index estimates.

1. 2. DEA/AR METHODOLOGY HIGHLIGHTS

In the spirit of Farrell [9], the DEA methodology developed by Charnes et al. [4, 5, 18], provides non-parametric efficiency measures (see, also, [1, 2]). DEA efficiency measures partition into classes [5]. Values may be introduced into the dual (multiplier) problem (see, e.g., [6, 20–24]). LCs link the input and output multiplier bounds; whereas, CRs do not link these bounds.[3] LC profit ratio multipliers, which embody market imperfections, may provide unique capital shares.

3. EXAMPLE SHOWING IMPORTANCE OF SLACKS IN MALMQUIST INDEXES

Let $P^1 = [p_1, p_2, p_3]$ represent a data domain D^1 at time t; and let $P^2 = [p_1, p_2, p_4]$ represent a data domain D^2 at time $t+1$. D^1 is regarded as the technology at time t; and D^2 is regarded as the technology at time $t+1$. Consider, e.g., the data domain matrix

$$P = \begin{bmatrix} 1 & 1 & 1 & 1 \\ -4 & -2 & -3 & -3 \\ -2 & -4 & -3 & -3 \\ -3 & -3 & -3 & -20 \end{bmatrix} = [p_1 \ p_2 \ p_3 \ p_4]$$

and consider two subdomains D^1 and D^2 with

$$P^1 = [p_1 \ p_2 \ p_3] \quad \text{and} \quad P^2 = [p_1 \ p_2 \ p_4].$$

Here, p_4 at time $t+1$ reflects the same activity as p_3 at time t but its third input is 17 units greater.

Consider the four DEA type problems (see, e.g., [5])

$$\begin{array}{ll} \min \theta & \max Z = u_1 y_0 \\ \text{subject to} & \text{subject to} \\ P^j\lambda - p_0(\theta) = S \geq 0 & w \geq 0 \\ \theta \text{ sign free} & x_0^T \nu = 1 \\ \lambda \geq 0 & w^T P^j = -T \leq 0, \end{array}$$

where

$$\begin{bmatrix} j \\ 0 \end{bmatrix} = \begin{bmatrix} 1 & 1 & 2 & 2 \\ 3 & 4 & 3 & 4 \end{bmatrix}$$

identifies the data subdomain and the DMU selected.

The optimal θ $(= Z)$ equals 1 for DMU_0 all four problems, as can be seen by considering an SCSC optimal solution (see, e.g., [5, 18]) for each of the four problems

$$\begin{bmatrix} 1 \\ 3 \end{bmatrix}, \begin{bmatrix} 1 \\ 4 \end{bmatrix}, \begin{bmatrix} 2 \\ 3 \end{bmatrix}, \begin{bmatrix} 2 \\ 4 \end{bmatrix}.$$

The SCSC solutions used are:

$$\begin{bmatrix} \lambda & T \\ S & w \end{bmatrix} = \begin{bmatrix} 1/3 & 0 \\ 1/3 & 0 \\ 1/3 & 0 \\ 0 & 1 \\ 0 & 1/12 \\ 0 & 1/12 \\ 0 & 1/6 \end{bmatrix} \begin{bmatrix} 1/3 & 0 \\ 1/3 & 0 \\ 1/3 & 0 \\ 0 & 1 \\ 0 & 1/6 \\ 0 & 1/6 \\ 17 & 0 \end{bmatrix} \begin{bmatrix} 1/2 & 0 \\ 1/2 & 0 \\ 0 & 17/4 \\ 0 & 1 \\ 0 & 1/24 \\ 0 & 1/24 \\ 0 & 1/4 \end{bmatrix} \begin{bmatrix} 9/20 & 0 \\ 9/20 & 0 \\ 1/10 & 0 \\ 0 & 1 \\ 0 & 1/6 \\ 0 & 1/6 \\ 153/10 & 0 \end{bmatrix}$$

Numerical verification of feasibility for the four primal-dual pairs establishes their respective optimalities. The SCSC conditions are obviously satisfied. Since $\theta^0 = 1$ for all four problems, we have,

$$\theta(t,t) = \theta(t,t+1) = \theta(t+1,t) = \theta(t+1,t+1) = 1.$$

Hence, the Malmquist index for DMU$_0$ is 1. But, note that $s_3^- = 17$ for $[\frac{1}{4}]$; whereas, $s_3^- = 0$ for $[\frac{1}{3}]$. Ignoring slacks as large as $s_3^- = 17$, in comparison to other entries, may not be reasonable in measuring TFP growth. Actually, replacing $x_3 = 20$ by $x_3 = 200$ in p_4 would magnify the problem of ignoring slacks. Is it meaningful to regard the performance of DMU$_0$ as unchanged in the two periods? This seems noble indeed. Clearly, ignoring slacks may bias the Malmquist indexes and, in turn, measures of TFP growth (see also Table 2 verification below).

4. INPUT/OUTPUT DATA AND MULTIPLIER BOUNDS

Let $y = q$, $x_1 = k$, and $x_2 = L$ below to facilitate use of DEA. Purchasing Power Parity (PPP) monetary units are analyzed.

4.1. *Output/Inputs*

Output y. Domestic product (DP) is the sum of private and government consumption and adjusted net savings, i.e., net savings plus net current transaction adjustment. Also below, Gross Domestic Product (GDP) is analyzed as an alternative output y.

Inputs. x_1 is a nation's gross fixed capital stock; x_2 is a nation's total employment.

4.2. *Multiplier Bounds*

For y, the AR multiplier bounds were specified to be one, i.e., a dollar of DP is worth a dollar. For x_1, the AR multiplier bounds were based on the Wilshire 5000 equity index. For x_2, the AR multiplier bounds were based on U.S. total compensation per employee adjusted to reflect relative compensation levels in each of the other nine nations analyzed.

5. DEA/AR ANALYSIS OF DOMESTIC PRODUCT, CAPITAL, AND LABOR

5.1. *Efficiency and Slacks*

For 1980, the capital and labor plot of the data normalized on domestic product is illustrated in Figure 1. Japan, Germany, and the U.S. clearly determined the DEA-efficiency frontier.

For 1980, 1985, and 1990, the measures of DEA radial efficiency and their classifications are presented in Table 1; classifications are also provided.

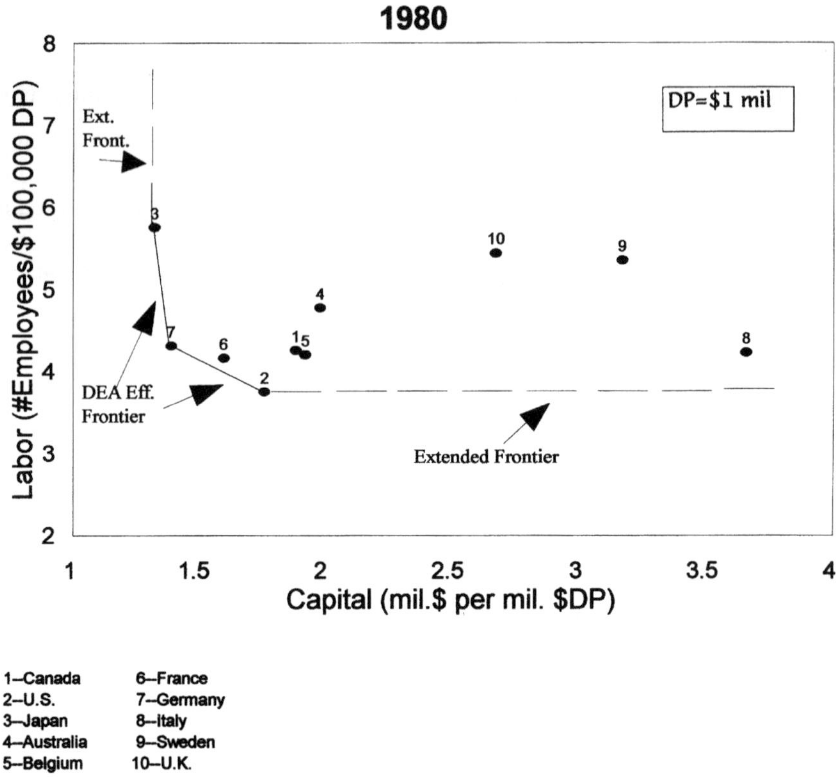

Fig. 1. Labor employment vs. capital intensity per unit domestic product, 10 leading industrial nations.

Recall that, the NF class indicates some positive primal slacks; several decision units, i.e., nations, were so classified.

AR-Efficiency. The U.S. was the AR-efficient nation in 1980, 1985, and 1990.[4] None of the other OECD nations analyzed was AR-efficient in any of these three years.

Malmquist Indexes Slacks. Non-proportionality in the adjustment process was verified in the primal slack computations (see Table 2). Some positive input slacks were found in each of the four linear programs (LPs) used to compute the Malmquist indexes for each decision unit.

5.2. *Linked-Cone AR Maximum (MPR) and Minimum (mPR) Profit Ratios*

The U.S. provided the maximum of the MPRs and also the maximum of the mPRs across the 10 nations in each of the three years analyzed. Inferentially,

TABLE 1

DEA radial efficiency measures (θ^0), 10 OECD countries in 1980, 1985, and 1990, DEA CCR ratio model*

DMU		1980		1985		1990	
Name	#	θ	Class	θ	Class	θ	Class
Canada	1	0.85	NE'	0.89	NE'	0.83	NE'
U.S.	2	1	E	1	E	1	E
Japan	3	1	E	1	E	0.96	NF
Australia	4	0.78	NE'	0.73	NE'	0.67	NF
Belgium	5	0.84	NE'	0.92	NF	0.97	NF
France	6	0.96	NE'	0.98	NF	0.99	NE'
Germany	7	1	E	1	E	1	E
Italy	8	0.83	NF	0.87	NF	0.92	NF
Sweden	9	0.63	NF	0.68	NF	0.66	NF
UK	10	0.66	NF	0.75	NF	0.72	NF

*NF class indicates some positive primal slacks; the other identified classes have no positive primal slacks.

the U.S. was the best place to invest for the true entrepreneur, as reflected in the MPR, and also for the risk-averse, as reflected in the mPR.

6. Measures of TFP Growth for the United States

A linear approximation of (1) provides:

$$\begin{aligned}\frac{\dot{A}}{A} &\simeq (\ln y^{t+1} - \ln y^t) - (\ln x_2^{t+1} - \ln x_2^t)\\ &- w[(\ln x_1^{t+1} - \ln x_1^t) - (\ln x_2^{t+1} - \ln x_2^t)],\end{aligned} \tag{3}$$

where

$$w_k = \left(\frac{\Delta y}{\Delta x_1}\right)\left(\frac{x_1}{y}\right) = v_1^0\left(\frac{x_1}{y}\right).$$

In the 1980–1990 period, the unique optimal solutions to the U.S. MPR and mPR capital multipliers v_1^0 provided comparable estimates of TFP growth for the U.S.; these two TFP estimates differed by less than 1/10%. Accordingly, for the U.S., the MPR and mPR were averaged to estimate the U.S. LC TFP growth rate (see Table 3). The LC estimate indicates, relative to the inflation rate, no real TFP growth (0%/yr) for the U.S. from 1981–1985, some modest

TABLE 2

Input slacks in application in four LPs used to compute Malmquist indexes*

	Input Slacks							
	Within Period LPs				Inter-Period LPs			
	LP1		LP2		LP3		LP4	
DMU	x_1	x_2	x_1	x_2	x_1	x_2	x_1	x_2
1980 v. 1985								
1	0	0	0	0	0	0	2.125E+5	0
2	0	0	0	0	0	0	2.4778E+6	0
3	0	0	0	0	0	2.1775E+4	0	0
4	0	0	0	0	0	0	0	1.0563E+5
5	0	0	1.5217E+4	0	0	0	9.5435E+4	0
6	0	0	0	0	0	0	2.8567E+5	0
7	0	0	0	0	0	3.5399E+3	1.5504E+5	0
8	6.846E+5	0	1.1397E+6	0	2.9144E+5	0	1.9314E+6	0
9	3.2687E+4	0	6.0445E+4	0	0	0	1.4645E+5	0
10	3.5637E+4	0	2.0704E+4	0	0	0	4.4579E+5	0
1985 v. 1990								
1	0	0	0	0	0	140.2	1.6146E+5	0
2	0	0	0	0	0	0	2.0058E+6	0
3	0	0	0	6.8495E+3	0	2.6081E+4	0	0
4	0	0	831.66	0	0	66.0	9.0093E+4	0
5	1.5217E+4	0	3.6665E+4	0	0	0	1.0823E+5	0
6	0	0	0	0	0	1.8273E+3	2.5988E+5	0
7	0	0	0	0	0	4.7302E+3	0	0
8	1.1397E+6	0	1.7278E+6	0	7.1112E+5	0	2.5134E+6	0
9	6.0445E+4	0	8.8801E+4	0	1.7284E+4	0	1.619E+5	0
10	2.0704E+4	0	1.4204E+5	0	0	0	5.0165E+5	0

*See Note 1 for identification of four Malmquist index components.
Also, see Table 1 for nation corresponding to each decision making unit (DMU).

real TFP growth (0.9%/yr) from 1986–1990, and slight real TFP growth (0.1%/yr) from 1981–1990.

Standard Approach estimates of U.S. TFP growth were made using a capital share estimate ($w_k = 0.4$) from a 1982 U.S. Input-Output Table. This Standard Approach estimate was 1.2%/yr less than the LC estimate from 1981–1985; it was 1.5%/yr less than the LC estimate from 1985–1990; and it was 1.2%/yr less than the LC estimate from 1981–1990. The Standard Approach showed negative real economic growth in all three cases.

TABLE 3

TFP growth rates for United States, 1980–1985 and 1985–1990

	Standard Approach (%/yr)	Malmquist Index (%/yr)	LC Approach (%/yr)	U.S. Price Inflation Rate* (%/yr)
1981–1985	3.5	3.8	5.7	5.7
1986–1990	3.1	3.8	4.6	3.7
1981–1990	3.3	3.8	4.5	4.4

*Implicit GNP Deflator, Economic Report of the President, 1994.

Using the AR-efficiency measures in the Malmquist indexes, which eliminates some but not all of the primal slack problem (see Note 3), the Malmquist index estimates of TFP were in-between those of the Standard Approach and those of the LC Approach, but they were generally closer to the Standard than the LC estimates; negative real economic growth was shown from 1981–1985 and 1981–1990. Slight positive real economic growth was shown from 1986–1990.

Standard Approach estimates appear to assume perfect factor markets; clearly, Malmquist indexes assume perfect factor markets. Allowance for imperfect factor markets in the LC TFP estimates may well explain the higher TFP growth rates found by the LC Approach than by the Standard Approach and also by Malmquist indices.

7. Variations in the DEA/AR Analysis

The LC measures of U.S. TFP growth using GDP as the output were very comparable to those using DP as the output. Also, the BCC convex modeling [1, 2] measures of efficiency were uniformly in accordance with the CCR ratio modeling measures.

8. Summary and Conclusions of DEA/AR Analysis for Ten Nations

The LC U.S. TFP growth estimates were greater than the corresponding estimates using standard growth accounting procedures and also Malmquist indexes. LC profit ratio estimates of TFP growth allow for imperfect factor markets. Alternative output measure did not noticeably affect the U.S. estimates of LC TFP growth. The presence of positive primal slacks in Malmquist indexes may bias such estimates of TFP growth.

ACKNOWLEDGEMENTS

The authors are indebted to some helpful data responses by D. Blades, OECD, Paris, and also to some helpful review comments by W.W. Cooper on an earlier version of the working paper. Data, supporting documentation, and additional references may be found in Rice University Jones School Working Paper No. 115, 1996 by the authors.

NOTES

1. Fåre et al.'s [8] Malmquist index may be stated as follows:

$$M_0(x^{t+1}, y^{t+1}), x^t, y^t) = D_0^{t+1}(x^{t+1}, y^{t+1})/D_0^t(x^t, y^t)$$

$$\times \left[\frac{D_0^t(x^{t+1}, y^{t+1})}{D_0^{t+1}(x^{t+1}, y^{t+1})} \times \frac{D_0(x^t, y^t)}{D_0^{t+1}(x^t, y^t)} \right]^{1/2},$$

   where $D_0^t(x^t, y^t)$ is the reciprocal of the DEA-efficiency measure in year t.
2. The reason for this flaw may be traced partly back to the Malmquist index developments by Caves et al. [3] who assumed an Implicit Production Function and used the Implicit Function Theorem to derive their fundamental findings. Possible positive slacks were not considered. Further, all of their findings hold only in local neighborhoods, i.e., in the "small". Fåre et al. [8] applied their theory in the "large" globally across the production possibility set. As shown by example and verified in the application below, this generalization from the "small" to the "large" does not necessarily hold, as might be expected.
3. An AR which requires every u, v multiplier to be positive implies all of the ordinary primary slacks S must be zero. However, additional "slack" terms in the modified primal reflecting the dual of the AR must be accounted for; they are not necessarily zero. In fact, exactly one of these new slacks was positive for each of the AR-inefficient nations in 1980, 1985, and 1990; however, all of these new slacks, plus the original primal slacks were zero for the U.S. This left only some positive slacks for the U.S. in the inter-period LPs. Clearly, further research is required to "fix" the Malmquist index (in the context of a DEA production possibility set) to soundly measure TFP growth.
4. For all of the AR-inefficient decision units (nations), not only the original primal slacks, but also the dual multipliers were unique (see, e.g., [7]) in each of the three years. Thus, the multipliers represented marginal values of labor and capital. This extension of efficiency pricing from the frontier to the interior of the production possibility set permits more fully use of the pricing system (see Koopmans [13]). Similar extensions apply to DEA-inefficiency estimates when unique. Also, see, e.g., Thompson et al. [21] for further demonstration of importance of slacks and uniqueness.

REFERENCES

1. Banker, R.D., A. Charnes, and W.W. Cooper, 1984, 'Some models for estimation technical and scale efficiencies in data envelopment analysis', *Management Science* 30(9), 1078–1092.
2. Banker, R.D., 1984, 'Estimating most productive scale size using data envelopment analysis', *Management Science* 30(9), 1078, 1092.

3. Caves, D.W., L.R. Christensen, and W.E. Diewert, 1982, 'The economic theory of index numbers and the measurement of input, output, and productivity', *Econometrica* 50(6), 1393–1414.
4. Charnes, A., W.W. Cooper, and E. Rhodes, 1978, 'Measuring the efficiency of decision making units', *European Journal of Operational Research* 2, 429–444.
5. Charnes, A., W.W. Cooper, and R.M. Thrall, 1991, 'A structure for classifying and characterizing efficiencies and inefficiencies in data envelopment analysis', *The Journal of Productivity Analysis* 2, 197–237.
6. Charnes, A., W.W. Cooper, A.M. Huang, and D.B. Sun, 'Polyhedral cone-ratio DEA models with an illustrative application to large commercial banks', *Journal of Econometrics* 46(1/2), 73–91.
7. Cooper, W.W., S. Kumbhakar, R.M. Thrall, and Xuelin Yu, 1995, 'DEA and stochastic frontier analyses of the 1978 Chinese economic reforms', *Socio-Economic Planning Sciences* 29(2), 85–112.
8. Fare, R., S. Grosskopf, M. Norris, and Z. Zhang, 1994, 'Productivity growth, technical progress, and efficiency change in industrialized countries', *The American Economic Review* 84(1), 66–83.
9. Farrell, M.J.,1957, 'The measurement of productive efficiency', *Journal of Royal Statistical Society* A120, 251–281.
10. Golany, B. and S. Thore, 1996, 'The competitiveness of nations', IC^2 Institute Working Paper #94-05-03, Austin, April 1994, in W.W. Cooper, D. Gibson, F. Phillips, and S. Thore (Eds), *Impact: How IC^2 Research Affects Public Policy and Business Markets*, Westport, CT: Greenwood, pp. 191–210, to appear.
11. Hickman, B.G., 1992, 'International productivity and competitiveness: An overview', in B.G. Hickman (Ed.), *International Productivity and Competitiveness*, New York: Oxford University Press, pp. 3–32.
12. Klein, L.R., 1992, 'Restructuring of the world economy', in B.G. Hickman (Ed.), *International Productivity and Competitiveness*, New York: Oxford University Press, pp. 33–48.
13. Koopmans, T.C., 1951, 'Efficient allocation of resources', *Econometrica* 19, 455–465.
14. Krugman, R.R. and R.Z. Lawrence, 1994, 'Trade, jobs, and wages', *Scientific American* 270(4), 44–49.
15. Lovell, C.A.K., 1993, 'Production frontiers and productive efficiency', in H.O. Freid, C.A.K. Lovell, and S.S. Schmidt, (Eds), *The Measurement of Productive Efficiency*, New York: Oxford University Press.
16. Lovell, C.A.K. and J.T. Pastor, "Macroeconomic Performance of Sixteen Ibero-American Countries Over the Period 1980-1991," Unpublished Paper, Available from Authors Upon Request, Oct. 1994.
17. Melyn, W. and W. Moesen, 1991, 'Towards a synthetic indicator of macroeconomic performance: Unequal weighing when limited information is available', Public Economics Discussion Paper No. 17, Center for Economic Studies, Katholieke Universiteit Leuven, Belgium.
18. Seiford, L.M. and R.M. Thrall, 1990, 'Recent developments in DEA: The mathematical programming approach', *Journal of Econometrics* 46(1/2), 7–38.
19. Solow, R.M., 1957, 'Technical change and the aggregate production function', *The Review of Economics and Statistics* 39(3), 312–320.
20. Thompson, R.G., P.S. Dharmapala, and R.M. Thrall, 1995, 'DEA linked-cone efficiency and profitability potential with application to Illinois Coal Mines', *International Journal of Production Economics* 39, 99–115.
21. Thompson, R.G., P.S. Dharmapala, E.J. Gatewood, S. Macy, and R.M. Thrall, 1996, 'DEA/Assurance region SBDC efficiency and unique projections', *Operations Research, OR Practice* 44(4), 1–10.

22. Thompson, R.G., L. Langemeier, C-T Lee, E. Lee, and R.M. Thrall, 1990, 'The role of multiplier bounds in efficiency analysis with an application to Kansas farming', *Journal of Econometrics* 46, 93–108.
23. Thompson, R.G., F.D. Singleton, Jr., B.A. Smith, and R.M. Thrall, 1986, 'Comparative site evaluations for locating high energy lab in Texas', *TIMS Interfaces*, 1380–1395.
24. Thompson, R.G. and R.M. Thrall, 1994, 'Polyhedral assurance regions with linked constraints', in *New Directions in Computational Economics*, Boston/Dordrecht: Kluwer Academic Publishers, pp. 121–133.
25. Waltz, E.A. and R.G. Thompson, 1995, 'International relative technical efficiency analysis of a U.S. commitment to lunar solar power', in *Alternative Power from Space Conference Proceedings*, Albuquerque, NM.

KAORU TONE

Several Algorithms to Determine Multipliers for Use in Cone-Ratio Envelopment Approaches to Efficiency Evaluations in DEA

ABSTRACT. In this paper, we will discuss subjects related to virtual multipliers in the cone-ratio model in DEA. Usually, there exists ambiguity in the virtual multipliers in the polyhedral cone-ratio method when some exemplary efficient DMUs' multipliers are employed as the admissible directions of the cone. We will propose three practical methods for resolving this ambiguity, along with an example. Then, we will discuss possible applications of vertex enumeration software, based on the Double Description Method.

1. INTRODUCTION

Data Envelopment Analysis (DEA) introduced by Charnes et al. (1978) has been widely applied in evaluating the relative efficiency of decision making units (DMUs) with multiple inputs and outputs. Relative efficiency is measured by a ratio scale of the virtual input vs. the virtual output, which are the weighted sums of inputs and outputs, respectively. The weights to inputs and outputs are usually nonnegative and are decided according to which are most preferable to the DMU concerned, via a linear programming solution. Since the original Charnes, Cooper and Rhodes (CCR) model, many studies have been developed to cope with the real life problems. One such study researched the feasible region of the weights and has actually imposed some additional constraints to the weights. Such studies resulted in the Assurance Region (AR) model and the Cone-Ratio (CR) model. The initial example of an AR as developed by Thompson et al. (1986) confines the feasible region of the weights by imposing lower and upper bounds to the ratio of some selected pairs of weights. (See also Thompson et al. (1990, 1994), and Roll and Golany (1993).) On the other hand, in early applications of the CR, the sum form was emphasized. Thus, Sun (1987) and Charnes et al. (1989, 1990)

H. Amman et al. (eds.), Computational Approaches to Economic Problems, 91–109.

solve the CCR model first and choose a few exemplary efficient DMUs from among all the efficient ones by consulting with experts on the problem. Then, the corresponding optimal weights to the selected efficient DMUs are used to construct a convex cone as the feasible region of the weights. However, usually the optimal weights are not uniquely determined and hence there is ambiguity in selecting the weights to form the cone.

In an effort to overcome this problem, in Section 2, we will introduce three principles for deciding the convex cone. Then, in Section 3, we will propose three practical algorithms for resolving the ambiguity based on three principles, i.e. the most restricted, the most relaxed and the central. We will give an example of the proposed method in Section 4. Finally, in Section 5, the possible applications of Fukuda's vertex enumeration software (1993), which is based on the Double Description Method of Motzkin et al. (1958), will be discussed. It will be seen that this software will open a rich field of research and applications in DEA.

2. Assurance Region and Cone-Ratio Models

Suppose there are n DMUs with m inputs and s outputs. The i-th input and the r-th output of the j-th DMU are denoted by x_{ij} and y_{rj}, respectively. Let the input and output matrices X and Y be

$$X = (x_{ij}) \in R^{m \times n} \quad \text{and} \quad Y = (y_{rj}) \in R^{s \times n}. \tag{1}$$

We assume $X > 0$ and $Y > 0$. The virtual input and output for DMU$_j$ are defined by

$$V_j = \sum_{i=1}^{m} v_i x_{ij} \qquad (j = 1, \ldots, n) \tag{2}$$

and

$$U_j = \sum_{r=1}^{s} u_r y_{rj} \qquad (j = 1, \ldots, n), \tag{3}$$

where (v_i) $((u_r))$ is the the *weight* (or *multiplier*) to the input (output) i (r). Again, we assume $v_i > 0$ $(\forall i)$ and $u_r > 0$ $(\forall r)$.[1]

Now, we observe the ratio of the virtual input vs. output:

$$R_j = \frac{U_j}{V_j} = \frac{\sum_r u_r y_{rj}}{\sum_i v_i x_{ij}} \qquad (j = 1, \ldots, n). \tag{4}$$

The CCR efficiency θ_o^* $(o = 1, \ldots, n)$ is evaluated by the optimal solution of the following fractional program:

$$\max \theta_o = \frac{\sum_r u_r y_{ro}}{\sum_i v_i x_{io}} \tag{5}$$

$$\text{subject to } \frac{\sum_r u_r y_{rj}}{\sum_i v_i x_{ij}} \le 1 \qquad (j = 1, \ldots, n) \tag{6}$$

$$\boldsymbol{v} \ge \boldsymbol{0}, \qquad \boldsymbol{u} \ge \boldsymbol{0}. \tag{7}$$

This progam can be transformed into an equivalent linear program (LP), by Charnes and Cooper transformation (1962), as follows:

$$\max \boldsymbol{u}\boldsymbol{y}_o \tag{8}$$

$$\text{subject to } \boldsymbol{v}\boldsymbol{x}_o = 1 \tag{9}$$

$$-\boldsymbol{v}X + \boldsymbol{u}Y \le \boldsymbol{0} \tag{10}$$

$$\boldsymbol{v} \ge \boldsymbol{0}, \qquad \boldsymbol{u} \ge \boldsymbol{0}, \tag{11}$$

where $\boldsymbol{x}_o$ ($\boldsymbol{y}_o$) is the input (output) vector of DMU$_o$ and $\boldsymbol{v}$ ($\boldsymbol{u}$) the input (output) weight row vector.

Let an optimal solution of this LP be $(\boldsymbol{v}^*, \boldsymbol{u}^*)$. Then, the set of $(\boldsymbol{v}^*, \boldsymbol{u}^*)$ forms a convex polyhedron, which we call the (optimal) *VU set* or *cell* for DMU$_o$. In applying DEA to actual problems, we should be conscious of the economic and socioeconomic aspects of the problems, which are closely related with the virtual multiplier (weight) $\boldsymbol{v}$ ($\boldsymbol{u}$) to the input (output) items. Although the original DEA models impose no restriction on $\boldsymbol{v}$ and $\boldsymbol{u}$ except positivity (or nonnegativity), we can introduce the relative importance of weights by restricting their feasible regions. In this regard, two notable models have been proposed, i.e. the assurance region (AR) and the cone-ratio (CR) models.

2.1 Assurance Region Model

One AR model imposes lower and upper bounds to the ratio of some selected pairs of weights. For example, we may add a constraint on the ratio of weights to Input 1 and Input 2 as follows:

$$l_{12} \le \frac{v_2}{v_1} \le u_{12}, \tag{12}$$

where l_{12} and u_{12} are the lower and upper bounds to the ratio, respectively. Thompson et al. (1994) named this model 'CR-PIP', since it is an intersection form polyhedral cone ratio model defined by pairwise comparisons (see also Thompson and Thrall, 1995; Thompson et al., 1995).

Likewise, similar constraints may be added to pairs of some output multipliers and even to multipliers between some selected input and output multipliers (Thompson et al. (1990) named this type *linkage constraints*). See Thompson and Thrall (1995), Thompson et al. (1986, 1990, 1994, 1995) and Roll and

Golany (1993) for more details and further extensions. The constraint such as (12) restricts the feasible region of multipliers to a polyhedral cone.

2.2. The Sum Form Cone-Ratio Model

On the other hand, in the cone-ratio model, especially in the polyhedral cone-ratio model, some exemplary DMUs will be chosen from among the CCR efficient DMUs as a result of expert knowledge. Then, the optimal weights corresponding to the selected DMUs will be used to form a polyhedral cone for an admissible region of multipliers. We will now briefly describe the sum form of the polyhedral cone-ratio model (see Charnes et al. (1990) for details). Let us assume that the feasible input weight $\boldsymbol{v}$ is in the polyhedral convex cone spanned by the k admissible nonnegative direction (row) vectors $\boldsymbol{a}_j \in R^m$ $(j = 1, \ldots, k)$. Thus, a feasible $\boldsymbol{v}$ can be expressed as

$$\begin{aligned} \boldsymbol{v} &= \sum_{j=1}^{k} \alpha_j \boldsymbol{a}_j \quad \text{with} \quad \alpha_j \geq 0 \ (\forall j) \\ &= \boldsymbol{\alpha} A, \end{aligned}$$

where $A^T = (\boldsymbol{a}_1^T, \ldots, \boldsymbol{a}_k^T) \in R^{m \times k}$ and $\boldsymbol{\alpha} = (\alpha_1, \ldots, \alpha_k)$.

Let the convex cone thus defined be

$$V = \{\boldsymbol{v} | \boldsymbol{v} = \boldsymbol{\alpha} A, \ \boldsymbol{\alpha} \geq \boldsymbol{0}\}. \tag{13}$$

Likewise, based on the l admissible nonnegative direction (row) vector $\boldsymbol{b}_j \in R^s$ $(j = 1, \ldots, l)$, we assume that the feasible output weight $\boldsymbol{u}$ is in the polyhedral convex cone defined by

$$U = \{\boldsymbol{u} | \boldsymbol{u} = \boldsymbol{\beta} B, \ \boldsymbol{\beta} \geq \boldsymbol{0}\}, \tag{14}$$

where $B^T = (\boldsymbol{b}_1^T, \ldots, \boldsymbol{b}_l^T) \in R^{s \times l}$ and $\boldsymbol{\beta} = (\beta_1, \ldots, \beta_l)$.

Then, the cone-ratio model for evaluating the relative efficiency of the n DMUs coincides with the CCR model that evaluates the same DMUs with the following transformed data set $(\bar{X}, \bar{Y})$.

$$\bar{X} = AX \in R^{k \times n} \quad \text{and} \quad \bar{Y} = BY \in R^{l \times n}. \tag{15}$$

This corresponds to the CR model in 'sum form' ('CR-PS' in Thompson and Thrall, 1995) as the direct product of V and U, i.e. the components $\boldsymbol{v}$ and $\boldsymbol{u}$ range independently over the input and output cones. Thus, the sum form CR model evaluates the relative efficiency of DMU$_o$ by the following primal and dual linear programs:

$$(\text{CRP}_o) \quad \max \boldsymbol{u} \bar{\boldsymbol{y}}_o \tag{16}$$

$$\text{subject to} \quad \boldsymbol{v} \bar{\boldsymbol{x}}_o = 1 \tag{17}$$

$$-v\bar{X} + u\bar{Y} \leq \mathbf{0} \tag{18}$$

$$v \geq \mathbf{0}, \qquad u \geq \mathbf{0}. \tag{19}$$

$$(\text{CRD}_o) \quad \min \theta \tag{20}$$

$$\text{subject to } \theta \bar{x}_o - \bar{X}\boldsymbol{\lambda} - s_x = \mathbf{0} \tag{21}$$

$$\bar{y}_o - \bar{Y}\boldsymbol{\lambda} + s_y = \mathbf{0} \tag{22}$$

$$\boldsymbol{\lambda} > \mathbf{0}, \quad s_x \geq \mathbf{0}, \quad s_y \geq \mathbf{0}. \tag{23}$$

2.3. Three Principles for Choosing Cones

It is not easy to choose the admissible directions, since usually the optimal virtual weights for an efficient DMU are not uniquely determined. Therefore, we need some other criteria for selecting a reasonable point in the optimal VU set. There may be at least three principles for this purpose. The first one, the most restricted case, is to choose the cone as the minimum diameter convex set which makes the exemplary DMUs efficient. The next one, the most relaxed case, is to choose the cone as the convex hull of the VU set of the exemplary DMUs. The last one chooses the cone generated by the 'central points' of each exemplary VU set.

However, from computational points of view, the above three principles cannot be easily implemented. In fact, the first two might be NP-hard problems and the last one depends on the method of choosing the central point for each cell.

3. Practical Methods for the Three Cases

Corresponding to the above mentioned general principles, we will propose three practical methods which approximately implement them.

3.1. The Most Restricted Case

Let the chosen exemplary DMUs be $\text{DMU}_{\alpha_1}, \ldots, \text{DMU}_{\alpha_p}$. We solve the following fractional program (FP_k) for each DMU_{α_k} ($k = 1, \ldots, p$).

$$(\text{FP}_k) \quad \max \frac{\sum_{r=1}^{s} u_r \sum_{j \neq k} y_{r\alpha_j}}{\sum_{i=1}^{m} v_i \sum_{j \neq k} x_{i\alpha_j}} \tag{24}$$

$$\text{subject to } \sum_{i=1}^{m} v_i x_{i\alpha_k} = \sum_{r=1}^{s} u_r y_{r\alpha_k} = 1 \tag{25}$$

$$\sum_{i=1}^{m} v_i x_{ij} \geq \sum_{r=1}^{s} u_r y_{rj} \qquad (j = 1, \ldots, n) \tag{26}$$

$$v_i \geq 0 \quad (\forall i), \qquad u_r \geq 0 \quad (\forall r). \tag{27}$$

The objective of this fractional program is to find a point $(\boldsymbol{v}^*, \boldsymbol{u}^*)$ among the optimal points for DMU$_{\alpha_k}$ that maximizes the ratio scale of the DMU formed by aggregating other exemplary DMUs.

The optimal objective value in (FP)$_k$ is not greater than one and attains one if, and only if, the intersection of the cells corresponding to DMU$_{\alpha_1}, \ldots,$ DMU$_{\alpha_p}$ is not empty. In this case, it is sufficient to solve only (FP$_1$) and the vertex found will be used as the cone, (actually the ray) for the cone-ratio model. Otherwise, we will solve (FP$_k$) for $k = 1, \ldots, p$ and find optimal vertices $(\boldsymbol{v}_1^*, \boldsymbol{u}_1^*), \ldots, (\boldsymbol{v}_p^*, \boldsymbol{u}_p^*)$ which will be used to form the cone. The objective term in (FP)$_k$ corresponds to the aggregated DMU with $(\sum_{j \neq k} x_{i\alpha_j}, \sum_{j \neq k} y_{r\alpha_j})$ and hence the scaling of each component $(\boldsymbol{x}_{\alpha_j}, \boldsymbol{y}_{\alpha_j})$ deserves consideration. In any case, there remains ambiguity in the optimal solution if it is degenerate.

The fractional program (FP$_k$) can be solved as a linear programming problem via the Charnes and Cooper transformation (1962) (see also Charnes et al., 1991), which is briefly described in Appendix A.

3.2. The Most Relaxed Case

Instead of maximizing the objective function in (FP$_k$), we try to minimize it, subject to the same constraints. Thus the objective is:

$$\text{minimize } \frac{\sum_{r=1}^{s} u_r \sum_{j \neq k} y_{r\alpha_j}}{\sum_{i=1}^{m} v_i \sum_{j \neq k} x_{i\alpha_j}}. \tag{28}$$

This program will find a vertex in the optimal VU set of DMU$_k$ which is, in a sense, farthest from the other exemplary DMUs. Let the optimal solution be $(\bar{\boldsymbol{v}}_k^*, \bar{\boldsymbol{u}}_k^*)$ $(k = 1, \ldots, p)$, which will be utilized to form the cone for the cone-ratio model.

3.3. The Central Case

This case corresponds to finding a central (relatively interior) point for each CCR-efficient DMU.

The CCR model is formulated for each DMU_o $(o = 1, \ldots, n)$ as the following LP:

$$(\text{CCR}_o) \quad \max \boldsymbol{u}\boldsymbol{y}_o \tag{29}$$

$$\text{subject to } \boldsymbol{v}\boldsymbol{x}_o = 1 \quad (30)$$

$$-\boldsymbol{v}X + \boldsymbol{u}Y \leq \mathbf{0} \quad (31)$$

$$\boldsymbol{v} \geq \mathbf{0}, \qquad \boldsymbol{u} \geq \mathbf{0}. \quad (32)$$

The computation is usually done on the dual side of (CCR_o) which is :

$$(\text{LP}_o) \quad \min \theta \quad (33)$$

$$\text{subject to } \theta\boldsymbol{x}_o - X\boldsymbol{\lambda} - \boldsymbol{s}_x = \mathbf{0} \quad (34)$$

$$\boldsymbol{y}_o - Y\boldsymbol{\lambda} + \boldsymbol{s}_y = \mathbf{0} \quad (35)$$

$$\boldsymbol{\lambda} \geq \mathbf{0}, \quad \boldsymbol{s}_x \geq \mathbf{0}, \quad \boldsymbol{s}_y \geq \mathbf{0}. \quad (36)$$

Let optimal solutions for (CCR_o) and (LP_o) be $(\boldsymbol{v}^*, \boldsymbol{u}^*)$ and $(\theta^*, \boldsymbol{\lambda}^*, \boldsymbol{s}_x^*, \boldsymbol{s}_y^*)$, respectively, for which we have the complementarity:

$$\boldsymbol{v}^*\boldsymbol{s}_x^* = \mathbf{0} \quad \text{and} \quad \boldsymbol{u}^*\boldsymbol{s}_y^* = \mathbf{0}. \quad (37)$$

Furthermore, for a CCR-efficient DMU, we have

$$\theta^* = 1, \quad \boldsymbol{s}_x^* = \mathbf{0} \quad \text{and} \quad \boldsymbol{s}_y^* = \mathbf{0}.$$

However, by the strong theorem of complementarity, it can be seen that for a CCR-efficient DMU, there exists, in addition, an optimal solution of (CCR_o) with

$$\boldsymbol{v}^* > \mathbf{0} \quad \text{and} \quad \boldsymbol{u}^* > \mathbf{0}. \quad (38)$$

We will present two methods for finding a strictly complementary solution for a CCR-efficient DMU.

3.3.1. The Primal-Dual Interior Point Method

The primal-dual interior point methods for linear programming (see Kojima et al. (1989), McShane et al. (1989) and Choi et al. (1990), among others) will theoretically converge to the center of the optimal facet of the problem and the solution is strictly complementary. However, practical implementations of interior point methods usually employ a long step size to the boundary of the feasible region for attaining the next interior iterate, and hence the optimal solution is strictly complementary but not central. Therefore, in order to follow the central trajectory, we need to take special care in choosing the step size.

In the numerical experiments in the next section, we interpret the 'central solution' as related with the complementarity conditions in (37) as follows (see Kojima et al. (1989), for more details):

[The Central Solution]
An optimal solution $(\boldsymbol{v}^*,\ \boldsymbol{u}^*)$ for (CCR$_o$) is called *central*, if it satisfies, with the corresponding dual slack $(\boldsymbol{s}_x^*, \boldsymbol{s}_y^*)$ and for a sufficiently small positive number ε,

$$v_i^* s_{x_i}^* = \varepsilon \qquad (i = 1, \ldots, m) \tag{39}$$

and

$$u_r^* s_{y_r}^* = \varepsilon \qquad (r = 1, \ldots, s). \tag{40}$$

3.3.2. The Parametric Linear Programming Approach
If a strictly complementary solution, i.e. $\boldsymbol{v}^* > 0$ and $\boldsymbol{u}^* > 0$, is required instead of the central one, we can obtain one by a simplex based method, as follows:

If a CCR-efficient solution is not strictly complementary, we will solve the following parametric linear program in a scalar t:

$$\max w = t(\boldsymbol{e}\boldsymbol{s}_x + \boldsymbol{e}\boldsymbol{s}_y) \tag{41}$$

$$\text{subject to } \boldsymbol{x}_o = X\boldsymbol{\lambda} + \boldsymbol{s}_x \tag{42}$$

$$\boldsymbol{y}_o = Y\boldsymbol{\lambda} - \boldsymbol{s}_y \tag{43}$$

$$\boldsymbol{\lambda} \geq \boldsymbol{0}, \quad \boldsymbol{s}_x \geq \boldsymbol{0}, \quad \boldsymbol{s}_y \geq \boldsymbol{0}. \tag{44}$$

Since we have the optimal solution $w^* = 0$ for $t = 0$ at the end of the (CCR$_o$) solution, we try to make t positive, while keeping $\boldsymbol{s}_x = \boldsymbol{0}$ and $\boldsymbol{s}_y = \boldsymbol{0}$. A positive t^* is guaranteed to exist by the strong theorem of complementarity, which turns out, in the (CCR$_o$) side, positive weights such that

$$\boldsymbol{v}^* \geq t^*\boldsymbol{e} > \boldsymbol{0} \quad \text{and} \quad \boldsymbol{u}^* \geq t^*\boldsymbol{e} > \boldsymbol{0}. \tag{45}$$

From the $(\boldsymbol{v}^*, \boldsymbol{u}^*)$, we can get a strictly complementary solution for (CCR$_o$).

4. An Example

Table 1 exhibits data for 14 general hospitals operated under similar environments. As input items, we employ the working hours per month of doctors and nurses, while as outputs the amounts of medical expense insurance for outpatients and inpatients are used.

The CCR-efficiency, along with weights to inputs and outputs, is shown in Table 2. At this stage, by experts' opinion, we chose H6 and H10 as exemplary

TABLE 1

Data of general hospital

Hospital	Input		Output	
	Doctor	Nurse	Outpatient	Inpatient
H1	3008	20980	97775	101225
H2	3985	25643	135871	130580
H3	4324	26978	133655	168473
H4	3534	25361	46243	100407
H5	8836	40796	176661	215616
H6	5376	37562	182576	217615
H7	4982	33088	98880	167278
H8	4775	39122	136701	193393
H9	8046	42958	225138	256575
H10	8554	48955	257370	312877
H11	6147	45514	165274	227099
H12	8366	55140	203989	321623
H13	13479	68037	174270	341743
H14	21808	78302	322990	487539

TABLE 2

Efficiency and weight by CCR model

Hospital	CCR Eff.	Doctor v_1	Nurse v_2	Outpatient u_1	Inpatient u_2	Reference Set	
H1	0.955	0.332E-03	0	0.959E-05	0.167E-06	H2	H6
H2	1	0.242E-03	0.140E-05	0.714E-05	0.225E-06	H2	
H3	1	0.104E-03	0.204E-04	0.339E-05	0.325E-05	H3	
H4	0.702	0.282E-03	0.128E-06	0	0.699E-05	H6	H8
H5	0.827	0	0.245E-04	0	0.384E-05	H10	
H6	1	0.784E-04	0.154E-04	0.256E-05	0.245E-05	H6	
H7	0.844	0.133E-03	0.102E-04	0	0.505E-05	H3	H6
H8	1	0.209E-03	0.458E-07	0.111E-07	0.516E-05	H8	
H9	0.995	0	0.233E-04	0.426E-05	0.136E-06	H2	H10
H10	1	0.319E-04	0.149E-04	0.215E-05	0.143E-05	H10	
H11	0.913	0.162E-03	0.739E-07	0	0.402E-05	H6	H8
H12	0.969	0.793E-04	0.611E-05	0	0.301E-05	H3	H6
H13	0.786	0	0.147E-04	0	0.230E-05	H10	
H14	0.974	0	0.128E-04	0	0.200E-05	H10	

TABLE 3

Efficiency measured by the sum form cone-ratio models

Hospital	Restricted	Relaxed	Central	Fukuda
H1	0.8910	0.9546	0.9137	0.8870
H2	0.9434	1	0.9816	0.9359
H3	1	1	0.9961	1
H4	0.5456	0.7018	0.5251	0.5826
H5	0.7418	0.8270	0.7991	0.7812
H6	1	1	1	1
H7	0.7361	0.8441	0.7146	0.7601
H8	0.8428	1	0.8962	0.9033
H9	0.9318	0.9946	0.9652	0.9452
H10	1	1	1	1
H11	0.8276	0.9125	0.8402	0.8556
H12	0.8701	0.9690	0.8498	0.8921
H13	0.6096	0.7859	0.6110	0.6576
H14	0.6929	0.9742	0.8051	0.7937
Average	0.8309	0.9260	0.8498	0.8567

among the five CCR-efficient DMUs. The three approaches mentioned in the preceding section would give the following results.

4.1. The Most Restricted Case

We solved the fractional program (FP) in Section 3.1 for H6 and obtained the optimal solution:

$$v_1^* = 7.8408 \times 10^{-5}, \quad v_2^* = 1.5401 \times 10^{-5}$$

$$u_1^* = 2.5567 \times 10^{-6}, \quad u_2^* = 2.4503 \times 10^{-6},$$

with the optimal objective value $= 1$.

Thus, the cells of H6 and H10 have the above common vertex, which was used as the admissible direction for solving the sum form cone-ratio model. The results are exhibited in the 'Restricted' column of Table 3.

4.2. The Most Relaxed Case

We solved the fractional program (FP) with the minimizing objective function (28) for H6 and H10 and obtained the following results:

For H6

$$v_1^* = 1.8601 \times 10^{-4}, \quad v_2^* = 0$$

$$u_1^* = 5.3658 \times 10^{-6}, \quad u_2^* = 9.3452 \times 10^{-8},$$

with the optimal objective value = 0.8863.

For H10

$$v_1^* = 0, \quad v_2^* = 2.0427 \times 10^{-5}$$

$$u_1^* = 0, \quad u_2^* = 3.1961 \times 10^{-6},$$

with the optimal objective value = 0.9065.

The two directions thus obtained were used to form the sum form cone and the results are exhibited in the 'Relaxed' column of Table 3.

4.3. The Central Case

For the central case, we used the solutions obtained by a primal-dual interior point code 'NUOPT 2.0'. This was developed by Mathematical Systems Institute Inc. (Yamashita, 1992). Table 4 shows the optimal primal-dual solutions for H6 and H10. The numbers in the column 'Complementarity' designate the product of the optimal primal and dual (slack) values. Both solutions are sufficiently central in the sense that the complementary slackness conditions between each variable and slack turned out to give almost equal values. Using these two directions, we have the 'Central' column of Table 3. On an average, the restricted case is the most severe in efficiency and the central case is between the restricted and the relaxed cases. Numbers in the last column 'Fukuda' will be explained in the next section.

5. Enumeration of Optimal Vertices

It is interesting to identify all the vertices $(\boldsymbol{v}, \boldsymbol{u})$ of the convex polyhedron, which makes a DMU efficient, not only for the purposes mentioned in the preceding sections but also in order to arrive at an understanding of the overall positioning of the efficient DMU in the $(\boldsymbol{v}, \boldsymbol{u})$ space.

Recently, Fukuda (1993) has developed an algorithm and software[2] for enumerating all vertices of a convex polyhedron defined by a system of linear inequalities, base on the Double Description Method (1958). This software is useful for the above mentioned purposes in several ways.

TABLE 4

The central solutions for H6 and H10

H6			
	Primal	Dual (Slack)	Complementarity
v_1	0.1653365483D-03	0.5570273948D-12	0.9209698676D-16
v_2	0.2959126680D-05	0.3112293210D-10	0.9209669872D-16
u_1	0.3546108830D-05	0.2597124867D-10	0.9209687423D-16
u_2	0.1620134799D-05	0.5684524764D-10	0.9209696387D-16
H10			
	Primal	Dual (Slack)	Complementarity
v_1	0.1592371450D-04	0.7923392020D-10	0.1261698324D-14
v_2	0.1764454185D-04	0.7150641665D-10	0.1261697961D-14
u_1	0.2130784631D-05	0.5921283146D-09	0.1261697912D-14
u_2	0.1443378578D-05	0.8741282332D-09	0.1261697966D-14

5.1. Enumeration of Optimal Vertices for Selected DMUs

Let the convex polyhedron corresponding to a CCR-efficient DMU$_o$ be

$$C_o = \{(\boldsymbol{v}, \boldsymbol{u}) \mid \boldsymbol{v}\boldsymbol{x}_o = \boldsymbol{u}\boldsymbol{y}_o = 1, \boldsymbol{v}\boldsymbol{x}_j \geq \boldsymbol{u}\boldsymbol{y}_j (\forall j), \boldsymbol{v} \geq \mathbf{0}, \boldsymbol{u} \geq \mathbf{0}\}.$$

We can apply this software to enumerate all the vertices of the convex polyhedron C_o.It works efficiently for medium size problems. In fact, for an actual problem with 42 DMUs, 4 inputs and 2 outputs, all vertices of an efficient DMU could be obtained instantly on the SUN SparkServer 1000 and in 15 seconds on the Mac Powerbook Duo 210 (68030, 25 MHz). The problem has 6 efficient DMUs among the total of 42 DMUs and the polyhedron corresponding to the said DMU has 22 vertices. It has been observed that the number of vertices increases exponentially with the number of tight (active) constraints in the optimal solution of (CCR$_o$). It increases also as the number of inputs and outputs does.

We applied this software to the sample problem above, especially for DMUs H6 and H10 and obtained 6 and 5 vertices for H6 and H10, respectively, as exhibited in Table 5 (CPU-time was negligible).

For the purpose of comparing vertices of the polyhedra corresponding to different DMUs, it is convenient to normalize $(\boldsymbol{v},\ \boldsymbol{u})$ so that

$$\sum_{i=1}^{m} v_i + \sum_{r=1}^{s} u_r = 1.$$

TABLE 5
All vertices of H6 and H10

All Vertices of H6				
No.	v_1	v_2	u_1	u_2
1	1.8542E-4	8.4472E-8	0	4.5953E-6
2	1.8601E-4	0	1.9038E-8	4.5793E-6
3	1.8601E-4	0	5.3658E-6	9.3452E-8
4	1.2090E-4	9.3195E-6	0	4.5953E-6
5	7.3557E-5	1.6095E-5	4.0202E-6	1.2224E-6
6	7.8408E-5	1.5401E-5	2.5567E-6	2.4503E-6
All Vertices of H10				
No.	v_1	v_2	u_1	u_2
1	5.5037E-5	1.0810E-5	1.7946E-6	1.7199E-6
2	5.1905E-5	1.1357E-5	2.8369E-6	8.6257E-7
3	0	2.0427E-5	3.7409E-6	1.1890E-7
4	0	2.0427E-5	0	3.1961E-6
5	3.2349E-5	1.4774E-5	0	3.1961E-6

Table 6 shows the normalized vertices for H6 and H10.

It is observed that H6 and H10 have two vertices in common ((No. 5 in H6 and No. 2 in H10) and (No. 6 in H6 and No. 1 in H10)) and 'the most restricted case' in Section 4.1 identified the second of these. The last two columns of Table 6 show the CCR-ratio scale of H6 and H10 for each vertex, respectively. As expected, 'the most relaxed case' in Section 4.2 found the vertex that gives the lowest score to the counterpart DMU, in this example.

From Table 5, we can obtain a 'center' (or a kind of the center of gravity), as the average of each coordinate value, for each polyhedron as shown in Table 7. By using these two directions as admissible for the cone, we obtained the CCR efficiency as denoted in the columns 'Fukuda' in Table 3.

5.2. *Enumeration of All Optimal Vertices*

Instead of enumerating all vertices corresponding to selected DMUs, we can enumerate optimal vertices $(\boldsymbol{v}, \boldsymbol{u})$ of all efficient DMUs as follows.

Let us define the convex polyhedron C by

$$C = \{(\boldsymbol{v}, \boldsymbol{u}) \mid \boldsymbol{v}\boldsymbol{x}_j \geq \boldsymbol{u}\boldsymbol{y}_j (\forall j), \boldsymbol{v} \geq \mathbf{0}, \boldsymbol{u} \geq \mathbf{0}\}. \tag{46}$$

TABLE 6

Normalized vertices of H6 and H10

No.	Normalized Vertices of H6 v_1	v_2	u_1	u_2	Efficiency H6	H10
1	0.9754	0.0004	0.0000	0.0242	1.0000	0.9041
2	0.9759	0.0000	0.0001	0.0240	1.0000	0.9035
3	0.9715	0.0000	0.0280	0.0005	1.0000	0.8863
4	0.8968	0.0691	0.0000	0.0341	1.0000	0.9647
5	0.7751	0.1696	0.0424	0.0129	1.0000	1.0000
6	0.7935	0.1559	0.0259	0.0248	1.0000	1.0000
No.	**Normalized Vertices of H10 v_1**	**v_2**	**u_1**	**u_2**	**Efficiency H6**	**H10**
1	0.7935	0.1559	0.0259	0.0248	1.0000	1.0000
2	0.7751	0.1696	0.0424	0.0129	1.0000	1.0000
3	0.0000	0.8411	0.1540	0.0049	0.9239	1.0000
4	0.0000	0.8647	0.0000	0.1353	0.9065	1.0000
5	0.6429	0.2936	0.0000	0.0635	0.9543	1.0000

TABLE 7

'Center' of polyhedron

No.	v_1	v_2	u_1	u_2
H6	1.3838E-4	6.8166E-6	1.9936E-6	2.9227E-6
H10	2.7858E-5	1.5559E-5	1.6745E-6	1.8187E-6

C is a convex cone pointed to $(\mathbf{0},\ \mathbf{0})$ and represented by a set of extreme rays $\{(\boldsymbol{v}_{r_i},\ \boldsymbol{u}_{r_i})\}$. If an extreme ray $(\boldsymbol{v}_{r_i},\ \boldsymbol{u}_{r_i})$ satisfies the relation $\boldsymbol{v}\boldsymbol{x}_k = \boldsymbol{u}\boldsymbol{y}_k$ for some k, then the DMU $(\boldsymbol{x}_k,\ \boldsymbol{y}_k)$ is CCR-efficient and the $(\boldsymbol{v}_{r_i},\ \boldsymbol{u}_{r_i})$ corresponds to an optimal vertex for the DMU$_k$. Table 8 shows the list of all twelve optimal extreme rays that make at least one DMU efficient. Notice that the rays are normalized so that the sum of elements is equal to one. Fukuda's software *cdd* provides several useful options, of which we will mention two functions (i) to identify the incidence relations between the vertices/rays and the inequalities that are satisfied by equality, and (ii) to find the adjacent vertices/rays for each vertex/ray. The column 'DMUs' in Table 8

TABLE 8

Enumeration of all optimal vertices

No.	v_1	v_2	u_1	u_2	DMUs			Adjacency		
V1	0.0000	0.8411	0.1540	0.0049	H2	H10		V3	V5	V12
V2	0.7935	0.1559	0.0259	0.0248	H3	H6	H10	V3	V4	V8
V3	0.7751	0.1696	0.0424	0.0129	H2	H6	H10	V1	V2	V9
V4	0.6429	0.2936	0.0000	0.0635	H3	H10		V2	V5	V8
V5	0.0000	0.8647	0.0000	0.1353	H10			V1	V4	
V6	0.9754	0.0004	0.0000	0.0242	H6	H8		V7	V8	V10
V7	0.9759	0.0000	0.0001	0.0240	H6	H8		V6	V9	V10
V8	0.8968	0.0691	0.0000	0.0341	H3	H6		V2	V4	V6
V9	0.9715	0.0000	0.0280	0.0005	H2	H6		V3	V7	V11
V10	0.9759	0.0000	0.0000	0.0241	H8			V6	V7	
V11	0.9715	0.0000	0.0285	0.0000	H2			V9	V12	
V12	0.0000	0.8412	0.1588	0.0000	H2			V1	V11	

exhibits DMUs that are efficient for the corresponding vertex and the column 'Adjacency' shows the list of adjacent vertices. The graph of the optimal vertices are displayed in Figure 1, where the efficient DMUs correspond to the facets.

5.3. *From Cone-Ratio to Hull-Constraints*

The 'hull' option of Fukuda's *cdd* does the reverse operation. That is, given a set of rays, this option finds a minimal system of linear inequalities to represent the convex cone spanned by the rays. As a matter of course, the given set of rays must be full dimensional.

5.3.1. *The Separate Cones Case*

Let the admissible input and output directions of $\boldsymbol{v}$ and $\boldsymbol{u}$ be $\{\boldsymbol{a}_j\}$ ($j = 1, \ldots, k$) and $\{\boldsymbol{b}_j\}$ ($j = 1, \ldots, l$), respectively. (The corresponding cones V and U are defined by (13) and (14).) We assume that $\{\boldsymbol{a}_j\}$ ($\{\boldsymbol{b}_j\}$) spans the $m(s)$ dimensional space. By applying the 'hull' option, we obtain the equivalent linear inequalities representation of cones as

$$\boldsymbol{v}H \leq \boldsymbol{0} \quad \text{and} \quad \boldsymbol{u}G \leq \boldsymbol{0}. \tag{47}$$

Thus, the cone-ratio model for evaluating DMU_o can be expressed by the following primal and dual programs

(Primal) $\max \boldsymbol{u}\boldsymbol{y}_o$

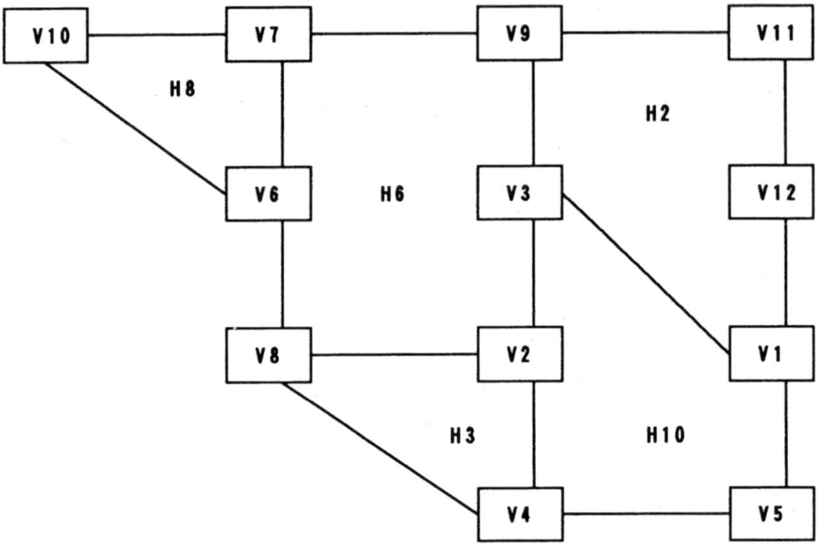

Fig. 1. Graph of all optimal vertices.

$$\begin{aligned} &\text{subject to } \boldsymbol{v}\boldsymbol{x}_o = 1 \\ &-\boldsymbol{v}X + \boldsymbol{u}Y \leq \mathbf{0} \\ &\boldsymbol{v}H \leq \mathbf{0} \\ &\boldsymbol{u}G \leq \mathbf{0} \\ &\boldsymbol{v} \geq \mathbf{0}, \quad \boldsymbol{u} \geq \mathbf{0}. \end{aligned} \tag{48}$$

$$\begin{aligned} &\text{(Dual)} \quad \min \theta \\ &\text{subject to } \theta \boldsymbol{x}_o - X\boldsymbol{\lambda} + H\boldsymbol{\mu} - \boldsymbol{s}_x = \mathbf{0} \\ &\boldsymbol{y}_o - Y\boldsymbol{\lambda} - G\boldsymbol{\nu} + \boldsymbol{s}_y = \mathbf{0} \\ &\boldsymbol{\lambda} \geq \mathbf{0}, \quad \boldsymbol{\mu} \geq \mathbf{0}, \quad \boldsymbol{\nu} \geq \mathbf{0}, \quad \boldsymbol{s}_x \geq \mathbf{0}, \quad \boldsymbol{s}_y \geq \mathbf{0}. \end{aligned} \tag{49}$$

EXAMPLE 5.3.1. Let the two admissible directions for input weights be

$$\boldsymbol{a}_1 = (0.7935,\ 0.1559) \quad \text{and} \quad \boldsymbol{a}_2 = (0.7751,\ 0.1696).$$

Then, we have the hull expression as follows:

$$v_1 - 5.090v_2 \leq 0 \quad \text{and} \quad -v_1 + 4.570v_2 \leq 0.$$

Hence, the matrix H is given by

$$H = \begin{pmatrix} 1 & -1 \\ -5.090 & 4.570 \end{pmatrix}.$$

Let the two admissible directions for output weights be

$$\boldsymbol{b}_1 = (0.0259,\ 0.0248) \quad \text{and} \quad \boldsymbol{b}_2 = (0.0424,\ 0.0129).$$

Then, we have the hull expression as follows:

$$u_1 - 3.287u_2 \leq 0 \quad \text{and} \quad -u_1 + 1.044u_2 \leq 0.$$

Hence, the matrix G is given by

$$G = \begin{pmatrix} 1 & -1 \\ -3.287 & 1.044 \end{pmatrix}.$$

5.3.2. Notes on Hull Representation

Theoretically, the cone form DEA is equivalent to the hull form one, if the matrix of the admissible directions is full dimensional. However, the hull form is more directly connected to the original DEA problem, in that the optimal solution can be interpreted within the framework of the original input/output data, similarly to the assurance region model.

6. CONCLUDING REMARKS

In the first half of this paper, we proposed three approaches to the sum form cone-ratio model with respect to the virtual input/output multipliers. The choice of the admissible directions for the cone is crucial to the successful application of the cone-ratio model. If expert knowledge on the virtual multipliers (weights) could be combined with the three cases proposed, progress could be made in the evaluation of the relative efficiency of DMUs. Extensions to other cone-ratio models, i.e. linked cones (Thompson and Thrall, 1995) would be an interesting future research subject. In the latter half of the paper, we described the possible applications of Fukuda's vertex enumeration algorithm for efficient DMUs, which would be useful for better understanding of the structure of solutions.

ACKNOWLEDGEMENTS

I would like to thank Komei Fukuda and Hiroshi Yamashita for applying their software 'cdd.c' and 'NUOPT 2.0' to my DEA problems and would encourage others to use these efficient programs. Also, I am grateful to Professors

W.W. Cooper and R.M. Thrall for their helpful comments and corrections. This research was supported by Grant-in-Aid for Scientific Research (C), the Ministry of Education, Science and Culture, Japanese Government.

Appendix A. Solution of Fractional Programming

The fractional program (FP$_k$) can be transformed into equivalent linear program as follows:

$$(\mathrm{LP}_k) \quad \max \sum_{r=1}^{s} U_r \sum_{j \neq k} y_{r\alpha_j} \tag{50}$$

$$\text{subject to} \quad \sum_{i=1}^{m} V_i \sum_{j \neq k} x_{i\alpha_j} = 1 \tag{51}$$

$$\sum_{i=1}^{m} V_i x_{i\alpha_k} = \sum_{r=1}^{s} U_r y_{r\alpha_k} = t \tag{52}$$

$$\sum_{i=1}^{m} V_i x_{ij} \geq \sum_{r=1}^{s} U_r y_{rj} \qquad (j = 1, \ldots, n) \tag{53}$$

$$V_i \geq 0 \quad (\forall i), \qquad U_r \geq 0 \quad (\forall r), \qquad t \geq 0. \tag{54}$$

Let an optimal solution of (LP$_k$) be $(\boldsymbol{V}^*,\ \boldsymbol{U}^*,\ t^*)$. Then we have the optimal solution of (FP$_k$) by

$$\boldsymbol{v}^* = \boldsymbol{V}^*/t^* \quad \text{and} \quad \boldsymbol{u}^* = \boldsymbol{U}^*/t^*. \tag{55}$$

Notes

1. For computational purposes, we can relax these positive constraints to nonnegativity. See Charnes et al. (1991) and Tone (1993).
2. The free software 'cdd.c' is available via anonymous ftp from ftp.epfl.ch (directory incoming/dma).

References

Charnes, A. and W.W. Cooper, 1962, 'Programming with linear fractional functionals', *Naval Research Logistics Quarterly* 15, 333–334.

Charnes, A., W.W. Cooper, Z.M. Huang, and D.B. Sun, 1990, 'Polyhedral cone-ratio DEA models with an illustrative application to large commercial banks', *Journal of Econometrics* 46, 73–91.

Charnes, A., W.W. Cooper, and E. Rhodes, 1978, 'Measuring the efficiency of cecision making units', *European Journal of Operational Research* 2, 429–444.

Charnes, A., W.W. Cooper, and R.M. Thrall, 1991, 'A structure for classifying and characterizing efficiency and inefficiency in data envelopment analysis', *The Journal of Productivity Analysis* 2, 197–237.

Charnes, A., W.W. Cooper, Q.L. Wei, and Z.M. Huang, 1989, 'Cone ratio data envelopment analysis and multi-objective programming', *International Journal of System Sciences* 20, 1099–1118.

Choi, I.C., C.L. Monmma, and D.F. Shanno, 1990, 'Further development of a primal-dual interior point method', *ORSA Journal on Computing* 2, 304–311.

Fukuda, K., 1993, 'cdd.c : C-implementation of the double description method for computing all vertices and extremal rays of a convex polyhedron given by a system of linear inequalities', Department of Mathematics, Swiss Federal Institute of Technology, Lausanne, Switzerland.

Kojima, M., S. Mizuno, and A. Yoshise, 1989, 'A primal-dual interior point method for linear programming', in *Progress in Mathematical Programming: Interior-Point and Related Methods*, N. Megiddo (Ed.), New York: Springer-Verlag, pp. 29–48.

McShane K.A., C.L. Monma, and D.F. Shanno, 1989, 'An implementation of a primal-dual interior point method for linear programming', *ORSA Journal on Computing* 1, 70–83.

Motzkin, T.S., H. Raiffa, G.L. Thompson, and M.R. Thrall, 1958, 'The double description method', in *Contribution to the Theory of Games*, Vol. 2, H.W. Kuhn and A.W. Tucker (Eds), Annals of Mathematics Studies, No. 28, Princeton: Princeton University Press, pp. 81–103.

Roll, Y. and B. Golany, 1993, 'Alternate methods of treating factor weights in DEA', *OMEGA International Journal of Management Science* 21, 99–109.

Sun, D.B., 1987, 'Evaluation of managerial performance of large commercial banks by data envelopment analysis', Unpublished Ph.D. dissertation (Graduate School of Business, University of Texas, Austin, Texas).

Thompson, R.G., P.S. Dharmapala, L.J. Rothenberg, and R.M. Tharll, 1994, 'DEA ARs and CRs applied to worldwide major oil companies', *Journal of Productivity Analysis* 5, 181–203.

Thompson, R.G., L.N. Langemeier, C.-T. Lee, E. Lee, and R.M. Thrall, 1990, 'The role of multiplier bounds in efficiency analysis with application to Kansas farming', *Journal of Econometrics* 46, 93–108.

Thompson, R.G., F.D. Singleton, Jr., R.M. Thrall, and B.A. Smith, 1986, 'Comparative site evaluations for locating a high-energy physics lab in Texas', *Interfaces* 16, 35–49.

Thompson, R.G., E.A. Waltz, D.S. Dharmapala, and R.M. Thrall, 1995, 'DEA/AR measures and Malmquist indexes applied to ten OECD nations', Working Paper No. 115, Jesse H. Jones Graduate School of Administration, Rice University, Houston, Texas 77251.

Thompson, R.G. and R.M. Thrall, 1995, 'Assurance region and cone ratio', Paper presented at the First International Conference of the Society on Computational Economics, May 21–24, 1995, Austin, Texas.

Tone, K., 1993, 'An ε-free DEA and a new measure of efficiency', *Journal of the Operations Research Society of Japan* 36, 167–174.

Yamashita, H., 1992, revised 1994, 'A globally convergent primal-dual interior point method for constrained optimization', Technical Report, Mathematical Systems Institute Inc., Tokyo, Japan.

PART TWO

Computational Methods in Finance

RAMAPRASAD BHAR AND CARL CHIARELLA

The Estimation of the Heath–Jarrow–Morton Model by Use of Kalman Filtering Techniques

ABSTRACT. A fairly flexible functional form for the forward rate volatility is applied to the Heath–Jarrow–Morton model of the term structure of interest rates to reduce the system dynamics to Markovian form. The resulting stochastic dynamic system is cast into a form suitable for estimation by use of nonlinear filtering methodology. The technique is applied to 90 day bank bill and 3 year treasury bond data in the Australian market.

1. Introduction

The modern theory of the term structure of interest rates and the pricing of interest rate sensitive contingent claims involves expressing the bond price dynamics in terms of an equivalent probability measure which renders them arbitrage free. As a consequence both the drift and the diffusion coefficients of the stochastic differential equations describing bond price dynamics become functions of a maturity dependent volatility function. The genesis of this approach is the work of Heath, Jarrow and Morton (Heath et al. 1992a).

Analogously to the Black–Scholes equity option pricing model, the main input in the HJM approach is the entire term structure of the underlying asset and its volatility. Given the current term structure, the volatility function describes how it subsequently evolves over time. Heath et al. (1992b) describe how this model can be used to price and hedge the entire interest rate derivative book of a financial institution and thus offer a consistent approach to the management of interest rate exposure. At the very heart of this technique is the choice of the volatility function. In the HJM context, the volatility function describes the fluctuations of each part of the term structure. Thus the modelling of the term structure of volatility becomes of crucial importance in modelling term structure of interest rates and in contingent claims pricing. Many of the forms of the volatility functions reported in the literature have been chosen for analytical convenience rather than being based on any empirical evidence.

H. Amman et al. (eds.), Computational Approaches to Economic Problems, 113–126.

Apart from the study of Heath et al. (1990), there has not been a great deal of empirical research into the appropriate form of the volatility function to be used in the arbitrage free class of models. This paper seeks to address this gap. The parameters of a postulated functional form of the volatility function are estimated using the observed bond prices by applying Kalman filtering methodology. This requires transformation of the HJM model to finite-dimensional state space form. The complexity of this step is determined by the functional form of the volatility function and, in particular, whether it is dependent on the state variable. The data sets used for the empirical study are the 90-day bill futures contracts trading on the Sydney Futures Exchange (SFE) and the prices of 3-year Australian Treasury bonds traded between banks. The former instrument, for all intents and purposes, is the coupon-free bond of the theoretical development and thus any errors introduced by coupon stripping procedures are avoided.

The remainder of the paper is organised as follows. In Section 2, the essential framework of the HJM model relevant to this study is reviewed. Section 3 reviews how the model may be expressed in finite dimensional state space form when certain functional forms for the volatility function are adopted. Section 4 shows how the state space form may be used to apply Kalman filtering methodology to estimate the parameters of the volatility function. In Section 5, the data set is described in detail, whereas Section 6 describes the empirical results. Section 7 concludes the paper.

2. The Basic Framework

Based on the general framework of Heath et al. (1992a) we assume that the forward rate $f(t,T)$ (the rate contracted at time t for instantaneous borrowing at time $T \geq t$) is driven by the one factor stochastic integral equation

$$f(t,T) - f(0,T) = \int_0^t \alpha(v,T)dv + \int_0^t \sigma(v,T)dW(v). \tag{1}$$

Here $\alpha(t,T)$, $\sigma(t,T)$ are respectively the drift and diffusion coefficients at time t for an instrument maturing at time T, $f(0,T)$ is the initial forward rate curve (observed from the market determined yield curve) and dW are the increments of the single Wiener process driving the stochastic fluctuations of the forward rate curve.

Heath et al. show (see Bhar and Chiarella (1996) for a succinct summary) that if the economy is arbitrage free then the drift cannot be chosen independently of the volatility function. As a consequence the stochastic process for the forward rate becomes which may also be written as the stochastic differential equation

$$f(t,T) = f(0,T) + \int_0^t \sigma(v,T) \int_v^T \sigma(v,y)dydv + \int_0^t \sigma(v,T)d\tilde{W}(v), \quad (2)$$

which may also be written as the stochastic differential equation

$$\begin{aligned} df(t,T) &= \left(\sigma(t,T) \int_t^T \sigma(t,y)dy\right) dt + \sigma(t,T)d\tilde{W}(t), \\ &\equiv \mu_f(t,T)dt + \sigma(t,T)d\tilde{W}(t). \end{aligned} \quad (3)$$

Here $d\tilde{W}$ are the increments of a Wiener process from the equivalent martingale probability measure which arises in the HJM theory by application of Girsanov's theorem.

The corresponding stochastic differential equation for the instantaneous spot rate of interest ($r(t) = f(t,t)$) is given by

$$\begin{aligned} dr(t) &= \left[f_2(0,t) + \frac{\partial}{\partial t}\int_0^t \sigma(v,t) \int_v^t \sigma(v,y)dydv + \int_0^t \sigma_2(v,t)d\tilde{W}(v)\right] dt \\ &\quad + \sigma(t,t)d\tilde{W}(t). \end{aligned} \quad (4)$$

If $P(t,T)$ denotes the price at time t of a pure discount bond maturing at time T then it can be shown by application of Ito's lemma that, $B(t,T) \equiv \ln P(t,T)$, is driven by the stochastic differential equation

$$\begin{aligned} dB(t,T) &= \left[r(t) - \frac{1}{2}\sigma_B^2(t,T)\right] dt - \int_t^T \sigma(t,v)dvd\tilde{W}(t) \\ &\equiv \mu_B(t,T)dt + \sigma_B(t,T)d\tilde{W}(t). \end{aligned} \quad (5)$$

The principle difficulty in application of the HJM model lies in the third term in the expression for the drift in Equation (4). This expression involves an integral over the history of the shock process up to time t and so makes the stochastic process driving bond prices non-Markovian. Most applications of the HJM approach seek some simplification which renders the driving dynamics Markovian.

3. Reduction to a Markovian System

It is shown in Bhar and Chiarella (1996) that by assuming for the forward rate volatility the specific functional form:

$$\sigma(t,T) = a_0 e^{-\lambda(T-t)} r(t)^{\gamma}, \quad (6)$$

then the dynamics, driving $r(t)$ and $B(t,T)$ turn out to be Markovian. Here a_0, λ are parameters to be determined and γ will be set at 0.5 or 1 in the empirical analysis below.

It is further shown in Bhar and Chiarella (1996) that the non-Markovian stochastic dynamics system (4), (5) for $r(t)$, $B(t,T)$, with $\sigma(t,T)$ given by (6) can be expressed as the Markovian stochastic differential system

$$dS(t) = [J(t) + H(S(t),t)S(t)]dt + V(S(t),t)d\tilde{W}(t), \tag{7}$$

where

$$S(t) \equiv [B(t,T), r(t), \phi(t)]^T, \tag{7a}$$

$$J(t) \equiv [0, f_2(0,t) + \lambda f(0,t), 0]^T, \tag{7b}$$

$$V(S(t),t) \equiv [a_0 r(t)^\gamma (e^{-\lambda(T-t)} - 1)/\lambda, a_0 r(t)^\gamma, 0]^T, \tag{7c}$$

$$H(t) = \begin{bmatrix} 0 & h_{12} & 0 \\ 0 & -\lambda & a_0^2 \\ 0 & h_{32} & -2\lambda \end{bmatrix}, \qquad \begin{aligned} h_{12} &= 1 - \tfrac{1}{2}\, r(t)^{2\gamma-1}[e^{-\lambda(T-t)} - 1]^t/\lambda^2, \\ h_{32} &= r(t)^{2\gamma-1}, \end{aligned} \tag{7d}$$

and

$$\phi(t) \equiv \int_0^t r(u)^{2\gamma} e^{-2\gamma(t-u)} du. \tag{7e}$$

The state variable $\phi(t)$, which summarises characteristics of the path history of the instantaneous spot rate process is not readily observable. The instantaneous spot rate $r(t)$ itself is also assumed not to be directly observable in this study. The shortest rate that could be used in Australia would be a 30-day rate. Data on overnight rates exist but are considered too "noisy" for reliable empirical work. So the only element of the state vector $S(t)$ which is considered observable is the log bond price $B(t,T)$, hence we have the observation vector (in this case a scalar)

$$Y(t) = CS(t) + \varepsilon(t), \tag{8}$$

where

$$C = [1,0,0] \quad \text{and} \quad \varepsilon(t) \sim N(0, \sigma_\varepsilon).$$

We add a measurement error term to the observations in (8) to cater for effects such as bid-ask spread, thin trading and model misspecification.

It should be pointed out that similar reductions to a Markovian system have been found by Carverhill (1994) and Ritchken and Sankarasubramanian (1995).

4. Nonlinear Filter Estimation

Under the assumed specification of the volatility function, the problem of estimating the unknown parameters (a_0, λ) essentially implies solving the stochastic differential system represented by Equation (7). Since, this system contains the unobserved variables $r(t)$, $\phi(t)$ and the only observed variable $B(t,T)$ enters the system through the measurement Equation (8), the approach to solving this problem is based on nonlinear filtering.

For ease of exposition, Equation (7) is expressed as

$$dS(t) = F(S(t);\theta)dt + V(S(t);\theta)d\tilde{W}(t), \tag{9}$$

whcrc

$$\theta = [a_0, \lambda].$$

In general, $F(\cdot)$ and $V(\cdot)$ will be nonlinear in both the state variables as well as the parameters. Estimation of the parameter θ in Equation (9) will involve some form of discretisation from which the conditional moments over successive time intervals can be calculated.

Our approach to estimating the parameter vector θ consists is seeking the probability of the set of observations $\Pr(Y_1, Y_2, \ldots, Y_n, \theta)$ and maximising this quantity with respect to θ. This probability in turn is the product of the transition probabilities $\Pr(Y_{k+1} \mid Y_k;\theta)$ which can be calculated by the Kalman filter (see Harvey (1989) for an exposition) on the assumption of conditional normality over each subinterval (t_k, t_{k+1}).

We use $\hat{S}_{k+1|k}$ to denote the best forecast of $S(t_{k+1})$ madc at t_k bascd on the observation vector Y_k and $\hat{S}_{k+1|k+1}$ to denote the best estimate of $S(t_{k+1})$ based on knowledge of the observation vector Y_{k+1} at t_{k+1}. The essence of the Kalman filter technique is to recursively calculate $\hat{S}_{k+1|k}$, $\hat{S}_{k+1|k+1}$ via a sequence of updating equations which we reproduce here for completeness.[1]

A number of approaches to the discretisation of Equation (9) are possible using some of the schemes for the numerical solution of stochastic differential equations, outlined in Kloeden and Platen (1992). Here we shall use the Milstein scheme which is an order 1.0 strong Taylor scheme. We employ a strong scheme as these generate pathwise approximations which are necessary for Monte Carlo studies of the estimators. In applying this scheme we approximate the volatility vector over each subinterval by its most recent filter estimate.

The Milstein scheme discretises the stochastic differential Equation (9) as

$$\begin{aligned} S_{k+1} &= [S_k + F(S_k;\theta)\delta_k] + V(S_k;\theta)\sqrt{\delta_k}\,\zeta_k \\ &\quad + \frac{1}{2}\,V'(S_k;\theta)V(S_k;\theta)\delta_k[(\zeta_k)^2 - 1]. \end{aligned} \tag{10}$$

where $\zeta_k \sim N(0,1)$ and $\delta_k = t_{k+1} - t_k$.

Here V' is the matrix of derivatives of the elements of the vector V with respect to elements of the state vector S. Using $V^{(i)}$ to denote the ith element of V then

$$V' = \begin{bmatrix} \dfrac{\partial V^{(1)}}{\partial B} & \dfrac{\partial V^{(1)}}{\partial r} & \dfrac{\partial V^{(1)}}{\partial \phi} \\[2ex] \dfrac{\partial V^{(2)}}{\partial B} & \dfrac{\partial V^{(2)}}{\partial r} & \dfrac{\partial V^{(2)}}{\partial \phi} \\[2ex] \dfrac{\partial V^{(3)}}{\partial B} & \dfrac{\partial V^{(3)}}{\partial r} & \dfrac{\partial V^{(3)}}{\partial \phi} \end{bmatrix} = \begin{bmatrix} 0 & a_0(e^{-\lambda(T-t)} - 1)\gamma r^{\gamma-1}/\lambda & 0 \\ 0 & a_0\gamma r^{\gamma-1} & 0 \\ 0 & 0 & 0 \end{bmatrix}. \tag{11}$$

Since S_{k+1} is conditionally normal within (t_k, t_{k+1}) we obtain from Equation (10)

$$E(S_{k+1} \mid S_k) = S_k + F(S_k;\theta)\delta_k,$$

and

$$\begin{aligned} \mathrm{Cov}(S_{k+1} \mid S_k) &= V(S_k;\theta)V^T(S_k;\theta)\delta_k \\ &\quad + \frac{1}{2}\,(V'VV^T + VV^TV'^T)\delta_k^{3/2}E(\zeta_k^3) \\ &\quad + \frac{1}{4}\,V'VV^TV'\delta_k^2(E(\zeta_k^4) - 1). \end{aligned} \tag{12}$$

From the above two equations, the best forecast of S at t_{k+1} made at t_k (knowing Y_k at t_k) is

$$\hat{S}_{k+1|k} = \hat{S}_{k|k} + F(\hat{S}_{k|k};\theta)\delta_k,$$

and the best forecast of variance of $S_{k+1|k}$ is

$$P_{k+1|k} = \exp[A_k\delta_k]P_{k|k}(\exp[A_k\delta_k])^T + Q_{k+1}, \tag{13}$$

where Q_{k+1} is given by (12). The estimation error over (t_k, t_{k+1}) is then calculated as

$$Y_{k+1} - C\hat{S}_{k+1|k}, \tag{14}$$

and its variance is

$$v_{k+1} = CP_{k+1|k}C^T + \sigma_\varepsilon. \tag{15}$$

The Kalman filter updating equation for the state vector is

$$\hat{S}_{k+1|k+1} = \hat{S}_{k+1|k} + K_{k+1}[Y_{k+1} - C\hat{S}_{k+1|k}], \tag{16}$$

where K_{k+1}, the Kalman gain matrix, is given by

$$K_{k+1} = P_{k+1|k}C^T v_{k+1}^{-1}. \tag{17}$$

(Note that v_{k+1} in this case is a scalar.)

The recursion for the error covariance completes the specification of the Kalman filter updating equations

$$P_{k+1|k+1} = [I - K_{t+1}C]P_{k+1|k}[I - K_{k+1}C]^T + K_{k+1}\sigma_\varepsilon K_{k+1}^T. \tag{18}$$

Under the assumption of normal distribution as incorporated in Equations (11) and (12), the transition probability density function for the state vector S_k to S_{k+1} can be written for a given set of observations (T) with the help of the updating Equations (15–18). Following the argument in Harvey (1989) the prediction error decomposition form of the likelihood function is given by

$$\log L = -\frac{n}{2}\log 2\pi - \frac{1}{2}\sum_{k=1}^{n}\log|v_k| - \frac{1}{2}\sum_{k=1}^{n} e_k^2 v_k^{-1}, \tag{19}$$

where $e_k = Y_k - \hat{Y}_{k|k-1}$.

To estimate the parameter vector θ of the volatility function of the forward rates, the likelihood function in (19) can be maximised using a suitable numerical optimisation procedure.

Maximising L with respect to θ yields consistent and asymptotically efficient estimators $\hat{\theta}$. That is (see Lo 1988) $p\lim_{n\to\infty}\hat{\theta} = \theta$ and $\sqrt{n}\,(\hat{\theta} - \theta) \sim N(0, I^{-1}(\theta))$, where the asymptotic covariance matrix $I^{-1}(\theta)$ is the inverse of the information matrix $I(\theta)$ given by

$$I(\theta) = \lim_{n\to\infty}\frac{1}{n}\sum_{R=1}^{n} E\left[\frac{\partial^2}{\partial\theta\partial\theta'}\log L\right].$$

The Milstein scheme is one of a number of discretisation schemes which could be used. In Bhar and Chiarella (1995) we have also employed the method of local linearisation and the Euler–Maruyama method. From the perspective of parameter estimation we have not found any significant differences between these alternative schemes.

5. The Data Set

Our 90-day bank bill futures data is based on the Australian Bank Bill Market.The physical bank accepted bills market is an important short term financial market in Australia. These bills are issued on a discount basis and those for 90 days are the most actively traded. Periods of up to 180 days are also traded on the exchange. These bills have a face value of \$500,000 and are usually traded in lots of \$5 million. Discount rates are quoted as an index derived from (100 – yield p.a.) and the convention of 365 days in a year is used.

The futures market in bank bills started trading on the Sydney Futures Exchange (SFE) in 1979 and is the most important futures contract traded in the Australian market. The futures contract is for delivery of bills of face value \$500,000 and of maturity of 85–95 days and the delivery months are March, June, September and December. Contracts for delivery for up to 36 months are not uncommon. Discount rates are also quoted as an index as for the physical bank bills. Settlement dates for these futures contracts are the second Friday of the delivery months, although trading terminates on Wednesday prior to this second Friday.

The data set used in this study consists of end-of-day bank bill futures prices reported by the SFE for the contracts deliverable in March quarter of 1991. There are 250 observations for this contract in the sample. For the purpose of this study all discount bank bill futures prices have been standardised to \$1 of face value and the relationship between the yield and the price per dollar face value of these contracts is, $1/(1 + \text{yield} * 90/365)$.

In addition to this short-term contract, long-term (i.e. 3 year Australian Treasury bonds) bond data[2] has also been used in the estimation of the coefficients of the volatility function. Since these bonds are coupon paying bonds, a coupon stripping procedure outlined in Hunt (1994) is first applied to produce an equivalent zero coupon bond price series. Details of the coupon bond pricing mechanism are also described in that paper. This data set consists of weekly observations and thus there are 156 observations in this set.

6. The Empirical Results

We recall that the functional form assumed for $\sigma(t, T)$ is that given in Equation (6). Two different values of γ have been adopted in this study, namely $\gamma = 0.5$ and $\gamma = 1$.

The estimation process also requires specification of the initial forward rate function $f(0, T)$. This is done using a polynomial fitting procedure and is described in detail in Bhar and Hunt (1993). The initial value of the spot rate is obtained from $f(0, T)$ by setting $T = 0$.

The maximisation of the forecast error decomposition form of the likelihood function is carried out in GAUSS™ using the secant method BFGS and the variation of the golden section BRENT as the step search method.

Table 1 shows the estimated coefficients together with the value of the log likelihood functions. The standard errors are also reported however these should be treated with caution because of the small sample size. Below we

TABLE 1

Estimated coefficients and other statistics.

	a_0	λ	$\log L$	Implied Spot Rate Mean	Implied Spot Rate Stdv.
90-Day Bill					
($\gamma = 0.5$)	0.017189	0.014599	–1168.07	0.110073	0.00547
	(4.69E-06)	(0.000687)			
($\gamma = 1.0$)	0.175446	0.065338	–1294.18	0.182097	0.06771
	(2.50E-06)	(0.010265)			
3-Year Bonds					
($\gamma = 0.5$)	0.003937	–0.047981	–891.38	0.111405	0.00825
	(1.23E-06)	(0.002790)			
($\gamma = 1.0$)	0.010162	–0.014577	–899.89	0.110962	0.00824
	(1.88E-08)	(0.000872)			

Number of data points in 90-Day Bill dataset is 250, and in 3-Year Bond dataset is 156. The numbers in parentheses under the coefficients represent standard errors. These result from the covariance matrix obtained by the inversion of the last Hessian computed during the optimisation process.

discuss a Monte-Carlo bootstrap approach to an analysis of the statistical confidence intervals. The sample statistics of the implied instantaneous rate of interest, $r(t)$, are also included in this table.[3] It should be remembered that $r(t)$ has been generated under the equivalent measure and the mean $r(t)$ can be compared with the real interest rate of that period to obtain some idea about the market price of risk for that period. However, the volatility estimates of $r(t)$ are same in both the equivalent measure and the "real world" measure. The question of the value of γ that fits the data best is left for future research. The plot of the estimated volatility functions for the forward rate as well as of the bonds (for the 3-year treasury bond data and $\gamma = 0.5$) are shown in Figure 1. As expected the bond price volatility falls towards zero with falling time to maturity. For $\gamma = 1.0$ the behaviour of the volatility function (not shown) is very similar to that in Figure 1. It is interesting to note that the sample statistics of $r(t)$ for both values of γ are quite comparable but it is not so for the other data set.

In order to be able to comment on the statistical confidence intervals of the estimated parameters we employ the Monte-Carlo bootstrap technique to determine the distribution of the estimated parameters. All of these distributions have been calculated for the 3-year Australian Treasury bond data in the $\gamma = 0.5$ case.

The bootstrap samples are generated as follows:

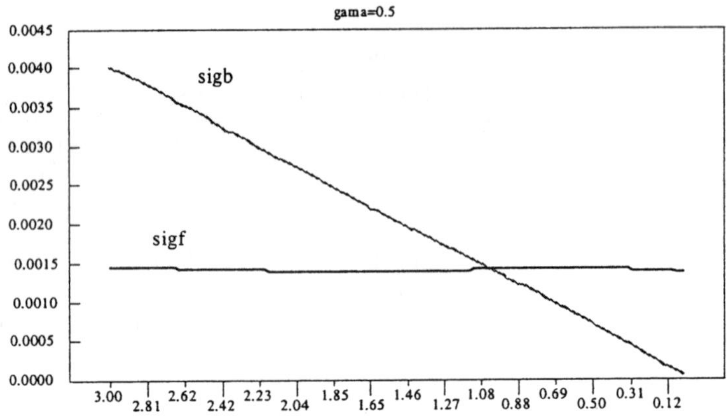

Fig. 1. Volatility function of forward rate and bond price.
Volatility functions for the 3-year Treasury bond data.

(i) Using the original data set, the parameters are estimated as explained in the paper by maximising the prediction error decomposition form of the likelihood function.
(ii) The prediction error vector is stored.
(iii) The prediction error vector is sampled via uniformly distributed random numbers and added back to the original data to generate one instance of the bootstrap sample.
(iv) Using the simulated data obtained in the third step, the parameters are estimated as in step one.
(v) The steps three and four are repeated 1000 times and a histogram of the distribution of the estimated parameters is obtained.

In Figures 2 and 3 the distributions of the estimated parameters using the Milstein scheme are shown.[4] The quantile distributions are also given as a measure for the confidence interval. The estimated value of a_0 lies within the peak block of the distribution for a_0 whereas the estimated value of λ lies one standard deviation to the left of the peak block of the distribution for λ.

However these Monte-Carlo bootstrap distributions for the estimates are subject to median bias as discussed by Effron (1987). This bias problem can be overcome by considering, amongst a number of other methods, the pivotal quantity. This quantity is in essence a distribution of the t-statistic of the estimate. For an estimate of a parameter θ ($= a_0$ or λ) it is defined as

$$\text{Pivotal Quantity}(\theta) \equiv \text{PQ}(\theta) = (\theta^B - \theta)/\text{SE}(\theta^B),$$

where θ = the postulated estimate (i.e. the estimates in Table 1), θ^B = the mean of the bootstrap sampling distribution and $\text{SE}(\theta^B)$ = the standard error of the bootstrap sampling distribution.

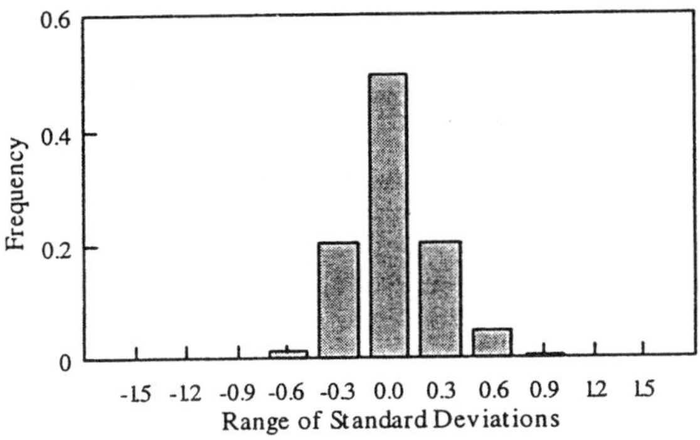

Percentile	
0.025	-0.0019
0.050	-0.0012
0.100	0.0009
0.500	0.0058
0.900	0.0102
0.950	0.0153
0.975	0.0176

Fig. 2. Bootstrap sampling distribution (a_0). Frequency distribution of the parameter from 1000 bootstrap resampling using 3-year Treasury bond data. Highly nonuniform distribution indicating median bias. Possible improvements may be achieved by examining the distribution of a pivotal statistic, e.g. bootstrap-t and/or applying bias correction due to Efron (1987). Mean and standard deviation of the distribution are 0.00772 and 0.01669, respectively.

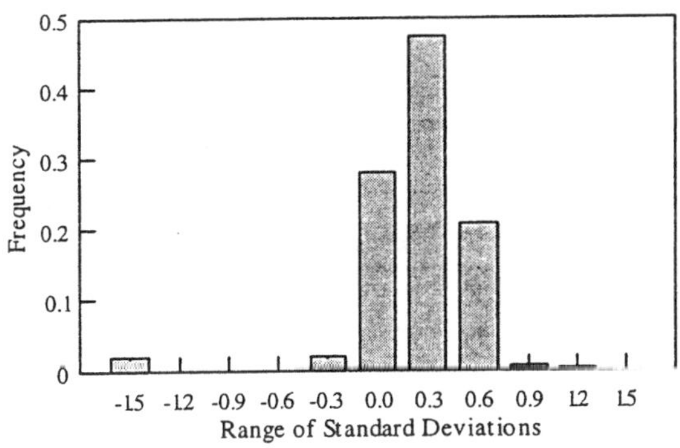

Percentile	
0.025	-0.1152
0.050	-0.0906
0.100	-0.0801
0.500	-0.047[illegible]
0.900	-0.006[illegible]
0.950	0.0082
0.975	0.0108

Fig. 3. Bootstrap sampling distribution (λ). Frequency distribution of the parameter from 1000 bootstrap resampling using 3-year Treasury bond data. Highly nonuniform distribution indicating median bias. Possible improvements may be achieved by examining the distribution of a pivotal statistic, e.g. bootstrap-t and/or applying bias correction due to Efron (1987). Mean and standard deviation of the distribution are -0.06087 and 0.13257, respectively.

Figures 4 and 5 display the bootstrap distribution of the pivotal statistics as explained in the footnotes. From Figure 2 we calculate PQ(a_0) to be 0.24 which according to Figure 4 is within the 95% confidence interval, whilst from Figure 3 we calculate PQ(λ) to be -0.1 which according to Figure 5 is in the 95% confidence interval.

Thus the pivotal quantity confirms the statistical significance of the estimates in the case $\gamma = 0.5$ for the Milstein method. Bhar and Chiarella (1995) discuss estimation results by the Euler–Maruyama method of discretisation and by local linearisation, but find similar results to those reported here.

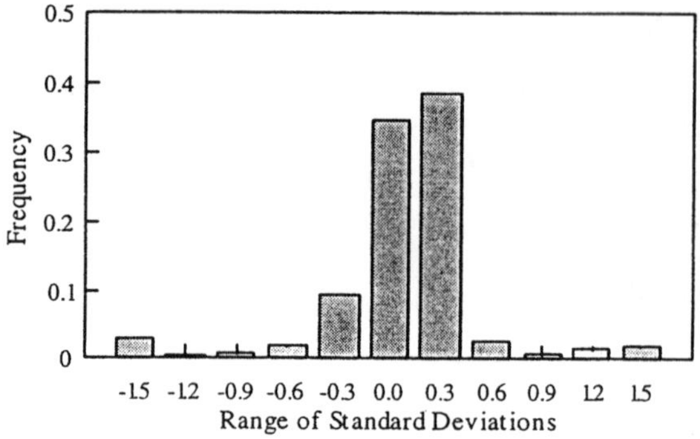

Percentile(*E+03)	
0.025	-87.02
0.050	-37.47
0.100	-23.23
0.500	-3.59
0.900	11.96
0.950	54.62
0.975	79.59

Fig. 4. Bootstrap sampling distribution (pivotal quantity). Frequency distribution of the pivotal quantity defined below from 1000 bootstrap resampling using 3-year Treasury bond data. Pivotal quantity = Bootstrap-t = $(a_0^B - a_0)/SE(a_0^B)$. The superscript B denotes bootstrap bootstrap estimate and SE stands for standard error.

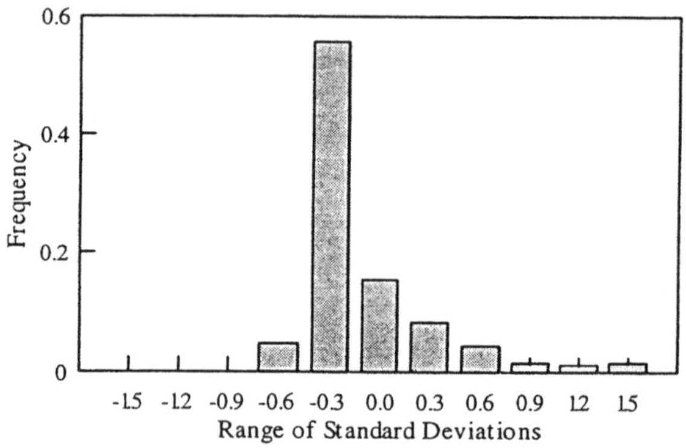

Percentile	
0.025	-6.47
0.050	-5.32
0.100	-3.98
0.500	3.35
0.900	60.57
0.950	115.46
0.975	148.22

Fig. 5. Bootstrap sampling distribution (pivotal quantity). Frequency distribution of the pivotal quantity defined below from 1000 bootstrap resampling using 3-year Treasury bond data. Pivotal quantity = Bootstrap-t = $(\lambda^B - \lambda)/SE(\lambda^B)$. The superscript B denotes bootstrap bootstrap estimate and SE stands for standard error.

7. Conclusion

We have discussed how the assumption for the forward rate volatility of a certain deterministic function of time multiplied by a function of the spot rate allows the reduction of the (non-Markovian) dynamics of the Heath–Jarrow–Morton model to a Markovian system. We have expressed the resulting Markovian system in state-space form and shown how the problem of estimating the parameters of the forward rate volatility function can be viewed as a nonlinear filtering problem. By using discretisations based on the Milstein scheme we have approached the estimation problem by means of the extended Kalman filter.

In this study we estimate a forward rate volatility function involving two parameters using 90 day bank bill futures and 3 year Australian Treasury bond data from the Australian markets.

In the case of the 3-year Australian Treasury bond data we have used Monte-Carlo bootstrap simulation of the parameter estimates as well as of their pivotal quantities to determine that the estimates are statistically significant.

We conclude in favour of the viability the general approach which we advocate. Namely that of choosing forward rate volatility functions which allow a reduction of the Heath–Jarrow–Morton system to Markovian form and then approaching the parameter estimation problem by use of the extended Kalman filter.

Further research needs to consider a number of issues. Firstly extend the results to larger data sets to determine the stability of the parameter estimates. Secondly estimate the parameter γ (see Equation (6)) and examine its stability. Thirdly the significance of the incorporation of more maturity dependent terms in the expression for the forward rate volatility (i.e. more a_i coefficients). Fourth, recast the system dynamics in terms of market quoted periodic rates (weekly, monthly etc.) rather than the idealised instantaneous rates of the theoretical development of HJM. This is possible by appropriate use of Ito's lemma. Fifth, use nonlinear filtering methods based on density approximation techniques as discussed for example by Tanizaki (1993) to overcome approximation errors and biases which may have been introduced by the discretisation scheme considered here. Sixth, allow for the forward rate volatility functional forms dependent upon the forward rate itself. Unfortunately in this case reduction of the system dynamics to a Markovian system is not possible. It then becomes necessary to consider infinite dimensional filtering problems. The early work of Falb (1967) may provide a starting point to this difficult problem.

ACKNOWLEDGEMENT

Financial support from the ARC grant A79132090 in the development of this work is gratefully acknowledged.

NOTES

1. Note that $P_{k+1|k} = \text{Var.}(\hat{S}_{k+1|k}, P_{k+1|k+1} = \text{Var.}(\hat{S}_{k+1|k+1})$.
2. The data was collected partially from the Australian Financial Review (which publishes a Reserve Bank of Australia collation of prices from bond market dealers) and partially from Australian Gilt Securities Pty Ltd.
3. These statistics are simply the mean and standard deviation of the time path for $r(t)$ generated by the state equations with the estimated value of θ.

4. The skewed distributions seen in Figures 2 and 3 appear to confirm similar findings by Stoffer and Wall (1991) in their study to investigate the properties of parameter estimates from state-space models by Kalman filter.

REFERENCES

Berndt, E.K., B.H. Hall, R.E. Hall, and Hausman, J.A., 1974, 'Estimation and inference in non-linear structural models', *Annals of Economic and Social Measurement* 3, 653–665.

Bhar, R. and C. Chiarella, 1996, 'Transformation of Heath–Jarrow–Morton models to Markovian systems', *The European Journal of Finance* (forthcoming).

Bhar, R. and C. Chiarella, 1995, 'The estimation of the Heath–Jarrow–Morton model by use of Kalman filtering techniques', Working Paper No. 54, University of Technology, Sydney.

Bhar, R. and B.F. Hunt, 1993, 'Predicting the short-term forward interest rate structure using a Parsimonious model', *Review of Futures Markets* 12(3), 577–590.

Carverhill, A., 1994, 'When is the short rate Markovian', *Journal of Mathematical Finance* 4, 305–312.

Efron, B., 1987, 'Better bootstrap confidence intervals', *J. American Statistical Assoc.* 82, 171–200.

Falb, P.L., 1967, 'Infinite-dimensional filtering: The Kalman–Bucy filter in Hilbert space', *Information and Control* 11, 102–137.

Harvey, A.C., 1989, *Forecasting, Structural Time Series Models and the Kalman Filter*, Cambridge: Cambridge University Press.

Heath, D., R. Jarrow, and A. Morton, 1990, 'Contingent claim valuation with a random evolution of interest rates', *Review of Futures Markets* 9(1), 54–82.

Heath, D., R. Jarrow, and A. Morton, 1992a, 'Bond pricing and the term structure of interest rates: A new methodology for contingent claims valuation', *Econometrica* 60(1), 77–105.

Heath, D., R. Jarrow, and A. Morton, 1992b, 'Easier done than said', *RISK* 5(9), 77–80.

Hunt, B.F., 1994, 'Testing alternative methods of modelling yields on coupon paying bonds', Paper presented at the *First Annual Coneference, Asia-Pacific Finance Association*, Sydney, September 28, 1994.

Kloeden, P.E. and E. Platen, 1992, *Numerical Solution of Stochastic Differential Equations*, Berlin: Springer-Verlag.

Lo, A.W., 1988, 'Maximum likelihood estimation of generalised Ito processes with discretely sampled data', *Econometric Theory* 4, 231–247.

Maddala, G.S., C.R. Rao, and H.D. Vinod, 1993, *Handbook of Statistics*, Vol. 11, Amsterdam: Elsevier.

Ozaki, T., 1992, 'Identification of nonlinearities and non-Gaussianities in time series', in D. Brillinger et al. (Eds), *New Directions in Time Series Analysis*, Part 1, Berlin: Springer-Verlag.

Ritchken, P. and L. Sankarasubramanian, 1995, 'Volatility structures of forward rates and the dynamics of the term structure', *Journal of Mathematical Finance* 5, 55–72.

Stoffer, D.S. and K.D. Wall, 1991, 'Bootstrapping state-space models: Gaussian maximum likelihood estimation and the Kalman filter', *Journal of American Statistical Association* 86, 1024–1033.

Tanizaki, H., 1993, *Nonlinear Filters: Estimation and Applications*, Berlin: Springer-Verlag.

EMILIO BARUCCI, UMBERTO CHERUBINI AND LEONARDO LANDI

Neural Networks for Contingent Claim Pricing via the Galerkin Method

ABSTRACT. We use Neural Networks as a Semi-NonParametric technique to approximate, by means of the Galerkin method, contingent claim prices defined by a no-arbitrage Partial Differential Equation. The Neural Networks' weights are determined as to satisfy the no-arbitrage Partial Differential Equation. A general solution procedure is developed for European Contingent Claims. The main feature of the Neural Network is that its weights are time varying, they change as the time to expiration of the claim changes. The method has been evaluated for option pricing in the standard Black and Scholes framework.

1. Introduction

Contingent claim pricing is a central topic in modern mathematical finance. In many cases, because of the complexity of the contingent claim contract, it is difficult to find out "the price" of the asset. The no-arbitrage condition is the "invisible hand" which enables us to price a contingent claim, the price is obtained by ruling out arbitrage opportunities from the market. Such no-arbitrage price turns out to be characterized by the features of the contract and of the stochastic process of the underlying asset price.

Black and Scholes in their 1973 seminal paper (Black and Scholes 1973) provide the basic framework to define the no-arbitrage price of a contingent claim. In their setting, the underlying asset price S is supposed to follow a lognormal diffusion process

$$dS = \mu S dt + \sigma S dz, \tag{1}$$

where μS represents the drift term, σS is the diffusion term and z is a standard Brownian motion.

H. Amman et al. (eds.), Computational Approaches to Economic Problems, 127–141.

The no-arbitrage price of an European contingent claim written on the underlying asset is characterized by the following second order partial differential operator

$$L(y(S,\tau)) = \frac{1}{2}\sigma^2 S^2 \frac{\partial^2 y}{\partial S^2} + rS\frac{\partial y}{\partial S} - \frac{\partial y}{\partial \tau} \tag{2}$$

with the boundary conditions

$$y(0,\tau) = 0, \qquad y(S,\tau) \sim S \text{ as } S \to \infty,$$

where τ is the time to expiration of the contingent claim ($\tau = T - t$, T is the expiration date of the contingent claim), and r is the risk free interest rate.

The price of an European contingent claim with payoff $g(S)$ at time T is given by the solution of the following *Cauchy problem*

$$L(y(S,\tau)) - ry(S,\tau) = 0 \tag{3}$$

with the final condition

$$y(S,0) = g(S). \tag{4}$$

Specifically for an European Call Option we have

$$y(S,0) = \max(S - E, 0),$$

where E is the strike price. The price of all kinds of European contingent claims can be obtained by specifying suitable functional forms for the final condition.

According to the fundamental asset pricing principle, see (Duffie 1992, Harrison and Kreps 1979, Harrison and Pliska 1981), we have that if markets are complete then there must exist a probability measure such that all of the European contingent claims, expressed in terms of a risk-neutral numeraire, i.e., discounted, satisfy the martingale principle:

$$y(S,\tau) = e^{-r\tau}\tilde{E}(y(S,0)) = e^{-r\tau}\tilde{E}(g(S(T))). \tag{5}$$

The expectation operator $\tilde{E}(\cdot)$ denotes the conditional expectation under the risk neutral measure defined by the stochastic process (1) with the drift changed to rS. The simplicity of expression (5) should not be misleading; it is in fact the solution of the Cauchy problem (3–4) which may not have a closed form solution, depending on the contingent claim contract and on the underlying stochastic process. If a closed form solution does not exist, numerical techniques become the last resort. In this case, the possibility to represent the equilibrium pricing relationship by *Semi-NonParametric* (SNP) techniques has been investigated. With this approach, the expected value is approximated by a sequence of functions; the approach goes back to the so called "method of sieves" (Grenander 1981), and includes orthogonal polynomial representations (Gallant and Tauchen 1989), and *Neural Networks* (NNs) (Gallant and White 1990), as particular cases.

The SNP approach to asset pricing was motivated by different questions. The first is whether these techniques, in particular NNs, can be useful in approximating a contingent claim pricing formula; the analysis in (Hutchinson et al. 1994) showed that NNs may reconstruct the Black and Scholes option pricing formula by learning an observed set of data. A second question is related to the restrictions to be imposed on the SNP representation to ensure consistency with the no-arbitrage requirement. Madan and Milne addressed this problem assuming that price functions are in Hilbert space and using a Hermite polynomial basis as an approximation for all the contingent claims in the economy (Madan and Milne 1994). Bansal and Viswanathan use an NN to approximate the pricing kernel of an economy imposing the no-arbitrage restriction on the sample equivalents of moments (Bansal and Viswanathan 1993).

Here we follow a different route. We propose to approximate the no-arbitrage contingent claim price by an NN architecture to which we impose to satisfy the no-arbitrage PDE driving all of the asset prices in the economy. The technical tool that enables us to impose the PDE restriction to our SNP representation of prices is the Galerkin method, a *weighted residuals* technique which is very popular among heat and fluid dynamics scholars, but which is almost unknown in finance. The Galerkin method requires to postulate a flexible functional form of the solution, i.e. an expansion in basis functions. Such functional form can be interpreted as an NN whose weights are chosen as to satisfy the PDE, see (Meade and Fernandez 1994a, 1994b). The interesting thing is that the PDE restriction shows up in time-varying, rather than constant, weights: weights change as the time to expiration changes. Thus, a standard NN with constant weights does not seem to be consistent with the no arbitrage requirement since the weights are required to follow a well defined time path through expiration.

The paper is organized as follows. In Section 2 we describe the Galerkin method. In Section 3 we apply the Galerkin method to no-arbitrage contingent claim pricing when the underlying asset price follows a general diffusion process. In Section 4 we apply the method to evaluate European options under very general assumptions about the diffusion process. In Section 5 we evaluate the numerical accuracy of the method in the standard Black and Scholes framework.

2. THE GALERKIN METHOD

The Galerkin method is extensively applied to fluid and heat dynamics problems described by a PDE but, to the best of our knowledge, it has never been applied in finance. It belongs to the class of weighted residuals methods, see

(Fletcher 1984, 1991). The peculiarity of weighted residuals methods with respect to *finite difference* methods is that they assume that the exact or the approximate solution of a PDE can be expressed analytically in terms of a set of functions, i.e. *trial functions*. This enables us to give an interpretation, also from an economic point of view, to the solution in terms of a basis.

Let us consider a differential equation

$$L(y) = 0,$$

where $y \in \Gamma \subset \Re$ with the corresponding initial conditions $I(y) = 0$ and boundary conditions $H(y) = 0$ for $y \in \partial\Gamma$. The operator $L(y)$ can be the second order operator of the type defined in (2). A weighted residuals method starts by assuming that the solution, deemed *trial solution* or *approximating solution*, is of the following form

$$y_a(x,t) = y_0(x,t) + \sum_{j=1}^{N} a_j(t)\phi_j(x),$$

where $\phi_j(x)$, $j = 1, \ldots, N$, are known analytic functions and are called trial functions, $y_0(x,t)$ is a function properly chosen to satisfy the boundary and initial conditions. The coefficients $a_j(t)$, $j = 1, \ldots, N$, are determined requiring that the integral of weighted residuals over the computational domain Γ be zero, and by the linearity of the $L(\cdot)$ operator we have

$$\int_\Gamma L(y_a) f_k(x) dx = 0, \qquad k = 1, \ldots, N,$$

where $f_k(x)$ are the *weight functions*. The Galerkin technique is characterized by weight functions which are the trial functions themselves, so the method requires to solve the problem

$$\int_\Gamma L(y_a) \phi_k(x) dx = 0, \qquad k = 1, \ldots, N.$$

Different kinds of Galerkin techniques can be developed assuming that the boundary conditions or the differential equation or neither of the two are exactly satisfied, i.e., *boundary, interior, mixed methods*. In the following we restrict our attention to interior and mixed methods. Depending on the domain of the trial functions both *spectral* and *finite elements* techniques can be implemented through the Galerkin technique. In the first case the trial functions span over the entire domain Γ, in the second case they are defined locally.

Given its features, the Galerkin method enables us to find out the closed form solution of a contingent claim pricing problem, if it exists, an approximate solution in terms of a basis expansion, as well as to provide an accurate

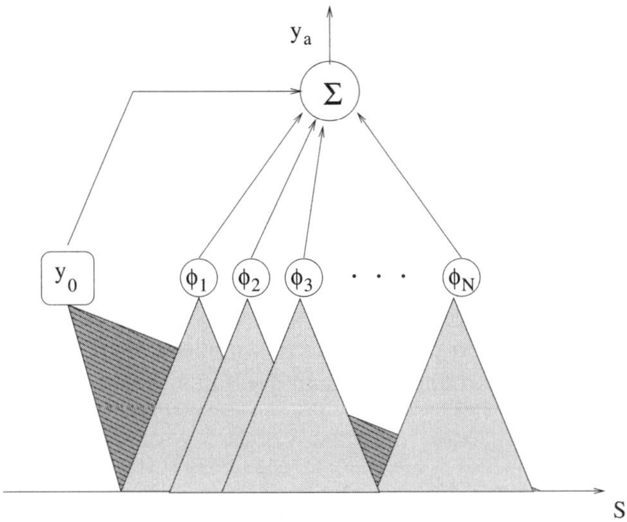

Fig. 1. Architecture of the NN used to approximate the PDE solution.

numerical solution as last resort. To achieve the first goal, the trial functions should be chosen according to the theoretical results about the solution. In the second case, besides empirical comparisons, an important result states that there is always a Galerkin method which corresponds to a variational method, i.e., the Rayleigh–Ritz method. This equivalence is quite important because it has been proved that the Rayleigh Ritz solution converges under some conditions to the exact solution as the number of functions approaches infinity, see (Fletcher 1984). The Rayleigh–Ritz method, see (Kantorovich and Krilov 1958, Mikhlin 1971), has been proved to converge to the minimizing solution of the variational problem provided that it is a solution with minimum energy and that the trial functions are linearly independent and complete in energy, i.e. a linear combination of the trial functions can be found which is able to approximate arbitrarily well both the function and the first derivative. In many cases, the equivalence between the Galerkin method and the Rayleigh–Ritz variational method is assured resorting to the Sturm–Liouville theory, see (Courant and Hilbert 1989, vol. I, chapter VI). This is the case of our problem.

To the approximating solution, provided that the trial functions are properly chosen, an interpretation as NN can be given, see (Meade and Fernandez 1994a, 1994b). Specifically, $y_a(x,t)$ can be interpreted as an NN with one hidden layer augmented by the term $y_0(x,t)$; in our interpretation a trial function is a neuron, see Figure 1.

The Galerkin method provides solutions with a high level of accuracy. Among weighted residuals methods it is shown to be the most efficient, see

(Fletcher 1984, pp. 32–38). With respect to finite difference methods, which are often used in finance, it has been proved that for a heat equation similar to the one used in asset pricing, the degree of accuracy of the Galerkin method is considerably higher even though at some computational cost, see (Panton and Sallee 1975).

3. Neural Networks for No-Arbitrage Contingent Claim Pricing

Assuming that an asset price S follows a stochastic process with $\nu(S)S^2$ denoting the diffusion term and rS the risk-adjusted drift, the partial differential operator characterizing European contingent claim prices defined on the asset becomes

$$L(y(S,\tau)) = \frac{1}{2}\,\nu(S)S^2\frac{\partial^2 y}{\partial S^2} + rS\frac{\partial y}{\partial S} - \frac{\partial y}{\partial \tau}\,.$$

The price of an European Call Option is given by the solution of the following Cauchy problem:

$$L(y(S,\tau)) - ry(S,\tau) = 0 \tag{6}$$

with the initial condition

$$y(S,0) = \max(S - E, 0).$$

As approximating solution of the no-arbitrage price we employ the following

$$y_a(S,\tau) = y_0(S,\tau) + \sum_{i=1}^{N} w_i(\tau)\phi_i(S). \tag{7}$$

$y_a(S,\tau)$ can be interpreted as a one hidden layer NN with time varying weights, the NN is augmented by adding $y_0(S,\tau)$ which is just a fixed weight node. The time varying feature of the solution representation (7) is given by the fact that the weights depend on the time to expiration of the contingent claim.

In the following we will apply the Galerkin method in its mixed version, we do not care explicitly about the boundary conditions; interior methods would instead require the boundary conditions to be satisfied exactly. However, by properly choosing $y_0(S,\tau)$ and resorting to "hat" activation functions defined on a bounded domain we can possibly obtain good results complying with the boundary conditions, see Section 4 for the European Call Option case.

To implement the method with $\Gamma = [0,\infty)$, we restrict, for computational needs, the domain to the range $\Gamma_b = [0,b]$. A set of equally spaced knots, S_i such that $S_i - S_{i-1} = \Delta S > 0$, $i = 1,\ldots,N$, is chosen in the domain Γ_b

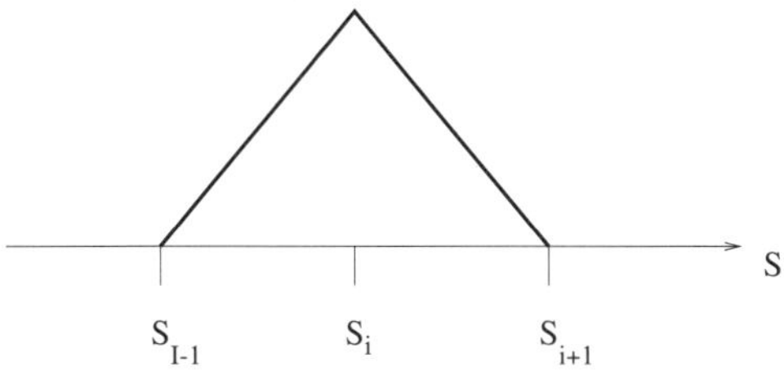

Fig. 2. The hat function.

and a trial function is defined for each knot. The trial function employed in our analysis is the so called "hat" function (see Figure 2)

$$\phi_i(S) = \begin{cases} \frac{S-S_{i-1}}{S_i-S_{i-1}} & \text{for } S_{i-1} \leq S \leq S_i \\ \frac{S_{i+1}-S}{S_{i+1}-S_i} & \text{for } S_i \leq S \leq S_{i+1} \\ 0 & \text{for } S < S_{i-1}, S > S_{i+1} \end{cases}, \tag{8}$$

where $\phi_i(S)$ is centered at the i-th knot, S_i. Please note that, even if this is not done in this paper, the architecture used in this application allows the estimation of the parameters of the NN by the means of standard learning procedures such as Back-Propagation (Rumelhart et al., 1986).

To apply a *weighted residuals* method we substitute the candidate solution (7) in the PDE (6) describing the no-arbitrage pricing condition, so that we get the following

$$L\left(\sum_{i=1}^{N} w_i\phi_i\right) - r\sum_{i=1}^{N} w_i\phi_i + L(y_0) - ry_0 = 0.$$

Applying the Galerkin method and exploiting the linearity of the $L(\cdot)$ operator, we get

$$\sum_{i=1}^{N} w_i\left(L(\phi_i), \phi_k\right) - \sum_{i=1}^{N} \dot{w}_i\left(\phi_i, \phi_k\right)$$

$$-r\sum_{i=1}^{N} w_i\left(\phi_i, \phi_k\right) + \left(L(y_0) - ry_0, \phi_k\right) = 0, \tag{9}$$

where $(\cdot, \cdot)$ represents the inner product and $\dot{w}_j = \partial w_j(\tau)/\partial\tau, j = 1, \ldots, N$. From (9) we obtain a linear system of differential equations in τ:

$$M\dot{\mathbf{w}}(\tau) = A\mathbf{w}(\tau) - rM\mathbf{w}(\tau) + \mathbf{c},$$

where $\mathbf{w}$ is the weights vector, the matrices $M = \{m_{jk}\}$ and $A = \{a_{jk}\}$ are defined as

$$m_{jk} = (\phi_j, \phi_k) \quad, a_{jk} = \left(L(\phi_j), \phi_k\right), \quad j, k = 1, \ldots N \tag{10}$$

and the vector $\mathbf{c}$ is defined as

$$c_k = (L(y_0) - ry_0, \phi_k), \qquad k = 1, \ldots, N.$$

So, the no-arbitrage condition requires the following path for the NN weights:

$$\dot{\mathbf{w}}(\tau) = M^{-1}A\mathbf{w}(\tau) - r\mathbf{w}(\tau) + M^{-1}\mathbf{c}. \tag{11}$$

Notice that the solution in (11) is nothing but an application of the separation of variables principle, as the basis functions depend only on the state variable, while the weights are assumed to depend only on the time to expiration τ.

The similarity between this approach and an NN architecture shows up clearly, as suggested in (Meade and Fernandez 1994a, 1994b), noting that the "hat" trial function $\phi_i(S)$ results by "hardwiring" two neighboring piecewise linear functions in a very straightforward way. Let us remark that the "hat" function $\phi_i(S)$ overlaps only with its closest neighbors $\phi_{i-1}(S)$ and $\phi_{i+1}(S)$ so that the matrix A is tridiagonal while M is tridiagonal and symmetric. Different choices could be made concerning the shape of such hardwired functions using for example sigmoid functions (squasher) in which case we will produce a bell shaped function.

In order to recover a solution for the weights we obviously need an initial condition. Initialization is straightforward, at expiration time $\tau = 0$ the contingent claim must be worth $g(S)$. Using this condition the initial set of weights $\mathbf{w}(0)$ can be directly obtained by interpolation. Notice that the function $\phi_i(S)$ is triangular and centered on S_i, where it is worth 1. It may be easily verified that if the final payoff $g(\cdot)$ is piecewise linear and the kinks are all set on the knots $(S_1, \ldots, S_N)$, then the payoff at expiration of the contingent claim y is exactly replicated by (7).

Let us remark that our basis representation provides a complete description of the economy. In fact we have

$$\tilde{E}(dy) - ry = \dot{\mathbf{w}}'\Phi(S) = [(M^{-1}A - rI)\mathbf{w}(\tau)]'\mathbf{\Phi}(\mathbf{S}) + (\mathbf{M}^{-1}\mathbf{c})'\mathbf{\Phi}(\mathbf{S}),$$

where $\mathbf{\Phi}(\mathbf{S})$ is the column vector made up of the basis functions and I is the identity matrix.

Let us remark that y_0 and $\mathbf{c}$ are arbitrarily chosen to satisfy the boundary conditions, so the matrix A uniquely provides a complete description of the assets in the market. Substituting the candidate solution we obtain

$$\tilde{E}(dy) = (M^{-1}A\mathbf{w}(\tau))'\mathbf{\Phi}(\mathbf{S}) + \mathbf{ry_0} + (\mathbf{M}^{-1}\mathbf{c})'\mathbf{\Phi}(\mathbf{S}).$$

In other words the matrix A determines the risk adjusted expected return of the contingent claim $y(S, \tau)$. This path depends crucially on the volatility term $\nu(S)$ which determines the elements of the matrix A.

To understand in which sense our model is a generalization of the standard framework, notice that it provides a local analysis of the price and of the risk-adjusted return of the contingent claim: at a knot S_i the contingent claim mostly depends on the i-th row of the matrix A and on the immediately surrounding rows, as well as on the value of the i-th component of $\mathbf{w}$ upon initialization. So, the expected risk-adjusted return on $y(S,\tau)$, as well as its value, crucially depends on the local volatility of the underlying asset. Assume for example the volatility function behaves according to the law $\nu(S) = k_i\sigma^2$ where k_i is a constant parameter across the interval between knot $i-1$ and knot i and σ^2 is a constant, say for example $\sigma^2 = \min \nu(S)$. The case in which $k_i = 1$, $i = 1, \ldots, N$, obviously represents the standard Black and Scholes framework, but we see that our NN representation may accommodate any model with state dependent volatility, just by letting the diffusion parameter vary across the knots.

Notice that the idea of allowing for volatility dependence on the state variable, i.e. on the underlying asset, may contribute to account for the so called "smile effect", that is the dependence of the implied volatility on the strike price, a phenomenon which is well known among practitioners, see (Dupire 1993). Along the same lines our methodology could be amended to account for the other well known phenomenon of dependence of implied volatility on the time to exercise, simply by setting $\nu(S,t)$, even though this would make the system in (11) nonlinear.

To conclude, our SNP framework provides an interesting tool to extend no-arbitrage pricing in order to allow for volatility time and state dependence.

4. Pricing European Options with Neural Networks

Let us consider the case of an European Call Option. As the *trial functions* are hat functions centered on knots chosen in Γ_b, in order to satisfy approximately the boundary conditions it is straightforward to set $y_0(S,\tau) = S$.

In order to use Equation (11) to compute the evolution of the weights over time, it is necessary to compute the elements of the matrices M, A and of the vector $\mathbf{c}$ in (10). In this special case, being $y_0(S,\tau) = S$ we have

$$c_k = (L(y_0), \phi_k) = 0.$$

In order to make easier the computation of the numerical solution we proceed to integrate by parts the term

$$\left(\nu(S)S^2\frac{\partial^2[\phi_j]}{\partial S^2}, \phi_k\right) = \int_0^b \nu(S)S^2\frac{\partial^2[\phi_j]}{\partial S^2}\phi_k dS$$

$$= \nu(S)S^2\frac{\partial\phi_j}{\partial S}\phi_k\Big|_0^b - \left(\frac{\partial\phi_j}{\partial S}, \frac{d}{dS}\left(\nu(S)S^2\phi_k\right)\right).$$

Let us analyze the last two terms in the above expression: the first term is zero when evaluated at $S = 0$ while the second term can be decomposed in two parts. As a result, the integration by parts gives the following:

$$\left(\nu(S)S^2\frac{\partial^2[\phi_j]}{\partial S^2},\phi_k\right) = \nu(S)S^2\frac{\partial\phi_j}{\partial S}\phi_k\Big|^b - \left(\frac{\partial\phi_j}{\partial S},\frac{d[\nu(S)S^2]}{dS}\phi_k\right) - \left(\frac{\partial\phi_j}{\partial S},\nu(S)S^2\frac{d\phi_k}{dS}\right).$$

Please note that the first term in the above expression turns out to be different from zero only for $j = k = N$. As a result the term a_{jk} is as follows

$$\begin{aligned} a_{jk} &= \frac{1}{2}\,\nu(S)S^2\,\frac{\partial\phi_j}{\partial S}\phi_k\Big|^b - \frac{1}{2}\left(\frac{\partial\phi_j}{\partial S},\frac{d[\nu(S)S^2]}{dS}\phi_k\right) \\ &\quad - \frac{1}{2}\left(\frac{\partial\phi_j}{\partial S},\nu(S)S^2\frac{d\phi_k}{dS}\right) + r\left(S\frac{\partial[\phi_j]}{\partial S},\phi_k\right), \end{aligned}$$

$j, k = 1, \ldots N$. Initial conditions are computed choosing the values $w_i(0)$ as to satisfy the condition:

$$\max(S - E, 0) = y_0(S) + \sum_{i=1}^{N} w_i(0)\phi_i(S).$$

In this framework, initialization of the weights is straightforward since we have:

$$w_i(0) = \begin{cases} -E & \text{if } E < S_i \\ -i\Delta S & \text{if } E \geq S_i \end{cases}.$$

Notice that it is very easy to represent arbitrage relationships under our NN representation. To take the most trivial example, consider the price of a put option with the same strike price E. We can immediately see that the price of the put option has about the same representation as that of the call. In fact, exploiting the put-call parity relationship $P = C - S + E\exp(-r\tau)$, we get

$$P = Ee^{-r\tau} + \sum_{i=1}^{N} w_i(\tau)\phi_i(S),$$

where the weights and the basis functions are those used for the call option.

This framework may be extended with the same simplicity to more general arbitrage relationships and composite option trading strategies. Among these, the so called *calendar spreads* are really built-in in our approach. In fact, since these option strategies are made up by a long and short position in call or put options with the same strike price but different exercise dates, their prices are really handled under our time varying NN representation. Other composite trading positions, in which the strike prices of the options are different, are more difficult to handle. To see this, take the case of a spread, say a *Bullish Vertical Spread* (BVS), which is constructed by buying a call with exercise price E_1 and selling a call with the same exercise date but strike price E_2, where $E_2 > E_1$. In our framework, it is easy to see that the no-arbitrage requirements implies that the BVS is priced as

$$\mathrm{BVS}(S, \tau, E_1, E_2) = \sum_{i=1}^{N} w_i(\tau)\phi_i(S),$$

where w_i are new equilibrium weights. As before, such a no-arbitrage requirement entails two steps. First, the weights have to be initialized as:

$$w_i(0) = \begin{cases} E_2 - E_1 & \text{if } E_2 < S_i \\ i\Delta S - E_1 & \text{if } E_1 \leq S_i \leq E_2 \\ 0 & \text{if } S_i < E_1 \end{cases} .$$

Finally, the no-arbitrage requirement restriction is completed by imposing to the weights to follow the time path described by the differential system that characterizes the economy.

5. Numerical Results

In this section we describe some numerical results of the application of the Galerkin method to compute the parameters $\mathbf{w}(\tau)$ of the solution of an European Call Option in the standard Black and Scholes framework. The European Call Option no-arbitrage price is

$$C(S, t) = SN(s_1) - Ee^{-r\tau}N(s_2),$$

where

$$s_1 = \frac{\log(S/E) + (r + \frac{1}{2}\sigma^2)\tau}{\sigma\sqrt{\tau}},$$

$$s_2 = \frac{\log(S/E) + (r - \frac{1}{2}\sigma^2)\tau}{\sigma\sqrt{\tau}} = s_1 - \sigma\sqrt{\tau}$$

and $N(\cdot)$ is the cumulative distribution function for a standardized normal distribution:

$$N(x) = \frac{1}{\sqrt{2\pi}} \int_{-\infty}^{x} e^{-0.5y^2}\, dy .$$

TABLE 1

Function $y_a(S, \tau)$ for $E = 1, t - T = 1.0, r = 0.1$, $\sigma^2 = 0.1$.

n. functions	Error for y_a $\|\bar{E}\|$	$\sigma^2_{\|E\|}$	$\|E\|_{\max}$
5	0.088780	0.006653	0.295461
6	0.072927	0.003944	0.248193
9	0.024451	0.000796	0.112527
10	0.016682	0.000369	0.082772
11	0.012508	0.000177	0.060899
21	0.011810	0.000183	0.053360
31	0.010123	0.000143	0.041194
41	0.009342	0.000102	0.023435

We use the “hat" functions described in (8). The system of differential equations to be solved in order to compute the parameters of the approximate solution is

$$\dot{\mathbf{w}}(\tau) = (M^{-1}A - rI)\mathbf{w}(\tau).$$

The elements of the matrices M and A are computed using the integration Romberg's method which is highly recommended in (Press et al. 1992, chapter 4.3) Once the matrix M has been computed, this is inverted exploiting the Lower triangular–Upper triangular (LU) decomposition (Press et al., chapter 2).

Assuming $\tau_0 = 0$, the parameter vector $\mathbf{w}$ is computed solving the linear system of differential equations, whose solution is

$$\mathbf{w}(\tau) = e^{(M^{-1}A - rI)\tau}\mathbf{w}(0),$$

where the exponential term has been evaluated by the means of a Taylor expansion.

The performance indexes considered are the mean absolute error $|\bar{E}|$, the error variance σ^2_E and the maximum absolute error $|E|_{\max}$. In the following, results are listed for $\tau = T - t = 1$, $E = 1$, $r = 0.1$ and the price asset variance $\sigma^2 = 0.1$. The asset price has been assumed to be in the range $[0, 10]$ so that the basis functions are equally distributed over this range. However, performance indexes have been measured over half of that range, i.e., $S \in [0, 5]$.

In Table 1, results of the approximate solution are listed; in Table 2, results of the derivative of the approximate solution with respect to the asset price

TABLE 2

Function $\Delta = \partial y_a(S,\tau)/\partial S$ for $E = 1, t-T = 1.0$, $r = 0.1$, $\sigma^2 = 0.1$.

n. functions	Error for Δ		
	$\lvert\bar{E}\rvert$	$\sigma^2_{\lvert E\rvert}$	$\lvert E\rvert_{\max}$
5	0.200020	0.048932	0.722113
6	0.181004	0.041761	0.635617
9	0.091278	0.018474	0.526652
10	0.079555	0.016230	0.825527
11	0.075196	0.017354	0.936559
21	0.086615	0.016926	1.013829
31	0.071810	0.015432	0.921434
41	0.060451	0.013434	0.834530

TABLE 3

Function $\Theta = \partial y_a(S,\tau)/\partial \tau$ for $E = 1, t-T = 1.0$, $r = 0.1$, $\sigma^2 = 0.1$.

n. functions	Error for Θ		
	$\lvert\bar{E}\rvert$	$\sigma^2_{\lvert E\rvert}$	$\lvert E\rvert_{\max}$
5	0.071804	0.003126	0.189560
6	0.040977	0.001155	0.166592
9	0.048445	0.000813	0.105266
10	0.042749	0.000517	0.113438
11	0.037999	0.000685	0.119617
21	0.021726	0.000602	0.102771
31	0.020398	0.000567	0.101340
41	0.018340	0.000502	0.092834

S ($\Delta = \partial y_a(S,\tau)/\partial S$) are reported. In Table 3, results of the derivative of the approximate solution with respect to τ ($\Theta = \partial y_a(S,\tau)/\partial\tau$) are listed. In Figure 3 the curve of the approximate solution is displayed.

6. Conclusions

We have provided an NN-based framework for contingent claim pricing. The NN's weights are computed according to the Galerkin technique as to satisfy

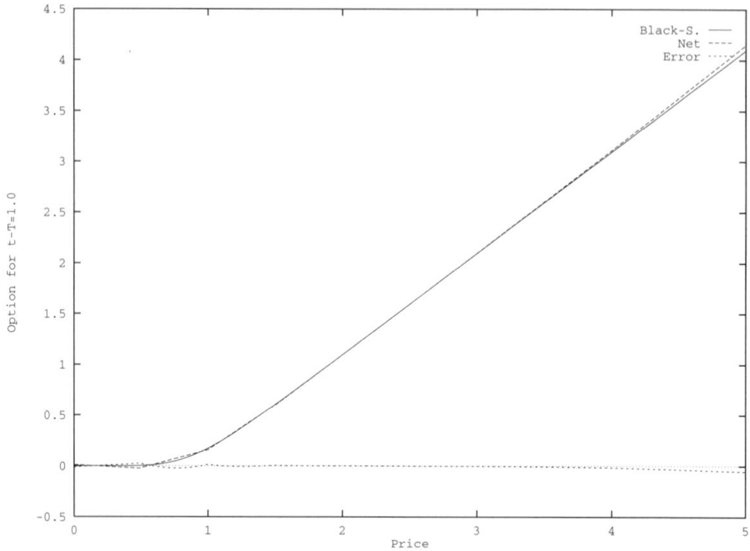

Fig. 3. Function $y_a(S,\tau)$ for $E = 1$, $t - T = 1.0$, $r = 0.1$, $\sigma^2 = 0.1$ computed with 31 knots.

the no-arbitrage PDE defining the contingent claim equilibrium price. The solution obtained allows the computation of the weights as a function of the time to expiration of the contingent claim by solving a system of linear differential equations. The approach used in this paper completes the one proposed in (Meade and Fernandez 1994a, 1994b) where NNs with constant weights are used to solve a PDE and it provides the right framework to apply NNs to option pricing.

The method has performed quite well in computing the Black and Scholes pricing formula. We have shown that it can be used in more complex cases allowing, for example, state-dependent volatility.

References

Bansal, R. and S. Viswanathan, 1993, 'No arbitrage and arbitrage pricing: A new approach', *Journal of Finance* XLVIII(4), 1231–1262.

Black, F. and M. Scholes, 1973, 'The pricing of options and corporate liabilities', *Journal of Political Economy* 81, 637–654.

Courant, R. and D. Hilbert, 1989, *Methods of Mathematical Physics*, New York: Wiley.

Duffie, D., 1992, *Dynamic Asset Pricing Theory*, Princeton: Princeton University Press.

Dupire, B., 1993, 'Pricing and hedging with smiles', in *Proceedings of the AFFI Conference*, La-Baule.

Fletcher, C., 1984, *Computational Galerkin Methods*, New York: Springer-Verlag.

Fletcher, C., 1991, *Computational Techniques for Fluid Dynamics, Vols. I–II*, New York: Springer-Verlag.

Gallant, A. and G. Tauchen, 1989, 'Semi-nonparametric estimation of conditionally constraint heterogenous processes: Asset pricing implications', *Econometrica* 57, 1091–1120.

Gallant, A. and H. White (1990), 'Connectionist non-parametric regression: Multi-layer feed-forward networks can learn arbitrary mappings', *Neural Networks* 3, 535–550.

Grenander, U. (1981), *Abstract Inference*, New York: Wiley

Harrison, M.J. and D.M. Kreps, 1979, 'Martingales and arbitrages in Multiperiod securities markets', *Journal of Economic Theory* 20, 381–408.

Harrison, M.J. and S. Pliska, 1981, 'Martingales and stochastic integrals in the theory of continuous trading', *Stochastic Processes and Applications* 11, 215–260.

Hutchinson, J.M., A.W. Lo, and T. Poggio, 1994, 'A nonparametric approach to pricing and hedging derivatives securities via learning networks', *Journal of Finance* 49(3), 851–889.

Kantorovich, L.V. and V.I. Krilov, 1958, *Approximate Methods of Higher Analysis*, New York: Noordhoff, Gröningen and Interscience.

Madan, D.B. and F. Milne, 1994, 'Contingent claims valued and hedged by pricing and investing in a basis', *Mathematical Finance* 4(3), 223–245.

Meade, A. and A. Fernandez, 1994a, 'The numerical solution of linear ordinary differential equations by feedforward neural networks', *Mathematical and Computer Modelling* 19, 1–25.

Meade, A. and A. Fernandez, 1994b, 'Solution of nonlinear ordinary differential equations by feedforward neural networks', *Mathematical and Computer Modelling*, to appear.

Mikhlin, S.G., 1971, *The Numerical Performance of Variational Methods*, Wolters-Noordhoff.

Panton, R.Z. and H.B. Sallee, 1975, *Computers and Fluids*, Vol. 3, pp. 257–269, New York: Springer-Verlag.

Press, W.H., S.A. Teukolsky, W.T. Vetterling, and B.P. Flannery, 1992, *Numerical Recipies in C*, Cambridge: Cambridge University Press.

Rumelhart, D.E., G.E. Hintos, R.J. Williams, 1986, 'Learning internal representation by error propagation', in *Parallel Distributed Processing: Exploration in the Microstructure of Cognition. Vol. 1: Foundations*, D. Rumelhart and J. McClelland (Eds), Cambridge, MA: MIT Press.

DIEM HO

Asset Liability Management

ABSTRACT. Asset Liability Management (ALM) is a decisional tool that helps to manage interest rate risks and their correlated risks, with the objective of sustaining the profit or enriching the institution. The difficulty with the endeavor comes from the inadequate data system, the complexity of financial products; in particular, on the embedded options and the credit risks. In this paper, we shall present a complete feasible solution to ALM, from practical experiences, by modelling the cash flows of all products and providing the optimization for restructuring of the balance sheet to meet the risk/return objective of the management. Discussions on strategies and ALM organization are also given to assure a smoothly running ALM solution.

1. Introduction

In recent years, the finance industry has witnessed unprecedented interest rate volatility and has seen its traditional markets become the focus of intense competition due to the globalization and the deregulation of the market as well as the restructuring of business operations thanks to the advent of high technologies. The consequence has been higher risks and lower margins for all participants. The market competition induces the banks and insurance companies to price their products more competitively to reflect closely the market condition, their investment incomes and their liability costs. This leads to increased efforts to manage the credit risk, interest rate risk and foreign exchange risk in a global environment. The market volatility has a direct impact on the insurance and the bank portfolios on both asset and liability sides, in particular on the induced liquidity risk. Financial institutions are forced to look at the total return on surplus or equity instead of only the asset return as usually done with insurers or only with the net interest incomes for banks. These elements call for a global asset liability management system (see, for example, Platt 1986, Langen 1989, Gualandri 1991, Fabozzi and Konishi 1991, Ho 1992).

H. Amman et al. (eds.), Computational Approaches to Economic Problems, 143–159.

ALM can be considered as one of the most challenging and important tasks due to the complexity of the financial products, in particular, the uncertainty on liabilities for insurers, the erratic returns and demanding constraints on investments as well as the unpredictable impacts of economic and financial environments.

The paper will cover, in Section II, the objectives of Asset Liability Management (ALM). In Section III, we propose a feasible solution to ALM. The conclusions follow in Section IV. Although we presented the numerical results at the Computing in Economics and Finance meeting last May 21–24, 1995 in Austin, we shall not cover them in this paper due to the cumbersome and lengthy explanations on the detailed balance sheet and the effects of its scenario restructuring.

2. Objectives of Asset Liability Management

The ALM solution is designed to provide the management of a bank or an insurance company an effective tool

1. to manage risks:
   - to monitor risks,
   - to control their impacts,
   - to hedge the bank's risk exposures,
   - and to simulate different optimal strategies,
2. to sustain or to enhance its profits,
3. to master its growth,
4. and to comply with government regulations.

Historically, the ALM risk management has concentrated mainly on *interest rate risks* (IRR) on the current earnings. That can be seen by the fact that most of ALM solutions have used the gap approach for the net interest income (NII) based on the accounting values (book values) as a target account to be managed. With the advent of advanced information technology (IT), software and hardware, more sophisticated modeling such as stochastic simulations can be easily done, the risk management in ALM has taken on the correlated risks such as the embedded options in the banking or insurance products to truly represent the change in the product cash flows with respect to the interest rate shift. That induces the need to deal with the real market values of the products. In fact, by doing this, the bank or the insurance company is interested not only in their current earnings but also in the economic perspectives of their businesses. In addition, during the 1980s the regulatory authority began to ask for reporting on the market values. The saving and loan crisis in the US has also had an impact on the banking community. The accurate assessment of their market value portfolios, by concentrating on both interest rate risk and credit risk, has become inevitable. The real cash flow of a loan, for example, has to take into account the default risk of that class of loans to generate the real risk-adjusted cash flow.

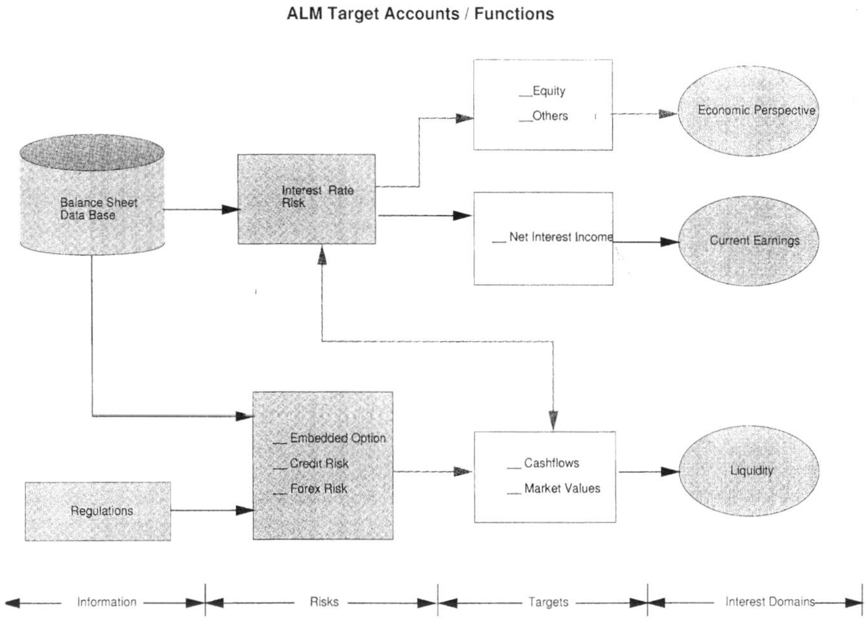

Fig. 1. ALM target accounts/functions.

As a result, the actual ALM solution also takes into account the *credit risks* as a correlated risk. It should be noted that the correlated risks have not been usually measured correctly or even ignored completely by many institutions (Toevs and Haney 1986).

In addition, foreign currency based businesses are increasing for many financial institutions with the globalization of their market. Their assets and liabilities may have foreign currency portfolios too. Thus the ALM should provide the capacity to handle the *foreign exchange (forex) risks* to truly report their positions on their local currency based balance sheet.

With the detailed cash flows for all balance sheet positions, the ALM can inevitably be also an effective tool to manage the *liquidity risks* as well.

The ALM target accounts/functions are shown in Figure 1. As indicated, from the balance sheet positions, one can look at interest rate risks to estimate the impact on the net interest income. If the credit risks and embedded options can be properly taken into account, the real cash flows can be generated for both liabilities and assets. We can then evaluate the market values of different products or positions on the balance sheet. With the realistic risk adjusted and optioned adjusted cash flows, the management can manage the liquidity risk more effectively. In addition, with the market values, the economic perspectives of the financial institution can be easily assessed through its portfolio equity or surplus. Figure 1 shows the functional flow of the required information, the risks to be assessed for different targets in different interest domains.

An ALM solution nowadays can deal primarily with *interest rate risks* and effectively with *credit risks*, *foreign exchange risks* and *liquidity risks*.

Due to the requirements of the regulatory authorities at the national level or supranational level, and the business requirements, the ALM should be flexible enough to allow the management to control any strategic target account in a timely fashion for current earnings, economic perspectives, or liquidity imperative. Information on other less strategic accounts (secondary) can also be easily obtained and monitored as the bank wishes. Typically, the target accounts can be:

- the net interest income (NII),
- the equity (or surplus) market value as a function of the balance sheet structure and of the interest rate sensitive assets and liabilities,
- the economic leverage or the equity/asset (or surplus/liability) ratio,
- the total return on equity (surplus) for a given investment horizon,
- the return on total assets,
- etc.

Different interest rate scenarios and yield curves are used to evaluate the market values of all assets and liabilities to help the management with the what-if simulation.

To maximize the profit or to optimize the growth, the optimization is used to propose the best set of financial instruments to hedge the target account or to restructure the balance sheet positions to the desired level of risk/return. To do so, the detailed characteristics of all balance sheet and off balance sheet positions must be known along with their effective yields. That means, all embedded options, default rates and recovery rates for different classes of products must be calculated to generate the option adjusted and credit risk adjusted cash flows, hence the market values and their effective yields. Scenario simulation is provided to help the institution's management to select the best strategy.

Figure 2 shows a schematic ALM solution which deals with the five problem areas:

1. customers,
2. market,
3. products or services,
4. operations,
5. regulations.

It consists of at least a database system to provide accurate and timely information. The analytics module is for modeling and evaluating all products with respect to the current market environment. The decision tool, in this case, is an optimizer, designed to provide the best strategy to meet the risk/return objective of the management. The whole ALM solution targets the profit, the efficiency and the competitiveness for the financial institution.

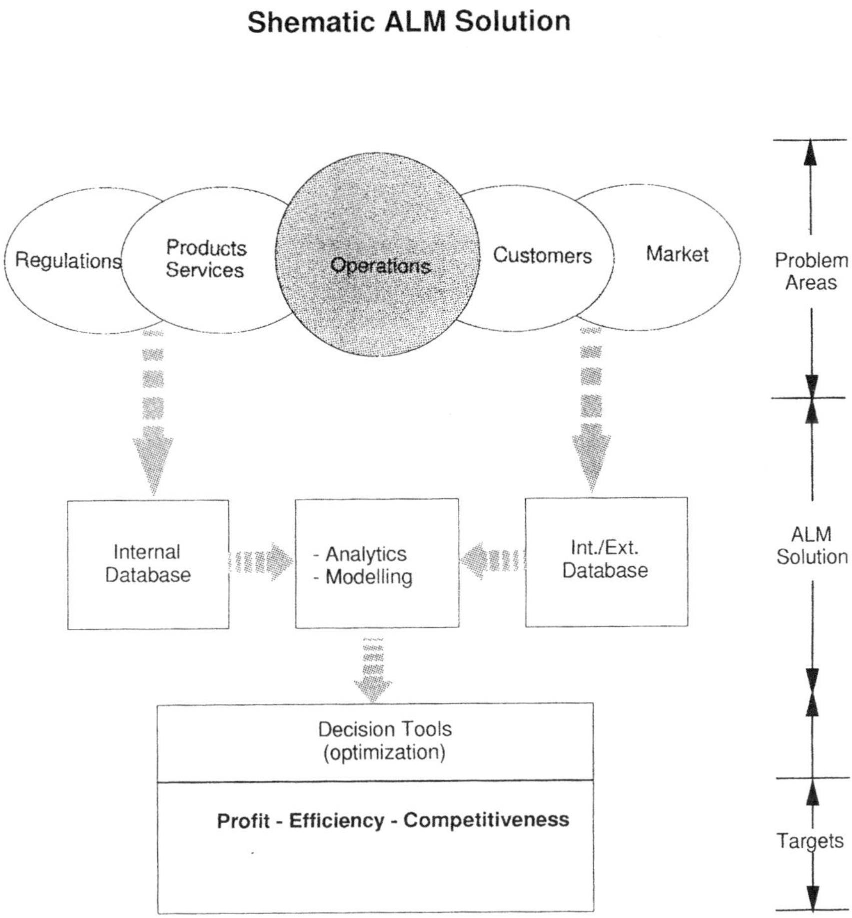

Fig. 2. Schematic ALM solution.

3. A Feasible ALM

In this section, the discussion will be more banking oriented; however, many features are also applicable to insurance business.

3.1. *Approaches*

There are three generic approaches for ALM often seen in literature as well as on the market.

3.1.1. *Maturity Gap and Periodic Gap*

This model focuses primarily on the net interest income as the target account. The model derives its name from the difference or the gap between the values of rate-sensitive assets and rate-sensitive liabilities. The model objective is to set this gap to zero to hedge against rate changes. This approach does not take into account the difference of the repricing times of assets and liabilities. To improve this shortcoming, the Periodic Gap model was developed. It measures gaps for a number of sequential time periods (maturity buckets). This approach can provide analysis on the short term liquidity risk and the net interest income.

Its deficiencies are its

- failure to reveal risk exposure for large period,
- restrictive choices in the control of interest risk for small periods,
- inability of managing simultaneously many target accounts,
- inaccurate assumption on the identical behavior of assets and liabilities *versus* interest rate changes,
- inability of handling embedded options, credit risks,
- inability to measure the appreciation or depreciation of assets and liabilities, thus their market values and the economic perspectives.

3.1.2. *Simulation*

This model was developed to correct certain deficiencies of the periodic gap model in a dynamic forward-looking context. It designs the simulation model based on detailed assumptions on managerial behaviors, loan and deposit demands and future interest rate paths, etc. It can provide the market values *versus* the interest rate shifts, complex cash flows with embedded options, short term liquidity analysis and the net interest income.

Although the approach is appealing, there exists a number of disadvantages:

- time consuming,
- black box with probably unappropriate hypotheses,
- requirement of highly skilled experts.

This is a powerful technique but it should only be used as the last resort due to its complexity. In the case of what-if simulation, the result may be quite subjective. The search for scenarios may not be exhaustive.

3.1.3. *Duration*

This model is based on the measurement of duration, a measure of interest sensitivity of any cash flow series, or the price sensitivity to interest rate shift (e.g. Bierwag et al. 1983, Toevs 1986). The duration and convexity used in this paper are the modified duration and convexity referred to in literature. The advantages of this model are that it takes into account both the amplitude and the timing of these flows and it can avoid the deficiencies of other approaches. For example, it does not require exact matching, as restricted in the periodic gap model, instead it matches duration and gives the manager more flexibility. The convexity can take into account the adverse behaviors of assets and liabilities with respect to interest rate changes (Ho 1990). Duration analysis may be performed simultaneously on many target accounts. The model yields a consistent measure of risk exposure for multiple target accounts. This information may help executives to assess quickly the market values and their associated risks with respect to the interest rate shifts. And, the management can take appropriate countermeasures. The duration gap model also reveals a large number of asset and liability choices capable of incrementally improving the risk exposure to the desired levels. The optimization procedure can be used to pick the optimal hedge. Correlated risks can also be easily taken into account by this model. The disadvantages of this model are that it requires a high level of mathematics and optimization, but this requirement may also be needed by the simulation approach. However, mathematical complexity may be justified by the duration model's flexibility and its associated higher returns. It might not accurately measure certain abrupt random risks or influences of new business lines. Frequent verifications and readjustments may eliminate these potential risks and might even provide certain gains.

A practical solution requires us to assess the market values or the present worth of all financial products; that means the economic perspective of the bank portfolio. As a result, we have to use the duration as a risk measure along with simulation to analyze systematically all possible scenarios. Both what-if simulation and Monte Carlo (stochastic) simulation should be available for subjective judgments as well as objective assessments of the market. The convexity is taken into account to reduce the readjustment frequency. Gap analysis is also necessary for evaluating the NII, for liquidity analysis (short term cash-flows) and for reporting to regulatory authorities. Simulations should be done objectively with scenarios, well thought out or well founded, based on some consensus forecasting. Hedging can be done by optimization based on a list of all available hedging instruments or on those that the bank is willing to use. The hedging can also be done by directly manipulating the balance sheet by selling or buying assets and liabilities to meet the risk objective. Financial instruments such as swaps, options, futures, caps/floors, etc., can be used to obtain the desired duration and performance for the portfolio. Synthetic products can also be generated to synthesize unavailable instruments or to meet certain specific criteria. Since the performance profiles or the profit/loss profile of all financial product families, as well as the total bank's portfolio, are available, both micro and macro-hedging are possible.

To arrive at this solution, the ALM system should have four basic components: a data system, an analytics module for financial modelling and cash flow generation, an optimizer for optimal restructuring or strategic planning, and a user-friendly interface to render the system friendly and transparent to users.

3.2. *Data System*

This is the information management system. It is a very important part of the ALM. If the information is not reliable or consistent, the result will be misleading or even meaningless. To have reliable information we should have accurate data on the cash-flows of all elements of assets and liabilities and their associated contingent claims; for example, the embedded options in a mortgage or a certificate of deposit. That requires accurate information on current positions, product characteristics and customer's behaviors. Certain historical data is necessary to determine functional relationships between different yields with respect to the base rates (e.g. riskless treasury rates) or to determine the rate volatilities. Historical data can also be used for forecasting, in particular for projecting future inflows or outflows not currently present. The market data is also needed to define the actual financial environment that we are in and to give us the market values of products traded on the market. Macro-economic information is also necessary for the financial modeling.

3.3. *Analytics Module*

As mentioned above, all the items (products) on the balance sheet are priced. The market value, the effective return, the option adjusted spread, the duration and convexity have to be calculated. If the market values exist, their associated spreads have to be calculated to take into account the credit risk and/or the liquidity risk. In order to compute these elements, a financial environment must be defined. The financial modeling of all instruments has to be done to generate the cash-flows associated with the instruments. The cash flows are option adjusted and credit risk adjusted. Each cash flow consists of interest income and principal payment. The cash flow, discounted by its current market rate, should give the net present value or the option adjusted spread (OAS) if its market value exists.

3.3.1. *Environment*

The environment file contains up-to-date information for the users to manage their current balance sheet; typically,

- the term structure of IRs and their volatilities,
- mortgage prepayment rates for different market segments,
- redemption (early withdrawal) rate of different deposit classes and market environments,
- default rates and recovery rates for different credit classes and market environments.

For a constitutional view of interest rates, we shall need the term structure of interest rates and their volatilities. The IR term structure is the yield curve of zero coupon bonds. We also use the yield to maturity, an effective average of the term structure rates, for each product. We also need the prepayment models for different segments of mortgages, the redemption models, and the default rate models for different credit instruments on the balance sheet and their associated recovery rates from historical data.

It should be noted that the term structure of interest rates is considered as the consensus view of interest rates. The state bond market data should be used to derive the interest rates for different maturities because of their liquidity and credit quality. The term structure of interest rates provides a basis for estimating forward interest rates. This estimation would depend on the term structure theory used. We do not assume that these forward rates will be correct in the future, but at least it provides a coherent view of the future. The ALM solution should be flexible enough to allow users to simulate any variation of the interest rate curve to fit the users' view of the future in their search for the best strategy.

3.3.2. *Financial Modeling and Cash-Flow Generator*

All instruments are modelled to calculate the cash-flows, the present values, their effective yields, the spreads, and the risk parameters such as durations and convexities. The spread is a measure which represents the effects of prepayment, credit, and/or liquidity risk of the product.

Typically, for treasury bonds and depending on their nature whether they have coupons or not, at floating rates or fixed rates, different models have to be designed to calculate their durations, convexities, effective yields and the spreads. If it is a floating rate bond, the term structure of interest rates has to be used. Attention has to be paid to the lag time between the reset time and the coupon time. The coupon time is one period before the coupon payment dates. There may also be other options attached to the instruments such as a cap, floor, collar, drop-lock, put-call, conversion, etc. The option has to be appropriately calculated to generate the correct cash flow for the bond and its market value.

For commercial and industrial loans, the credit risk may modify the cash flow. The credit risk arises when certain customers fail to pay by insolvency or by bankruptcy. Historical data can provide, for a class of customers in a sector, the number of such cases or the percentage of loan volume lost over a given time period. This default risk can be influenced by a number of factors including the economic environment, sector performance, product lines and their competitiveness on the market, the financial structure of the enterprise and the loan, and the entrepreneur himself. When such an event happens, the banks, as lenders, may take certain legal measures to recover their loans. Thus we have different default rates and recovery rates for different classes of customers. With this information, an appropriate model should be designed to generate the risk adjusted cash flow of the loan; its present value or market value, duration and convexity are calculated using the current market rates of similar products.

For mortgages, the pricing is complicated due to the fact that there is always a prepayment option embedded in the product whose risk is not usually well assessed. And customers can exercise it to the disadvantage of the issuers. The same argument can equally be applied to the Certificates of Deposit (CD) with their early withdrawal (redemption) option. Normally, when there exists a substantial negative difference between the actual mortgage rate and the contract rate, customers may choose to refinance their debts at a lower rate. The decision to prepay does not depend only on the rate differential but also on other factors such as the profile of the customer and the age of the mortgage. It should be noted that the prepayment exists even when the actual rate is higher than the contract rate. In this situation, the prepayment can be advantageous to the banks. For this, a Monte Carlo simulation based on the term structure of interest rates and their volatilities can be used to generate different cash flow scenarios for a mortgage basket. For each scenario, we discount the cash flows by the market rate to obtain its present value. The market value is the weighted sum of these present values. If there were no prepayment option, the cash flow would be a constant coupon series defined by the contract rate. The present value of the prepayment option can be obtained by taking the difference between these two discounted cash flows. With the presence of the prepayment option, the duration is much less than if there were no option. In addition, the convexity may no longer be positive but might experience a downward trend called *negative convexity*. Similar analysis can be carried out for a CD. The prepayment or early withdrawal provision in banking products can represent a serious problem to a financial institution and needs to be effectively hedged. The banks are often forced to give these facilities to customers due to government requirements or marketing strategy, however, they need not do so free of charge. They can hedge the risk through the use of off-balance sheet financial instruments or by levying a service charge appropriate to the level of refinancing and the rate differential. The prepayment option can also be calculated by using a binomial model instead of a fully fledged simulation.

Another type of mortgage is the adjusted rate mortgage, in which the payments are indexed to a reference. It also has the life cap and floor, margin and periodic cap to provide certain security to customers. The pricing can be done by the simulation technique described above. Since it is readjusted periodically based on the referenced index, the option value is not of the same importance as that of the fixed rate case.

On the liability side, typically, for a certificate of deposit at fixed rate, we have to establish a functional relationship between the market rate of this instrument and the treasury rate. The cash-flow defined by the contractual characteristics of the product can be generated. Modeling for early withdrawal (account termination) should be incorporated, in particular when the treasury rate is substantially higher than the contractual rate. This is very much like the prepayment option of a mortgage. In establishing the functional relationship between the CD market rate and the treasury rate, care should be taken to model the time lag in resetting the CD rates with respect to a change in treasury rates. This lag may have an asymmetric behavior when rates increase or decrease.

In the above example, we have discussed the modeling and the analytics of some typical products to show the stake of product pricing and its complexity when accurate market values, durations, convexities and effectives yields are to be calculated. It should be noted that the credit risk accounted for in this explanation only helps to assess the forward-looking credit risk positions of the bank, in contrast to the provision of bad loans, which accounts for what has already happened to the bank's portfolio. In the next section, we will show the optimization process, in which the effective yields are used. That means high credit risk activities may be reduced under the bank's profit policy. In that case, some improvement on the credit quality can be obtained. However, the real improvement must come from the filtering of bad customers at the outset by a performant credit rating system.

3.4. *Optimizer: Hedging and Strategic Planning*

The main objective of the ALM hedging is to protect a portfolio value at a desired level against IR shifts. With the information calculated by the analytics module, an optimization procedure can be used to select the best strategy for this purpose. We may keep the actual balance sheet structure and use a basket of derivative products to create a strategy to satisfy our objective and constraints. Or, we can modify the actual structure along with a basket of derivative products for our restructuring or strategic planning purpose. In the actual situation in Europe, where the derivatives are not yet popular instruments, the modification of the balance sheet structure becomes more important. And securitization may be one of the means for the balance sheet restructuring (Bhattacharya 1991).

It would defeat the purpose of ALM, if after all complex modeling to expose the potential risk is done, the management were not provided with a decision tool to deal with the exposures. That explains why optimization must be an essential part of the ALM.

3.4.1. *Objective Function and Constraint Set*

The objective function, for most of the time, will be maximizing the profit (for a given time horizon), which is defined as the difference between the asset yields (product of the assets and their effective returns) and the liability costs, net of the market value of the hedging strategy and the restructuring cost. The restructuring cost can be considered as the incremental overhead cost, that means the additional cost incurred when the business volume of that activity changes. This information is usually available from the bank's profitability analysis. In fact we can also define the objective function as minimizing a deviation error from a desired performance profile or a profit/loss profile of a portfolio subject to a series of constraints including the level of cost. If a quadratic tracking error is sought after, the correlations among assets and liabilities can be taken into account.

The constraints are divided into five categories:

- Structure: those constraints that do not change with time or environment. For example, the equity is the difference between assets and liabilities net of the marking-to-market of the off-balance sheet products.
- Policy: constraints that change with time and relate to policies or strategies of the institution or management. For example, the minimum level of cash in the portfolio or how much funding to industrial loans or commercial loans should come from CDs. Caps and floors for each type of products or business lines can be defined here.
- Regulation: constraints imposed by regulatory authorities; typically, constraints related to credit risks or risk-weighted assets. In 1995, additional sets of global constraints relating to interest rate will also be imposed (known as the Capital Adequacy Directives, CAD, see for example, Elderfield 1994, Gualandri 1997). Constraints on capital adequacy and reserves belong to this category. The risk weight for each balance sheet position must be identified. The risk weight is the quantity assigned to each type of products by the regulatory authority to represent the credit risk and the IRR associated with that class of products. As mentioned above, the newly imposed CAD must be a coherent part of the ALM solution.
- Interest rate and foreign exchange: typically, conditions on duration and convexity, for different target accounts. For foreign exchange, if a series of cash flows in foreign currencies is converted by a transfer, a swap, or a series of future contracts into domestic currency, the effect of domestic IR shifts should be taken into account. Normally, the foreign assets do not have to be hedged completely if we want to take advantage of the correlations among local assets, foreign assets and foreign exchanges (Kritzman 1990).
- Liquidity: This constraint relates to the assurance of the liquidity condition of the bank. One of the simple measures for this is to assign a percentage of liquid assets to the total liabilities. However, a detailed cash-flow model can be used for a time horizon decided by management to ensure that the asset side can well cover the liability side. This is called the dedication procedure.

3.4.2. *Hedging Instrument Set*

A certain number of derivative products such as options, forwards, futures or swaps can be used for hedging purpose if available and acceptable to the regulators or the management. The characteristics of these instruments must be specified or calculated, such as their sensitivity to IR shifts (duration and convexity), their performance profiles *versus* the IR shifts, and their risk weights. These parameters will be needed in the constraint set of the optimization.

3.4.3. *Simulation and Optimal Strategy*

With the objective function, the feasible constraint set and a permissible hedging instrument set, the optimal solution can be found. If we change the constraints, the hedging instrument set, or the assumed financial environment typified by the term structure of interest rates, we can obtain different optimal strategies. The ALM system should allow the user to simulate a wide range of scenarios with different target accounts and the system will provide the optimal solution for each one. If the user has a firm feeling of what the future IR term structures should be, he can go back and change the environment as he sees fit and can again simulate new scenarios and obtain new optimal strategies.

3.5. *I/O User Interface*

This is a complex solution, and to be effective, we need an extremely user-friendly system. It should help users to navigate the application with ease. It should provide successive menu screens for the selection of different options or tasks in the solution. It should allow users to compute or simulate different scenarios at different levels of aggregation in the product lines. The balance sheet can be broken down into subsets of geographic regions or network branches. And finally, it should be transparent to users.

3.5.1. *User Friendly Hierarchical Menu-Driven I/O Interface*

At the top layer or level, we may have a consolidated balance sheet with different selection menus. The system allows users to set the environment for simulation or to compute the current state of the balance sheet. It should allow the user, from this level, to restructure the balance sheet to meet all constraints and objectives of the bank's management. Results can be displayed in different ways to help the decision making process. Graphic displays, tables and reports of different types can be generated and printed out. Information on the initial position, optimal structure and characteristic variables associated with different classes of products and instruments are displayed. The variables consist of effective yield, incremental overhead cost, credit risk, risk weight, duration and convexity. This information should provide users with a quick assessment of the risk adjusted return of each class of products, its sensitivity to IR and its risk weighted capital. On each product line, users can click forward to go down to a lower level of aggregation just to the lowest level.

At each level, the system can compute the yield, duration, convexity, credit risk etc., from that level down on that branch. Users can go back to a higher level of aggregation, the parent node. The environment parameters can also be easily accessed and modified for different scenarios.

3.5.2. *Report Generator*

The ALM solution should provide the analytical interest rate risk measures that may be reported in a structured or unstructured way according to the user's needs. The system provides the outputs consolidated at different levels based on geographic areas or product families.

The application allows you to build graphic outputs and specific reports for each kind of target accounts that you want to control. Finally, the system can provide some useful reports such as

- the present value or the market value and the risk measure of each balance sheet position,
- the cash-flow projection for each maturity date and the corresponding liquidity level,
- the duration and the convexity of each balance sheet position,
- the balance sheet restructuring that meets the interest rate risk objective,
- the list of scenario assumptions,
- the proposed strategies to hedge interest rate risks,
- the projection of each future balance sheet position and the related net interest income,
- benefit margin for each financial product or activity,
- etc.

3.6. *Strategy*

The institution management must be able to articulate clearly the objective of their risk management. What target accounts do they want to manage? Sometimes, it is necessary to define an intermediate or temporary objective, or an achievable goal for the ALM because the primary objective can be too hard to achieve immediately. This is why the ALM system should have the capability of incremental hedging. Depending on the strategy of the institution at the moment, the target account may be, for example, the net interest income, the total return on equity, the market value of equity or the economic leverage. The traditional ALM system always concentrates on the net interest income. It should be noted that the net interest income is no longer considered sufficient for a good ALM. This is particularly true from the regulator's viewpoint, because the net interest income does not take into account the market value of the bank portfolio or its economic perspective. To look only at net interest income is a sure way of providing misleading information, unless the bank can look at the net interest income for many periods in the future, thus taking into account the market appreciation of the bank asset liability position. In addition, the regulator may require reports on the assessment of the performance profiles of the market value changes with respect to the interest rate shifts. One may also have multiple target accounts provided that they are not inconsistent. For example, one cannot immunize market value of equity and total return on equity simultaneously. In fact, to hedge the equity may come into conflict with the position of net interest income. The strategy identification should have the consensus within the institution to be effective. This leads us to a discussion of the last issue of the ALM solution, the organization role in the ALM implementation.

3.7. *Organization*

The organization for an ALM system usually consists of an ALM committee, or ALCO, and an ALM cell or department.

1. The ALM committee

   The ALCO is the decision making body. It should be chaired by the chairman or a member of the board of directors, and should include representatives from different departments affected by the ALM; typically
   - Treasury and Securities,
   - Planning,
   - Accounting,
   - Management Control,
   - Information Technologies,
   - Credit,
   - Risk Management,
   - a secretary.

   Other alternate members from other services can participate as problems arise. In particular, the commercial departments should be involved in case of new product choice or change in volume of actual concerned activities. The chairman of the ALCO should have the jurisdiction over all organizational components. His presence along with the representatives of different departments will help to define the objective properly and keep the operations of the ALM cell running smoothly. The ALCO must assure the efficiency and the responsiveness in its decision process and it should be in charge of the main activities of the bank management. The secretary is also the leader of the ALM cell. The secretary of the committee keeps track of decision discussions, decision papers, presents options and analysis on outstanding questions from the previous meeting. The ALCO should meet at least once a month for strategic decisions, extraordinary meetings can also be convened at the discretion of the chairman, in particular, when there is an important turbulence on the market or an urgent matter detected by the ALM cell.
2. The ALM cell

   The functions of the ALM cell consist of collecting pertinent data and information, monitoring the balance sheet, running scenario simulations, preparing options and analysis on outstanding questions of the previous meeting and for new situations for decision, and implementing the decisions along with other departments. The cell should consist of at least the following members/functions:

- Group leader, (secretary of ALCO),
- Financial analyst, modeler
- Analyst/programmer, database specialist

This ALM cell should run the ALM daily for monitoring or when new information is updated. Simulations on different crisis scenarios should be run to detect any urgent matter for the management. The maintenance and the updating of the system should also be a responsibility of this group. Weekly reports should be prepared for members of the ALCO.

4. Conclusions

Every economic activity is concerned with the efficient management of cash flows. In particular, a bank has an important competitive advantage if it can improve its control over risks and profitability of its financial flows or react timely and effectively to changes in interest rates.

The ALM system should provide an accurate assessment of IR risks and the correlated risks on earnings, total market and replacement value of every item on the balance sheet. It can enhance long term profitability by detailed pricing of assets, liabilities and off-balance sheet elements. It also provides the best restructuring strategy to the bank if the current performance profile is not desired. That means it provides profit, efficiency and competitiveness.

Altogether, the ALM is a decisional tool for IRR but it can be used for foreign exchange risk, credit risk and liquidity risk. The data and analytics available in the ALM solution can be extended to cover the global risks and the duration based solution for the CAD.

Acknowledgements

The author gratefully acknowledges the contributions and collaborations of many European banks, in particular from Dr. A. Ceola, Dr. G. Baldassi of Banca Popolare Veneta and Dr. J.M.P.M. Boavida of Caixa Geral de Depositos. I would like to thank also my colleagues in France, Italy and Portugal for their collaborations. The figures are done by Marilia Salazar.

References

Bhattacharya, A.K., 1991, 'Overview of asset/liability management models and interest rate risk control', in F.J. Fabozzi and A. Konishi (Eds), *Asset/Liability Management*, Chicago, IL: Probus, pp. 99–122.

Bierwag, G.O., G. Kaufman, and A. Toevs, 1983, 'Duration: Its development and use in bond portfolio management', *Financial Analysis Journal* July–August, 15–35.

Elderfield, M., 1994, 'Developments in EC and international capital adequacy regulations', *J. Finan. Reg. Compl.* 2(4), 314–322.

Fabozzi, F.J. and A. Konishi, 1991, *Asset/Liability Management*, Chicago, IL: Probus.

Gualandri, E., 1991, 'The approaches to interest risk of supervisory authority and financial institutions', *Revue de la Banque* 1, 20–33.

Gualandri, E., 1997, 'Asset & liability management: Regulatory guidelines on interest rate risk control and their impacts on financial institutions', in D. Ho and T. Schneeweis (Eds), *Advanced Applications in Finance, Investment and Banking*, to be published.

Ho, D., 1992, 'A practical approach to asset liability management', *Finan. Syst. J.* 3, 142–150.

Ho, T.S.Y., 1990, *Strategic Fixed Income Investment*, Homewood, IL: Dow Jones-Irwin.

Kritzman, M.P., 1990, *Asset Allocation for Institutional Portfolios*, Homewood, IL: Business One Irwin.

Langen, D., 1989, 'An (interactive) decision support system for bank asset liability management', *Decision Support System* 5, 389–401.

Platt, R.B., 1986, *Controlling Interest Rate Risk. Applications for Money Management*, New York: Wiley.

Toevs, A.L., 1986, 'Uses of duration analysis for the control of interest rate risk', in R.B. Platt (Ed.), *Controlling Interest Rate Risk*, New York: Wiley, pp. 28–61.

Toevs, A.L. and W.C. Haney, 1986, 'Measuring and managing interest rate risk: A guide to asset/liability models used in banks and thrifts', in R.B. Platt (Ed.), *Controlling Interest Rate Risk*, New York: Wiley, pp. 256–350.

SOREN S. NIELSEN

An Efficient Parallel Implementation of a Lattice Pricing Model

ABSTRACT. A two-factor model for the valuation of default risk implicit in US corporate bonds is developed and implemented on a parallel computer. The model is discretized and implemented as a trinomial lattice. The model is used for the least-squares estimation of implicit parameters of volatility and correlation, consistent with the observable term structures of several corporate bond categories, across several trading days.
Although the non-linear optimization is compute-intensive, the pricing step is easily parallelizable on a shared-memory, symmetric multiprocessor system. It is here implemented on the Convex Exemplar SPP–1200 parallel computer, and numerical results are presented.

1. Introduction

We present in this paper a two-factor model for the valuation of default risk in corporate bonds. The model is used for the estimation of implicit volatility and correlation parameters, which involves a compute-intense non-linear optimization. The paper presents a parallel implementation of this model on a Convex Exemplar SPP-1200 computer. The paper illustrates that even a serial implementation of the model can be efficiently parallelized on this architecture with a minimum of programmer effort. We briefly introduce the model and its financial underpinnings below, but the main focus of this paper is on the model's suitability for parallel computing. The model is further developed (for the valuation of default risk in interest-rate swaps and swaptions) and motivated in Nielsen and Ronn (1996), who also give an analysis of the financial results (as opposed to the numerical timings given here) of the model.

The background for the model is as follows. The first factor is the instaneous risk-free short-term rate, r, which can be viewed as the yield on short-term government securities (Treasuries). We use observable market data to calibrate the model so it correctly prices such securities (i.e., is a no-arbitrage model).

H. Amman et al. (eds.), Computational Approaches to Economic Problems, 161–173.

In addition, we consider corporate bonds belonging to two ratings categories. These bonds have higher yields than Treasuries, presumably due to higher inherent default risk. The spread between the risk-free rate and the risky yields, s, is the second factor of our model. In continuous time, the model can be written:

$$\begin{aligned} dr &= \mu_t r\,dt + \sigma_r r\,dz_1 \\ ds &= \sigma_s s\,dz_2, \end{aligned} \tag{1}$$

where r is the instantaneously-riskless rate of interest; μ_t is the expected change in dr; μ_t is chosen to precisely match the observable term structure of interest rates; σ_r is the volatility of r; s is the instantaneous yield spread for risky corporate asset; σ_s is the volatility of s and $\mathrm{Corr}(dr, ds) = \rho\,dt$.

A key assumption of our development is that the spread s is a market-efficient indicator of default risk. Let λ be the default rate, i.e., $\lambda\,dt$ the chance of default during the time interval dt, and let D be the post-default recovery rate (recovery per unit face value). Invoking an argument of risk-neutral valuation (see, e.g., Hull 1997), these three quantities can be linked together as follows: A risk-neutral investor is indifferent between investing at the risk-free rate r, and a risky investment with a $\lambda\,dt$ chance of D, plus a $1 - \lambda\,dt$ chance of a unit payoff, discounted at the risky rate, $r + s$:

$$\exp\{rdt\} = \exp\{(r+s)\,dt\}[D \cdot \lambda\,dt + (1 - \lambda\,dt)],$$

which, substituting $\exp\{s\,dt\} \approx 1 + s\,dt$ and ignoring terms of order dt^2, yields the relationship $\lambda = s/(1-D)$.

Some intuition for this model follows:

- The corporation's bond prices are presumed to drift downward as default becomes increasingly likely (e.g., as they are downgraded).
- Given the default event has occurred, the bond sells at a post-default price of D, some fraction of face value.
- We allow for a correlation in changes between r and s, and perform period-by-period discounting using riskless rates of interest.
- Over the next interval, if the security does not default, it will pay a return in excess of the riskfree rate; otherwise, it will sell at a price D.

The valuation of default risk goes back to Merton (1974), who modeled the default event as depending upon the value of the firm, F, presumed to follow geometric Brownian motion, and default triggered by this value dropping below some threshold, $F \leq B$. In contrast with Merton's model, the present model follows more recent research (Jarrow and Turnbull 1992, Jarrow et al. 1994, Lando 1993, Madan and Unal 1994, Duffie and Singleton 1994) in not assuming knowledge of an unobservable firm value. Rather, our model allows us to estimate implicitly the volatilility parameters (σ_r, σ_s, ρ) based upon our implementation of the two-factor model, with the two processes centered around directly observable market data (treasury yields and spreads, respectively).

The remainder of the paper is organized as follows: The data for our model and the estimation procedure employed are described in Section 2. The discretization and implementation of the model in a lattice structure is described in Section 3. Section 4 presents results of a parallel implementation, and finally, Section 5 concludes the paper.

2. DATA: TREASURY AND CORPORATE BOND TERM STRUCTURES

The data for our analysis consists of the term structures of Treasury bonds and three ratings classes of corporate bonds (rated AAA-AA, A-BBB and BB-C), obtained as Merrill Lynch & Co. bond indices. These term structures were observed through maturities of up to 10 years. Although we have data for the entire years 1993–1994, only data from the 20 trading days of December 1994 are used in the present study. Treasury and corporate bonds pay coupons every half year, and those epochs constitute the natural dates upon which corporate bonds may default. We hence discretize our model into intervals of $\Delta = 1/2$ year, and assume the existense of 20 par bonds with maturities of 1/2, 1, 1 1/2, ..., 10 years from *each* of the three ratings categories, and for *each* trading date. The data allow us to perform pricing analyses of the corporate bond categories separately, or jointly for 2 or all 3 categories, and for individual dates or jointly across the time period of interest.

The default-risk parameter estimation amounts to a non-linear minimization of pricing errors relative to known (treasury or corporate) bond prices, which are by construction at par (i.e., the price of a \$1 face value bond is \$1). Each bond has a known value at maturity, and known coupon payments every half year, unless the bond defaults, in which case there is a one-time payment of D. Pricing the bond on the lattice then consists of calculating its risk-neutral, expected value as standard. and we seek to estimate the implied parameters such as to minimize the total pricing error. The number of parameters over which the minimization is performed depends on the number of corporate bond ratings categories involved: The parameter σ_r pertains to the risk-free Treasuries, and for each corporate bond category added, two additional parameters (σ_c and ρ_c, where subscript c refers to the appropriate spread process, separate for each category, but assumed constant across the time period in question). With $n = 1, 2$ or 3 categories, the minimization is hence over 3, 5 or 7 parameters.

Specifically, let $\mathcal{U} \subseteq \{\text{AAA-AA, A-BBB, BB-C}\}$ be the set of ratings categories used, and let $\mathcal{D}$ be the set of dates for which term structures are used. Let also

$$V_t^{cd}(\sigma_r, \sigma_c, \rho_c), c \in \mathcal{U},\ d \in \mathcal{D}$$

be the price, as evaluated on the lattice, of the corporate bond with maturity $t = 1/2, 1, 11/2, \ldots, 10$ years of category c on date d. Then the complete estimation problem is:

$$\min_{(\sigma_r,\sigma_c,\rho_c),c\in\mathcal{U}} \sum_{d\in\mathcal{D}} \sum_{c\in\mathcal{U}} \sum_{t=1/2}^{10} [1 - V_t^{cd}(\sigma_r, \sigma_c, \rho_c)]^2. \tag{2}$$

For further information on the data involved, the statistical properties of the above estimator, and an extension of the model to also take into account interest rate swaps and swaptions, refer to Nielsen and Ronn (1996).

3. A Trinomial Lattice Implementation

The continuous-time system (1) is now discretized to allow a lattice-implementation. As explained, the resulting lattice will cover a 10-year time period in intervals of $\Delta = 1/2$ years, and hence have 20 time steps.

The quadrinomial lattice proposed for this process is:

$$\begin{bmatrix} r(t+\Delta) \\ s(t+\Delta) \end{bmatrix} = \begin{cases} \begin{bmatrix} r(t)\exp\left\{\mu(t)\Delta + a_0\sqrt{\Delta}\right\} \\ s(t)\exp\left\{b_0\sqrt{\Delta}\right\} \end{bmatrix} & \begin{matrix}\text{with Prob.} \\ p_0 = \lambda(s)\Delta\end{matrix} \\ \begin{bmatrix} r(t)\exp\left\{\mu(t)\Delta + a_1\sqrt{\Delta}\right\} \\ s(t)\exp\left\{b_1\sqrt{\Delta}\right\} \end{bmatrix} & \begin{matrix}\text{with Prob.} \\ p_1\end{matrix} \\ \begin{bmatrix} r(t)\exp\left\{\mu(t)\Delta + a_2\sqrt{\Delta}\right\} \\ s(t)\exp\left\{b_2\sqrt{\Delta}\right\} \end{bmatrix} & \begin{matrix}\text{with Prob.} = \\ p_2\end{matrix} \\ \begin{bmatrix} r(t)\exp\left\{\mu(t)\Delta + a_3\sqrt{\Delta}\right\} \\ s(t)\exp\left\{b_3\sqrt{\Delta}\right\} \end{bmatrix} & \begin{matrix}\text{with Prob.} = \\ p_3\end{matrix} \end{cases} \tag{3}$$

where p_0 is the default probability, and the $p_j \geq 0, j = 0, \ldots, 3$ and sum to unity.

The parameter set $\{a_i, b_i, p_i, i = 0, 3\}$ is chosen to satisfy the mean, variance and covariance conditions implied in Equation (1). Specifically, we require that, under the risk-neutral probability measure,

$$E\begin{bmatrix} dr/r \\ ds/s \end{bmatrix} = \begin{bmatrix} \mu_t \\ 0 \end{bmatrix} dt \tag{4}$$

$$\text{Var}\begin{bmatrix} dr/r \\ ds/s \end{bmatrix} = \begin{bmatrix} \sigma_r^2 \\ \sigma_s^2 \end{bmatrix} dt \tag{5}$$

$$\text{Cov}\left(\frac{dr}{r}, \frac{ds}{s}\right) = \sigma_{rs}\, dt \tag{6}$$

For a general introduction to the principles underlying there requirements, and for the use of the resulting tree for valuation purposes, see, e.g., Hull (1997). Restated in terms of (3), the system (4–6) can be written:

$$\begin{aligned}
\sum_{i=0}^{3} p_i a_i &= 0, \\
\sum_{i=0}^{3} p_i b_i &= 0, \\
\sum_{i=0}^{3} p_i a_i^2 &= \sigma_r^2, \\
\sum_{i=0}^{3} p_i b_i^2 &= \sigma_s^2, \\
\sum_{i=0}^{3} p_i a_i b_i &= \sigma_{rs}.
\end{aligned}$$

As demonstrated in Nielsen and Ronn (1996), this system can be shown to have the following solution:

$$\begin{aligned}
p_0 &= \lambda(s)\Delta, \quad p_1 = p_2 = 1/4, \quad p_3 = 1/2 - \lambda(s)\Delta, \\
a_0 &= a_3 = 0, \\
b_0 &= b_3 = \sigma_s \sqrt{1-\rho^2}\,, \\
a_1 &= -\sqrt{2}\,\sigma_r, \\
b_1 &= -\sigma_s \left(\sqrt{2}\,\rho + \sqrt{1-\rho^2}\right), \\
a_2 &= \sqrt{2}\,\sigma_1, \\
b_2 &= \sigma_s \left(\sqrt{2}\rho + \sqrt{1-\rho^2}\right),
\end{aligned}$$

where $\rho \equiv \sigma_{rs}/(\sigma_r \sigma_s)$. There are indeed multiple solutions to the system; a bonus of the solution given here is that, since $a_0 = a_3$ and $b_0 = b_3$, the processes emanating from the first and fourth branch of each tree node are identical from then on, and we hence do not need to store nodes corresponding to both of these subtrees. This conveniently allows us, by treating the default event explicitly, to implement the above tree as a trinomial tree instead of a quadrinomial, resulting in a big reduction in the storage and computational requirements. Consequently, we henceforth label the emaning branches by 1, 2 and 3, respectively.

The tree's computational efficiency may be observed as follows. At time $t + n\Delta$,

$$r\,(t + n\Delta) = r(t) \exp \left\{ \sum_{i=1}^{n} \mu\,(t + i\Delta)\,\Delta + (n_1 a_1 + n_2 a_2 + n_3 a_3)\,\sqrt{\Delta} \right\}$$

$$s\,(t + n\Delta) = s(t) \exp \left\{ (n_1 b_1 + n_2 b_2 + n_3 b_3)\,\sqrt{\Delta} \right\}$$

The values of (r, s) at each tree node hence depends only on the number of up-, middle-, and down-branches taken to that node, not the order (or path). Thus, the tree is recombining, and both $r(t + n\Delta)$ and $s(t + n\Delta)$ depend only on n_1, n_2 and $n_3 = n - n_1 - n_2$. The tree is illustrated in Figure 1.

4. Parallel Implementation

The trinomial lattice developed is now implemented on a parallel computer. We describe first the computer, then our parallel implementation. Timings are given and discussed.

4.1. The Convex Exemplar Parallel Computer

The Convex Exemplar SPP–1200 Scalable Computing system is a multi-processor, parallel computer with from 8 to 128 processors. Each processor, which is a Hewlett-Packard PA7200 RISC processor, runs at 120 MHz, allowing for a 128-processor peak performance of 30.7 GFLOPS. The machine to which we have access has 16 processors, of which 14 are available for user jobs (the last two are used for system management etc.).

The Exemplar is an example of an SMP (Symmetric Multi-Processing) computer where there is no distinction between processors. At any point in time, there is available a number of user processes requesting processing, and within each user process there is a number of *threads*, or subprocesses, which can all be executed in parallel. The computer has a global, shared memory, augmented with per-processor high-speed local cache memory. Every access to global memory results in a memory page being swapped into the requesting processor's cache. The Exemplar features an advanced, hard-ware based *cache coherency* scheme, by which data modified by one processor (and residing in its local cache) when referenced by another processor is automatically written back to global memory, then a fresh copy provided to

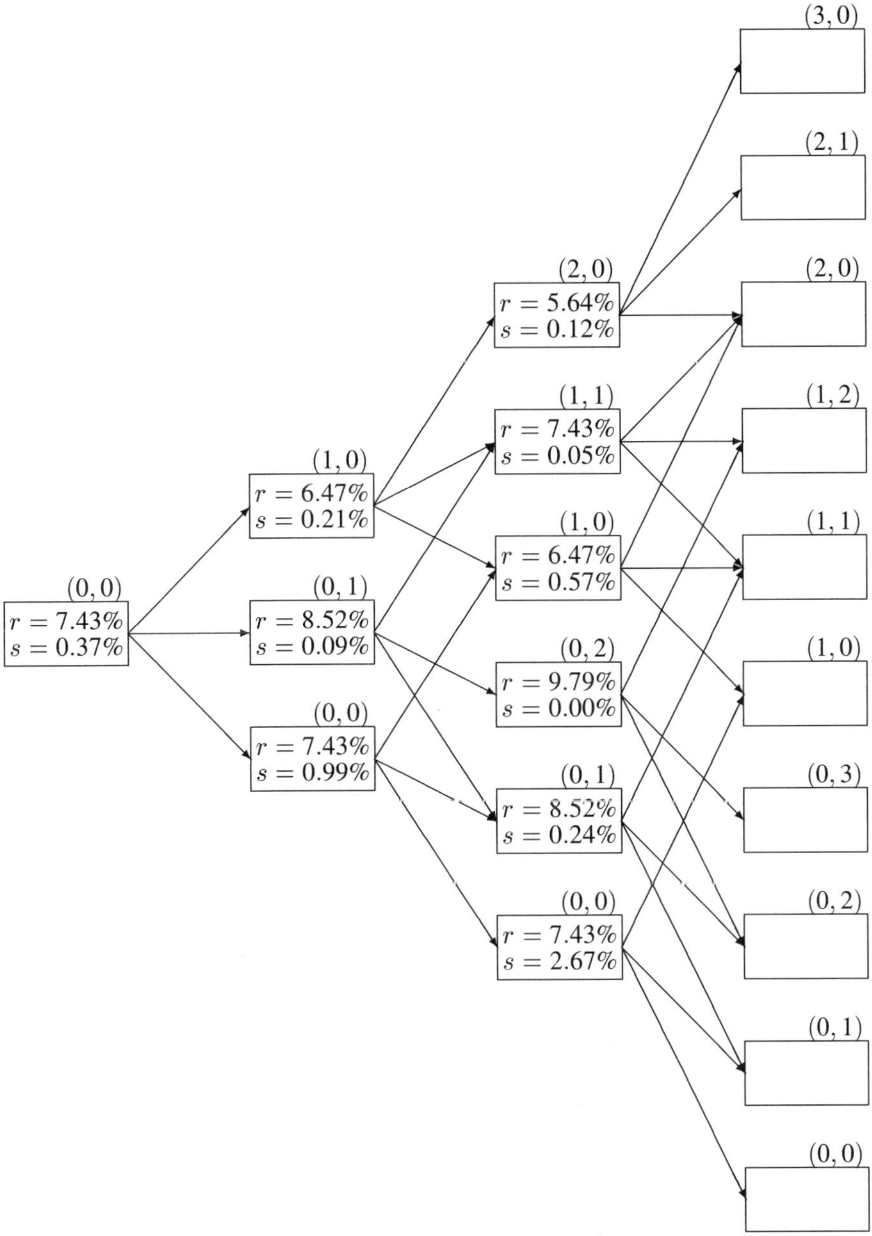

Fig. 1. The quadrinomial tree shown without the top (default) branches for $n = 3$ time periods. There are $(n+1)(n+2)/2$ nodes at time $n\Delta$, labeled by $(n_1, n_2), 0 \leq n_1 + n_2 \leq n$, indicating the number of "up-" and "middle-" branches taken to reach the node.

any other processors requesting it. This process is completely transparent to the programmer.

Several communication schemes between user threads are supported, including explicit message passing (e.g., using PVM, Geist et al. 1994), or shared-memory communication. The latter, which we use here, allows the parallelization of C, C++ or Fortran programs by the use of compiler directives which either specify separate sections of the program to be executed in parallel, or that loop iterations should be executed in parallel by separate threads. In both cases the compiler ensures synchronization of the threads at the end of the parallel region, and allows threads to communicate through global variables protected by critical regions.

One aim or this project is to show the suitability of this architecture for the lattice model with minimal programming effort. Starting with a sequential code, we identified a loop which could be parallelized easily (i.e. where the local calculations were independent across iterations). This loop, corresponding to the summations over c and d in (2) is part of the function evaluation. Hence, any speed-up resulting from this parallelization would be realized by any algorithm used to perform the minimization.

4.2. Numerical Results

The code was tested on three different problems, involving the joint estimation of implied parameters for 20, 40 or 60 categories of bonds, across 20 trading days during December, 1994, with either one (AAA-AA), two (AAA-AA, A-BBB) or three (AAA-AA, A-BBB and BB-C) ratings levels. Each of these categories leads to a set of processes (r, s) where r is centered on the forward rate curve of the day in question, and s is centered on the observable spread for the date and ratings level in question. Hence, each of the 20 (40, 60) categories require their own lattice evaluation, consisting of the pricing of 20 bonds with maturities of $0.5, 1, 1.5, \ldots, 10$ years.

We use three different versions of the code:

1. A strictly sequential version compiled with the optimization option -O2. This option invokes the Convex C compiler's most advanced scalar optimization, including common subexpression elimination, constant and copy propagation, strength reduction and special techniques for improving the efficiency of loops, such as strip mining and loop interchange and unrolling.
2. A version compiled with -O3, which allows the compiler to automatically parallelize certain loop constructs, particularly those where iteration counts will be known at run-time, and where successive iterations have no data dependencies. This option provides a means to achieve a program employing parallelism with no intervention from the programmer.
3. Finally, a version (also compiled with -O3) where certain loops were explicitly made parallel by the inclusion of a compiler directive. The aim

TABLE 1

Timings for parameter estimations for 1, 2 or 3 bond ratings ratings categories, each jointly for 20 dates (hence 20, 40 or 60 categories), and each comprising 20 bonds of different maturities. These times (from the shell time command) do not take into account processor idle time.

Number of Categories	Program Version -O2		-O3		Parallel	
20	110.4	98%	197.8	176%	152.7	813%
40	497.7	99%	655.1	139%	500.1	1290%
60	1900.3	99%	2429.1	154%	2220.7	1358%

was to achieve a high degree of parallelism with minimal programming effort. Hence, only one loop was parallelized, namely the pricing of the 20 bonds for each category. For our three test cases, this leads to the creation of 20 (40, or 60) separate threads.

The Convex C compiler will parallelize any loop preceded by a directive to that effect, regardless of whether the resulting code is correct. This required a slight rewriting of the original (sequential) source code, because local variables in blocks within the loop body are, by default, shared among the separate threads, which obviously leads to incorrect results. However, local variables within subroutines called from the loop body are private to each thread (in fact, each thread has its own stack). Hence, the entire body of the loop in question was converted to a subroutine, taking the loop index as a parameter. In addition, each thread was given the address of a unique location where to store the calculated result, which were then processed serially after termination of all threads. Newly developed programs could easily be written using this method of making parallelization safe, but even for our existing code this change was very easy. Results are presented in Tables 1–3.

Table 1 shows, for each combination of number of bond ratings categories and program version, the CPU time used (total for all processors used, in seconds), and the CPU utilization factor, in units of 1 CPU = 100%. These numbers were obtained with the shell's time command, and require careful interpretation. First, we note that CPU usage increases when moving from -O2 to the somewhat parallel -O3 version. With -O3, between 1.39 and 1.76 CPU's are used on average. This increase in CPU usage can only be attributed to the overhead of managing the compiler-generated parallelism. The manually parallelized version utilizes from 8.13 to 13.58 CPUs, and the total time is comparable to the -O3 version.

However, the Convex is a time-shared machine, and it appears that the numbers given above reflect only times accumulated when each CPU had a

TABLE 2

Wall clock times (min:sec) and number of function calls.

Number of Categories	Program Version -O2	-O3	Parallel	Number of Function Calls
20	1:52	1:53	0:19	6,880
40	8:19	7:52	0:39	30,720
60	31:43	31:43	2:44	118,520

TABLE 3

Wall clock comparisons between -O2 and manually parallelized versions, and actually achieved as well as maximum possible efficiency.

Number of Categories	-O2/Parallel Time Ratio	Realized Efficiency	Max. Poss. Efficiency
20	5.9	42.1%	71.4%
40	12.8	91.4%	95.2%
60	11.6	82.9%	85.7%

thread to execute. Hence, they do not account for differences in load-balancing among CPUs (where presumably idle CPUs could execute other user processes). A truer picture of speed-up emerges when we consider wall-clock times elapsed (we had exclusive use of the machine during these tests), see Table 2. There is no significant difference between the elapsed -O2 and -O3 times. In essence the compiler manages to utilize more processors with -O3, but that is almost exactly balanced out by the increased run-time overhead, ending up just spending more machine resources. Of course, for codes that contain more easily parallelizable loops, for instance with dense linear algebra, the difference with -O3 should be much greater.

We finally compare the actually realized speed-up between the -O2 and manually parallelized versions, based on the wall clock times. Table 3 shows the ratios of wall clock times, which, on a dedicated machine, is the truest measure of speed-up, and on this machine is bounded by 14. Dividing this measure by 14 yields the efficiency, i.e., actual CPU utilization achieved. We compare this number to the maximum efficiency possible, when taking into account that our load balancing is not perfect. Hence, the last column in Table 3, $(n/m)/\text{ceil}(n/m)$, where $n = 20, 40, 60$ is the number of tasks, and

TABLE 4

Serial vs. Parallel input.

Times	Program Version		
	-O2	-O3	Parallel
CPU usage (sec)	1.0	45.4	21.9
CPU usage (%)	58%	358%	563%
Wall Clock	0:02	0:13	0:04

$m = 14$ is the number of processors. This comparison shows, especially for the two largest computations, that the speed-up actually achieved is within a few percent of the maximum which could be expected.

An analysis such as this indicates that it would probably not, for this program, be worthwhile to attemp further parallelism, except possibly if many small jobs must be solved. In this case, the sequential part of the program may become a bottleneck. The main part of this is the initial input of large data files, and we now ask whether this could be parallelized with advantage.

4.3. Parallelizing Input

The initialialization of the program includes reading 16 files containing the bond yield curves for the period covered. These data are then used to calculate, for each category separately, the forward rates μ_t, along which the short rate process, r, is centered. We investigate whether the sequential reading of these files is a substantial serial bottleneck in the program, and whether it is advantageous to perform the input in parallel. This was done by running the program up to and including input, then terminating it. Results are reported in Table 4.

At the lowest level of optimization, -O2, a serial read of the files takes only 2 seconds, and hence do not influence the figures of the previous section seriously. When automatic parallelization (-O3) is invoked, however, times increase dramatically. Subsequent investigation of this phenomenon revealed what appears to be a Convex software problem, which future updates of the operating system may alleviate. Note that the -O3 option does not cause parallel file reads.

When parallel file reads are used, the wall clock time increases (compared to using -O2) to 4 seconds. Assuming that this number is not influenced by system software problems, this can be explained by the heavy, parallel access to system input-output routines, which are likely to be protected by critical regions. Whenever a process enters a critical region, any other process that tries to enter it (i.e., perform input-output) “busy waits”, or spins, until it gets access, hence leading to the high CPU time of 21.9 seconds. Also, simultaneously reading from several different files may compromise the caching and sequential read-ahead schemes of the disk I/O system. The conclusion clearly is that code segments with heavy I/O should not be parallelized indiscriminantly.

5. Conclusion

Models for pricing financial instruments can be compute-intensive when they comprise large numbers of instruments over long time horizons, especially when they are embedded in optimization procedures for the purpose of estimating implied parameters. This makes them attractive candidates for implementation on parallel computers. However, parallel computing is oftentimes cumbersome and requires substantial specialized knowledge on part of the programmer.

In this paper it is shown, by using a two-factor model for the pricing of default risk in corporate bonds, that substantial speed-ups, almost identical to the number of processors, can be realized with a minimal programming effort. This was done on a shared-memory Convex Exemplar SPP–1200 system with 14 processors, where, just by parallelizing a single loop, speed-ups close to the maximum expected were easily realized.

Acknowledgements

Access to the Convex Exemplar SPP–1200 was provided by the Applied Research Laboratories at the University of Texas at Austin. Data were provided by Merrill Lynch & Co. Helpful comments and suggestions on the model were received by numeral individuals, and participants at seminars at the University of Maryland, the University of Texas at Austin, Southern Methodist University, and the University of Copenhagen.

References

Duffie, D. and K.J. Singleton, 1994, 'Econometric modeling of term structures of defaultable bonds', Working Paper, Stanford University.

Geist, A., A. Beguelin, J. Dongarra, W. Jiang, R. Manchek, and V. Sunderam, *PVM, Parallel Virtual Machine, A User's Guide and Tutorial for Networked Parallel Computing*, Cambridge, MA: MIT Press.

Hull, J.C., 1997, *Options, Futures, and Other Derivative Securities*, Third Edition, Englewood Cliffs, NJ: Prentice Hall.

Jarrow, R.A., D. Lando, and S. Turnbull, 1994, 'A Markov model for the term structure of credit risk spreads', *Working Paper*, Cornell University and Queen's Univesity.

Lando, D., 1993, 'A continuous-time Markov model of the term structure of credit spreads', Working Paper, Graduate School of Management, Cornell University.

Madan, D.B. and Unal, H., 1994, 'Pricing the risks of default', Working Paper, College of Business, University of Maryland.

Merton, R.C., 1974, 'On the pricing of corporate debt: The risk structure of interest rates', *Journal of Finance* 29, 449–470.

Nielsen, S.S. and E. Ronn, 1996, 'The valuation of default risk in corporate bonds and interest rate swaps', Working Paper, University of Texas at Austin.

ANNA NAGURNEY AND STAVROS SIOKOS

Projected Dynamical Systems for International Financial Policy Modeling and Computation

ABSTRACT. In this paper, we present a projected dynamical systems approach for international financial policy modeling and computation. The dynamic model incorporates taxes that depend both on the origin and on the type of investing sector, and price policy interventions that allow the monetary authorities to set upper and lower prices for all instruments and currencies. The stationary point yields the optimal composition of assets and liabilities for each sector of each country, as well as the equilibrium prices of the instruments, and the exchange rates, in terms of a basic currency. We present qualitative properties of the continuous time model, in terms of stability analysis, and propose a discrete time algorithm, along with convergence results, and a numerical example. This paper may be viewed as a contribution to the internationalization of tools for financial analysis.

1. Introduction

In this paper, we present a modeling approach for competitive, imperfect market, international financial problems in a dynamic setting. The methodology utilized is that of the theory of projected dynamical systems (Nagurney and Zhang 1996).

In particular, the dynamic model developed in this paper describes the adjustment process of the sectors of the countries that, in equilibrium, yields the optimal composition of assets and liabilities in each portfolio. In addition, the adjustments of the prices of the instruments in each currency, as well as the exchange rate prices for each currency, in terms of a basic currency, are also described. In this paper, we relax the perfect market assumption and we take transaction costs and policy interventions into consideration. The suggested dynamic international financial model has the flexibility of containing as many countries, currencies, sectors, and financial instruments as mandated by the application in question, with the theoretical limit being bounded solely by the memory of the computer utilized for solution.

H. Amman et al. (eds.), Computational Approaches to Economic Problems, 175–191.

The transaction costs that we treat include taxes and fees that an investor has to pay for each individual international investment. For example, one type of transaction cost that is handled by the model covers costs that are related to the origin and to the identity of both the sectors and the instruments, so that each sector can be charged differently from the others according to its portfolio. This type of transaction cost gives the monetary authorities the ability to apply different fees and taxes to investors in distinct countries. The second type of transaction cost that can be handled is related only to the instrument and currency prices and is a special case of the previous one. This type of transaction cost can be seen as a VAT (value added tax) type of transaction cost. There are some papers in the existing literature that look at a similar environment in which the transaction costs (e.g., taxation) are uniform across investors, but are differentiated among the particular type of instrument, that is, between stocks and bonds, as in Miller (1977). However, the proposed models, thus far, provide limited information as to the equilibrium patterns.

The price policy interventions that the model incorporates include ceiling and floor prices, for both instruments and currencies, imposed by the governments. We assume that all the transaction costs, as well as the price ceilings and floors, are constants with known values.

Our goal in this paper is to make a contribution to the internationalization of financial analysis tools since it is now recognized (Hufbauer and Schott 1993, Rosenthal and Cafruny 1993, Silva and Sjorgen 1990, Adler and Dumas 1983, Grubel 1968, Lessard 1973, Solnik 1974) that many investors do diversify their portfolios internationally and, moreover, such investments offer new opportunities. In addition, the existing literature deals principally with a small number of countries and instruments (see, e.g., Eun and Janakiramanan 1986) without deriving currency or instrument prices or proposes mathematical models that apply only to perfect markets (cf. Nagurney 1994, and the references therein). Finally, we note that although finite-dimensional variational inequality theory (Nagurney and Siokos 1996a) can handle large-scale and complex international financial equilibrium problems, it does not enhance the understanding of disequilibrium behavior.

This paper is organized as follows. In Section 2, we present the dynamic imperfect market international financial model and show that the financial adjustment process is a projected dynamical system. In Section 3 we study the stability of the international financial adjustment process and provide conditions that guarantee the stability and the asymptotical stability of the adjustment process. In Section 4 we propose a discrete time method, the Euler method, for the solution of the model and provide conditions for convergence. We then present a numerical example for illustrative purposes.

2. The Dynamic International Financial Model with Transaction Costs and Policy Interventions

In this section we develop a dynamic international financial model with transaction costs and policy interventions and we study the adjustment process and the projected dynamical system that describes the dynamic behavior of the financial sectors and that of the instrument and currency prices.

We consider an economy consisting of N countries with a typical country denoted by j. Each country, in turn, has F sectors with a typical sector denoted by f. We also consider M currencies with a typical currency denoted by i. In each currency there are K instruments with a typical instrument denoted by k. Denote the volume of instrument k in currency i, held as an asset by sector f of country j, by $X_{i,k}^{j,f}$, and group the assets of a sector in a country into the MK-dimensional column vector $X^{j,f}$. Similarly, denote the volume of instrument k in currency i, held as a liability by sector f of country j, by $Y_{i,k}^{j,f}$ and group the liabilities of each sector in each country into an MK-dimensional column vector $Y^{j,f}$.

Let $r_{i,k}$ represent the price of instrument k in currency i and group the instrument prices into an MK-dimensional column vector r. Let e_i denote the rate of appreciation of currency i against the basic currency, which can be interpreted as the rate of return earned because of exchange rate fluctuations. These rates are then grouped into an M-dimensional column vector e.

Furthermore, from the policy interventions aspect, denote the price ceiling associated with instrument k of currency i as $r_{i,k}^C$ and the exchange rate price ceiling associated with currency i as e_i^C. Similarly, denote the price floor associated with instrument k in currency i as $r_{i,k}^F$ and the price floor associated with currency i as e_i^F. Group the instrument and currency price floors and ceilings, respectively, into the MK-dimensional column vectors r^F and r^C. Similarly, group the exchange rate price floors and ceilings, respectively, into the M-dimensional column vectors e^F and e^C. We assume that the price floors and, hence, the ceilings, are nonnegative. We further assume that each sector will behave as if it has no influence on the prices of the instruments and the exchange rates, or on the behavior of the other sectors. Hence, the assumption here is one of perfect competition.

Finally, denote the given tax rate levied on the net yield of sector f in country j on financial instrument k of currency i as $\phi_{i,k}^{j,f}$ and group the tax rates into an $MNFK$-dimensional column vector ϕ. We assume that all the transaction costs $\phi_{i,k}^{j,f}$ (or taxes) are constants with known values and lie in the interval $[0, 1)$. These costs depend both on the sector and the country that holds liabilities or assets in this instrument or currency. The model, hence, gives the local governments the flexibility to apply distinct tax rates across instruments in their area of authorization. Note that the model includes, as a special case, VAT type taxes, which only depend on the instrument and the currency. For example, a VAT tax on instrument k and currency i can be handled in our framework by setting $\phi^{j,f}_{i,k} = \tau_{i,k}$, for all j and f.

Associate now with each asset held in instrument k of currency i a positive coefficient $\alpha_{i,k}$, and with each liability a positive coefficient $\beta_{i,k}$, which are assumed to incorporate the unit transaction costs $c^x_{i,k}$ and $c^y_{i,k}$, respectively, and which, in turn, are assumed to lie in the interval $[0, 1)$. For example, one possible form of $\alpha_{i,k}$ is: $\alpha_{i,k} \equiv 1 + c^x_{i,k}$ and of $\beta_{i,k}$ is: $\beta_{i,k} \equiv 1 - c^y_{i,k}$.

We assume that each sector f of every country j seeks to maximize its utility, where the utility function is denoted by $U^{j,f}(X^{j,f}, Y^{j,f}, r, e; \phi)$ and is assumed to be a strictly concave function with respect to $(X^{j,f}, Y^{j,f})$. Hence, the sectors are assume to be risk averse. We further assume that this function has bounded second order derivatives for all its entries in the feasible set. We assume that the accounts of each sector must balance and denote the total financial volume held by sector f of country j by $S^{j,f}$.

The portfolio optimization problem of each sector in each country can then be expressed as:

$$\text{Maximize } U^{j,f}(X^{j,f}, Y^{j,f}, r, e; \phi), \tag{1}$$

subject to:

$$\sum_{i=1}^{M} \sum_{k=1}^{K} \alpha_{i,k} X^{j,f}_{i,k} = S^{j,f} \tag{2a}$$

$$\sum_{i=1}^{M} \sum_{k=1}^{K} \beta_{i,k} Y^{j,f}_{i,k} = S^{j,f}, \tag{2b}$$

$$X^{j,f}_{i,k}, Y^{j,f}_{i,k} \geq 0, \quad \forall i \in (1, M), \quad \forall k \in (1, K). \tag{3}$$

For each sector $f \in (1, F)$ in country $j \in (1, N)$ we let

$$\bar{X}^{j,f} = \left\{ X^{j,f} \in R^{MK}_{+} : \sum_{i=1}^{M} \sum_{k=1}^{K} \alpha_{i,k} X^{j,f}_{i,k} = S^{j,f} \right\} \tag{4}$$

denote the constraint set of its assets, and, similarly, we let

$$\bar{Y}^{j,f} = \left\{ Y^{j,f} \in R^{MK}_{+} : \sum_{i=1}^{M} \sum_{k=1}^{K} \beta_{i,k} Y^{j,f}_{i,k} = S^{j,f} \right\} \tag{5}$$

denote the constraint set for its liabilities. Then the feasible set for the assets and the liabilities of each sector of every country is a Cartesian product denoted by $\kappa^{j,f}$, where $\kappa^{j,f} \equiv \{\bar{X}^{j,f} \times \bar{Y}^{j,f}\}$. We define the feasible set for the assets of all sectors from all countries as:

$$\bar{X} \equiv \bar{X}^{1,1} \times \cdots \times \bar{X}^{j,f} \times \cdots \times \bar{X}^{N,F}$$

and, similarly, for the liabilities: $\bar{Y} \equiv \bar{Y}^{1,1} \times \cdots \times \bar{Y}^{j,f} \times \cdots \times \bar{Y}^{N,F}$, with $\kappa \equiv \{\bar{X} \times \bar{Y}\}$.

The optimization problem for each sector of each country can be interpreted as an effort to adjust its asset and liability pattern in a direction that maximizes its utility function, while maintaining the accounting and nonnegativity constraints. In particular, it is obvious that the ideal direction for the maximization of this utility function in the unconstrained case is given by: $(\nabla_{X^{j,f}} U^{j,f}, \nabla_{Y^{j,f}} U^{j,f})$, where:

$$\nabla_{X^{j,f}} U^{j,f} \equiv \left(\frac{\partial U^{j,f}}{\partial X_{1,1}^{j,f}}, \ldots, \frac{\partial U^{j,f}}{\partial X_{i,k}^{j,f}}, \ldots, \frac{\partial U^{j,f}}{\partial X_{M,K}^{j,f}} \right) \tag{6}$$

and

$$\nabla_{Y^{j,f}} U^{j,f} \equiv \left(\frac{\partial U^{j,f}}{\partial Y_{1,1}^{j,f}}, \ldots, \frac{\partial U^{j,f}}{\partial Y_{i,k}^{j,f}}, \ldots, \frac{\partial U^{j,f}}{\partial Y_{M,K}^{j,f}} \right), \tag{7}$$

where $\nabla_{X_{j,f}}$ denotes the gradient with respect to the variables in the vector $X^{j,f}$ with $\nabla_{Y^{j,f}}$ defined accordingly.

However, this "idealized" direction needs to be revised in order to incorporate the fact that the assets and liabilities must lie in the feasible set for each sector of each country. Consequently, the best-realizable direction of sector f of country j is the projection of the idealized direction $(\nabla_{X^{j,f}} U^{j,f}, \nabla_{Y^{j,f}} U^{j,f})$, onto the constraint set, $\kappa^{j,f}$, at its current portfolio $(X^{j,f}, Y^{j,f})$.

This best-realizable direction for a sector f in country j can be mathematically expressed as:

$$\Pi_{\kappa^{j,f}}((X^{j,f}, Y^{j,f}), (\nabla_{X^{j,f}} U^{j,f}, \nabla_{Y^{j,f}} U^{j,f})), \tag{8}$$

where for any closed convex set $S \in R^n$, $Z \in S$, and $v \in R^n$, the projection of the vector v at Z (with respect to S) is defined by:

$$\Pi_S(Z, v) = \lim_{\delta \to 0} \frac{P_S(Z + \delta v) - Z}{\delta} \tag{9}$$

and P_S is the norm projection defined by:

$$P_S(Z) = \arg \min_{Z' \in S} \|Z' - Z\|. \tag{10}$$

It should be pointed out that:

$$\text{If } Z \in \text{int } S \Rightarrow \Pi_S(Z, v) = v, \tag{11}$$

that is, if Z lies in the interior of the feasible set S, then the projection in the direction v is simply v. For additional background, see the book by Nagurney and Zhang (1996).

In view of (8), the asset and liability volumes for sector $f \in (1, F)$ of country $j \in (1, N)$ are adjusted, hence, according to the following process over time:

$$\dot{X}^{j,f} = \Pi_{\bar{X}^{j,f}}(X^{j,f}, \nabla_{X^{j,f}} U^{j,f}), \quad \dot{Y}^{j,f} = \Pi_{\bar{Y}^{j,f}}(Y^{j,f}, \nabla_{Y^{j,f}} U^{j,f}). \tag{12}$$

Moreover, the instrument and currency prices also change through time, adjusting to their supply and demand fluctuations. We assume that the prices of all instruments and all currencies follow the supply-demand rule, that is, the price of an instrument or currency will increase when the demand exceeds its supply, and will decrease, otherwise, within the imposed floors and ceilings.

More precisely, we define $\rho_{i,k}$ as minus the difference between supply and demand for instrument k in currency i, and ϵ_i as minus the difference between supply and demand for currency i, that is,

$$\rho_{i,k} \equiv \sum_{j=1}^{N} \sum_{f=1}^{F} -(1 - \phi_{i,k}^{j,f})(\alpha_{i,k} X_{i,k}^{j,f} - \beta_{i,k} Y_{i,k}) \tag{13a}$$

and

$$\epsilon_i \equiv \sum_{k=1}^{K} \sum_{j=1}^{N} \sum_{f=1}^{F} -(1 - \phi_{i,k}^{j,f})(\alpha_{i,k} X_{i,k}^{j,f} - \beta_{i,k} Y_{i,k}^{j,f}). \tag{13b}$$

The instrument price $r_{i,k}$ changes according to:

$$\dot{r}_{i,k} = \begin{cases} \max\{0, \rho_{i,k}\}, & \text{if } r_{i,k} = r_{i,k}^F \\ \rho_{i,k}, & \text{if } r_{i,k}^F < r_{i,k} < r_{i,k}^C \\ \min\{0, \rho_{i,k}\}, & \text{if } r_{i,k} = r_{i,k}^C, \end{cases} \tag{14}$$

which is equivalent to:

$$\dot{r}_{i,k} = \Pi_{[r_{i,k}^F, r_{i,k}^C]}(r_{i,k}, \rho_{i,k}). \tag{15}$$

The currency price e_i, in turn, changes according to:

$$\dot{e}_i = \begin{cases} \max\{0, \epsilon_i\}, & \text{if } e_i = e_i^F \\ \epsilon_i, & \text{if } e_i^F < e_i < e_i^C \\ \min\{0, \epsilon\}, & \text{if } e_i = e_i^C, \end{cases} \tag{16}$$

which is equivalent to:

$$\dot{e}_i = \Pi_{[e_i^F, e_i^C]}(e_i, \epsilon_i). \tag{17}$$

The financial adjustment process that derives the allocation of assets and liabilities for each sector f of country j along with the prices of each instrument and each currency can now be formulated, in view of (6), (7), (15), and (17), as:

$$\begin{cases} \dot{X}^{j,f} = \Pi_{\bar{X}^{j,f}}(X^{j,f}, \nabla_{X^{j,f}} U^{j,f}); & \forall j \in (1,N), \ \forall f \in (1,F) \\ \dot{Y}^{j,f} = \Pi_{\bar{Y}^{j,f}}(Y^{j,f}, \nabla_{Y^{j,f}} U^{j,f}); & \forall j \in (1,N), \ \forall f \in (1,F) \\ \dot{r}_{i,k} = \Pi_{[r_{i,k}^F, r_{i,k}^C]}(r_{i,k}, \rho_{i,k}); & \forall i \in (1,M), \ \forall k \in (1,K) \\ \dot{e}_i = \Pi_{[e_i^F, e_i^C]}(e_i, \epsilon_i); & \forall i \in (1,M). \end{cases} \tag{18}$$

For simplicity, and in order to maintain a compact mathematical formulation, we introduce the following notation: Let $B = 2MNFK + MK + M$, $\Omega \equiv \kappa \times \bar{B}$, where

$$\bar{B} = \prod_{i=1,k=1}^{M,K} \left[r_{i,k}^F, r_{i,k}^C \right] \times \prod_{i=1}^{M} \left[e_i^F, e_i^C \right]$$

and define the column vector $Z = (X, Y, r, e) \in \Omega$, and the column vector $F(Z)$:

$$F(Z)^T = \left[F_1(Z), \ldots, F_b(Z), \ldots, F_B(Z) \right]^T, \tag{19}$$

which is equal to:

$$\begin{bmatrix} -\nabla_X U(X,Y,r,e;\phi) \\ -\nabla_Y U(X,Y,r,e;\phi) \\ \sum_{j=1}^N \sum_{f=1}^F (1-\phi_{1,1}^{j,f})(\alpha_{1,1} X_{1,1}^{j,f} - \beta_{1,1} Y_{1,1}^{j,f}) \\ \vdots \\ \sum_{j=1}^N \sum_{f=1}^F (1-\phi_{M,K}^{j,f})(\alpha_{M,K} X_{M,K}^{j,f} - \beta_{M,K} Y_{M,K}^{j,f}) \\ \sum_{k=1}^K \sum_{j=1}^N \sum_{f=1}^F (1-\phi_{1,k}^{j,f})(\alpha_{1,k} X_{1,k}^{j,f} - \beta_{1,K} Y_{1,k}^{j,f}) \\ \vdots \\ \sum_{k=1}^K \sum_{j=1}^N \sum_{f=1}^F (1-\phi_{M,k}^{j,f})(\alpha_{M,k} X_{M,k}^{j,f} - \beta_{M,k} Y_{M,k}^{j,f}) \end{bmatrix}_{B \times 1}^T . \tag{20}$$

In view of Proposition 1 in Dong et al. (1996), and, taking into consideration the new notation, the international financial adjustment process can be succinctly expressed mathematically as:

$$\dot{Z} = \Pi_\Omega(Z, -F(Z)). \tag{21}$$

According to Dupuis and Nagurney (1993), we have the following theorem.

THEOREM 1. *Equation (21) well defines a dynamical system, in that there exists a unique solution path to (21) for any boundary condition,* $Z(0) = Z_0 \in \Omega$.

It is easy to see that the dynamical system defined in (21) is a nonclassical system due to the discontinuity of the projection map Π_Ω at the boundary of Ω (see Dupuis and Nagurney 1993). Such discontinuities arise because of the constraints underlying the application(s) in question. System (21) was first termed a "projected dynamical system" or PDS(F, Ω) by Zhang and Nagurney (1995). For additional background and applications, see the book by Nagurney and Zhang (1996).

We now make the connection between stationary points of the projected dynamical system (21), the solutions to a variational inequality problem, and the equilibrium conditions governing the international financial model. In particular, we show the equivalence among the stationary points, the solutions to a variational inequality problem, and the equilibrium points defined by the equilibrium conditions.

THEOREM 2 (Dupuis and Nagurney 1993). *The stationary points of the projected dynamical system* PDS(F, Ω)*, that is,* Z^* *satisfying*

$$0 = \Pi_\Omega(Z^*, -F(Z^*)) \tag{22}$$

correspond to the solutions of the variational inequality problem VI(F, Ω) *defined by:*

Determine $Z^* \in \Omega$*, such that*

$$\langle F(Z^*)^T, Z - Z^* \rangle \geq 0, \quad \forall Z \in \Omega, \tag{23}$$

where $\langle \cdot, \cdot \rangle$ *denotes the inner product in* R^B*, since* Ω *is a convex polyhedron.*

We now write down the variational inequality problem (23) explicitly, utilizing (19) and (20): Determine $(X^*, Y^*, r^*, e^*) \in \Omega$, such that:

$$-\sum_{j=1}^{N}\sum_{f=1}^{F}\left[\nabla_{X^{j,f}} U^{j,f}(X^{j,f^*}, Y^{j,f^*}, r^*, e^*; \phi)\right] \times [X^{j,f} - X^{j,f^*}]$$

$$-\sum_{j=1}^{N}\sum_{f=1}^{F}\left[\nabla_{Y^{j,f}} U^{j,f}(X^{j,f^*}, Y^{j,f^*}, r^*, e^*; \phi)\right] \times [Y^{j,f} - Y^{j,f^*}]$$

$$+\sum_{i=1}^{M}\sum_{k=1}^{K}\left[\sum_{j=1}^{N}\sum_{f=1}^{F}(1 - \phi_{i,k}^{j,f})(\alpha_{i,k} X_{i,k}^{j,f^*} - \beta_{i,k} Y_{i,k}^{j,f^*})\right] \times [r_{i,k} - r_{i,k}^*]$$

$$+\sum_{i=1}^{M}\left[\sum_{k=1}^{K}\sum_{j=1}^{N}\sum_{f=1}^{F}(1-\phi_{i,k}^{j,f})(\alpha_{i,k}X_{i,k}^{j,f^*}-\beta_{i,k}Y_{i,k}^{j,f^*})\right]\times[e_i-e_i^*]\geq 0,$$

$$\forall (X,Y,r,e)\in\Omega. \tag{24}$$

In Nagurney and Siokos (1996a) it is shown that the solution to the variational inequality (24) coincides with the equilibrium solution that guarantees optimality of the portfolios and that the market clears for both the financial instruments and the currencies if the respective prices are not at the imposed floors or ceilings. The above dynamic model generalizes the model in Nagurney and Siokos (1996b) by incorporating policies and transaction costs. It also generalizes the model of Dong (1996) by extending it to the international domain and by incorporating transaction costs.

3. Stability Analysis

In this section we provide conditions under which a disequilibrium pattern of assets, liabilities, instrument and currency prices will reach an international financial equilibrium state under the adjustment process (21). For consistency, and in order to simplify the study of the asymptotic behavior of the dynamic international financial model, we present the following definitions. The theorems are presented without proofs since they are straightforward adaptations of the stability theorems that are found in Dong et al. (1996), Nagurney and Siokos (1996b), and Dong (1996).

DEFINITION 1. *The international financial adjustment process is stable if each financial equilibrium, $Z^*=(X^*,Y^*,r^*,e^*)$, is a monotone attractor, that is, for any initial asset, liability, and instrument and currency price pattern, (X_0,Y_0,r_0,e_0), the distance, $\|(X(t),Y(t),r(t),e(t))-(X^*,Y^*,r^*,e^*)\|$, is nonincreasing in time t, where $(X(t),Y(t),r(t),e(t))$ satisfies the adjustment process (21).*

In other words, if an international financial adjustment process is stable, then any state of disequilibrium will remain close to an equilibrium pattern forever.

DEFINITION 2. *The international financial adjustment process is asymptotically stable if it is stable and for any initial asset, liability, and price pattern, (X_0,Y_0,r_0,e_0), the financial adjustment process starting with (X_0,Y_0,r_0,e_0) converges to some equilibrium pattern (X^*,Y^*,r^*,e^*); namely,*

$$\lim_{t\to\infty}(X_0(t),Y_0(t),r_0(t),e_0(t))\to(X^*,Y^*,r^*,e^*). \tag{25}$$

Asymptotic stability can then be interpreted as the case that any international financial disequilibrium will eventually approach equilibrium.

THEOREM 3 (Stability of International Financial Adjustment Process). *If the utility function $U^{j,f}$ of each sector f from every country j is twice differentiable and concave in $X^{j,f}$ and $Y^{j,f}$, and the utility function has the following form:*

$$U^{j,f}(X^{j,f}, Y^{j,f}, r, e) = u^{j,f}(X^{j,f}, Y^{j,f}) + \sum_{i=1}^{m} \sum_{k=q}^{K} (1 - \phi_{i,k}^{j,f})(r_{i,k} + e_i)(X_{i,k}^{j,f} - Y_{i,k}^{j,f}) \tag{26}$$

and all $\alpha_{i,k}$ and $\beta_{i,k} = 1$, then the international financial adjustment process is stable.

THEOREM 4. *If we assume that all sectors f in countries j have a strictly concave utility function with respect to the assets and liabilities, then all financial equilibria are comprised of unique asset and liability patterns X^* and Y^*.*

THEOREM 5. *If we assume that all sectors f in countries j have a strictly concave utility function with respect to the asset and liability pattern, $(X^{j,f}, Y^{j,f})$, the utility functions are twice continuously differentiable, and of the form (26), then the financial adjustment process is asymptotically stable, provided that all $\alpha_{i,k}$ and $\beta_{i,k} = 1$.*

Note that the sum of the second and third terms on the right-hand side of the equality in (26) represents the value of the asset holdings minus the value of the liability holdings. An important special case of (26) is given by the quadratic utility function:

$$U^{j,f}(X^{j,f}, Y^{j,f}, r, e; \phi) = - \begin{pmatrix} X^{j,f} \\ Y^{j,f} \end{pmatrix}^T Q^{j,f} \begin{pmatrix} X^{j,f} \\ Y^{j,f} \end{pmatrix} + \sum_{i=1}^{M} \sum_{k=1}^{K} (1 - \phi_{i,k}^{j,f})(r_{i,k} + e_i)(X_{i,k}^{j,f} - Y_{i,k}^{j,f}), \tag{27}$$

where $Q^{j,f}$ is the symmetric $2MK \times 2MK$ variance/covariance matrix representing the risk associated with the portfolio choice.

4. A Discrete Time Algorithm

In this section, we present a discrete time algorithm, the Euler method, for the computation of the international financial equilibrium pattern. This algorithm may also be viewed as a discrete time approximation or discrete time adjustment process for the continuous time model given by (21). The Euler method is a special case of the general iterative scheme introduced in Dupuis and Nagurney (1993). For completeness, and easy reference, we now state the general iterative scheme applied to the international financial model: At each iteration τ, one must compute:

$$Z^{\tau+1} = P_\Omega(Z^\tau - a_\tau F_\tau(Z^\tau)), \tag{28}$$

where $\{a_\tau\}$ is a positive sequence, to be discussed later, along with an interpretation, P_Ω is the projection operator defined in (10), and F_τ is some suitable approximation of $F(Z)$ defined in (19) and (20).

In the case of the Euler method, we have $F_\tau = F$, and, hence, the iterative step takes the form:

$$Z^{\tau+1} = P_\Omega(Z^\tau - a_\tau F(Z^\tau)), \tag{29}$$

which is equivalent (Nagurney 1993) to the solution of the variational inequality problem:

Determine $Z^{\tau+1} \in \Omega$, satisfying:

$$\langle (Z^{\tau+1} + a_\tau F(Z^\tau) - Z^\tau)^T, Z - Z^{\tau+1}\rangle \geq 0, \quad \forall Z \in \Omega. \tag{30}$$

We now write down (30) explicitly for our problem.

Compute $(X^{\tau+1}, Y^{\tau+1}, r^{\tau+1}, e^{\tau+1}) \in \Omega$ by solving the variational inequality problem:

$$\sum_{j=1}^{N}\sum_{f=1}^{F}\sum_{i=1}^{M}\sum_{k=1}^{K}\Bigg[X_{i,k}^{j,f\,\tau+1} + a_\tau\Bigg(-\frac{\partial u^{j,f}(X^{j,f\,\tau}, Y^{j,f\,\tau})}{\partial X_{i,k}^{j,f}}$$

$$-(1-\phi_{i,k}^{j,f})(r_{i,k}^\tau + e_i^\tau)\Bigg) - X_{i,k}^{j,f\,\tau}\Bigg] \times [X_{i,k}^{j,f\,\prime} - X_{i,k}^{j,f\,\tau+1}]$$

$$+\sum_{j=1}^{N}\sum_{f=1}^{F}\sum_{i=1}^{M}\sum_{k=1}^{K}\Bigg[Y_{i,k}^{j,f\,\tau+1} + a_\tau\Bigg(-\frac{\partial u^{j,f}(X^{j,f\,\tau}, Y^{j,f\,\tau})}{\partial Y_{i,k}^{j,f}}$$

$$+(1-\phi_{i,k}^{j,f})(r_{i,k}^\tau + e_i^\tau)\Bigg) - Y_{i,k}^{j,f\,\tau}\Bigg] \times [Y_{i,k}^{j,f\,\prime} - Y_{i,k}^{j,f\,\tau+1}]$$

$$+\sum_{i=1}^{M}\sum_{k=1}^{K}\left[r_{i,k}^{\tau+1} + a_\tau\left[\sum_{j=1}^{N}\sum_{f=1}^{F}\left(\alpha_{i,k}X_{i,k}^{j,f\,\tau} - \beta_{i,k}Y_{i,k}^{j,f\,\tau}\right)\right] - r_{i,k}^\tau\right]$$

$$\times [r'_{i,k} - r_{i,k}^{\tau+1}]$$

$$+\sum_{i=1}^{M}\left[e_i^{\tau+1} + a_\tau\left[\sum_{k=1}^{K}\sum_{j=1}^{N}\sum_{f=1}^{F}\left(\alpha_{i,k}X_{i,k}^{j,f\,\tau} - \beta_{i,k}Y_{i,k}^{j,f\,\tau}\right)\right] - e_i^\tau\right]$$

$$\times [e_i' - e_i^{\tau+1}] \geq 0, \qquad \forall (X', Y', r', e') \in \Omega. \tag{31}$$

In the context of the international financial problem, the projection operation entails the solution of a quadratic programming problem, which in view of the feasible set, which is a Cartesian product, is further decomposable in the assets, the liabilities, and in the prices. Moreover, since the constraints are linear and the objective function is separable the problems can be solved exactly and in closed form (Nagurney and Siokos 1996a). To conclude this section, the following theorem provides the convergence of the proposed Euler method in the context of the international financial problem.

THEOREM 6. *Suppose that the utility functions U are strictly monotone decreasing and of the form (26). Let $\{a_\mathcal{T}\}$ be a sequence of positive real numbers that satisfies*

$$\lim_{\mathcal{T} \to \infty} a_\mathcal{T} = 0 \tag{32}$$

and

$$\sum_{\mathcal{T}=1}^{\infty} a_\mathcal{T} = \infty. \tag{33}$$

Then the Euler method given by

$$Z^{\tau+1} = P_\Omega(Z^\tau - a_\tau F(Z^\tau)), \tag{34}$$

where $F(Z)$ is the vector defined in (19) and (20) converges to some international financial equilibrium pattern, provided that all $\alpha_{i,k}$ and $\beta_{i,k} = 1$.

Proof. According to Dupuis and Nagurney (1993, Theorem 7), the sequence $\{Z^\tau\}$ generated by (34) converges to some solution to the variational inequality problem (24), equivalently, to a stationary point of the projected dynamical system (21)), provided that the following assumption is satisfied. Consequently, it converges to some equilibrium pattern.

ASSUMPTION. Fix an initial condition $Z^0 \in \Omega$ and define the sequence $\{Z^\tau, \tau \in N\}$ by (34). Assume the following conditions.

1. $\sum_{\mathcal{T}=0}^{\infty} a_\mathcal{T} = \infty, \quad a_\mathcal{T} > 0, \quad a_\mathcal{T} \to 0, \quad$ as $\quad \tau \to \infty$.
2. $d(F_\tau(Z), \bar{F}(Z)) \to 0$ uniformly on compact subsets of Ω as $\tau \to \infty$, where $d(Z, A) = \inf\{\|Z - y\|, y \in A\}$.
3. Define ϕ_y to be the unique solution to $\dot{Z} = \Pi_\Omega(Z, -F(Z))$ that satisfies $\phi_y(0) = y \in \Omega$. The $\omega-$limit set

   $$\cup_{y \in \Omega} \cap_{t \geq 0} \cup_{s \geq t} \{\phi_y(s)\}$$

   is contained in the set of stationary points of $\dot{Z} = \Pi_\Omega(Z, -F(Z))$.
4. The sequence $\{Z^\tau, \tau \in N\}$ is bounded.

5. The solutions to $\dot{Z} = \Pi_{\Omega}(Z, -F(Z))$ are stable in the sense that given any compact set Ω_1 there exists a compact set Ω_2 such that $\cup_{y\in\Omega\cap\Omega_1}\cup_{t\geq 0}\{\phi_y(t)\} \subset \Omega_2$.

Notice that condition (1) is already met by the chosen sequence according to (32) and (33). Condition (2) is also satisfied because $F(Z)$ is continuous and $F_\mathcal{T} = F$. By Theorem 5, the international financial adjustment process is asymptotically stable, and, hence, every ω-limit point of the projected dynamical system (21) is an equilibrium pattern. This verifies condition (3) of that assumption. Condition (4) becomes trivial, with notice to the fact that the feasible set is compact. Finally, condition (5) of the assumption holds true because the financial adjustment process (21) is asymptotically stable and, therefore, it is bounded. The proof is complete.

5. A Numerical Example

The Euler method was coded in FORTRAN and implemented on an IBM SP2. The CPU time for the example is reported exclusive of input/output times. We solved the subproblems using exact equilibration (Nagurney 1993).

In the example we initialized the algorithm as follows: $X^{j,f}_{i,k} = S^{j,f}/MK$ and $Y^{j,f}_{i,k} = S^{j,f}/MK$ for all j, f; $r_{i,k} = 1$ for all i, k and $e_i = 1$ for all i with $S^{1,1} = S^{1,2} = S^{2,1} = S^{2,2} = 1$; $S^{3,1} = S^{3,2} = 2$. In order to maintain feasibility, we set: $X^{j,f}_{1,1} = S^{j,f}/\alpha_{1,1}$, $Y^{j,f}_{1,1} = S^{j,f}/\beta_{1,1}$, for all j, f; all remaining $X^{j,f}_{i,k}$ and $Y^{j,f}_{i,k}$ were set to 0.

The convergence criterion that we utilized was that the absolute difference between two successive iterates was less than ϵ with ϵ set to 0.001. We set $\{a_\mathcal{T}\} = 0.2\{1, 1/2, 1/2, 1/3, 1/3, 1/3, \ldots\}$.

The example consisted of 3 countries, 2 sectors, 2 currencies, and 2 instruments. The variance-covariance matrices were as follows, with the variance-covariance matrices for the first country's sectors given by:

For country 1, sector 1:

$$Q^{1,1} = \begin{pmatrix} 1.0 & 0.2 & 0 & 0 & -0.2 & -0.3 & 0 & 0 \\ 0.2 & 1.0 & 0 & 0 & -0.1 & -0.2 & 0 & 0 \\ 0 & 0 & 1.0 & 0 & 0 & 0 & -0.1 & 0 \\ 0 & 0 & 0 & 1.0 & 0 & 0 & -0.1 & 0 \\ -0.2 & -0.1 & 0 & 0 & 1.0 & 0.4 & 0 & 0 \\ -0.3 & -0.2 & 0 & 0 & 0.4 & 1.0 & 0 & 0 \\ 0 & 0 & -0.1 & -0.1 & 0 & 0 & 1.0 & 0 \\ 0 & 0 & 0 & 0 & 0 & 0 & 0 & 1.0 \end{pmatrix},$$

For country 1, sector 2:

$$Q^{1,2} = \begin{pmatrix} 1.0 & 0.3 & 0.2 & 0 & 0 & 0 & -0.1 & -0.2 \\ 0.3 & 1.0 & 0 & 0 & 0 & -0.15 & 0 & 0 \\ 0.2 & 0 & 1.0 & 0.5 & -0.1 & 0 & 0 & 0 \\ 0 & 0 & 0.5 & 1.0 & 0 & -0.3 & 0 & 0 \\ 0 & 0 & -0.1 & 0 & 1.0 & 0 & 0.2 & 0 \\ 0 & -0.15 & 0 & -0.3 & 0 & 1.0 & 0.3 & 0 \\ -0.1 & 0 & 0 & 0 & 0.2 & 0.3 & 1.0 & 0 \\ -0.2 & 0 & 0 & 0 & 0 & 0 & 0 & 1.0 \end{pmatrix}.$$

The variance-covariance matrices for the sectors in the second country were given by:

For country 2, sector 1:

$$Q^{2,1} = \begin{pmatrix} 1.0 & 0 & 0.3 & 0 & -0.1 & -0.1 & 0 & 0 \\ 0 & 1.0 & 0.1 & 0 & 0 & 0 & -0.2 & 0 \\ 0.3 & 0.1 & 1.0 & 0 & -0.3 & 0 & 0 & 0 \\ 0 & 0 & 0 & 1.0 & -0.4 & 0 & 0 & 0 \\ -0.1 & 0 & -0.3 & -0.4 & 1.0 & 0 & 0 & 0 \\ -0.1 & 0 & 0 & 0 & 0 & 1.0 & 0.5 & 0 \\ 0 & -0.2 & 0 & 0 & 0 & 0.5 & 1.0 & 0.1 \\ 0 & 0 & 0 & 0 & 0 & 0 & 0.1 & 1.0 \end{pmatrix},$$

For country 2, sector 2:

$$Q^{2,2} = \begin{pmatrix} 1.0 & 0.4 & 0 & 0 & -0.2 & 0 & 0 & 0 \\ 0.4 & 1.0 & 0 & 0 & 0 & -0.1 & 0 & 0 \\ 0 & 0 & 1.0 & 0 & -0.3 & 0 & 0 & 0 \\ 0 & 0 & 0 & 1.0 & 0 & 0 & -0.4 & 0 \\ -0.2 & 0 & -0.3 & 0 & 1.0 & 0 & 0 & 0 \\ 0 & -0.1 & 0 & 0 & 0 & 1.0 & 0.3 & 0 \\ 0 & 0 & 0 & -0.4 & 0 & 0.3 & 1.0 & 0.1 \\ 0 & 0 & 0 & 0 & 0 & 0 & 0.1 & 1.0 \end{pmatrix}.$$

The variance/covariance matrices for the third country were given by:

For country 3, sector 1:

$$Q^{3,1} = \begin{pmatrix} 1.0 & 0.1 & 0 & 0 & 0 & 0 & 0 & -0.1 \\ 0.1 & 1.0 & 0.2 & 0 & -0.2 & 0 & 0 & 0 \\ 0 & 0.2 & 1.0 & 0 & 0 & -0.3 & 0 & 0 \\ 0 & 0 & 0 & 1.0 & 0 & 0 & 0 & 0 \\ 0 & -0.2 & 0 & 0 & 1.0 & 0.5 & 0 & 0 \\ 0 & 0 & -0.3 & 0 & 0.5 & 1.0 & 0 & 0 \\ 0 & 0 & 0 & 0 & 0 & 0 & 1.0 & 0.4 \\ -0.1 & 0 & 0 & 0 & 0 & 0 & 0.4 & 1.0 \end{pmatrix},$$

For country 3, sector 2:

$$Q^{3,2} = \begin{pmatrix} 1.0 & 0 & 0.2 & 0 & -0.1 & -0.2 & 0 & 0 \\ 0 & 1.0 & 0.3 & 0 & 0 & -0.4 & 0 & 0 \\ 0.2 & 0.3 & 1.0 & 0 & 0 & 0 & -0.1 & 0 \\ 0 & 0 & 0 & 1.0 & 0 & 0 & 0 & 0 \\ -0.1 & 0 & 0 & 0 & 1.0 & 0.4 & 0 & 0 \\ -0.2 & -0.4 & 0 & 0 & 0.4 & 1.0 & 0 & 0 \\ 0 & 0 & -0.1 & 0 & 0 & 0 & 1.0 & 0.6 \\ 0 & 0 & 0 & 0 & 0 & 0 & 0.6 & 1.0 \end{pmatrix}.$$

We set the $\phi_{i,k}^{j,f}$ as follows: $\phi_{1,1}^{1,1} = 0.15$, $\phi_{1,2}^{1,1} = 0.02$, $\phi_{2,1}^{1,1} = 0.10$, $\phi_{2,2}^{1,1} = 0.20$, $\phi_{1,1}^{1,2} = 0.20$, $\phi_{1,2}^{1,2} = 0.01$, $\phi_{2,1}^{1,2} = 0.25$, $\phi_{2,2}^{1,2} = 0.10$, $\phi_{1,1}^{2,1} = 0.30$, $\phi_{1,2}^{2,1} = 0.05$, $\phi_{2,1}^{2,1} = 0.10$, $\phi_{2,2}^{2,1} = 0.10$, $\phi_{1,1}^{2,2} = 0.15$, $\phi_{1,2}^{2,2} = 0.05$, $\phi_{2,1}^{2,2} = 0.10$, $\phi_{2,2}^{2,2} = 0.20$, $\phi_{1,1}^{3,1} = 0.30$, $\phi_{1,2}^{3,1} = 0.15$, $\phi_{2,1}^{3,1} = 0.10$, $\phi_{2,2}^{3,1} = 0.20$, $\phi_{1,1}^{3,2} = 0.10$, $\phi_{1,2}^{3,2} = 0.05$, $\phi_{2,1}^{3,2} = 0.10$, $\phi_{2,2}^{3,2} = 0.25$.

The price floors and ceilings were: $r_{1,1}^F = 0.1$, $r_{1,1}^C = 0.5$, $r_{1,2}^F = 0.1$, $r_{1,2}^C = 0.5$, $r_{2,1}^F = 0.0$, $r_{2,1}^C = 1.0$, $r_{2,2}^F = 0.05$, $r_{2,2}^C = 0.5$. $e_1^F = 0.05$, $e_1^C = 1$, $e_2^F = 0.05$, $e_2^C = 1$.

The transaction costs were: $\alpha_{1,1} = 1.1, \alpha_{1,2} = 1.2, \alpha_{2,1} = 1.1, \alpha_{2,2} = 1.3$, $\beta_{1,1} = 0.6, \beta_{1,2} = 0.7, \beta_{2,1} = 0.8, \beta_{2,2} = 0.9$.

The algorithm converged in 183 iterations and .10 seconds of CPU time yielding the following solution:

Instrument Prices: $r_{1,1} = 0.225, \ r_{1,2} = 0.275, \ r_{2,1} = 0.100, \ r_{2,2} = 0.267$,

Exchange Rate Prices: $e_1 = 0.499, \ e_2 = 0.804$,

Asset and Liability Pattern:

$$X_{1,1}^{1,1} = 0.099, \quad X_{1,2}^{1,1} = 0.226, \quad X_{2,1}^{1,1} = 0.276, \quad X_{2,2}^{1,1} = 0.243,$$

$$X_{1,1}^{1,2} = 0.192, \quad X_{1,2}^{1,2} = 0.212, \quad X_{2,1}^{1,2} = 0.000, \quad X_{2,2}^{1,2} = 0.411,$$

$$X_{1,1}^{2,1} = 0.000, \quad X_{1,2}^{2,1} = 0.088, \quad X_{2,1}^{2,1} = 0.330, \quad X_{2,2}^{2,1} = 0.408,$$

$$X_{1,1}^{2,2} = 0.132, \quad X_{1,2}^{2,2} = 0.087, \quad X_{2,1}^{2,2} = 0.322, \quad X_{2,2}^{2,2} = 0.305,$$

$$X_{1,1}^{3,1} = 0.127, \quad X_{1,2}^{3,1} = 0.122, \quad X_{2,1}^{3,1} = 0.359, \quad X_{2,2}^{3,1} = 0.246,$$

$$X_{1,1}^{3,2} = 0.500, \quad X_{1,2}^{3,2} = 0.680, \quad X_{2,1}^{3,2} = 0.142, \quad X_{2,2}^{3,2} = 0.367,$$

$$Y_{1,1}^{1,1} = 0.196, \quad Y_{1,2}^{1,1} = 0.281, \quad Y_{2,1}^{1,2} = 0.392, \quad Y_{2,2}^{1,2} = 0.433,$$

$$Y_{1,1}^{1,2} = 0.227, \quad Y_{1,2}^{1,2} = 0.353, \quad Y_{2,1}^{1,2} = 0.289, \quad Y_{2,2}^{1,2} = 0.422,$$

$$Y_{1,1}^{2,1} = 0.591, \quad Y_{1,2}^{2,1} = 0.194, \quad Y_{2,1}^{2,1} = 0.234, \quad Y_{2,2}^{2,1} = 0.365,$$

$$Y_{1,1}^{2,2} = 0.385, \quad Y_{1,2}^{2,2} = 0.199, \quad Y_{2,1}^{2,2} = 0.355, \quad Y_{2,2}^{2,2} = 0.391,$$

$$Y_{1,1}^{3,1} = 0.218, \quad Y_{1,2}^{3,1} = 0.395, \quad Y_{2,1}^{3,1} = 0.242, \quad Y_{2,2}^{3,1} = 0.437,$$

$$Y_{1,1}^{3,2} = 0.323, \quad Y_{1,2}^{3,2} = 1.014, \quad Y_{2,1}^{3,2} = 0.410, \quad Y_{2,2}^{3,2} = 0.843.$$

Note that the markets cleared for both the instruments and for the currencies since none of the prices in equilibrium were at the floors or at the ceilings.

Note also that although convergence was established only in the case that all $\alpha_{i,k}$ and $\beta_{i,k}$ were equal to 1, the Euler method still converged.

Acknowledgements

This research was supported, in part, by the National Science Foundation under grant DMS 902471 under the Faculty Awards for Women Program. The computational research was conducted using the resources of the Cornell Theory Center at Cornell University in Ithaca, New York. The hospitality of KTH is gratefully appreciated.

References

Adler, M. and B. Dumas, 1983, 'International portfolio choice and corporation finance. A synthesis', *The Journal of Finance* 38, 925–983.

Dong, J., 1996, 'Dynamic model and stability analysis of general financial equilibrium with policy interventions', presented at the Second International Conference on Computing in Economics and Finance, Geneva, Switzerland.

Dong, J., D. Zhang, and A. Nagurney, 1996, 'A projected dynamical systems model of general financial equilibrium with stability analysis', *Mathematical and Computer Modelling*, in press.

Dupuis, P. and A. Nagurney, 1993, 'Dynamical systems and variational inequalities', *Annals of Operations Research* 44, 9–42.

Eun, C. and S. Janakiramanan, 1986, 'A model of international asset pricing with a constraint on the foreign equity ownership', *The Journal of Finance* 41, 879–914.

Grubel, H., 1968, 'Internationally diversified portfolios: Welfare gains and capital flows', *American Economic Review* 58, 1299–1314.

Hufbauer, G. and J. Schott, 1993, *NAFTA: An Assessment*, Washington, DC: Institute of International Economics.

Lessard, D., 1973, 'World country industry relationships in equity returns: Implications for risk reduction through international diversification', *Financial Analysts Journal* 32, 2–8.

Miller, M., 1977, 'Debt and taxes', *Journal of Finance* 32, 261–275.

Nagurney, A., 1993, *Network Economics: A Variational Inequality Approach*, Boston, MA: Kluwer Academic Publishers.

Nagurney, A., 1994, 'Variational inequalities in the analysis and computation of multi-sector, multi-instrument financial equilibria,' *Journal of Economic Dynamics and Control* 18, 161–184.

Nagurney, A. and S. Siokos, 1996a, 'Variational inequalities for international general financial equilibrium modeling and computation', *Mathematical and Computer Modelling*, to appear.

Nagurney, A. and S. Siokos, 1996b, 'Dynamics of international financial networks: Modeling, stability analysis, and computation', in M. Beckmann, B. Johansson, F. Snickars, and R. Thord (Eds), *Knowledge and Networks in a Dynamic Economy*, Berlin: Springer-Verlag, to appear.

Nagurney, A. and D. Zhang, 1996, *Projected Dynamical Systems and Variational Inequalities with Applications*, Boston, MA: Kluwer Academic Pubishers.

Rosenthal, G. and A. Cafruny, 1993, *The State of the European Community. The Maastricht Debates and Beyond*, Boulder, CO: Liener Longman.

Silva, M. and B. Sjörgen, 1990, *Europe 1992 and the New World Power Game*, New York: Wiley.

Solnik, B., 1974, 'Equilibrium model of the international market', *Journal of Economic Theory* 8, 500–524.

Zhang, D. and A. Nagurney, 1995, 'On the stability of projected dynamical systems', *Journal of Optimization Theory and Applications* 85, 97–124.

EMMANUEL YASHCHIN, THOMAS K. PHILIPS, AND
DAVID M. STEIN

Monitoring Active Portfolios Using Statistical Process Control

ABSTRACT. We consider the problem of estimating the performance of a portfolio via an on-line algorithm; i.e. the return of the portfolio is measured at regular (typically monthly) intervals, and every time a new return for the portfolio is received, the estimate of the portfolio's current performance is updated. An alarm is raised when sufficient statistical evidence accrues to determine that the portfolio is not meeting some prespecified criterion of satisfactory performance.

1. INTRODUCTION

The measurement of investment performance is central to all investment operations, and a wide range of performance measurement techniques for actively managed portfolios can be found in the literature. Precise formulations of a number of these techniques can be found in Jensen (1969), Blake et al. (1993), Grinblatt and Titman (1989), Sharpe (1992) and the references contained therein. A common thread that links all these techniques is their emphasis on determining the performance of a portfolio over some *fixed* period of time: i.e., given the composition or the returns of the portfolio over some fixed period (typically the entire life of the portfolio) the performance measures for the period are extracted via a well defined algorithm.

In this paper we consider estimating measures of portfolio performance via an *on-line* algorithm; i.e., given an ongoing sequence of returns from a portfolio, we estimate the *current value* of the performance measure every time we are presented with a newly realized return. We then flag a warning when sufficient statistical evidence accumulates to indicate that the performance has deteriorated to an unsatisfactory level (under some suitable definition of what constitutes unsatisfactory performance). Our emphasis on estimating the performance dynamically is motivated by a desire to detect a deterioration

H. Amman et al. (eds.), Computational Approaches to Economic Problems, 193–205.

in performance in as short a time as possible. In particular, the use of this method allows us to detect poor performance caused by a static investment process that does not evolve to reflect changes in the market.

The techniques we bring to this problem are derived from the field of Statistical Quality Control (SQC). In the parlance of SQC, we wish to *monitor* the *current process level* or current value of a performance measure via a *monitoring scheme*. To do so, we must

1. Decide on a suitable measure of performance, and derive an on-line estimator for it,
2. Model the sequence of returns and specify regions for the model parameters that correspond to satisfactory and unsatisfactory performance,
3. Design a monitoring scheme that triggers an alarm once the evidence for unsatisfactory performance becomes statistically significant, and
4. Decide on the measures to be taken once an alarm is triggered.

The monitoring scheme we propose is based on the likelihood ratio approach to statistical hypothesis testing, and is known as the Cusum (an abbreviation of Cumulative Sum) procedure. The Cusum procedure has been proven to be optimal for a large class of models in that for a given rate of false alarms, it minimizes the time taken to detect unsatisfactory performance.

The remainder of this paper is structured as follows. In Section 2 we decide upon our measure of performance, derive an on-line estimator for it, and specify parameter regions that correspond to satisfactory and unsatisfactory performance. In Section 3 we develop the theory of the Cusum monitoring scheme. Section 4 is devoted to the design of the monitoring scheme and an example of the use of the Cusum technique. Finally, in Section 5, we draw our conclusions and make some suggestions for future research.

2. A Measure of Performance and Its Estimation

Define M_i to be the *net* return from the managed portfolio and B_i to be the return from the benchmark against which the managed portfolio is to be compared in time period $i = 1, 2, \ldots, N$. The logarithmic excess return of the managed portfolio over the benchmark is defined by

$$\Delta_i \triangleq \ln\left(\frac{1 + M_i}{1 + B_i}\right). \tag{1}$$

Δ_i is a random variable which we assume to be normally distributed with parameters μ and σ^2. We further assume that the terms of the sequence $\{\Delta_i\}$ are independent and identically distributed (i.i.d.). The above assumptions are supported by analysis of data corresponding to more than fifty funds observed for periods ranging from two to eight years. The use of the logarithm in our definition of the excess return allows us to write the multi-period log-excess return of the portfolio as the sum of its log-excess returns in each constituent period.

Given the efficiency of modern capital markets and the ability to invest large sums of money at low cost in the market portfolio, a measure of performance for actively managed portfolios must

1. Be positive when the managed portfolio outperforms the benchmark,
2. Be negative when the managed portfolio underperforms the benchmark,
3. Incorporate some measure of the portfolio's risk.

In addition, the current value of the performance measure must be readily estimated. This last condition necessitates the use of a measure that does not require the estimation of a portfolio's systematic (or non-systematic) risk. Estimates of systematic risk are typically derived via a regression, and do not adapt quickly to changes in a portfolio's composition and performance. We, therefore, suggest the use of the tracking error, or the standard deviation of the logarithmic excess returns as the measure of risk.

Our chosen performance measure is the Information Ratio $R \triangleq \mu/\sigma$. This measure meets all the above criteria, and its estimates are readily updated as each new data point is received. A detailed explanation of this measure and its properties can be found in Sharpe (1994). One of the reasons why we feel that information ratio is a suitable parameter to be monitored is because it measures the probability that the portfolio will outperform its benchmark. Indeed, consider a portfolio with parameters μ and σ and let N be the investor's horizon of interest. Then the probability that this portfolio outperforms its benchmark after N time units is given by $\Phi(\sqrt{N}\mu/\sigma)$ where $\Phi(\cdot)$ is the standard normal cumulative distribution function (cdf).

In accordance with the chosen criterion, our lines of indifference in (μ, σ) space are straight lines that pass through the origin, and our quality control procedure flags a warning when sufficient statistical evidence accumulates to suggest that the manager's information ratio is less than some acceptable level. We define the performance of a managed portfolio to be *satisfactory* if the Information Ratio $R > R_0$, and to be *unsatisfactory* if $R < R_1$, where R_0 and R_1 are predefined constants that satisfy the inequality $R_0 > R_1$. If $R_1 < R < R_0$, the performance is said to be neither satisfactory nor unsatisfactory. The three zones are shown in Figure 1.

As the true value of R is not known in advance, we now turn to the problem of estimating it from the data. We consider estimators of the form $\hat{\mu}_i/\hat{\sigma}_i$, where $\hat{\mu}_i$ and $\hat{\sigma}_i$ are the estimates of μ and σ after the incorporation of the ith period's return. In the special case when σ is known in advance to be some fixed constant σ_0, the maximum likelihood estimate of the mean of a normal random variable given a single observation is the observation itself, i.e.,

$$\hat{\mu}_i = \Delta_i, \tag{2}$$

so that the maximum likelihood estimate of the information ratio is given by

$$\hat{R}_i = \frac{\Delta_i}{\sigma_0}\,. \tag{3}$$

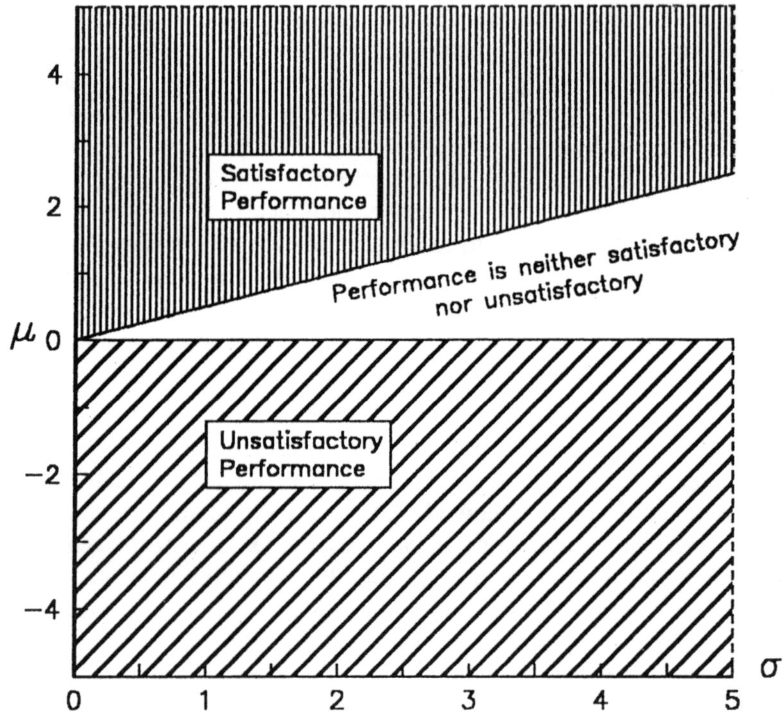

Fig. 1. Regions in the (μ, σ) plane that correspond to satisfactory and unsatisfactory performance. Both excess return and tracking error are annualized.

If σ is not known we substitute an estimate of σ_i into the denominator of (3). We use an estimator of σ_i that exploits the fact that $E[\Delta_i - \Delta_{i-1}]^2 = 2\sigma^2$. This estimator, which consists of geometrically discounted unbiased estimators of σ^2, adapts to a slowly changing process variance and is given by

$$\hat{\sigma}_0^2 = \hat{\sigma}_1^2 = \sigma_0^2$$

$$\hat{\sigma}_i^2 = \gamma\hat{\sigma}_{i-1}^2 + (1-\gamma)\frac{(\Delta_i - \Delta_{i-1})^2}{2}, \quad 0 < \gamma < 1, \quad i = 2, 3, \ldots \tag{4}$$

$$\hat{\sigma}_i = \sqrt{\hat{\sigma}_i^2}\,. \tag{5}$$

Choosing $\gamma = 1$ is equivalent to assuming that σ is known and equal to σ_0. This results in an improved estimate of the information ratio if the assumption is true, but one that is not robust to changes in the level of volatility or a misspecification of σ_0. By reducing the value of γ we get a poorer estimate of R when $\sigma = \sigma_0$, but gain the ability to adapt to time varying (or fixed but incorrectly initialized) levels of volatility. Clearly there is a trade-off to be made: lowering the value of γ decreases the response time at the expense of introducing noise into the estimate. In practice, values of γ between 0.8 and 0.95 yield acceptable results.

This estimator of volatility has two desirable properties:

1. If $E[\Delta]$ is time varying, it responds to a change in the mean within two observations.
2. If the variance of Δ is time varying, it adapts to a change in the volatility in time proportional to $1/(1-\gamma)$, and this can be varied to suit the process being monitored.

A detailed examination of the properties of this estimator can be found in Yashchin (1993b). Its fixed sample analog was discussed in Von Neumann et al. (1941). Given the current estimates of the mean and the variance of Δ, we define our sequence of estimates of the information ratio $\{\hat{R}_i\}$ via the equation

$$\hat{R}_i = \frac{\hat{\mu}_i}{\hat{\sigma}_{i-1}} = \frac{\Delta_i}{\hat{\sigma}_{i-1}} . \tag{6}$$

Observe that we divide Δ_i by $\hat{\sigma}_{i-1}$ rather than $\hat{\sigma}_i$. This reduces (and in practice almost completely removes) the correlation in the sequence $\{\hat{R}_i\}$ while increasing the sensitivity of the procedure to large changes in the information ratio. If the magnitude of the most recent observation Δ_i is large, it induces a large increase in the estimate of the variance, effectively slowing the response of our control procedure to sharp downward changes in the mean.

3. Cusum Schemes and Their Graphical Representation

The Cusum procedure is a particular implementation of the classical likelihood ratio test. A sequence of observations $\{x_i\}$ (estimates of the information ratio in our case) is assumed to be generated by a process (or portfolio manager) the state of which is acceptable, unacceptable, or neither acceptable nor unacceptable, corresponding to an information ratio that is greater than R_0, less than R_1 or lies in between R_0 and R_1. After the ith observation, we compute the quantity

$$T_i = \max_{1\leq j\leq i} \log \left[\frac{f[x_j, x_{j+1}, \ldots, x_i \mid \text{Process is in the unacceptable state}]}{f[x_j, x_{j+1}, \ldots, x_i \mid \text{Process is in the acceptable state}]} \right], \tag{7}$$

where $f(\cdot)$ is the probability density function of $\{x_i\}$.

The procedure stops and raises an alarm the first time T_i exceeds some fixed threshold h. At this point sufficient statistical evidence has accumulated to conclude that the state of the process is unacceptable. As the $\{x_i\}$ are random variables, the possibility exists that an alarm is raised when the process is not in the unacceptable state, and the rate of such false alarms is a function of the threshold h. Raise the threshold and the frequency of false alarms decreases while the time taken to detect an unacceptable state increases. Lower it, and false alarms are raised more often, but problems are detected earlier. The value of h is a design parameter for the Cusum scheme. If the sequence $\{x_i\}$ is independent, it is convenient to compute T_i via the recursion

$$\begin{aligned} T_0 &= 0 \\ T_i &= \left[T_{i-1} + \log\left(\frac{f[x_i \mid \text{Process is in the unacceptable state}]}{f[x_i \mid \text{Process is in the acceptable state}]}\right)\right]^+, \end{aligned} \tag{8}$$

where $x^+ = \max[0, x]$. A rather more complex recursion applies when $\{x_i\}$ is serially correlated.

The Cusum procedure is closely related to a Sequential Probability Ratio Test (SPRT) on two densities with log boundaries 0 and h, in which the test is applied to each successive new observation until a decision in favor of one of the densities is reached. The Cusum procedure may also be thought of as an SPRT that is run backwards in time, i.e. we stop as soon as we find a value of j for which the likelihood ratio of the sequence $x_j, x_{j+1}, \ldots, x_i$ exceeds the threshold h.

If $\{x_i\}$ is normally distributed, and the acceptable and unacceptable states differ only in that the mean of $\{x_i\}$ changes downward from μ_0 to $\mu_1, \mu_1 < \mu_0$, then (8) simplifies to

$$T_i = [T_{i-1} + \delta(-x_i + k)]^+, \tag{9}$$

where $\delta = (\mu_0 - \mu_1)/\sigma^2$, $k = (\mu_1 + \mu_0)/2$ and μ_0 and μ_1 are the means of the sequence $\{x_i\}$ in the acceptable and unacceptable states respectively. It is common practice to drop the multiplicative constant and to restate the recursion in the form

$$\begin{aligned} P_0 &= 0 \\ P_i &= [P_{i-1} - x_i + k]^+. \end{aligned} \tag{10}$$

Thus, the decision scheme is determined by the pair of parameters (h, k). The value k plays the role of an "anchor" that prevents the scheme from drifting towards signal level when the process is in acceptable state: when $E[x_i]$ is time invariant and greater than k, the rate of alarms triggered by the process $\{P_i\}$ is low. When $E[x_i] < k$, however, the scheme $\{P_i\}$ develops a linear trend that causes a signal approximately after $0.5 + h/(k - E[x_i])$ observations. The signal level h is used to achieve the desired trade-off between the rate of false alarms and sensitivity.

We note that the properties of (10) have been extensively studied, and not only in conjunction with its applications in statistical monitoring. For example, Equation (10) is known as Lindley's recursion in the field of Operations Research, and is used to model the behavior of dams and queueing systems (see Stoyan 1983).

The Cusum is plotted in one of two graphical formats. The first, which is known as Page's format after the pioneering work of Page (1954), plots the sequence $\{P_i\}$. The second, which is known as the Cusum format, plots the modified sequence

$$\begin{aligned} C_0 &= 0 \\ C_i &= C_{i-1} + x_i - t_0, \end{aligned} \tag{11}$$

where t_0 is an appropriate centering constant. In this work we set t_0 to 0.

In the Cusum format the *slope* of the Cusum plot is centered around $E[x_i] - t_0$. The law of large numbers assures that the slope of the Cusum plot converges to $E[x_i] - t_0$. Visually, changes in slope are readily apparent, allowing one to quickly estimate the current process mean and the time at which the process mean changed. In spite of the fact that the Cusum format differs from Page's format, it is possible to implement the control scheme via a visual tool. This tool consists of a V shaped mask (known as a V-mask) that is placed on top of the Cusum plot. An alarm is raised if any point on the Cusum plot lies outside the boundary of the V-mask. Kemp (1961) has shown that the Cusum plot triggers an alarm if and only if Page's procedure does so.

It is customary to characterize the performance of a control scheme via the concept of Average Run Length (ARL). Specifically, the rate of false alarms is measured in terms of ARL_0, the expectation of the time taken to trigger an alarm when the true value of the process mean is in the acceptable region. For a fixed value of ARL_0 the standard measure of the power of a control scheme is ARL_1, the expectation of the time taken to trigger an alarm when the true value of the process mean is located in the unacceptable region.

It is in this framework that the Cusum is an optimal monitoring scheme. For a given rate of false alarms, and starting from its worst case initial condition, no other procedure has a lower value of ARL_1. The proof of this theorem is complex: we refer the interested reader to the papers by Lorden (1971), Banzal and Papantoni-Kazakos (1986), and Moustakides (1986).

4. THE DESIGN OF THE MONITORING SCHEME AND SOME EXAMPLES OF ITS USE

We next consider the issues that arise in the design of our Cusum monitoring scheme. We set R_0, the satisfactory level for the information ratio, to be 0.144, (or $0.5 = \sqrt{12} * 0.144$ if the information ratio is defined as the ratio of the annualized excess return to the annualized tracking error). The probability that such a portfolio will have outperformed its benchmark at the end of a three year period is 0.807, and at the end of five years, this probability rises to 0.868. Our choice of R_0 is pragmatic: the annualized information ratio is expressible as a simple fraction, the probability of outperforming the index over a three to five year horizon is high, and we have found very few managers who can run portfolios with information ratios substantially larger than this for extended periods of time.

We set R_1, the unsatisfactory level for the information ratio to be 0, for in this case the excess return is 0, and we can better the long run results of the portfolio by simply investing in the benchmark portfolio and avoiding management fees and transaction costs. More often than not, the benchmark portfolio is the market portfolio, and this can be invested in at particularly low cost via the futures market. As k is chosen midway between R_0 and R_1, i.e. $k = R_0/2$, the problem of design reduces to finding the value of h for which ARL_0 has some pre-specified value.

When γ, the smoothing parameter for the estimator of variance is set to 1, the process $\{\hat{R}_i\}$ is normal with variance 1 and independent. Therefore, the sequence $\{P_i\}$ forms a Markov process running between an absorbing boundary at h and a reflecting boundary at 0. The Average Run Length of the scheme is then simply the first passage time of this process and can be computed using standard techniques.

When $\gamma < 1$, however, the sequence $\{\hat{R}_i\}$ is serially correlated, destroying the Markovian property of the sequence $\{P_i\}$. Even so, the distribution of the process $\{\hat{R}_i\}$ (and consequently that of $\{P_i\}$) depends only on the ratio μ/σ. To see this, let

$$Z_i = (\Delta_i - \mu)/\sigma. \tag{12}$$

The sequence $\{Z_i\}$ is independent and normally distributed with mean 0 and variance 1. We can represent the marginal distribution of $\hat{R}_i$ in the form

$$\text{Prob}(\hat{R}_i \le x) = \text{Prob}\left(\frac{Z_i + \mu/\sigma}{\tilde{\sigma}_{i-1}} \le x\right), \tag{13}$$

where $\{\tilde{\sigma}_i\}$ is defined in the same way as (5), i.e.

$$\begin{aligned}
\tilde{\sigma}_0^2 &= \tilde{\sigma}_1^2 = \sigma_0^2 \\
\tilde{\sigma}_i^2 &= \gamma\tilde{\sigma}_{i-1}^2 + (1-\gamma)\frac{(Z_i - Z_{i-1})^2}{2}, \quad 0 < \gamma < 1, \quad i = 2, 3, \dots \\
\tilde{\sigma}_i &= \sqrt{\tilde{\sigma}_i^2}\,.
\end{aligned} \tag{14}$$

Since the distribution of $\tilde{\sigma}$ depends only on the distribution of $\{Z_i\}$, the probabilities of events related to $\{\hat{R}_i\}$ can be expressed in terms of the distribution of the sequence $\{Z_i\}$ and the Information Ratio, μ/σ.

The complexity of the design problem when $\gamma < 1$ necessitates the use of simulation for the estimation of Average Run Lengths, though some analytic approximations are known (see, for example, Bagshaw and Johnson 1974,

TABLE 1

The Average Run Length vs. the Threshold h. The control scheme is (10) with $x_i = \hat{R}_i$ and $k = 0.072$. The values $\hat{R}_i$ are computed by using (5) with $\gamma = 0.9$ and (6).

h	ARL_0 (months)	ARL_1 (months)
6.81	84	41
6.29	72	37
5.72	60	32
5.08	48	27
4.33	36	22
3.41	24	16

1975, Yashchin 1993a). The latter paper shows how to find an i.i.d. sequence $\{\tilde{R}_i\}$ whose ARL_0 is approximately the same as that of the serially correlated sequence $\{\hat{R}_i\}$. Our computations and simulations were performed using CONTRD, a software package developed at the IBM T.J. Watson Research Center that allows one to design Cusum monitoring schemes. Once designed, the scheme is transferred to the related software package CONTRP for the generation of the control plots.

In our quality control scheme, we sample the returns of managed portfolios once a month and set the threshold h so as to allow one false alarm in 7 years, i.e. the average run length $\text{ARL}_0 = 84$ months. In Table 1 we display the results of a computation of the average run length for various values of h for the sequence $\{\hat{R}_i\}$ computed by using $\gamma = 0.9$ in (5) and under the assumption that the sequence $\{\Delta_i\}$ is i.i.d. The first column of Table 1 contains h, the level at which an alarm is triggered. The second column contains ARL_0, the average run length conditioned on the true Information Ratio being 0.144 (or 0.5 if the Information Ratio is annualized). The third column contains ARL_1, the average run length conditioned on the true information ratio being 0. Observe that an alarm is raised in roughly half the time when the information ratio is +0.5 as when it is 0.

In a practical implementation, one may want to incorporate a mechanism that triggers an alarm especially fast in response to an *initially present* unsatisfactory performance. One such mechanism is already there and is implemented via the proper choice of σ_0. This value can be considered as a "contracted volatility" and if the initial volatility is higher than σ_0 the manager is especially vulnerable to an alarm because his negative returns are measured against lower σ (in essence, the manager must "earn" the right to operate at a higher level of volatility by producing a large enough number of positive

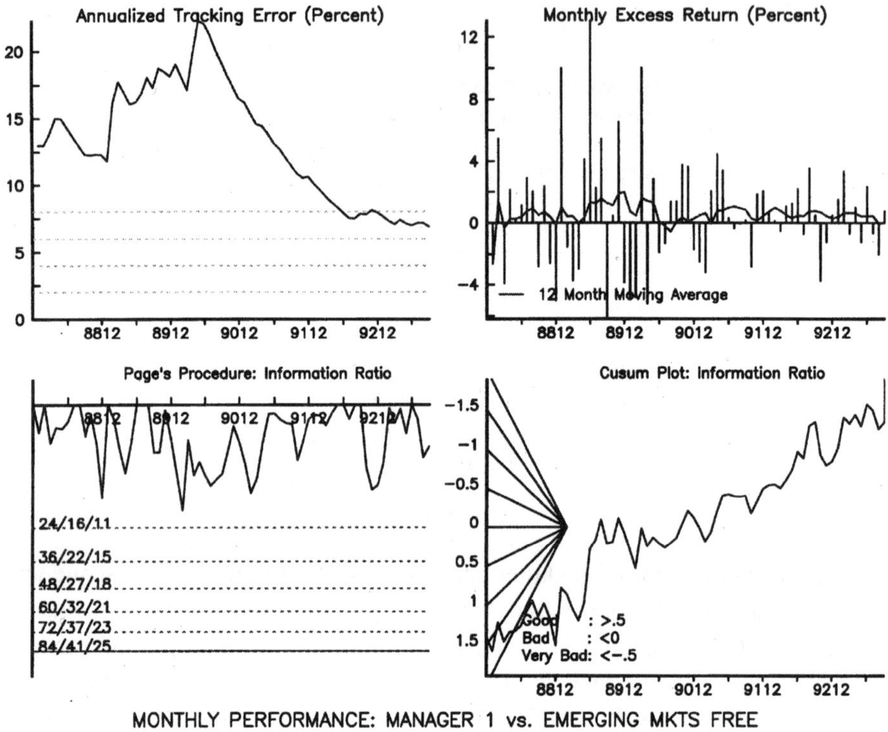

Fig. 2. Sample output generated for a Manager whose performance is satisfactory.

returns). Another mechanism can be implemented by initiating the scheme (10) not from zero, but from a *headstart* (see Lucas and Crosier 1982). The value $P_0 = h/2$ is usually recommended in the literature.

The sole remaining issue is that of the nature of the action that ought to be taken when an alarm is triggered. In particular, it is tempting to ask whether the money manager ought to be terminated as soon as an alarm is raised. It certainly behooves us to thoroughly investigate the manager's investment process, to check if the manager's underperformance was caused by an exposure to certain diversifiable risks, the loss of a key employee, or a poorly thought out investment process. The decision to terminate a manager should involve all of the above considerations, and we are reluctant to recommend termination on the basis of just the Cusum plot. A decision to terminate a manager ought to be as well thought out as the decision to hire that manager.

In Figures 2 and 3 we show the output produced by our implementation of the Cusum scheme described in this paper for two different portfolios. Each of these figures is derived from a real portfolio. The names of the managers have been removed to conceal their identity. At the top left, we display the current

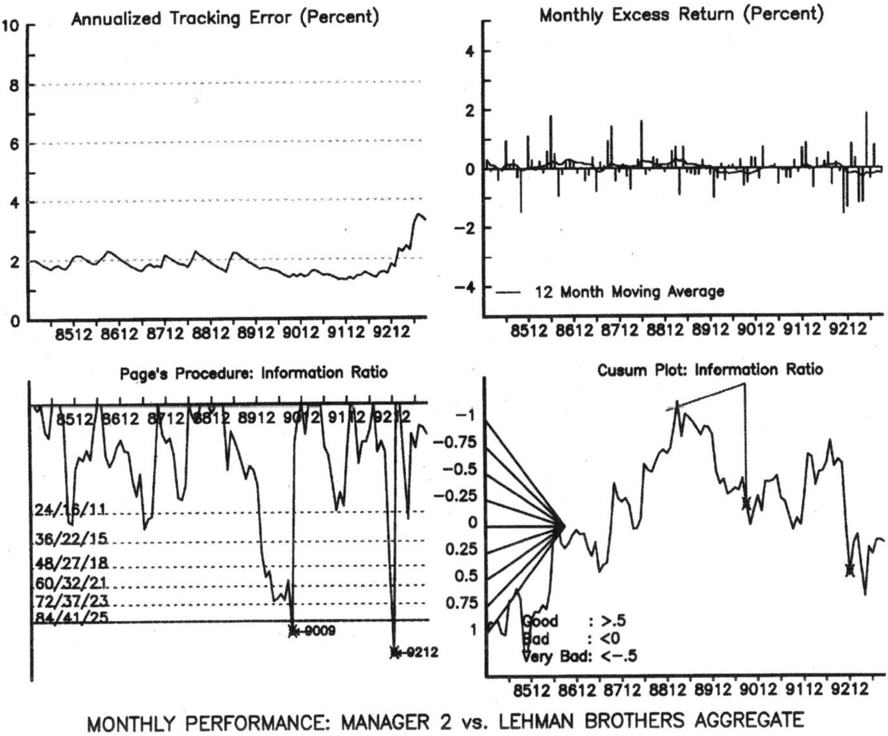

Fig. 3. Sample output generated for a Manager whose performance is unsatisfactory.

estimate of the portfolio's tracking error that is generated by Equation (5). The estimates are annualized (i.e., the sequence (5) is multiplied by $\sqrt{12}$). At the top right, we plot the sequence of logarithmic excess returns. At the bottom left, we plot the Cusum in Page's format, and each level is labelled with its corresponding value of ARL_0, ARL_1, and ARL_2, which are the average run lengths conditioned on the annualized information ratio being 0.5, 0 and -0.5, respectively. An alarm is raised when the Cusum crosses the lowest level, and as can be seen from the charts, the corresponding values of ARL_0, ARL_1, and ARL_2 are 84 months, 41 months and 25 months. Stated differently, a false alarm will be raised once in 84 months (7 years) on average, a manager who does not add value to his benchmark will be detected in 41 months (about 3 1/2 years) on average, and a manager with an information ratio of -0.5 will be detected in about 2 years on average. Finally, at the bottom right, we plot sequence $\{C_i\}$ in the Cusum format, and a protractor of slopes is drawn on the left hand side to enable one to estimate the slope of the Cusum at any point.

The first portfolio, whose performance is depicted in Figure 2, is an actively managed portfolio for which the benchmark is the Emerging Markets Index.

The performance of this portfolio is satisfactory over the entire monitoring period, as the portfolio consistently outperforms its benchmark with an information ratio close to 0.5. Observe that the slope of the Cusum plot is consistently close to 0.5, even as the manager's tracking error drops by a factor of 2.

The second portfolio, whose performance is depicted in Figure 3, is an actively managed fixed income portfolio for which the benchmark is the Lehman Brothers Aggregrate Index. The performance of this manager is unsatisfactory, as evidenced by the slope of the Cusum plot being approximately 0 and the alarm that is raised by the Cusum procedure. The manager was not terminated after the first alarm was raised and continued to perform poorly, leading to a second alarm being raised three years after the first.

If the information ratio of the second portfolio is computed over the entire time period, it will look satisfactory, as the good performance in the first four years will mask the poor performance over the next four years. The Cusum procedure, however, discards the irrelevant information in an intelligent way, preventing the good past performance from clouding our judgement on the current performance of the portfolio.

5. Conclusions

The Cusum procedure is a powerful tool for analyzing and monitoring data that is subject to abrupt changes at unknown points in time. This technique can be used to monitor non-normal, multivariate or serially correlated data streams by modifying the threshold h appropriately. We have shown how the Cusum procedure can be used to set up a monitoring system for actively managed portfolios that enables one to detect underperformance rapidly. We have used the procedure described in this paper for a number of years, and have found it to be extremely useful. As with any performance measurement methodology, some care in the use of the technique is called for: in particular, it is imperative that a manager not be terminated exclusively on the basis of an alarm. Instead, an alarm should be viewed as a statistically motivated cause for concern and should trigger a thorough investigation into the causes of underperformance.

References

Bagshaw, M. and R.A. Johnson, 1975, 'The effect of serial correlation on the performance of CUSUM TESTS II', *Technometrics* 17, 73–80.

Banzal, R.K. and P. Papantoni-Kazakos, 1986, 'An algorithm for detecting a change in a stochastic process', *IEEE Trans. Information Theory* IT-32(2), 227–235.

Blake, C.R., E.J. Elton, and M.J. Gruber, 1993, 'The performance of bond mutual funds', *Journal of Business* 66(3), 371–404.

Grinblatt, M. and S. Titman, 1989, 'Portfolio performance evaluation: Old issues and new insights', *Review of Financial Studies* 2, 393–421.

Johnson, R.A. and M. Bagshaw, 1974, 'The effect of serial correlation on the performance of CUSUM tests', *Technometrics* 16, 103–122.

Jensen, M., 1969, 'Risk, the pricing of capital assets, and the evaluation of investment portfolios', *Journal of Business* 42, 167–247.

Kemp, K., 1961, 'The Average Run Length of the cumulative sum chart when a V-mask is used', *Journal of the Royal Statistical Society, B* 23, 149–153.

Lorden, G., 1971, 'Procedures for reacting to a change in distribution', *Ann. Math. Stat.* 42, 1897–1908.

Lucas, J.M. and R.B. Crosier, 1982, 'Fast initial response for Cusum quality control schemes: Give your Cusum a head start', *Technometrics* 24, 199–205.

Moustakides, G.V., 1986, 'Optimal stopping times for detecting changes in distributions', *Ann. Stat.* 14(2), 1379–1387.

Page, E., 1954, 'Continuous inspection schemes', *Biometrika* 41, 100–115.

Sharpe, W.F., 1992, 'Asset allocation, management style, and performance measurement', *Journal of Portfolio Management* (Winter), 7–19.

Sharpe, W.F., 1994, 'The Sharpe ratio', *Journal of Portfolio Management* (Fall), 49–58.

Stoyan D., 1983, *Comparison Methods for Queues and Other Stochastic Models*, New York: John Wiley and Sons.

von Neumann, J., R.H. Kent, H.R. Bellinson, and B.I. Hart, 1941, 'The mean square successive difference', *Ann. Math. Stat.* 12, 153–162.

Yashchin, E., 1993a, 'Performance of Cusum control schemes for serially correlated observations', *Technometrics* 35, 37–52.

Yashchin, E., 1993b, 'Statistical control schemes: Methods, applications and generalizations', *International Statistical Review* 61, 41–66.

PART THREE

Computational Methods for a Social Environment

ALFRED NORMAN, GREG LEONARD, LEIGH LINDEN,
KARA MEYTHALER, KIM MURRAY, HERB NEWHOUSE,
NANCY TANTZEN, AND MICHAEL ZIEGLER

Ordering: Human versus Computer

ABSTRACT. Binary comparison operators form the basis of consumer set theory. When finding the preferred item from a set, humans frequently use a binary comparison operator. If humans could only perform binary comparisons, however, then any procedure a human might employ to make a complete preference ordering of n items would be bound from below in both cost and time by $O(n \log_2 n)$. Experimental evidence indicates that humans are capable of implementing a linear algorithm for small sets. This indicates that humans have an ordinal utility function.

1. Introduction

An important aspect of developing a procedural consumer theory, Simon (1976), is determining what strategies humans use to order a set of items. In this paper, we will compare theoretical computer algorithms to order sets with algorithms actually employed by humans.

Comparing computer algorithms with human algorithms is difficult. Computer algorithms are precisely defined with fixed time and cost steps, so that the complexity can be analyzed analytically. As we discovered, human algorithms have variable time and cost steps and the algorithms themselves are modified with experience. Moreover, the algorithm must be inferred from behavior. This makes assertions concerning asymptotic behavior difficult. A brief summary of complexity analysis is contained in Appendix A. For a survey of the literature on economic complexity, see Norman (1994).

The basis of consumer set theory is the binary ranking operator. In Section 2, we present an experiment that asks human subjects to find the best pen out of a set of pens. This experiment demonstrates that humans frequently do use a binary ranking operator.

If humans were limited to a binary ranking operator in determining a complete preference ordering for a set of items, then, for a complete preference ordering, efficient humans would need $O(n \log_2 n)$ binary ranking operations.

H. Amman et al. (eds.), Computational Approaches to Economic Problems, 209–223.

We discuss several of these sorting algorithms in Section 3. However, if consumers were able to construct an ordinal utility function over the alternatives, they could employ a conceptually simple bucket sort with no more than $O(n)$ operations.

In our two ordering experiments, we used several subsets of pens to investigate the types of algorithms humans use to make a preference ordering. The experimental procedure and the results are described in Section 4. Using regression analysis in Section 5, we demonstrate that humans use a linear algorithm which is a variation of a bucket sort. This result, plus discussion with the subjects, indicates that humans use an ordinal utility function for this task. Our data also indicate that humans are not consistent in their orderings.

In Section 6, we conclude.

2. BINARY COMPARISON OPERATOR

In this section, we characterize a binary comparison operator based on a fundamental assertion of modern utility theory: a consumer can rank any two alternatives. In addition, we assume the procedure requires the consumer to perform at least one information operation to determine the attributes of each good. We define an information operator $D(b_i) = a_i$ as well as a binary ranking operator, $R(a_i, a_j)$, which the consumer must execute to determine the preferences between two items, b_i and b_j.

We assume each type operator $D(b_i)$ and $R(a_i, a_j)$ incurs a cost of c_D and c_R respectively. These costs are considered to be constant both over time and over the entire set of items. We assume the consumer has a memory. In other words, once the consumer has performed an information operator on an item, he does not need to repeat the operation if he considers the item again.

In addition to being costly, the information operator, $D(b_i)$, and the binary ranking operation, $R(a_i, a_j)$, have the standard properties of completeness, reflexivity and transitivity. Consider a simple model of a consumer searching for a preferred item from a finite set of close substitutes $B = \{b_1, b_2, \ldots, b_n\}$. The goal of the search is to find a preferred item defined as follows: $b_i^* \in B$ such that for all $b_j \in B$ is $b_i^* \succeq b_j$. Finding a preferred item with a ranking operator is a variation of finding the largest number in a set of numbers. Compare the first item with the second, then compare the larger with the third, and so on.

ALGORITHM. Preferred Item Search

Step 1: pre $= 1, i = 1$ Perform $D(b_{\text{pre}})$.

Step 2: As long as $i < n$, repeat step 3.

Step 3: Let i increase by one. Perform $D(b_i)$. If $R(a_{\text{pre}}, a_i) \neq b_{\text{pre}} \succeq b_i$ then pre $= i$.

This algorithm is efficient. Finding a preferred item, a minor variation of finding the largest number in a list, has computational complexity n.

We designed the following experiment to determine whether humans use this efficient algorithm based on a binary comparison operator to find a preferred item.

Method: The subjects were 15 college students selected from the student body at the University of Texas at Austin.

The materials included:

1. A set of 20 pens, both new and used, that varied in size, thickness, color (red, blue, and black) and type of tip (felt, ball point, roller ball, and fountain).
2. A set of 10 new pens covered with gray duct tape. All of the pens in this set were approximately of the same length. No two pens were the same. The pens varied by the type of point, color (blue or black) and thickness.
3. Blank, white paper.

Procedure: We gave the first five subjects the set of 20 pens. The next ten subjects received the set of ten pens covered with tape. All subjects had white scratch paper. Each subject was asked to pick out the pen they preferred.

Experimental Results and Interpretation: None of the first five subjects wrote with all 20 pens. Subject one picked out a long, thin black pen, wrote with it, and declared it the preferred pen. When asked why, she explained she liked long thin black pens and the one she picked was the only one. Other subjects eliminated substantial numbers of the pens by criteria such as being ball points, and then, they wrote with the remainder to decide which pen they preferred. When the pens were not covered with duct tape, it was not obvious what sort of algorithm the subjects used.

When the pens were covered with duct tape, the subjects had to write with each pen in order to determine its qualities. From observation and discussion with the subjects, we conclude that these subjects used a binary comparison operator to find the preferred pen. Several subjects used the Preferred Item Search algorithm mentioned above. Subject two said that the first pen was the best, and he tested each pen against the first. The above algorithm was definitely not the only procedure adopted by the subjects. Subject three said that she compared all the pens with an ideal pen she imagined. She laid out the first five pens in a complete preference ordering. The sixth pen was close to the ideal pen, and she compared all the rest to the sixth. When asked what she would have done if she had not found an ideal pen, she said she would have processed the entire set a second time. Most subjects only wrote with each pen once. A few found two or three approximately equivalent pens and wrote with them several times to decide which pen they preferred.

From the two variations of this experiment, we conclude that under some circumstances humans do use a binary comparison operation to find a preferred item.

3. COMPUTER ORDERING

In this section, we examine the types of algorithms a human might use if limited to binary ranking operators without an ordinal utility function. Such algorithms are commonly known as sorting algorithms (Aho et al. 1974, Knuth 1973). Then we consider whether the capability of creating an ordinal utility function leads to a more efficient ordering technique. This examination provides a framework in order to evaluate the human ordering procedures used in the experiments.

If we assume that humans would use a conceptually simple search, we might expect humans to use a variation of a bubble sort to order a set of pens. A possible algorithm to order the pens in a complete preference ordering from left to right is as follows:

1. Write with the first pen, $D(P_1) = a_1$, and place at the right end point.
2. Write with the second pen, $D(P_2) = a_2$, and place to the left of the first.
3. Interchange the first and second pens if $R(a_1, a_2) = P_1 \succeq P_2$.
4. Repeat (5) and (6) until all pens are ordered.
5. Write with next pen, $D(P_{\text{next}}) = a_{\text{next}}$, and place to left of partial order.
6. Interchange next pen with pen to right as long as $R(a_{\text{next}}, a_{\text{right}}) = P_{\text{right}} \succeq P_{\text{next}}$.

Because this algorithm requires $1 + 2 + 3 + \ldots n - 1$ binary comparisons in the worst case and half that number in the expected case, it is $O(n^2)$ both in the worst and expected cases. From the perspective of writing code, this algorithm requires very few statements and efficiently orders small numbers of items because it incurs only a low initial cost. We reasoned that humans might use this algorithm because of its conceptual simplicity.

Efficient algorithms exist for ordering which are only $O(n \log_2 n)$ in the worst and expected value cases. Let us consider one of the algorithms efficient in the worst case, Mergesort. A human might employ this algorithm to order 16 pens in the following manner:

1. Write with all 16 pens.
2. Lay the pens in a row.
3. Merge the first with the second, the third with the fourth, . . ., the fifteenth with the sixteenth. Merging the first with the second requires comparing the first with the second and ordering them in a column with the preferred item first. This results in 8 columns of two members each.
4. Merge the first column with the second, the third with the fourth, . . ., the seventh with the eighth. This step results in four columns of 4 members each.
5. In a similar fashion, merge the four columns merged into two columns of 8 members each.
6. Merge the two columns into one ordered column.

Another efficient algorithm in the worst case is the Heapsort algorithm. Because we spent over half an hour understanding how this algorithm worked, we concluded it would be unlikely for any subject, not intimately familiar with ordering algorithms, to intuitively use this algorithm. A third algorithm, efficient in the expected value case, is the Quicksort algorithm. However, like Heapsort, Quicksort is not intuitively understandable and, thus, is not likely to be used by humans.

In analyzing sorting algorithms, computer scientists focus on minimizing the number of binary comparison operations. If this were the case for humans determining a complete preference ordering, we might expect to see some variation of the sorting algorithms discussed above.

If, however, we assume that humans can assign ordinal utility values to items in a set, then humans could use a more efficient algorithm. Consider the bucket ordering algorithm used to sort n integers all contained in the interval (k, l), where k and l are integers. This sorting process uses the following algorithm:

1. Establish $(l - k - 1)$ buckets, where $(l - k - 1)$ is the number of integers on the interval.
2. Pick an integer and determine its value.
3. Place it in the bucket with the corresponding value.
4. Continue (2) and (3) until all numbers have been assigned to buckets.

The integers are now sorted.

Thus, a human wishing to efficiently sort a set of integers could use a bucket sort. This idea, however, is not limited to sorting integers. Consider a human ordering n items in a set B. Assume a human can use an information operator $G(b_i)$ which determines the ordinal utility as an integer number from the attributes. This integer might serve as the index for a subjective classification scheme such as bad, poor, fair, good, and excellent. A human has the ability of creating a bucket for each new preference level as needed. Now, humans can use a placement operator $P(b_i)$ to place b_i in the correct bucket. The number of G and P operations is $O(n)$ for this bucket sort. Thus, if each item could be assigned an integer value, the bucket sort would be the most efficient sorting algorithm of the ones mentioned here.

4. HUMAN ORDERING

To determine how humans actually establish a complete preference ordering on a set of pens when given financial rewards for consistency, we conducted the following experiments.

First Experiment: The subjects were 21 college students selected from the University of Texas at Austin.

The materials included:

1. A set of 28 pens, both new and used, that varied in size, thickness, style, color (black, blue, green, orange, purple, and red) and type of tip (ball point, felt, fountain, and roller ball).

2. A stop watch.
3. Blank, white paper.
4. Cash to reward consistent behavior.

Procedure:

A. Each subject was asked to order sets of 4, 8, 12, and 16 pens. Before ordering any of the sets we read to each subject the instructions displayed in Appendix B. The procedure for each set of pens had the following steps. The subject entered the room and sat at the table where the set of pens to be ordered was placed together with a sheet of blank white paper. Upon completion of the timed task, we requested that he or she momentarily step outside of the room. We recorded the order of the pens described in B, the number of writes, and the duration of the ranking process. We created the next set of pens and asked the subject to return to order the next set.

B. The financial incentives were designed to encourage consistency. We assumed that if a subset of pens which the subject had already ordered was placed in the next set to be ordered, the focused subject would place these pens in the same relative order as before. Pens in positions 2 and 3 (2, 4, 5 and 7) [2, 4, 6, 7, 9 and 11] from the first (second) [third] set were randomly placed in the second (third) [fourth] set. For example, if in ordering set 2 the subject placed pen 3 from set 1 in a higher position than the pen 2 from set 1, it was counted as an inconsistency.

C. Upon conclusion of the experiment, we questioned some of the subjects about their ordering algorithm. We counted the number of inconsistencies in each group and deducted $0.25 for each inconsistency with a limit of 4 for each set. This kept the subjects' payoffs nonnegative. We paid the subjects, thanked them for their time, and asked that they not discuss the experiment with anyone.

Second Experiment: This variation of the experiment described above was designed to test the consistency of subjects' preference orderings over larger sets of pens. The subjects were ten undergraduates at the University of Texas at Austin. We used the same materials as before, except we increased the number of different pens to 51.

We used the same procedures as before except that the subjects were asked to order sets of 5, 10, 15, 20, and 25 pens. Pens in positions 2 and 4 (2, 4, 5, 7, 9) [2, 4, 6, 7, 9, 11, and 13] {2, 4, 6, 8, 10, 11, 13, 15, 17, 19} from the first (second) [third] {fourth} set were randomly placed in the second (third) [fourth] {fifth} set.

Each subject could earn $5, which we reduced by $0.25 for each of their inconsistencies in the relative ordering of the pens in the set of 10 and 15 and by $0.20 for each inconsistency in the relative orderings in the set of 20 and 25.

Experimental Results: In both experiments the majority of our subjects ordered the sets of pens in a sequential manner. After writing with each pen, the subject systematically placed the pen in its relative preference ordering.

We observed that after writing with a pen, the subjects usually looked one or two to the left and right of an "anchor pen" before placing the pen. This anchor pen was one chosen by the subject and was used to help the subject mark a place within the preference ordering. As the number of pens increased, we observed that, after writing with a pen, the subject's eyes often scanned a larger subset of the pens surrounding an anchor pen before placing the new pen. After this visual scan, the subject placed the pen into the partial ordering. Before placing the pen, some subjects wrote again with the pens on either side of the insertion point. Occasionally, a subject made some minor changes in the ordering.

Most of our subjects left open spaces between pens that possessed very different preference ratings. However, subject 21 placed each pen contingent to the already sorted pens, displacing the pens as required. In the absence of even a single rewrite, he performed with great interset consistency. He mentioned that he used anchor pens to which he made comparisons in the ordering.

When asked how they placed the pens, the subjects stated that after writing with a pen they formed a subjective rating, such as good, fair, or poor, based on the subjects' likes and dislikes regarding the pen's smoothness of writing, ink color, and pen style. They immediately knew approximately where in the partial ordering to place the new pen. Many subjects reported that the initial ordering was much more difficult than the following sets, demonstrating a learning curve.

Also, we observed subjects using variations in the algorithm in the preference orderings of the pens. In the sets of 12 and 16, subject nine initially sorted the pens into subgroups with common characteristics. Next, he ordered the pens within each subgroup. Finally, he integrated the ordered subgroups into a complete ordered set through preferences between the distinct subgroups.

Subject four executed a most unique and highly ineffective algorithm. First, he placed the pens in a random line. He then proceeded to write with each pen in a descending column, replacing each pen in its original position as he proceeded. Upon completion of this task, he regarded his work and located the writing that suited him best. After counting down the column, he counted across the pens to find the corresponding pen. He continued this process until he placed all pens in order. Without any rewrites, he correctly ordered the first set; however, when confronted with the two larger sets of pens, he became extremely confused and very inconsistent between set orderings.

Although many subjects only wrote with each pen once, each subject had the freedom to rewrite with any pen as many times as desired. Subjects varied greatly in the number of rewrites. Nevertheless, the number of rewrites appears to be an approximately linear function of the number of pens. However, the number of rewrites that a subject performed and the time it took for the subject to order the pens was not obviously related to the payment that the subject received. For example, subject nine took approximately 19 minutes to complete the preference ordering and made 60 extra writes beyond the required minimum. Subject six took approximately 6 minutes to complete the experimental ordering and made 30 extra writes. Nevertheless, subject nine made 7 inconsistent placings as opposed to 1 inconsistent placing by subject six.

It appears that as the number of pens increased, so did the difficulty level of the reordering. Subject 20 had definite preferences over the pens contained in the set of 12. However, in the set of 16 pens, he placed the second, fourth, sixth, and the seventh pens, that previously held distinct preferences, in a single indifferent position. The preferences should have remained consistent over the two sets.

In experiment two, the majority of our subjects used subgroups to help them in the ordering process with the largest two or in some cases three sets. These subjects usually wrote with each pen and placed it into a subgroup with similar characteristics.

For example, a subject created subgroups A, B, and C. Then, within each subgroup, the subject again wrote with each pen and ordered the subgroup. Finally, the subject ordered the subgroups, such as $\{a_1, a_2, \ldots, a_{n_1}, b_1, \ldots, b_{n_2}, c_1, \ldots, c_{n_3}\}$.

Subject 9B used a different subgroup method. He first wrote with each pen and created 3 distinct subgroups. Then, he wrote again with each pen in the first two subgroups and ordered them. However, after rewriting with each pen in the third subgroup, he created and ordered 3 new sub-subgroups. Unlike the other subjects who used subgroups, subject 9B did not keep these sub-subgroups distinct. For example, in the final order he obtained a sequence like $\{\ldots, c_{I_3}, c_{II_2}, c_{I_4}, \ldots\}$ where the c's refer to the third subgroup and I and II refer to the first and second sub-subgroups of C.

Subjects said that as the number of pens increased, they found it more difficult to formulate distinct preferences between all the pens. Sometimes, in ordering the larger subsets, subjects merged into a single indifference group, pens which the subjects had ordered separately in smaller subsets. Many subjects said that they used ink color to place the pens into indifference groups.

Most of our subjects wrote with each pen as it appeared in its random line-up. The one exception to this was subject 10B, who preselected the pens by sight. This indicates that she had pre-preferences for certain pens before writing. In the set of 25, she separated the pens into 4 subgroups prior to writing. Upon completion of writing with each pen, her final ordering contained 7 indifference groups.

5. Interpretation

From observing and talking with the subjects, it was obvious that none of the subjects were using any of the efficient binary comparison algorithms. It appeared that the subjects were using a variation of a bucket sort based on their ability to form an ordinal ranking of each pen after writing with it.

While it appears that the subjects were using a variation of a bucket sort, we can not simply assume that this is a linear algorithm in terms of human operations. As the experiment proceeded, a subject tended to write less with each pen to establish its quality, and as the number of pens increased, many used subsets to organize the data. These factors could be sublinear.

In contrast, the algorithm used by the subjects may contain higher than linear factors. For example, as the number of pens increased, the subjects appeared to look farther to each side of the insertion point of a new pen. This factor is not necessarily higher than linear because it could reach a limit independent of the number of pens.

To analyze these factors we examined several correlations of the data and then ran several regressions.

Correlations and Interpretations: First, we examined the correlation between time and various functions of the number of ordered pens. We constructed a table by aggregating each subject's time for each ranking (i.e. time to order 4 pens, time to order 5 pens, etc.) in one column. The other columns in the table were the values generated by each function of the number of pens ordered (i.e. $\ln n$, n, n^2, etc.). We then calculated the correlations between time and the various functions.

Correlations									
Variable	$\ln n$	n	$n \ln n$	$n^{1.2}$	$n^{1.3}$	$n^{1.4}$	$n^{1.5}$	n^2	n^3
Time	0.6996	0.7433	0.7461	0.7457	0.7462	0.7461	0.7456	0.7372	0.7030

It is clear from the table of correlations that the factors between n and n^2 all highly correlate with time. However, the sublinear factors ($\ln n$) and cubic factors seem less significant.

Next, we correlated the time to order each pen (the total time divided by the minimum number of writes), the time per write (the total time divided by number of writes), and percentage of possible money earned (as a surrogate for consistency) for the aggregate data and then for each of the experiments.

Correlations of Error			
Variable	Aggregate	Experiment I	Experiment II
Time to order – Time to write	0.61	0.62	0.60
Time to order – % Earned	0.03	0.09	–0.22
Time per write – % Earned	0.02	0.05	–0.40

It is extremely interesting to note the *negative* correlations between time to order and % earned and between time per write and % earned in the second experiment. These correlations are interesting because they seem to support our observations that subjects had different abilities to convert attributes to an ordinal utility. Some subjects had very clearly defined preferences over attributes, such as color, and were able to quickly and consistently order the pens. Other subjects' preferences of attributes were not as precisely defined; consequently, they required more time and were not as consistent. There is also the possibility that mental fatigue became a factor because we required the subjects to make at least 75 writes in the second experiment and only 40 in the first experiment.

Regression Analysis: From our observations, subjects appeared to use similar variations of a bucket sort. Thus, we can express the time it took to order a set of pens, T, as a linear function of the number of pens, X, as follows:

$$T_i = \beta_1 X_i + \epsilon_i,$$

where we assume ϵ_i to be distributed $N(0, \sigma_\epsilon)$. Regressing over our 134 observations (21 subjects sorting 4 groups of pens 4, 8, 12, 16 and 10 subjects sorting 5 groups 5, 10, 15, 20, 25) shows that $\beta_1 = 10.55$, $\sigma_{\beta_1} = 0.363$, and $t_{(133)} = 29.07$ with $1.96 < t_{0.05(133)} < 1.98$. ($R^2 = 0.864$.) We know that the function intersects the origin because each subject began working immediately and, thus, displayed no fixed cost. To test this, we estimated the equation $T_i = \beta_0 + \beta_1 X_i + \epsilon_i$. This yields $\beta_0 = 4.99$ ($\sigma_{\beta_0} = 10.64$) and $\beta_1 = 10.21$ ($\sigma_{\beta_1} = 0.798$). However, $t_{\beta_0(132)} = 0.469$ where $1.96 < t_{0.05(132)} < 1.98$ and thus, we fail to reject the hypothesis that $\beta_0 = 0$ at the 0.05 significance level. (For β_1, $t_{\beta_1(132)} = 12.81$.) Based on this, we conclude that excluding the constant term is reasonable.

Next, because of the high correlation between time and other functions of X, we tested these functions to determine how well they explained the variance in T by estimating the equation

$$T_i = \beta_2 f_n(X_i) + \epsilon,$$

where $n = 1, 2, 3, 4$ with $f_1(X) = X^2$, $f_2(X) = X^3$, $f_3(X) = \ln X$, $f_4(X) = X \log_2 X$. Each of these forms proved significant at the 0.05 significance level, but given the small values of X in our sample, a high degree of colinearity of exists between each $f_n(X)$ and X. (We tested this by regressing the function $X_i = \gamma_1 f_n(X_i) + \epsilon$.)

$f_n(X)$	β_2	σ_{β_2}	$t_{\beta_2(133)}$	R^2	γ_1	σ_{γ_1}	$t_{\psi_1(133)}$	R^2
X^2	0.55	0.02	22.0	0.79	0.052	0.001	35.3	0.90
X^3	0.024	0.001	15.9	0.65	0.002	0.0001	19.7	0.74
$\ln X$	57.04	2.37	24.1	0.81	5.40	0.12	45.1	0.94
$X \log_2 X$	2.57	0.095	27.2	0.85	0.243	0.003	83.6	0.98

So, despite the linearity of the subject's algorithms, the other functions of X may independently explain the variation in T because they act as a limited proxy for X. To discriminate between these possible explanations of T, we estimated the equation

$$T_i = \psi_1 X_i + \psi_2 f_n(X_i) + \epsilon_i$$

and tested the hypothesis $H_0 : \psi_2 = 0$ at the 0.05 significance level ($1.96 < t_{0.05(132)} < 1.98$). If the test is not significant, then we fail to reject the hypothesis, and conclude that $\psi_2 = 0$.

$f_n(X)$	ψ_1	σ_{ψ_1}	$t^*_{\psi_1}$	ψ_2	σ_{ψ_2}	$t^*_{\psi_2}$	Sig of* Regression	R^2
X^2	10.3	1.17	8.77	0.015	0.06	0.23	419.7	0.86
X^3	10.3	0.721	14.3	0.0008	0.0018	0.42	420.1	0.86
$\ln X$	10.29	1.47	7.00	1.50	8.19	0.183	419.6	0.86
$X \log_2 X$	10.8	2.66	4.05	–0.057	0.65	–0.087	419.5	0.86

*$3.04 < F_{0.05(2,132)} < 3.07$

Thus, within the 0.05 significance level, we can conclude that $\psi_2 = 0$. This means that T can be considered a linear function of X and that we can reasonably concluded that our subjects used a linear algorithm when sorting the pens.

6. Concluding Remarks

Economic theoreticians prefer consumer set theory over utility function consumer theory because they consider it more general. Our first experiment demonstrated that humans frequently use a binary ranking operator when selecting the preferred pen from a set. What is surprising is that a binary ranking operator is less efficient in creating a complete preference ordering. Humans have the ability to use an ordinal utility function to create a linear algorithm (n). If they only had binary ranking operators, they would be no more efficient than $n \log_2 n$.

We found the number of inconsistencies surprising. In the future we will examine this more closely and try to work with larger sets.

A. Information-Based Complexity

Computer scientists compare computer algorithms by the time required for execution, the cost involved, or the amount of memory needed. To make such comparisons, the time, cost or memory are usually parameterized with respect to an important attribute of the problem, such as n, the number of items to be ordered. We can make these comparisons with a finite n or make the comparisons asymptotically as n increases. Computer scientists find the later method advantageous because asymptotically, only the dominant factor in an algorithm matters.

We now present the framework for the information-based complexity analysis, a simplified case of Traub et al.'s (1988) information-based complexity. To define the cost function for an algorithm ω which solves a problem element $s \in S$, the problem set, we use the operators $\Upsilon = \{\upsilon_1, \upsilon_2, \dots \upsilon_m\}$. These operators are the information and computational operators used in the algorithm ω. For example, for the preferred item search, these operators would be $\Upsilon = \{D, R\}$. The cost function, C is:

$$C(\omega[s]) = \sum c_{\upsilon_i} \cdot (\text{number of } \upsilon_i \text{ operations}), \tag{1}$$

where c_l is the unit cost of executing υ_l. Similarly, we can also define a time function, T:

$$T(\omega[s]) = \sum t_{\upsilon_i} \cdot (\text{number of } \upsilon_i \text{ operations}), \tag{1a}$$

where t_l is the unit time of executing υ_l. For the rest of the discussion we shall just consider the cost function. The development of the time function would be the same.

For this discussion, we shall only consider the worst case analysis by defining the cost function for an algorithm ω which will solve all $s \in S$ as:

$$C(\omega[S])) = \sup_{s \in S} C(\omega[s]). \tag{2}$$

To solve S the consumer uses an efficient search, that is an algorithm ω^*;

$$\omega^*(S) = \inf_{\omega \in \Omega} C(S), \tag{3}$$

where Ω is the set of all algorithms which solve S. Establishing that the cost of an efficient consumer search algorithm has a particular cost (or time) function with respect to n is an example of information-based complexity analysis. It is desirable to use the concept of asymptotic information-based complexity in order to compare the characterization of the consumer search problem with other information-based problems. To define the asymptotically information-based complexity of S, let $Y = Y(n)$ be a nonnegative function which we wish to compare with the cost function, $C = C(n)$, which is an abbreviation of C_ω. Frequently Y is n, n^2 etc.

DEFINITION 1. C is upper order [lower order] Y, written $O(Y)[o(Y)]$, if there exist $i, j > 0$ such that $C(n) \leq [\geq] jY(n)$ for all $n > i$.

TABLE 1

Observed Data									
	Raw Times (sec) Number of Pens				Number of Writes Number of Pens				Pay
Sub	4	8	12	16	4	8	12	16	% Max
1	26.8	46.7	71.8	88.1	4	8	12	16	50
2	34.2	71.7	93.5	111.3	4	9	14	18	92
3	50.2	126.4	162.9	228.0	4	13	14	26	83
4	21.2	69.2	100.0	162.4	4	8	12	16	33
5	53	98	104	170	9	15	19	23	92
6	30	58	112	113	6	12	26	26	92
7	70	43	116	136	4	9	12	16	83
8	72.5	92.2	102.4	138.0	5	10	12	18	58
9	126	299	308	397	7	24	28	41	58
10	20	39	68	98	4	8	12	16	67
11	38	47	100	150	4	8	14	17	83
12	40.5	84.8	101.9	211.1	4	8	13	19	83
13	93.0	129.6	140.4	228.0	10	16	18	29	92
14	61.7	98.6	77.4	80.6	4	8	12	16	58
15	24.8	129.3	151.2	200.5	4	8	13	19	92
16	25.2	51.5	87	105	4	8	12	16	58
17	50.7	61.3	93.5	133.8	4	8	12	16	50
18	43.9	92.4	113.7	134.0	4	10	12	17	50
19	41.9	66.7	91.4	149.72	5	9	12	19	92
20	68.9	99.2	179.2	188.4	4	9	12	16	67
21	73.2	129.09	161.1	222.37	4	8	12	16	92
Ave	50.8	92.0	120.7	164.1	4.9	10.3	14.4	19.8	73

Definition 1 divides algorithms into equivalence classes. For example, for algorithms whose cost functions are polynomial in n, the equivalence classes are defined by the highest power of n. This definition can now be employed to characterize the information-based complexity of the consumer problem by applying the definition of upper and lower order to the cost functions of Ω.

DEFINITION 2. S has information-based complexity Y if there exists an algorithm $\omega_i \in \Omega$ such that C_{ω_i} is $O(Y)$ and for all algorithms $\omega_j \in \Omega$, C_{ω_j} is $o(Y)$.

TABLE 2

Observed Data

Sub	Raw Times (sec) Number of Pens 5	10	15	20	25	Number of Writes Number of Pens 5	10	15	20	25	Pay % Max
1	84	110	209	285	334	8	11	29	41	46	50
2	49	85	120	145	194	7	12	16	21	29	56
3	65	97	119	161	170	5	10	15	20	25	63
4	53	107	167	321	4634	5	10	15	33	37	58
5	40	57	128	174	308	8	10	27	29	50	65
6	44	65	84	110	168	5	10	16	20	27	85
7	48	104	112	223	266	9	15	16	29	26	75
8	32	63	99	167	195	5	10	15	20	28	35
9	93	182	244	336	362	8	14	29	44	55	60
10	82	122	185	224	258	7	13	17	21	27	35
Ave	59	99	146	215	272	7	12	20	28	35	58

The concept of information-based complexity divides information-based problems into equivalence classes to facilitate comparison of the "difficulty" in problem solving. With these definitions, problems can be identified as easy, (for example, members of the n equivalence class) or hard, (for example, members of the exponential equivalence class).

The basic problem with applying computer complexity theory to human algorithms is that the time and cost of the various steps in human algorithms appears variable. Second humans generally learn by doing and improve their algorithms as they proceed through the sets. We used regression analysis to test for linear, quadratic and $n \log_2 n$ factors.

B. Instructions to Subjects and Data

Instructions: The instructions given to each subject were: In this experiment, you will be asked to rank several sets of pens according to your preferences. You may use any factors or criteria you feel are relevant, but be sure to use the same criteria throughout the different rankings. We want you to write with each pen at least once, but you may write with any pen more than once if you feel that it is necessary. When making your rankings, order the pens from first, second, and so on down to the last. If you are indifferent between any pens, place them vertically like this. At the end of this experiment, you will be paid up to $3 based on the consistency of your rankings.

Data: The data obtained from the subjects is displayed in Tables 1 and 2.

REFERENCES

1. Aho, A.V., J.E. Hopcroft, and J.D. Ullman, 1974, *The Design and Analysis of Computer Algorithms*, Reading: Addison-Wesley.
2. Knuth, Donald E., 1973, *The Art of Computer Programming, Volume 3, Sorting and Searching*, Second Edition, Reading: Addison-Wesley.
3. Gujarati, Damodar N., 1995, *Basic Econometrics*, Third Edition, New York: McGraw-Hill.
4. Norman, Alfred L., 1994, 'Computability, complexity, and economics', *Computational Economics* 7, 1–21.
5. Simon, H.A., 1976, 'From substantive to procedural rationality', in S. Latsis (Ed.), *Method and Appraisal in Economics*, Cambridge: Cambrdige University Press.
6. Traub, J., G. Wasilkowski, and H. Woźniakowski, 1988, *Information Based Complexity*, Boston: Academic Press.

JASMINA ARIFOVIC

Strategic Uncertainty and the Genetic Algorithm Adaptation

ABSTRACT. This paper studies the behavior of the genetic algorithm in coordination games with strategic uncertainty that are characterized by the multiplicity of equilibria. The main objectives are to examine whether the genetic algorithm adaptation leads to coordination and what the long run properties of the dynamics are. The genetic algorithm behavior is compared to the evidence from the experiments with human subjects. The adaptation of genetic algorithm players results in coordination on an equilibrium. Which equilibrium is selected depends on the group size. The analysis of the long-run properties of the dynamics show that, as a result of the continuing effects of the genetic drift, the genetic algorithm can reach any of the equilibria of the game regardless of the group size. Simulations with large group treatments spend most of the time in Pareto-inferior equilibria, while simulations with small group treatments spend most of the time in Pareto-superior equilibria of the game.

1. Introduction

Coordination games with strategic uncertainty are generally characterized by the multiplicity of equilibria. Moreover, the presence of the strategic uncertainty introduces a possibility of coordination failures. Equilibrium refinements cannot reduce the set of Nash equilibria in these games and the theory provides neither the conditions under which some equilibria are more likely than others, nor the description of the environments in which coordination failures are more likely to occur.

The evidence from the experiments with human subjects (Van Huyck et al. 1990, Cooper et al. 1990) of the coordination games with Pareto-rankable multiple equilibria indicates that the observed pattern of behavior is consistent with the Nash equilibrium concept, but that the Pareto-dominant Nash equilibrium is not always an experimental outcome, i.e. coordination failures do arise in experimental economies. Van Huyck et al. experimental results show that the outcomes depend on the group size, i.e. on the number of players participating in a coordination game. Cooper et al. experimental evidence shows that dominated, cooperative strategies may influence the selection of an outcome from the set of Nash equilibria.

H. Amman et al. (eds.), Computational Approaches to Economic Problems, 225–236.

This paper studies the adaptation of a population of *boundedly rational* players in a version of the coordination game studied by Van Huyck et al. The genetic algorithm (Holland 1975) is used to model the evolution of players' decision rules. The objectives are to examine whether the genetic algorithm can capture qualitative results of Van Huyck et al. experiments and to examine the long-run properties of the dynamics which are observed under the genetic algorithm adaptation.

In economic modeling, the genetic algorithm describes the evolution of a population of rules, representing different possible beliefs, in response to experience. Rules whose application has been more successful are more likely to become more frequently represented in the population, through a process similar to natural selection in population genetics. Recombination of parts of rules and random mutations create new rules by changing certain features of rules previously represented in the population, thus allowing new ideas to be tried. Genetic algorithm and other computational techniques involving artificial intelligence are increasingly being employed by economists as a way of modeling the behavior of economic agents. (See Sargent (1993) for the overview.) The comparison between the genetic algorithm adaptation and the results of the experiments with human subjects has shown that the genetic algorithm learning successfully captures features of the behavior observed in the experimental economies (e.g. Arifovic 1994, 1995, 1996).

Evolutionary game theory analysis (Crawford 1991), as well as the two types of adaptive algorithms (Crawford 1995a, Roth 1995) have already been applied to Van Huyck et al. coordination game.

The description of the model and Van Huyck et al. experimental results are given in Section 2. This section also contains a summary of the results of the evolutionary game theory analysis and adaptive techniques that have been examined in this environment. The genetic algorithm application is described in Section 3. The results of the genetic algorithm simulations are presented in Section 4. Concluding remarks are given in Section 5.

2. Description of the Model

The behavior of the genetic algorithm is examined within the context of the game which Van Huyck et al. (1990) used for the laboratory experiments with human subjects. The game is a version of a model of team production with equal output shares and costly effort. If all players work equally hard, output more than repays players' effort costs. On the other hand, the minimum effort in the team creates a bottleneck. Thus if anyone shirks, the balance of the others' efforts is wasted.

Let $e_1, \ldots, e_n$ denote the levels of effort taken by n players. The game is defined by the following payoff function and strategy space for each of n players:

$$\pi(e_i, e_{\text{min}}) = a[\min(e_i, e_{\text{min}})] - be_i, \qquad a > b > 0, \tag{1}$$

where e_{min} equals $\min(e_1, \ldots e_n)$. Actions are restricted to the set of integers from 1 to $\bar{e}$ where $\bar{e}$ is the maximum feasible level of effort.

All feasible actions are potential Nash equilibrium outcomes which can be Pareto ranked. The payoff-dominant equilibrium is the one in which each player chooses maximum effort, $\bar{e}$. The equilibrium with the lowest payoff to each player is the one in which everyone chooses the least amount of effort, $e = 1$. If a selection principle is based on the "riskiness" of an equilibrium point, security selects the equilibrium with maximin actions, i.e. the equilibrium with the lowest payoff. The payoff-dominant selection principle, on the other hand, chooses an equilibrium with the maximum effort, $\bar{e}$, for each player i, $i \in [1, n]$.

In Van Huyck et al. experiments, groups of subjects played a series of one-stage simultaneous-move games, with no communication allowed before or during play. A minimum effort in the group was publicly announced after each stage.

Van Huyck et al. present evidence that security can undermine the salience of efficiency in repeated coordination games. The treatments with large groups ($G = 14$ and 15) converged to the maximin equilibrium actions. In the large group treatments in which b was set to zero, participants coordinated on the payoff-dominant equilibrium. The treatments with small groups where $G = 2$ resulted in the payoff-dominant equilibrium for the cases where pairs were fixed for T iterations. The outcome was indeterminate in those cases were players were randomly matched in each iteration of the game. These experimental results suggest that the large group size does introduce the amount of strategic uncertainty into the game sufficient to result in a selection of the minimum effort equilibrium and thus in a coordination failure. In addition, the payoff dominant equilibrium result observed in small group treatments suggests that the group size plays important role in coordination problems.

2.1. *Evolutionary Game Theory and Adaptive Techniques*

Crawford (1991) studies the minimum effort game using the evolutionary game theory in order to determine the stability of the minimum effort equilibria. The results of his analysis show that in large or finite populations the strategy configuration in which all players choose the lowest effort is the unique evolutionarily stable strategy (for $b > 0$). In these treatments, lower efforts always yield the same output shares as higher efforts, but at lower cost. Thus, in any population, large or finite, a mutation to an effort that is the minimum in the population then has higher payoff than all other efforts. The results of the Van Huyck at al. game in which b is set equal to 0 show that there is no evolutionarily stable strategy in this treatment.

For the values of the parameters used in Van Huyck et al. experiments, Crawford's random-pairing treatment results show that any pure strategy effort is monomorphic evolutionary stable strategy whenever the number of players, n, is greater than 4. For $n = 2$ and $n = 3$, he shows that only evolutionary stable strategy is the one with the lowest effort.

Crawford (1995a) follows the adaptive control literature in assuming that players' beliefs and strategy choices evolve according to a linear adjustment rule. On average, beliefs adjust part of the way toward the value suggested by the latest observation of the minimum effort. These average adjustments are perturbed each period by idiosyncratic shocks. Differences in players' beliefs and actions that result from these shocks introduce the strategic uncertainty into the model. The model that uses the behavioral parameters and variances estimated using experimental data from large group treatments reproduces the dynamics observed in experimental interactions and provides an adequate statistical summary of the behavior of subjects that participated in the experiments.

Crawford (1995b) discusses the results of the analysis when the methods of Kandori et al. (1993) and Young (1993) are applied to the model. In the long run, the process cycles perpetually among the pure-strategy equilibria of the underlying game, with their prior probabiities at any given time determined by the ergodic distribution. As the level of noise is allowed to approach zero, the ergodic distribution assigns the probability one of approaching the equilibrium with the lowest effort.

Roth (1995) describes the application of the Roth and Erev algorithm to the Van Huyck et al. game. The *common learning* version of their algorithm converges to the minimum effort equilibrium.

All of the above mentioned applications of the evolutionary game theory analysis and of the adaptive algorithms select the minimum effort equilibrium. These applications are successful in explaining the behavior observed in large group experimental treatments. However, these applications do not address the fixed pairs experimental treatments in which convergence to the payoff dominant equilibrium was observed.

3. The Genetic Algorithm Application

Players' decision rules are represented by a population of N binary strings. At each generation gen, players are randomly placed into groups of size g. Players within each group repeatedly play the game for T iterations. A player i, $i \in [1 \dots N]$, uses a binary string i to make a decision about his action at each iteration, t, $t \in [1 \dots T]$. A binary string consists of $\bar{e} + 1$ positions where $\bar{e} = 8$ is the maximum feasible action. Each position p_j, $j \in [0, \bar{e}]$, consists of l bits where l is the number of bits required to encode integer value $\bar{e}$. The total length of a string is $(\bar{e} + 1)l$ bits. The first position, p_0, encodes the action that player takes at iteration $t = 1$. A position p_j, $j \in [1, \bar{e}]$ encodes the action that player i takes at iteration $t > 1$, given that a minimum effort of his group at iteration $t - 1$, $e_{t-1,\min}$, was equal to j. Here is an example of a binary string that encodes integer actions in the interval $[1, 8]$ given the miminum action taken in the previous iteration:

position p_j	0	1	2	3	4	5	6	7	8
binary string:	001	100	001	111	001	010	000	100	110
action $e_{i,0}$	2								
action $e_{i,t}$:		5	2	8	2	3	1	5	7
$\bar{e}_{t-1,\min}$		1	2	3	4	5	6	7	8

The strategy encoded by this binary string is interpreted in the following way. At iteration $t = 1$, player i takes action $e_{i,0} = 2$. For $t > 1$, the player decides on effort 5 at iteration t if $e_{t-1,\min}$ was equal to 1; the player decides on effort 2 at t if $e_{t-1,\min}$ was equal to 2; and so on.

3.1. *The Implementation of Genetic Algorithm*

The algorithm is implemented in the following way:

1. At each generation gen, gen $\in [1, maxgen]$, players' groups, each of size g, are determined by randomly selecting players that will participate in each group. Each player's strategy is represented by a binary string. The size of the population of binary strings N divided by g, the group size, determines the number of groups.

2. Within each group, the players engage in the game that is repeated T iterations.

3. Each player i, $i \in [1, N]$, chooses his action. Initial action, at $t = 1$, is determined by decoding bits in the position p_0. For $t > 1$, $t \in [1, T]$, each player chooses his action at t by using the information about the minimum group effort from the previous, $t - 1$, iteration. Given the $t - 1$ minimum group effort, $e_{t-1,\min} = j$, $j \in [1, \bar{e}]$, the player looks up the jth position of his binary string and decodes the action that he takes at t.

4. Once each player chooses his action for iteration t, the minimum group effort of the current iteration is determined within each group.

5. The payoff for each player is computed using the information about the minimum effort and his own effort from Equation (1).

6. The payoffs are accumulated during T iterations of the game.

7. After T iterations, the average payoff for each player is computed as $\sum_{t=1}^{T} \pi_{i,t}/T$.

8. The binary strings are updated using the following genetic operators: reproduction, crossover and mutation. Two versions of the reproduction operator, roulette wheel and tournament selection, are implemented.

9. Steps 2 through 8 are repeated for $maxgen$ generations.

10. Initially, at gen $= 1$, a binary string for each player is chosen randomly.

3.2. *Description of Genetic Operators*

Reproduction makes copies of individual binary strings. The criterion used in copying is the value of the fitness function. The fitness of a string i at generation gen, $\mu_{i,\text{gen}}$, is equal to the average payoff that player i earned over T iterations,

$$\mu_{i,\text{gen}} = \frac{\sum_{t=1}^{T} \pi_{i,t}}{T}.$$

The effects of two different versions of the reproduction operator on the genetic algorithm behavior are examined. One is the reproduction that operates like a biased roulette-wheel where each binary string is allocated a slot sized in proportion to its fitness. The number of spins of the wheel is equal to the number of binary strings in a population. Each spin yields a reproduction candidate. Once a binary string is selected, its exact copy is made and it enters into a *mating pool.*

Another method is a tournament selection method. Two binary strings are randomly selected and their fitnesses (average payoffs) are compared. The binary string with a higher fitness value is copied and placed into the mating pool. Again, the tournament selection is repeated N times in order to obtain N copies of chromosomes.

Crossover operates on the pairs of randomly selected binary strings. First, two binary strings are selected from the mating pool at random. Secondly, a number k, $k \in [1, \ldots, l-1]$, is randomly selected and two new binary strings are obtained by swapping the bit values to the right of the position k. A total of $N/2$ pairs (where N is even integer) are selected. A probability that crossover will take place on a given selected pair i, $i \in [1, N/2]$ is equal to 0.6.

Mutation randomly changes the value of a position within a chromosome. Each position has a probability of 0.0033 of being altered by mutation, independent of other positions.

Given the updated set of binary strings, the algorithm proceeds to stage 2 for another generation of repeated games. Each simulation is conducted for a total of *maxgen* generations. Initial population of binary strings is randomly generated.

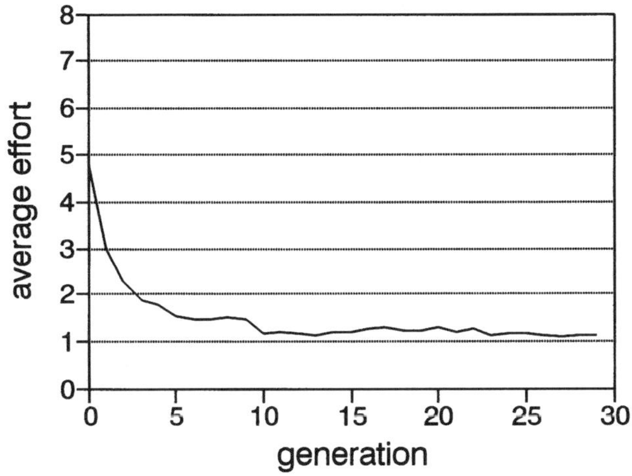

Fig. 1. Average effort, $g = 14$.

4. THE RESULTS OF SIMULATIONS

The first set of simulations was conducted using the group sizes $g = 2$, 3, 4, 5, 6, and 14. The population size was $N = 40$ for $g = 2, 4$, and 5, and $N = 42$ for $g = 3, 6$, and 14. The number of bits used to encode the value of effort at a position within a string was set equal to 3. This number determined the maximum feasible effort, $\bar{e} = 8$. The number of positions within a string was then equal to 8 and the total length of a string was $(8+1)3 = 27$ bits. Two sets of payoff parameter values that were implemented in Van Huyck at al. experiments were used. Five simulations with different random number generator seeds were conducted for each combination of the parameter values. In this set of simulations, the rate of mutation decreased exponentially following the generation at which the average effort was equal to the minimum or to the maximum feasible effort.

Simulations with group sizes $g = 2$, $g = 3$, and $g = 4$ converged to the payoff-dominant equilibrium, with all players choosing the maximum level of effort. On the other hand, simulations with group sizes $g = 5$, $g = 6$, and $g = 14$ converged to the secure equilibrium, with all players choosing the minimum level of effort. The results of simulations show that genetic algorithm players are able to solve individual coordination problem, i.e. they learn to coordinate on a particular equilibrium. The selected equilibrium is not necessarily the payoff-dominant equilibrium. In other words, the genetic algorithm players can exhibit coordination failures.

The results also show that the level of effort selected by the genetic algorithm for group sizes used in Van Huyck et al. experiments, $g = 2$ and $g = 14$ match the results observed in the experimental data, i.e. the payoff dominant

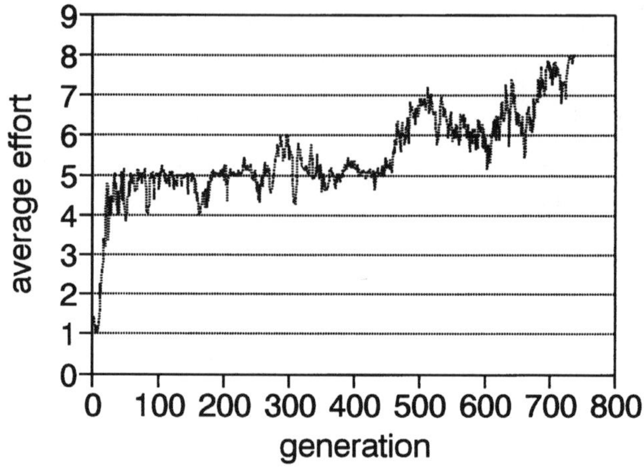

Fig. 2. Average effort $g = 2$, initialized at $e = 1.4$.

equilibrium level of effort was selected in small group treatments, with $g = 2$, while a secure equilibrium level of effort was selected in large group treatments, with $g = 14$. Figure 1 exhibits the behavior of the average effort in the simulation with $g = 14$. Average effort $\hat{e}$ is given by $\sum_{i=1}^{N}\sum_{t=1}^{T} e_{i,t}/TN$. Figure 2 exhibits the average effort in the simulation in which g was equal to 2. The simulation was initialized at a relaitvely low level of average effort equal to 1.4. The figure clearly shows how the adaptation takes place in stages, from the lower towards the higher levels of average effort.

The set of simulations conducted for the value of parameter b equal to 0 converged to the payoff dominant equilibrium for all group sizes. This matches the results from the Van Huyck experiments in which the payoff dominant equilibrium was selected in large group treatments when b was set to 0.

No qualitative difference in the results of simulations conducted with the application of roulette wheel and those conducted with the application of tournament selection were observed. In general, simulations with tournament selection took longer to converge. The results reported in this paper are from the simulations in which roulette wheel was applied.

In order to examine the issues related to the long-run features of the genetic algorithm dynamics, a second set of simulations for $g = 2$ and $g = 14$ was conducted. Each simulation lasted for $100,000$ generations. The rate of mutation was kept constant at the level set at the beginning of a simulation. (The values of all other simulation parameters were the same as those used in the first set of simulations.)

The analysis of the dynamics reveals that, if the rate of mutation is kept constant, a genetic algorithm population can reach any of the Nash equilibria

TABLE 1

Frequency distribution of average effort over 100,000 generations.

(a) $g = 2$								
e	1	2	3	4	5	6	7	8
frequency	0.000	0.000	0.002	0.016	0.085	0.190	0.440	0.267
(b) $g = 14$								
e	1	2	3	4	5	6	7	8
frequency	0.632	0.167	0.100	0.046	0.039	0.012	0.003	0.000

in the long run, regardless of the size of the group. Once the genetic algorithm population is close to one of the equilibria, it will not remain there due to the effects of the genetic drift. The drift will eventually move the population towards another equilibrium of the game. Thus, none of the equilibria are stable in the sense that once the population reaches it, it stays in its neighborhood forever. However, the group size does affect the frequency with which equilibria with different levels of effort are reached and the time spent in each one of them. Simulations with $g = 2$ will spend most of the time in equilibria with relatively high levels of effort, while simulations with $g = 14$ will spend most of the time in low effort equilibria.

Table 1 presents distributions of levels of average effort observed in simulations conducted for $100,000$ generations. The data show that in a simulation with $g = 2$, the average effort was 70% of time above 7. In a simulation with $g = 14$, the average effort was 80% of time below 2 (and 63% of time equal to 1).

To understand the dynamics of this evolutionary process, consider the following hypothetical example. Suppose that all players choose initial level of effort equal to 1, $e_{i,1} = 1$ for all i and that they choose $e_{i,t} = 1$ when $e_{min,t-1} = 1$ for $t \in [1, T]$. Thus, all players choose best response actions and the economy is in the minimum effort equilibrium. A positive rate of mutation will result in small deviations from best response, but strategies prescribing actions different from 1 at location 1 will be eliminated from the population. At the same time, mutation will result in the genetic drift in other parts of players' strategies, not currently used in the game. Over time, the drift will generate a number of strings that prescribe a level of effort j at some location j, $j > 1$. These changes will be irrelevant for the levels of effort that are actually chosen. But eventually, positions that encode initial levels of effort within these strings will also be affected by mutation, i.e. mutation will result in the initial levels of effort equal to j. When coupled with each other, these strings will choose higher levels of efforts and will accumulate higher payoffs than strings that are choosing the minimum effort. Reproduction will promote these strings and they will quickly overtake the population. Continuing effects of the genetic drift eventually bring the population to the highest level of effort. This process works in reverse as well, with population going to the lower level of chosen effort. For $g = 2$ this event has smaller probability of occurence than the event of going from the lower effort equilibrium to the higher effort equilibrium. If the strings prescribing lower amounts of effort are not to be wiped out of the population, their number has to be large enough to result in lower payoffs for high effort strings.

For large groups, $g = 14$, the same dynamics takes place. Due to the larger strategic uncertainty faced by players in these groups, higher levels of effort are less likely to be observed. Although there is a positive probability that groups of this size will reach the payoff dominant equilibrium, it takes around $90,000$ generations to observe this outcome. Using the same example which was used for $g = 2$, the jump from the minimum effort equilibrium to a higher effort equilibrium requires a formation of a group of 14 strings all playing higher level of effort. This event requires much higher level of mutation which is less likely than in the case of $g = 2$. If such event occurs, the accumulated fitness of these *high* effort strings will be larger than the fitness of strings that play in groups with lower minimum effort. Consequently, these *high* effort strings will obtain larger number of copies in the following generation. Since there is now a larger number of *high* effort strings in the population, the probability that there will be a group (or groups) of strings playing *high* effort becomes greater. On the other hand, the probability that these *high* effort strings will perform poorly in the subsequent generations is also greater for larger groups since the probability of playing in a group with a string that plays a lower level of effort is greater for larger groups. This adversely affects the survival rates of *high* effort strings. These are the reasons why the observed level of individual effort in large group simulations remains low most of the time.

The analysis of the long-run behavior of the economies which adapt under the genetic algorithm shows that, regardless of the group size, any equilibrium point can be reached. Due to the larger amount of strategic uncertainty present in the case of large group sizes and larger amounts of mutation required for equilibrium points with higher levels of effort, economies with larger group sizes will spend most of the time in low effort equilibria. Economies in which players play in small group sizes that are characterized by smaller strategic uncertainty spend more time in high effort equilibria. Also, smaller amount of mutation is required to move these economies from low to high effort equilibria. On the other hand, larger amount of mutation is required to move them from high to low effort equilibria.

The common feature of the behavior observed in simulations with both $g = 2$ and $g = 14$ is that a large fraction of genetic algorithm populations spends most of the time playing best response actions. This feature is present

TABLE 2

Frequency distribution of best response measure over 100,000 generations.

(a) $g = 2$

interval	0.1	0.2	0.3	0.4	0.5	0.6	0.7	0.8	0.9	1
frequency	0.00	0.00	0.00	0.00	0.01	0.02	0.04	0.14	0.25	0.47

(b) $g = 14$

interval	0.1	0.2	0.3	0.4	0.5	0.6	0.7	0.8	0.9	1
frequency	0.00	0.00	0.00	0.00	0.01	0.02	0.02	0.08	0.17	0.65

regardless of the group size. In order to examine how close an entire population of strings was to playing best response actions at each generation, the *best response measure*, br_{gen}, was calculated. It is given by

$$br_{i,\text{gen}} = 1 - \frac{\sum_{t=1}^{T} I_{i,t}}{NT},$$

where $I_{i,t}$ is an index variable equal to 0 when player's i effort at iteration t is equal to the minimum within the group in which he plays and 1 if it is greater than the minimum effort. Frequency distribution of this measure for $g = 2$ and $g = 14$ in simulations that were conducted for $100,000$ generations is given in Table 2. The frequency distribution shows that, regardless of the group size, the mass of the distribution is concentrated on the values of the measure close to one. This means that in both cases, for $g = 2$ and $g = 14$, the genetic algorithm populations spend most of the time close to the equilibria. More significant deviations, meaning lower values of the best response measure, occur only during brief periods of time while the transition from one equilibrium to the other takes place.

5. Concluding Remarks

Adaptation of genetic algorithm players results in coordination on an equilibrium. Simulations with large group treatments converged to the minimum effort equilibrium thus exhibiting coordination failures. Simulations with fixed pairs treatments reached the payoff-dominant equilibrium. These results indicate that the group size plays the crucial role in the equilibrium selection.

In the long-run, there is a positive probability that a genetic algorithm population may reach any of the equilibria of the game. This is a result of the continuing effects of the genetic drift. The drift causes changes in the parts of strategies which are irrelevant at a point in time. Since they do not affect the players' behavior, they are not subject to selection pressure. Over time, when the conditions change sufficiently, these parts of strategies become parts that are actually played. As a result, the economy transits to another equilibrium. Simulations with large group treatments spend most of the time in low effort equilibria, while simulations with fixed pairs treatments spend most of the time in high effort equilibria. The group size affects the probability that a simulation moves from a low to a high effort equilibrium such that the larger the group, the smaller the probability of moving from a low to high effort equilibria.

REFERENCES

Arifovic, J., 1994, 'Genetic algorithm learning and the Cobweb model', *Journal of Economic Dynamics and Control* 18, 3–28.

Arifovic, J., 1995, 'Genetic algorithms and inflationary economies', *Journal of Monetary Economics* 36, 219–243.

Arifovic, J., 1996, 'The behavior of the exchange rate in the genetic algorithm and experimental economies', *Journal of Political Economy* 104, 510–541.

Bryant, J., 1983, 'A simple rational expectations Keynes-type model', *Quarterly Journal of Economics* 98, 525–528.

Cooper, R. and A. John, 1988, 'Coordinating coordination failures in Keynesian models', *Quarterly Journal of Economics* 103, 441–463.

Cooper, R., D. De Jong, R. Forsythe, and Th. Ross, 1990, 'Selection criteria in coordination games', *American Economic Review* 80, 218–233.

Crawford, V., 1991, 'An 'evolutionary' interpretation of Van Huyck, Battalio, and Beil's experimental results on coordination', *Games and Economic Behavior* 3, 25–59.

Crawford, V., 1995, 'Adaptive dynamics in coordination games', *Econometrica* 63, 103–143.

Holland, J.H., 1975, *Adaptation in Natural and Artificial Systems*, Ann Arbor, MI: The University of Michigan Press.

Katz, M. and C. Shapiro, 1985, 'Network externalities, competition and compatibility', *American Economic Review* 75, 424–440.

Kiyotaki, N., 1988, 'Implications of multiple expectation equilibria under monopolistic competition', *Quarterly Journal of Economics* 103, 695–714.

Kandori, M., G. Mailath, and R. Rob, 1993, 'Learning, mutation, and long run equilibria in games', *Econometrica* 61, 29–56.

Roth, A., 1995, 'Introduction to experimental economics', in J. Kagel and A. Roth (Eds), *Handbook of Experimental Economics*, Princeton, NJ: Princeton University Press, pp. 3–109.

Sargent, T.J., 1993, *Bounded Rationality in Macroeconomics*, Oxford: Oxford University Press.

Van Huyck, J., R. Battalio, and R. Beil, 1990, 'Tacit coordination games, strategic uncertainty, and coordination failure', *American Economic Review* 80, 234–248.

Young, H.P., 1993, 'The evolution of conventions', *Econometrica* 61, 57–84.

BERNARDO A. HUBERMAN

Fluctuating Benefits and Collective Action

ABSTRACT. We show that when individuals confronted with a social dilemma contribute to the common good with an effort that fluctuates in time, they can make the group generate an average utility that actually decreases in time. This paradoxical behavior takes place in spite of the fact that typically individuals are found to be contributing at any given time. This novel phenomenon, which we verified in a number of computer experiments, is the result of an intermittency effect, whereby unlikely bursts of defection determine the average behavior of the group. Besides providing a dynamical theory for the lognormal distribution found in some sociological data, these results show that the typical behavior of individuals comprising a group can be inconsistent with its average properties.

INTRODUCTION

Social dilemmas are at the heart of the problem of generating cooperation among individuals confronted with conflicting choices. As such they have been studied for a number of years within the context of rational choice theory. As shown originally by Olson (1965), individuals having to choose between producing a public good and free riding on the effort of others face a dilemma when the benefit to be accrued by overall cooperation offsets individual costs, since rationality on the part of each individual leads to failure in achieving the common good (Hardin 1968, Schelling 1978, Hardin 1982, Glance and Huberman 1994). The resolution of such dilemmas underlie successful attempts at ongoing collective action, such as the functioning of large organizations (Bendor and Mookherjee 1987, Glance and Huberman 1993a, 1993b), the mobilization of political movements (Taylor 1976, Oliver and Marwell 1988) and the adoption of new technologies.

We have recently shown that for a broad set of beliefs and group characteristics cooperation can appear spontaneously in non-cooperative and diverse groups after long periods of time if delays in information are not important. Moreover, cooperation or defection appear suddenly and unexpectedly, with diversity acting as an additional source of uncertainty, thus shortening the time to an outbreak (Huberman and Glance 1993).

H. Amman et al. (eds.), Computational Approaches to Economic Problems, 237–247.

Studies of collective action usually make assumptions that not always reflect the behavior of realistic groups of people, such as the existence of a utility function that is the same for all individuals, or the constancy of the benefits and costs over long periods of time. Concerning the latter, it is well known that since cooperation is based on a person's effort, one never implements precisely the amount of cooperation that one intends to. There are always a number of reasons for this to be the case. An individual may be late returning from a meeting, and so can give less time for a cooperative endeavor than he had planned. Or, in situations where the production of the collective good demands some physical effort, it is reasonable to expect that individual contributions will vary over time. The same applies to cases where intellectual effort is required, such as clerical work in an organization. In those circumstances, it can be safely assumed that the benefit from cooperation will fluctuate around a mean value, with a dispersion determined by the variance of the appropriate distribution.

In this paper we study the effects of such fluctuating benefits on the possibility of obtaining sustained cooperation from a group of individuals confronted with a social dilemma. In spite of the fact that cooperation is optimal in either small groups or when individuals have long outlooks, in equilibrium some members of a cooperating group will occassionally choose to defect due to misinformation as to what the other members are doing (Glance and Huberman 1993a, 1993b). If in addition individual efforts also fluctuate, the benefit obtained by members of the group during those switchings could either encourage or discourage further switchings. Nevertheless, since these fluctuations lower the utility of the group, one expects that after a short period of time the group will revert to spontaneous cooperation.

A careful study of the resulting dynamics however, shows that this is not the case. Instead, variability in effort has a dramatic effect on the overall behavior of the system. We will show that a cooperating group of individuals can generate an average utility that *decreases* in time, even though the fluctuations in effort are small and with zero mean. This striking and paradoxical behavior is the result of a social intermittency effect, whereby unlikely bursts of defection determine the average behavior of the group, in spite of the fact that individuals are typically found to be cooperating at any given time. These predictions have been verified through a number of computer experiments.

This effect, although exhibited here within the context of collective action, is likely to be encountered in many other social situations characterized by equilibria punctuated with fluctuations. In certain cases it might even be possible for a large group of defectors to generate a utility that *increases* in time. Intermittency implies that in situations where the only available data is some average utility or other productivity measure, the inference that the individuals comprising the group act in ways consistent with the average behavior might be incorrect. If one had to summarize these findings in a simple vernacular sentence it would read: *"what you see is not what you get"*.

SOCIAL DILEMMAS

In a general social dilemma, each individual can either contribute (cooperate) to the production of a common good, or not (defect). While no individual can directly observe the effort of another, each member observes instead the collective output of the group or organization and can deduce overall group participation using knowledge of individual and group functions. In this process there is an amount of uncertainty in the relation between member's efforts and group performance. There are many causes for this uncertainty; for example a member may try but fail to contribute due to unforeseen obstacles. Another type of uncertainty might arise from the fact that individuals act with bounded rationality, occasionally making suboptimal decisions.

In a simple, but general limit, collective benefits increase linearly in the contribution of the members, at a rate b per cooperating member. Each contributing individual bears a personal cost, c. If k_i denotes whether member i is cooperating ($k_i = 1$) or defecting ($k_i = 0$) then the utility at time t for member i of a group of size n is given by (Bendor and Mookherjee 1987)

$$U_i(t) = b\frac{\hat{n}_c(t)}{n} - ck_i. \tag{1}$$

From knowledge of the functional form of the utility function, each individual can deduce the number of individuals effectively cooperating at some time t by inverting this equation and obtaning an estimate of the value of $\hat{n}_c$, or alternatively, by evaluating $\hat{f}_c(t) = \hat{n}_c(t)/n$, the fraction of individuals effectively cooperating at time t. Since the information available is not perfect, this estimate will differ from the actual number of individuals intending to cooperate.

When all members contribute successfully, each individual receives net benefits $bn/n - c = b - c$, independent of the group's size. The production of the collective good becomes a social dilemma when $b > c > b/n$. Thus, although the good of all is maximized when everybody cooperates ($b - c > 0$) the dominant strategy in a one shot interaction is to defect since additional gains from personal participation is less than the private cost ($b/n - c < 0$).

This logic changes when the interaction is ongoing since future expected utility gains will join present ones in influencing the rational individual's decision to cooperate or not in the production of the collective good. In particular, individual expectations concerning the future evolution of the game can play a significant role in each member's decisions. The barest notion of expectations comes from the economic concept of horizon length. The horizon length is how far an agent looks into the future, or how long the agent expects to continue interacting with the other members of the group. Within this framework, agents believe that their present actions will affect those of others in the future. In particular, individuals expect that defection encourages defection and cooperation encourages cooperation. But the degree to which this belief holds depends on the size of the group and the present level of production.

In earlier work we stated the benefits and costs to the individual associated with the two actions of cooperation and defection, i.e. contributing or not to the social good (Glance and Huberman 1993a, 1993b). We showed that if α is the rate at which individuals reevaluate their choices, and H is the horizon length that determines the discount of future returns, there is a strategy such that an individual will cooperate if the observed fraction cooperating exceeds a value f_{crit}, which is given by

$$f_{\text{crit}} = \frac{nc - b}{H\alpha(b - c)} \; . \tag{2}$$

Thus, individuals engage in conditional cooperation, cooperating when the fraction perceived as cooperating is greater than a critical amount, and defecting when it is lower than the critical amount. Although the precise functional form of f_{crit} can depend on specific sets of beliefs, there is a wide range of preference functions for which a critical fraction appears as the determinant of cooperation (Huberman and Glance 1991).

The dynamics of collective action is determined by the equation governing the fraction of agents cooperating at a given time. This equation was derived earlier, and it is given by (Glance and Huberman 1993a, 1993b)

$$\frac{d\hat{f}_c(t)}{dt} = -\alpha \left\{ \hat{f}_c(t) - \frac{1}{2}\left[1 + \text{erf}\left(\frac{(\langle \hat{f}_c(t)\rangle - f_{\text{crit}})}{\sigma\sqrt{2}}\right)\right]\right\} , \tag{3}$$

where erf denotes the error function, $\langle \hat{f}_c\rangle = p\hat{f}_c + (1-p)(1-\hat{f}_c)$, with p the probability that an agent intending to cooperate does so successfully, and σ determines the level of uncertainty in the system. This uncertainty is made up of two parts. One is related to the connection between intent and action that we just stated. The other refers to the variance in individual characteristics that make individuals have a diversity in their outlooks or in their benefit-cost ratios (Huberman and Glance 1993).

The fixed points of this equation, which are obtained by setting the right hand to zero, give the critical sizes beyond which cooperation can no longer be sustained. In our earlier work we showed that there is a sharp upper limit, n^*, to the size of a group which can support cooperation. Even if all members of a group larger than this size started cooperating, after a long time the whole group would switch to defection. Moreover, the outbreak of cooperation is sudden and unpredictable, taking place over a very short period of time. These predictions were observed in a number of computer experiments simulating social dilemmas.

FLUCTUATING EFFORTS

Although in the equilibrium state the number of cooperating agents does not change in time, occasional fluctuations take place whereby individuals might switch from cooperation to defection for short periods of time. These random events are due to the uncertainty that individuals have about the behavior of the others. This uncertainty can cause an individual to mistakenly perceive the amount of cooperation to be different than its actual value. Because of this misperception, an individual might act against the equilibrium condition of mutual cooperation or defection, causing the system to move away from the fixed point. The more uncertainty there is in the system, the more likely it is that there will be fluctuations away from the equilibrium state.

The situation becomes more complicated if one allows for the fact that individual efforts at contributing to the common good vary from time to time. This implies that superimposed on the occasional switchings from cooperation to defection and from defection to cooperation, there is an extra source of randomness stemming from the fact that benefits fluctuate in time, thus potentially creating a complex dynamical scenario.

When fluctuations take place, the group recovers in time according to an equation that governs the dynamics of fluctuations away from the equilibrium state. This equation can be obtained by performing a linear stability analysis of Equation (3) around the fixed point, which we will denote by $\hat{f}_o$. For the sake of simplicity, in what follows we will consider the case where the equilibrium corresponds to overall cooperation, so that $\hat{f}_o \cong 1$.That is the optimal situation for the case of small groups or when individuals have long horizons. The opposite case, that of a large group of defectors, can be treated by similar methods. Denoting a small deviation from the fixed point by δ_c, the fraction of individuals cooperating at any given time will be given by

$$\hat{f}_c = \hat{f}_o - \delta_c(t) \tag{4}$$

with $\delta_c \ll \hat{f}_o$. Replacing this expression in Equation (3) and performing a linear stability analysis around the fixed point, yields an equation for the dynamics of fluctuations around the cooperative equilibrium. As shown elsewhere (Huberman and Glance 1996), in the case of large uncertanties due to diversity one obtains

$$\frac{d\delta_c(t)}{dt} = -\alpha\delta_c(t)\left[A' - \frac{2}{\sigma^3\sqrt{2\pi}}\, f_{\text{crit}}\right] \tag{5}$$

with

$$A' = 1 + \frac{1}{\sigma\sqrt{2\pi}}\left(\frac{1}{2\sigma^2} - 1\right).$$

If the parameter values do not change with time, the expression inside the bracket of Equation (5) becomes a constant and the solutions of this equation correspond to exponential relaxation of any initial fluctuation to the state $\delta_c = 0$, i.e. overall cooperation. The characteristic relaxation time is given by the inverse of this constant bracket times the evaluation rate, α. The situation changes drastically however, when the cooperative output that an individual can produce fluctuates in time, making the utilities change accordingly. In what follows we will assume that the cooperative output is given by

$$b(t) = \bar{b} + \beta(t), \tag{6}$$

where $\bar{b}$ is the time independent benefit that results from cooperating, and the fluctuating component, $\beta(t)$, is a Gaussian random variable such that

$$\begin{aligned} \langle \beta(t) \rangle &= 0 \\ \langle \beta(t)\beta(t') \rangle &= 2\sigma' \delta(t - t'), \end{aligned} \tag{7}$$

where σ' denotes the variance in effort. Notice that the Gaussian character of the fluctuations implies that for all practical purposes the probability of observing an individual contributing a benefit above or below $\bar{b}$ by an amount exceeding three standard deviations is vanishingly small.

As shown in (Huberman and Glance 1996), fluctuations in benefits translate into a time dependent critical fraction that is given by

$$f_{\text{crit}}(t) = f_{\text{crit}} - \frac{\beta(t)}{H\alpha(b - c)} \tag{8}$$

with f_{crit} given by Equation (2), but with b replaced with $\bar{b}$. Substituting this expression in Equation (5), we obtain the equation governing the dynamics of fluctuations away from the cooperative fixed point. It is given by

$$\frac{d\delta_c(t)}{dt} = -A\delta_c(t) + B(t)\delta_c(t), \tag{9}$$

where $A = \alpha A' - \alpha f_{\text{crit}}/\sigma^3\sqrt{2\pi}$, and $B(t) = -\beta(t)/\sqrt{2\pi}\, H\sigma^3(b - c)$. It also follows that $B(t)$ is a Gaussian random variable with zero mean and with autocorrelation equal to $\langle B(t)B(t') \rangle = \bar{\sigma} = \sigma'/(\sqrt{2\pi}\, H\sigma^3(b - c))$.

With these properties of the random function $B(t)$, Equation (9) is a stochastic differential equation. In what follows we will obtain an exact solution of this equation and calculate the behavior of all the moments of δ_c.

Bursts of Defection

In order to study the role of fluctuations around the overall cooperative state, we now solve the stochastic differential equation given by Equation (9) by standard methods (Arnold 1992). Since the fluctuations in $B(t)$ are Gaussian, we can use the Stratonovich formalism (Stratonovich 1967) to find the time evolution of δ_c. It is given by

$$\delta_c(t) = \delta_c(0)e^{-At+w_t}, \tag{10}$$

where δ_c is the initial value of the fluctuation and w_t is a Wiener process such that $B(t) = dw_t/dt$, and with the property that

$$\begin{aligned} \langle w_t \rangle &= 0 \\ \langle w_t^2 \rangle &= \bar{\sigma} t. \end{aligned} \tag{11}$$

As can be seen from Equation (10), typical fluctuations away from the cooperative state relax exponentially fast to the fixed point, a result to be expected in thc case of small groups and large horizons.

A paradox appears however, when computing the moments of $\delta_c(t)$, which are given by

$$\langle [\delta_c(t)]^m \rangle = [\delta_c(0)]^m \langle e^{-(At+w_t)m} \rangle, \tag{12}$$

where m is the mth moment and $\delta_c(0)$ is the initial configuration of the fluctuating system. Using the fact that $\langle e^{mw_t} \rangle = e^{m^2 \sigma t}$, this equation becomes

$$\langle [\delta_c(t)]^m \rangle = [\delta_c(0)]^m e^{-Amt+m^2\bar{\sigma}t}. \tag{13}$$

From this expression, it is clear that the higher moments grow in time with increasing order, at a rate given by $m(m\bar{\sigma} - A)$. This happens while typical realizations of the fluctuations relax exponentially fast, as indicated by Equation (10). In particular, the average fraction of defecting agents, which is given by the first moment ($m = 1$) of $\delta_c(t)$, *increases* in time when the fluctuations in individual efforts exceed the value of A, which amounts to the condition

$$\bar{\sigma} > \alpha\sigma^2 H(b-c)(\sigma\sqrt{2\pi} - 1). \tag{14}$$

This behavior takes place in spite of the fact that typical fluctuations decay to zero, as shown by Equation (10). Even more striking, the average utility to an individual, which is given by $\langle U_i(t) \rangle = \langle b\hat{f}_c(t) \rangle - ck_i$ *decreases* in time as

$$\langle U_i(t) \rangle = \bar{b}[1 - \delta_c(0)e^{(\bar{\sigma}-A)t}] - ck_i. \tag{15}$$

Therefore, a measurement of the utility over a given time interval would lead to the wrong inference that defection is the prevalent strategy, for most inviduals are cooperating, as follows from Equation (10). Conversely, an increasing average utility might not necessarily signal increasing levels of cooperation in a large group.

In order to understand this paradox, it is useful to remember that the higher moments of $\delta_c(t)$ are related to the probability of very unlikely events.

The fact that the moments grow in time indicates that the behavior of the system is dominated by occasional bursts in which the number of individuals suddenly found to be defecting is very large, so large that the probability of their occurence would be practically zero if the fluctuations were Gaussian in nature. These intense peaks of defection happen in spite of the fact that fluctuations in effort are normally distributed around a mean value $\bar{b}$.

If these intermittent burst are non-Gaussian, we need to compute the quasistationary distribution of fluctuations that results from their evolution over a long time period. In order to so, divide both sides of Equation (9) by δ_c and integrate over a time interval T, to obtain, up to a constant,

$$\ln \frac{\delta_c(T)}{\delta_c(0)} = \sum_{0}^{T} B_n, \tag{16}$$

where the integral of $B(t)$ over time has been replaced by a sum over discrete time steps, at each of which the random quantity $B(t)$ acquires the value B_n.

Since the values of B_n are normally distributed random quantities with zero mean and variance $\bar{\sigma}^2$, the sum of the right hand side can be evaluated by invoking the Central Limit Theorem. Therefore, the logarithm of δ_c will be normally distributed with zero mean and variance $\bar{\sigma}^2$. In other words, δ_c is log-normally distributed according to

$$\text{Prob}[\delta_c] = \frac{1}{\delta_c \bar{\sigma} \sqrt{2\pi}} e^{-((\log \delta_c)^2 / 2\bar{\sigma}^2)}. \tag{17}$$

With the mean value of δ_c, μ, given by $\mu = e^{\bar{\sigma}^2}$, and its variance by $\mu^2(e^{\bar{\sigma}^2} - 1)$.

The log-normal distribution differs from the Gaussian one in two important aspects. The first one has to do with the fact that, unlike the normal distribution, the log-normal is quite asymmetric. Thus, typical realizations of the system do not coincide with its average behavior. Second, the tail of the log-normal distribution extends much further out than that of a normal distribution with comparable mean and variance. This can seen by noting the fact that for distributions with unit mean and variance the ratio of the log-normal to the normal distribution at six standard deviations is 33000, implying a finite probability for events which, when described by a normal distribution would have vanishing probability of occurring. That this anomolous events do determine the dynamics of ongoing collective action was verified in computer simulations of a social dilemma conducted in cooperation with Glance (Huberman and Glance 1996). By running event-driven Monte Carlo simulations of collective action, we were able to test the lognormality of the data, in agreement with the predictions of this theory.

DISCUSSION

In this paper we have shown how fluctuations in the effort to produce a public good can lead to a new social phenomenon characterized by rare and intense bursts of defection superimposed on a background of overall cooperation. This phenomenon is stochastic in nature. It leads to a paradoxical behavior of the average utility accrued by any individual, for it *decreases* in time in spite of the fact that typically all inviduals are found to be contributing the same average average amount of effort. Conversely, there can be cases where an equilibrium group of defectors can generate a utility that *increases* in time, although the conditions are more restrictive than in the case of cooperation.

This paradox was observed in computer simulations of social dilemmas and should also appear in real social settings corresponding to equilibria punctuated by fluctuations. If costs or benefits fluctuate, then one would observe the fact that typical, most probable, behavior is not the same as the average. This is also reflected in the nature of the statistical distribution of the data. Rather than obtaining the familiar bell-shaped curve corresponding to a normal distribution, one would observe an asymmetric distribution with a long tail. We emphasize that the detailed form of the critical fraction used in Equation (2) is not important for the existence of this effect. If the utility function has the general form given by Equation (1), then fluctuations in benefits will lead to intermittent bursts in cooperation and defection.

For the purpose of verifying these predictions, computer simulations have the advantage over social experiments that the variables and parameters can be precisely specified. Although computer simulations are no substitute for real social dynamics, their relative simplicity and clear outcomes can be used as a sign that this phenomenon can appear in real social settings, in particular those situations where the average behavior of quantities reflecting collective action seems at odds with what typical member of a group are doing.

An interesting application of these results is to provide a possible explanation for the so-called paradox of group size in political movements (Oliver and Marwell 1988). It has been documented that in certain cases (Marwell 1970) the larger the group the more likely it is to engage in collective action, a result that seems at odds with the common resolution of social dilemmas. This apparent paradox was explained by Oliver and Marwell (1988) by invoking the simple statistical fact that if what is needed to trigger a political movement is a minority of highly motivated individuals, a large group will be more likely to have such individuals than a smaller one (Schmidt 1977).

This paper presents a dynamical alternative to that view. If large temporal variations in effort exist in a social group, rare bursts of extreme cooperation could lead to an average utility that increases in time, so that individuals confronted with a social dilemma might construe a level of cooperation which is at odds with what typically everybody is doing. A test of this hypothesis could be performed by measuring the distribution of levels of effort in large political groups. Whereas the theory of Oliver and Marwell would predict that it is normally distributed around some mean value, our theory would lead to an asymmetric, log-normal type, distribution. If this were the case, it would provide a theoretical underpinng to the folk observation that in voluntary organizations ten percent of the people do fifty percent of the work.

On a normative vein, these results suggest that in order to secure cooperation within a group or organization, the requirements of long, diverse outlooks and small groups might not be enough. Since fluctuations in the effort of individuals are unavoidable, the choice of individuals with small variance in their outputs will be more successful at generating cooperative behavior than having a group of the same size made up of individuals with large temporal variations in effort. If that were not possible, the solution would then have to rely on either making controls and monitoring more efficient, or to organize the production of the common good in such a way that the overall utility due to cooperation increases faster than linear with the number of individuals in the organization. This can be the case when cooperation is used in the solution of complex problems (Clearwater 1991, Huberman 1990).

ACKNOWLEDGMENTS

This work profited from the computer exeperiments of N. Glance and from useful discussions with Jon Bendor and Mette Huberman.

REFERENCES

Arnold, Ludwig, 1992, *Stochastic Differential Equations: Theory and Applications*, Krieger Publications.

Bendor, Jonathan and Dilip Mookherjee, 1987, 'Institutional structure and the logic of ongoing collective action', *American Political Science Review* 81(1), 129–154.

Clearwater, Scott, Bernardo A. Huberman, and Tad Hogg, 1991, 'Cooperative solution of constraint satisfaction problems', *Science* 254, 1181–1183.

Glance, Natalie and Bernardo A. Huberman, 1994, 'The dynamics of social dilemmas', *Scientific American*, March, 76–81.

Glance, Natalie and Bernardo A. Huberman, 1993a, 'Organizational fluidity and sustainable cooperation', in K. Carley and M. Prietula (Eds), *Computational Organization Theory*, Lawrence Erlbaum Associates, pp. 217–240.

Glance, Natalie and Bernardo A. Huberman, 1993b, 'The outbreak of cooperation', *Journal of Mathematical Sociology* 17(4), 281–302.

Granovetter, Mark, 1978, 'Threshold models of collective behavior', *American Journal of Sociology* 83(6), 1420–1443.

Hardin, Garret, 1968, 'The tragedy of the commons', *Science* 162, 1243–1248.

Hardin, Russell, 1982, *Collective Action*, Johns Hopkins University Press.

Huberman, Bernardo A., 1990, 'The performance of cooperative processes', *Physica D* 42, 38–47.

Huberman, Bernardo A. and Natalie Glance, 1993, 'Diversity and collective action', in H. Haken and A. Mikhailov (Eds), *Interdisciplinary Approaches to Complex Nonlinear Phenomena*, Springer-Verlag, pp. 44–64.

Huberman, Bernardo A. and Natalie Glance, 1996, 'Fluctuating efforts and sustainable cooperation', in K. Carley and M. Prietula (Eds), *Simulating Organizations: Computational Models of Institutions*, MIT Press, to appear.

Huberman, Bernardo A. and Natalie Glance, 1997, 'Beliefs and cooperation', in P. Danielson (Ed.), *Modelling Rational and Moral Agents*, Oxford University Press, pp. 211–236.

Marwell, Gerald, 1970, 'Comment on Scott and El-Assal', *American Sociological Review* 35, 916.

Oliver, Pamela E. and Gerald Marwell, 1988, 'The paradox of group size in collective action: A theory of the critical mass. II', *American Sociological Review* 53, 1–8.

Olson, Mancur, 1965, *The Logic of Collective Action*, Harvard University Press.

Schelling, Thomas C., 1978, *Micromotives and Macrobehavior*, W.W. Norton and Company.

Schmidt, Steffen, James Scott, Carl Lande, and Laura Gausti, 1977, *Friends, Followers and Factions*, Berkeley: University of California.

Stratonovich, R.L., 1967, *Topics in the Theory of Random Noise*, Gordon and Breach.

Taylor, Michael, 1976, *Anarchy and Cooperation*, John Wiley and Sons.

LEIGH TESFATSION

A Trade Network Game with Endogenous Partner Selection *

ABSTRACT. This paper develops an evolutionary *trade network game* (TNG) that combines evolutionary game play with endogenous partner selection. Successive generations of resource-constrained buyers and sellers choose and refuse trade partners on the basis of continually updated expected payoffs. Trade partner selection takes place in accordance with a modified Gale–Shapley matching mechanism, and trades are implemented using trade strategies evolved via a standardly specified genetic algorithm. The trade partnerships resulting from the matching mechanism are shown to be core stable and Pareto optimal in each successive trade cycle. Nevertheless, computer experiments suggest that these static optimality properties may be inadequate measures of optimality from an evolutionary perspective.

1. INTRODUCTION

Evolutionary game studies typically focus on the optimality properties of strategy configurations when agents are matched randomly or deterministically by some extraneous device. The optimality properties of the matching mechanism per se are generally not considered [11, 14]. In contrast, optimal search studies focus on the optimality properties of preference-based agent matching mechanisms, but generally these studies are set in static contexts [18]. Since actual social interactions are often characterized both by evolutionary dynamics and by preference-based partner selection, studying both aspects together seems a logical and interesting next step to take.

This issue is addressed in Stanley et al. [20]. The standard evolutionary iterated prisoner's dilemma (IPD) is extended to an evolutionary IPD with choice and refusal (IPD/CR) by allowing players to choose and refuse game partners in each iteration on the basis of continually updated expected payoffs.[1]

---

* This paper is based on Tesfatsion [22]. An abbreviated version of this paper is scheduled to appear in the Proceedings Volume of the Fifth Annual Conference on Evolutionary Programming. The author is grateful to D. Fogel, M. Smucker, and N. Vriend for helpful comments.

H. Amman et al. (eds.), Computational Approaches to Economic Problems, 249–269.

The introduction of choice and refusal fundamentally alters the way in which players interact in the IPD and the characteristics that result in high payoff scores. Choice allows players to increase their chances of encountering other cooperative players, and refusal gives players a way to protect themselves from defections without having to defect themselves. The ostracism of defectors occurs endogenously as an increasing number of players individually refuse the defectors' game offers. Nevertheless, choice and refusal also permit opportunistic players to home in quickly on exploitable players and form parasitic relationships.

The computer experiments reported in [20] and in the subsequent studies by Ashlock et al. [1], Smucker et al. [19], and Hauk [8] indicate that the emergence of mutual cooperation in the standard evolutionary IPD is accelerated by the introduction of choice and refusal of partners. The underlying player interaction patterns induced by choice and refusal can be complex and highly path dependent, however, even when expressed play behavior is largely cooperative. Consequently, it has proved difficult to characterize the mapping from parameter configurations to evolutionary outcomes for the IPD/CR.

A potentially useful way to proceed, then, is to focus on more concrete settings which impose problem-specific constraints on agent interactions. In Tesfatsion [22] an evolutionary *trade network game* (TNG) is proposed for studying the interplay between evolutionary dynamics and endogenous preference-based partner selection under alternatively specified market structures.

The player set for the TNG consists of buyer and seller tradebots who choose and refuse trade partners on the basis of continuously updated expected payoffs. Buyers make trade offers to preferred sellers which the sellers either accept or refuse. A trade offer is an invitation to engage in a risky trade modelled as a two-player game. Each buyer and seller initially associates a prior expected payoff with each potential trade partner and adopts a random strategy for use in subsequent trades. The buyers and sellers then enter into a trade cycle loop consisting of successive rounds of partner matching, resource-constrained trading, and updating of expected payoffs. At the end of the trade cycle loop the buyers and sellers enter into an evolutionary step in which trade strategies successful in past trades are retained while trade strategies unsuccessful in past trades are replaced with variants of more successful strategies. A new trade cycle loop then commences.

The modular form of the TNG facilitates experimentation with alternative specifications for trade partner matching, trading, expectation updating, and trade strategy evolution. This paper presents preliminary experimental results obtained for the particular TNG module specifications outlined in Tesfatsion [22] using the C++ trade platform developed in McFadzean and Tesfatsion [16]. As will be clarified below, trade partners are determined in accordance with a *deferred choice and refusal* (DCR) mechanism, a modified Gale–Shapley matching mechanism [6] that retains the static optimality properties of the original Gale–Shapley mechanism. Expected payoffs are updated by means of a simple learning algorithm that yields consistent estimates. A trade is modelled as a prisoner's dilemma game, and trade (IPD) strategies are evolved by means of a standardly specified genetic algorithm.

Two types of markets are considered: buyer-seller markets; and two-sided markets. In the buyer-seller market, each tradebot is both a buyer and a seller in the sense that he can both make and receive trade offers. In the two-sided market, the set of buyers (tradebots who can make offers) is disjoint from the set of sellers (tradebots who can receive offers). For each type of market, attention is focused on the average fitness scores achieved by the tradebots as the market evolves and on the degree to which the tradebots engage in mutually cooperative behavior.

One interesting finding concerns the high transactions costs that agents can suffer under Gale–Shapley type matching mechanisms due to large numbers of refused offers. Specifically, for certain parameter specifications, the negative refusal payoffs accumulated under the DCR mechanism in both buyer-seller and two-sided markets can result in lower average fitness scores for the tradebots relative to other less sophisticated matching mechanisms. Another interesting finding concerns the evolutionary effects of the bias of Gale–Shapley type matching mechanisms in favor of those who actively make offers. Under the DCR mechanism, which inherits this bias, buyers in two-sided markets with relatively large seller acceptance quotas appear to be able to form long-term parasitic relations with sellers that reduce seller fitnesses relative to buyer fitnesses and hinder the emergence of mutually cooperative behavior. Overall, these experimental findings suggest that the conventional optimality properties used to evaluate agent matching mechanisms in static market contexts may be inadequate measures of optimality from an evolutionary perspective.

The TNG module specifications are detailed in Section 2. Static optimality properties of the DCR matching mechanism are developed in Section 3, and the evolutionary implications of the DCR matching mechanism are investigated in Section 4 by means of computer experiments. Concluding comments are given in Section 5.

2. The TNG Model

The set of players for the TNG is the union $V = B \cup S$ of a nonempty subset B of *buyer tradebots* who can submit trade offers and a nonempty subset S of *seller tradebots* who can receive trade offers, where B and S may be disjoint, overlapping, or coincident. For example, the buyers and sellers might represent customers and retail store owners, workers and employers, borrowers and lenders, or auction traders.

Each generation of tradebots participates in a *trade cycle loop* consisting of a fixed number of trade cycles. In each trade cycle, each buyer m can submit up to O_m trade offers to sellers, and each seller n can accept up to A_n trade offers from buyers, where O_m and A_n are strictly positive. One interpretation for the buyer offer quota O_m is that buyer m has a limited amount of resources (credit, labor time, collateral, ...) to trade in exchange for other items, and one interpretation for the seller acceptance quota A_n is that seller n has a limited amount of items (goods, job openings, loans, ...) to provide.

The tradebots determine their submission, acceptance, and refusal of trade offers in each trade cycle using a modifed version of the well-known Gale–Shapley deferred acceptance mechanism [6]. This modified mechanism, hereafter referred to as the *deferred choice and refusal* (DCR) mechanism, is discussed more carefully in Section 3 below. During the DCR matching process, any tradebot that has a trade offer refused is immediately penalized by receipt of a negative *refusal payoff*, R; the tradebot who does the refusing is not penalized. If a tradebot neither submits nor accepts any trade offers during this matching process, he receives a *wallflower payoff*, W.

A trade offer is an offer by a buyer to a seller to participate in a risky trade modelled as a prisoner's dilemma (PD) game. For example, the trade may involve the exchange of a good or service of a certain promised quality in return for a loan or wage contract entailing various payment obligations. A buyer participating in a trade may either cooperate (fulfill his trade obligations) or defect (renege on his trade obligations), and similarly for a seller. The range of possible payoffs is the same for each trade in each trade cycle: namely, L (the sucker payoff) is the lowest possible payoff, received by a cooperative tradebot whose trade partner defects; D is the payoff received by a defecting tradebot whose trade partner also defects; C is the payoff received by a cooperative tradebot whose trade partner also cooperates; and H (the temptation payoff) is the highest possible payoff, received by a defecting tradebot whose trade partner cooperates. More precisely, the payoffs are assumed to satisfy $L < D < 0 < C < H$, with $(L + H)/2 < C$. The payoff matrix for the PD game is depicted in Table 1.

The trade behavior of each tradebot, whether he is a pure buyer in $V - S$, a buyer-seller in $B \cap S$, or a pure seller in $V - B$, is characterized by a finite-memory pure strategy for playing a PD game with an arbitrary partner an indefinite number of times, hereafter referred to as a *trade strategy*. Each tradebot thus has a distinct trading personality even if he engages in both buying and selling activities. No tradebot knows any other tradebot's strategy a priori; he can only learn about it by engaging the other tradebot in repeated trades and observing the payoff history that ensues. Moreover, each tradebot's choice of an action in a current trade with a potential trade partner is determined entirely on the basis of the payoffs obtained in past trades with this same partner.

At the beginning of the initial trade cycle loop, before any actual trades have taken place, each tradebot v associates an exogenously given *prior expected payoff* $U_v^0(k)$ with each potential trade partner k. Throughout each

TABLE 1

Payoff matrix for the prisoner's dilemma game

		Player 2 c	Player 2 d
Player 1	c	(C,C)	(L,H)
Player 1	d	(H,L)	(D,D)

trade cycle, tradebot v then uses a simple variable-gain criterion filter [21] to update his current expected payoffs on the basis of the new payoffs he obtains from interactions with his potential trade partners. In particular, if tradebot v receives a payoff P from an interaction with a potential trade partner k, then v forms an updated expected payoff for k by taking a convex combination of this new payoff P and his previous expected payoff for k, where the inverse of the weight on P is 1 plus tradebot v's current payoff count with k. In this way, tradebot v keeps a running tab on the payoff outcomes of his interactions with k. As explained in Tesfatsion [22, Section 5], this updating procedure guarantees that the expected payoff tradebot v associates with k converges to the true average payoff tradebot v attains from interactions with k as the number of interactions between v and k becomes arbitrarily large.

At the end of a trade cycle loop, the fitness score of each tradebot is calculated as the average of all of the trade, refusal, and wallflower payoffs he received during this loop. The tradebots then enter into a *genetic step* in which the trade strategies used by the *elite* (the fittest tradebots) are retained while the trade strategies used by the remaining tradebots are replaced with variants of more successful trade strategies. A detailed discussion of the finite state machine (FSM) and standardly specified genetic algorithm (GA) used in the genetic step to represent and evolve the tradebots' trade strategies can be found in McFadzean and Tesfatsion [16]. Briefly, the GA is applied to a population of bit strings that encode the trade strategies (FSMs) of the tradebots. The GA employs two-point crossover with bit mutation, and parent strategies are chosen probabilistically in proportion to fitness. The particular FSM and GA parameter settings used in all experiments reported in this paper are detailed in the next section.

TABLE 2

TNG pseudo code

```
int main () {
  tngInit() ;                          // Construct initial tradebots
                                       //    with prior expected payoffs.
  For (G = 0,. . . ,GMAX-1) {          // Enter the generation loop.
    For (I = 0,. . . ,IMAX-1) {        // Enter the trade cycle loop.
      MatchTraders();                  // Determine trade partners,
                                       //    given expected payoffs,
                                       //    and record refusal and
                                       //    wallflower payoffs.
      Trade();                         // Implement trades and
                                       //    record trade payoffs.
      UpdateExp();                     // Update expected payoffs
                                       //    using newly recorded payoffs.
    }
    AssessFitness();                   // Record fitness scores.
    If (G < GMAX-1) {
      EvolveGen();                     // Genetic step: Evolve the
                                       //    current tradebots.
    }
  }
  Return 0 ; }
```

At the end of the genetic step the memories of the tradebots are reset to zero, their associated FSMs are reset to a fixed initial state, and their expected payoffs are reset to the prior expected payoff levels. A new trade cycle loop then commences. Table 2 depicts the overall logical progression of the TNG in pseudo-code.

Before reporting on analytical and simulation findings regarding the optimality properties of the DCR matching mechanism, three special cases of the TNG will be sketched to indicate the range of economic applications it encompasses.

Case 1: A Labor Market Modelled as an Assignment Game with Choice and Refusal

The set B consists of workers and the set S consists of employers, where B and S are disjoint. Each worker m can make work offers to a maximum of O_m employers, or he can choose to be unemployed and receive the known payoff W. Each employer n can hire up to A_n workers, and employers can refuse work offers. Once matched, a worker and employer engage in work site interactions modelled as a PD game.

This TNG special case extends the usual assignment problem [18] by incorporating subsequent strategic game play between matched pairs of agents and by having game play iterated over time. Assignment problems are commonly used by economists to model job-matching in labor markets as well as other economic processes, but the payoff outcome for each matched pair of agents is usually specified a priori.

Case 2: A Labor Market with Endogenously Determined Workers and Employers
The subsets B and S coincide, implying that each tradebot can both make and receive trade offers. Each tradebot v can make up to O_v work offers to tradebots at other work sites and receive up to A_v work offers at his own work site. The degree to which any accepted work offer results in satisfactory outcomes for the participant tradebots is determined by subsequent PD game play. Ex post, four pure types of tradebots can emerge: (1) pure workers, who work at the sites of other tradebots but have no tradebots working for them at their own sites; (2) pure employers, who have tradebots working for them at their own sites but who do not work at the sites of other tradebots; (3) unemployed tradebots, who make at least one work offer to a tradebot at another site but who end up neither working at other sites nor having tradebots working for them at their own sites; and (4) inactive (out of the work force) tradebots, who neither make nor accept any work offers.

Case 3: Intermediation with Choice and Refusal
The buyer subset B and the seller subset S overlap but do not coincide. The pure buyers in $V - S$ are the depositors (lenders), the buyer-sellers in $B \cap S$ are the intermediaries (banks), and the pure sellers in $V - B$ are the capital investors (borrowers). The depositors offer funds to the intermediaries in return for deposit accounts, and the intermediaries offer loan contracts to the capital investors in return for a share of earnings. The degree to which accepted offers are satisfactorily fulfilled is determined by subsequent PD game play.

3. Determination of TNG Trade Partners

The original Gale–Shapley matching mechanism [6] was designed for two-sided markets in which one subset of agents makes offers to a second disjoint subset of agents, with all offer quotas equal to 1. As detailed in Roth and Sotomayor [18], this mechanism continues to be the subject of numerous theoretical studies, and it has found practical application as well – most notably to the labor market for medical interns and residents.

The DCR mechanism extends the original Gale–Shapley mechanism to the more general TNG context in which the subsets of buyers (makers of offers) and sellers (receivers of offers) can be coincident, overlapping, or disjoint, with arbitrarily specified offer and acceptance quotas. The TNG tradebots use the DCR mechanism to determine their submission, acceptance, and refusal of trade offers conditional on their current preference rankings over potential trade partners. This section first provides a more careful description of the DCR mechanism. It is then shown that the DCR mechanism possesses the usual static optimality properties associated with Gale–Shapley type matching mechanisms: namely, core stability, and Pareto optimality for the subset of agents who actively make offers. Although trades in the TNG are currently modelled as prisoner's dilemma games, neither the definition of the DCR mechanism nor its static optimality properties depend on this specification.

For any tradebot v in V, let τ_v denote tradebot v's *minimum tolerance level*, and let $U_v(k)$ denote the expected payoff that tradebot v currently associates with a potential trade partner k. Tradebot k will be called *tolerable* for tradebot v if and only if $U_v(k) \geq \tau_v$. Also, given any two potential trade partners k' and k'', tradebot v will be said to *strictly prefer* to trade with k' rather than with k'' if $U_v(k') > U_v(k'')$ and to *equally prefer* trades with k' and k'' if $U_v(k') = U_v(k'')$.

The DCR Mechanism In Any Trade Cycle T:

Step 1: Each buyer m submits trade offers to a maximum of O_m most preferred sellers that he finds tolerable, with at most one trade offer going to any one seller. Each seller n then selects up to A_n most preferred trade offers received from tolerable buyers and places these offers on a waiting list. Seller n refuses all other trade offers received in Step 1. Buyers and sellers use random selection to break ties among equally-preferred trades.

Step K $(K \geq 2)$: If r sellers refused trade offers from buyer m in Step $K-1$, then buyer m submits up to r replacement trade offers in Step K to the most preferred and tolerable sellers who have not refused a trade offer from him during Steps $1, \ldots, K-1$. Each seller n then selects up to A_n most preferred and tolerable trade offers from among both the new trade offers he receives in Step K and the trade offers already on his waiting list from Step $K-1$, and he refuses the rest. These selected trade offers constitute seller n's waiting list for Step K. Buyers and sellers use random selection to break ties among tolerable equally-preferred trades.

Final Step K^**:* Step K^* is the final step if and only if no new trade offers are submitted in Step $K^* + 1$. If Step K^* is the final step, each seller accepts all trade offers on his Step K^* waiting list.

Under the DCR mechanism, two tradebots v and k can engage in zero, one, or two trades with each other in each trade cycle. Zero trades occur when neither tradebot submits an accepted trade offer to the other; one trade occurs when only one of the tradebots submits an accepted trade offer to the other; and two trades occur when each tradebot submits an accepted trade offer to the other. Note that this determination of trade partners requires the tradebots to pass messages back and forth to each other at event-driven times, a feature not present in standard economic models. This requirement is easily implemented by an object-oriented programming language such as C++.

Step K^* is the last step of the DCR mechanism in trade cycle T if and only if each buyer m either has had no trade offer refused in Step K^*, and hence has no desire to submit a new trade offer in Step $K^* + 1$, or is unable to submit a new trade offer in Step $K^* + 1$ because each seller that buyer m finds tolerable has already received a trade offer from him sometime during Steps $1, \ldots, K^*$. The first proposition provides an upper bound for K^*. The proofs for this proposition, and for all subsequent propositions, are detailed in Tesfatsion [22, Section 4].

PROPOSITION 3.1. *Let M denote the number of buyers in the buyer set B, and let N denote the number of sellers in the seller set S. In each trade cycle T, the DCR mechanism always ends at some Step K^* occurring on or before Step MN.*

DEFINITION 3.1. A buyer m and seller n will be said to form a *match* in trade cycle T, denoted by (m, n), if buyer m is tolerable for seller n, seller n is tolerable for buyer m, and buyer m and seller n engage in a trade during trade cycle T. A *matching outcome for trade cycle T* is then any listing of distinct matches (m, n) for trade cycle T such that each buyer m appears at most O_m times in the first position and each seller n appears at most A_n times in the second position. By construction, then, a matching outcome for trade cycle T is a list of trades that could feasibly take place during this cycle.

Note that the trades determined in any trade cycle T by the DCR mechanism always constitute a matching outcome for trade cycle T in the sense of Definition 3.1.

DEFINITION 3.2. (cf. Gale and Shapley [6, p. 10]) A matching outcome G for trade cycle T will be called *unstable* if the following conditions hold for some buyer m and seller n:

(a) m and n are *not* matched under G;

(b) m would prefer to be matched with n, in the sense that either there exists a match (m, n') under G such that $U_m(n) > U_m(n')$, or m is matched with fewer than O_m sellers under G and $U_m(n) \geq \tau_m$.

(c) n would prefer to be matched with m, in the sense that either there exists a match (m', n) under G such that $U_n(m) > U_n(m')$, or n is matched with fewer than A_n buyers under G and $U_n(m) \geq \tau_n$.

A matching outcome G for trade cycle T will be called *(pairwise) stable* if no such buyer m and seller n exist.

Intuitively, given conditions (a), (b), and (c), the buyer m and seller n could block the implementation of the matching outcome G by agreeing to play each other instead. Roth and Sotomayor [18] are careful to differentiate between group stable and pairwise stable matching outcomes, whereby the former they mean a matching outcome that is not blocked by *any* coalition of agents. In the TNG, each trader is assumed to have a preference ranking only over pairwise matches with other traders, and this preference ranking is unaffected by who else might be trading with these potential trade partners. Consequently, a matching outcome in the TNG is group stable if and only if it is also pairwise stable. Without risk of confusion, then, the qualifier "pairwise" will be omitted in all subsequent references to stable matching outcomes.

PROPOSITION 3.2. *Any matching outcome generated via the DCR mechanism is stable.*

The final proposition shows that the matching outcome generated by the DCR mechanism in each trade cycle is a best possible matching outcome from the viewpoint of the buyers, i.e., the tradebots who actively make offers, as long as buyers and sellers have strict preferences over their potential trade partners. The proof is a generalization of the optimality proof provided in Gale and Shapley [6, Thm. 2, p. 14] for their college admissions problem with B disjoint from S and offer quotas $O_m = 1$ for all agents m in B; see also Roth and Sotomayor [18, Chapter 5].

DEFINITION 3.3. A matching outcome G will be called *B-optimal* if: (a) G is a stable matching outcome; and (b) each buyer matched under G is at least as well off under G as under any other stable matching outcome.

PROPOSITION 3.3. *Suppose each buyer (seller) in some trade cycle T has a strict preference ranking over the sellers (buyers) he finds tolerable. Then the DCR mechanism yields the unique B-optimal matching outcome for trade cycle T.*

4. TNG Computer Experiments

In the previous section it is shown that the trade partnerships generated via the DCR mechanism exhibit the usual static optimality properties associated with

Gale–Shapley type matching mechanisms. Still to be determined, however, is the extent to which the DCR mechanism induces a high average payoff for the tradebots over evolutionary time. In particular, to what extent does the DCR mechanism encourage the emergence and persistence of mutually cooperative behavior?

Four types of computer experiments are discussed in the present section: (a) buyer-seller market experiments with sellers unconstrained by acceptance quotas; (b) buyer-seller market experiments with seller acceptance quotas set to 1; (c) two-sided market experiments with sellers unconstrained by acceptance quotas; and (d) two-sided market experiments with seller acceptance quotas set to 1. All experimental findings reported below were obtained using *TNG*, a C++ trade platform developed by McFadzean and Tesfatsion [16] which in turn is supported by the C++ abstract base classes developed by McFadzean [15] for a general artificial life platform, *SimBioSys*. These findings are preliminary in the sense that only average fitness scores are considered. A more thorough understanding of these findings will require delving more deeply into the underlying trade networks and the trade strategies that support these trade networks.

For each type of experiment, multiple runs from different initial random seeds are reported. The following features are set commonly across all of these experimental runs. The wallflower payoff W is set at 0, the refusal payoff R is set at -0.6, the PD trade payoffs are set at $L = -1.6$, $D = -0.6$, $C = 1.4$, and $H = 3.4$, and each tradebot's minimum tolerance level is set at $\tau = 0$. Each tradebot assigns the same prior expected payoff, $U^0 = C$, to each other tradebot, implying that he is initially indifferent concerning which trade partners he interacts with; and each tradebot assigns a negative prior expected payoff to himself, thus ensuring that he never trades with himself. Each buyer tradebot has an offer quota of 1, meaning that he can have at most one trade offer outstanding to sellers at any given time. The total number of tradebots is set at 24, and the 16 most fit tradebots in each generation are taken to be the elite. The number of trade cycles in each trade cycle loop is set at 150, and the number of generations is set at 50.

Each trade strategy is represented by a 16-state FSM with a fixed initial state and with memory 1. At the beginning of the first trade cycle loop, a bit string coding for each FSM is randomly generated. At the end of each trade cycle loop, the current population of trade strategies (FSMs coded as bit strings) is evolved by means of a genetic algorithm employing two-point crossover and bit mutation. The probability of crossover is set at 1.0 and the probability of a bit mutation is set at 0.005.

4.1. *Buyer-Seller Markets*

Each tradebot in these experiments was both a buyer and a seller, implying that he could both make and receive trade offers.

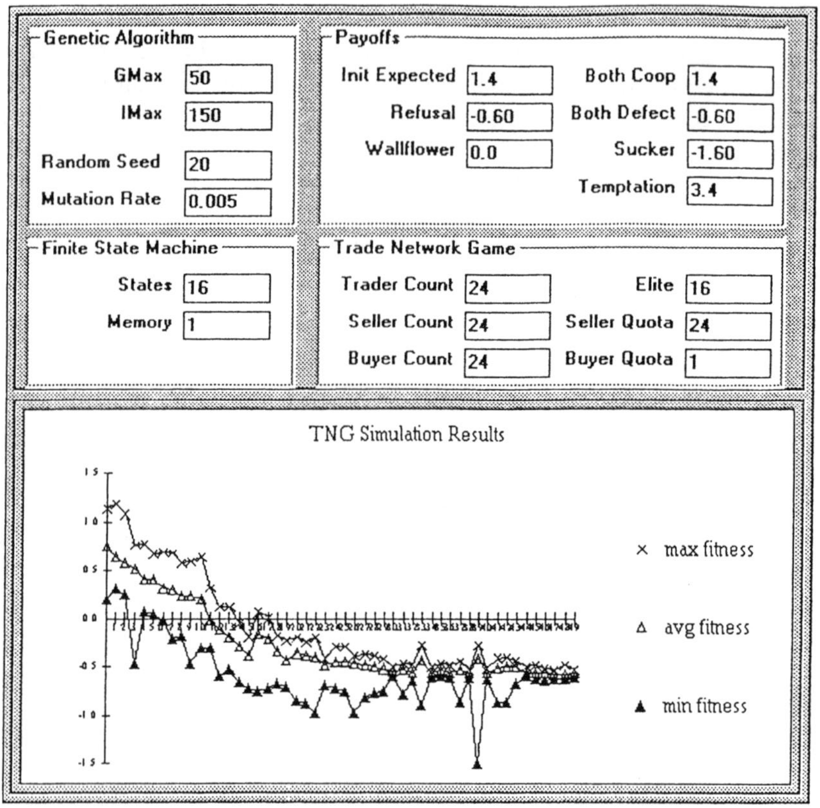

Fig. 1. Buyer-seller average fitness with random matching and seller quotas equal to 24.

In the first batch of buyer-seller experiments, the acceptance quota of each tradebot was set at 24, the total number of tradebots. Since offer quotas in these experiments were set at 1, the tradebots were then effectively unconstrained with regard to the number of trade offers they could have on their waiting lists at any given time.

As a benchmark, experiments were first run with random partner matching in place of the DCR matching mechanism. Random partner matching was effected by preventing the updating of the prior expected payoff $U^0 = C$ that each tradebot initially assigned to each potential trade partner, so that all tradebots remained indifferent concerning their potential trade partners and matching was accomplished by the default mechanism of a random draw. Although occasionally the average fitness score achieved by the tradebots under random matching rose to the mutual cooperation level, 1.4, a more typical outcome was a steady decline to the mutual defection level, -0.6 (see Figure 1).[2] The size of the refusal payoff is irrelevant for this finding,

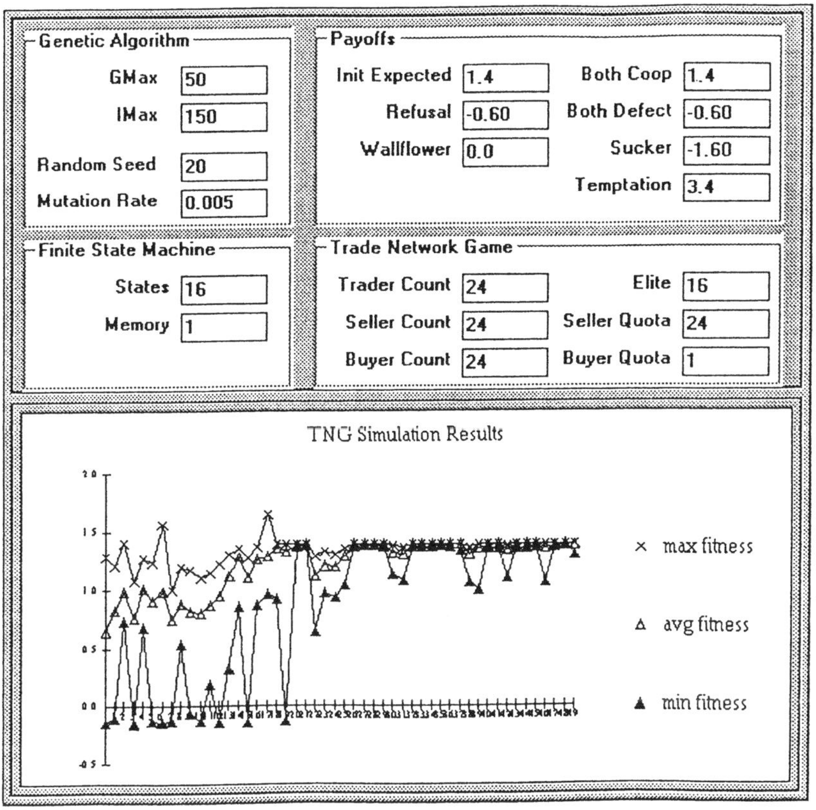

Fig. 2. Buyer-seller average fitness with DCR matching and seller quotas equal to 24.

since refusals never occur in TNG experiments with random matching and nonbinding acceptance quotas.

When the DCR matching mechanism was then restored, the average fitness score achieved by the tradebots typically evolved to the mutual cooperation level 1.4 (see Figure 2). These TNG experiments reinforce the previous IPD/CR findings of Stanley et al. [20] and Ashlock et al. [1] that a preference-based matching mechanism tends to accelerate the emergence of mutual cooperation in the IPD when each agent is permitted both to make and to refuse game offers, is unconstrained with regard to the number of received offers he can accept, and is permitted to have at most one offer outstanding at any given time.

In the second batch of buyer-seller experiments, the acceptance quotas were reduced from 24 to 1. Each tradebot could thus retain at most one trade offer on his waiting list at any one time; all other received trade offers had to be refused. Under random partner matching, the typical outcome was again the emergence of an average fitness score close to the mutual defection payoff level, −0.6. This same outcome obtained even when refusal payoffs were omitted from fitness scores, implying that refusal payoffs resulting from limited waiting lists were not a determining factor.

When the DCR matching mechanism was restored, however, the average fitness score typically leveled out at about 1.25 instead of evolving to the mutual cooperation payoff level 1.4, the outcome for the first batch of buyer-seller experiments. The explanation for this difference appears to lie in the changed nature of the refusal payoffs.

In the first batch of buyer-seller experiments, the acceptance quota (24) was large relative to the offer quota (1). In these circumstances, tradebots are generally refused by other tradebots only if the latter find them to be intolerable because of past defections. Negative refusal payoffs received in response to defections should rightly count against the fitness of the trade strategies generating the defections, for this induces changes in these strategies in the genetic step that tend to lead to higher future fitness scores. In the second batch of buyer-seller experiments, however, the acceptance quota (1) was much smaller in relation to the offer quota (1), implying that many more received trade offers had to be refused regardless of their desirability. In these circumstances, tradebots tend to accumulate large numbers of negative refusal payoffs purely as a consequence of the relatively small acceptance quota and the nature of the DCR mechanism, regardless of their trade strategies. Since neither the quotas nor the DCR mechanism are evolved in the current implementation of the TNG, penalizing the tradebots for these quota and DCR effects by including refusal payoffs in their individual fitness scores tends to lower their current average fitness score without inducing a higher average fitness score in the future.

As expected, the average fitness scores attained by the tradebots in the second batch of buyer-seller experiments markedly improved when refusal payoffs were removed from the calculation of the tradebots' individual fitness scores (see Figure 3). Improvement continued to occur when, in addition, the refusal payoffs were reduced in magnitude from −0.60 to −0.30; but a further reduction in magnitude to −0.06 and then to 0 resulted in increasingly volatile maximum and minimum average fitness scores with no discernible improvement in average fitness scores.

The probable cause of this increased volatility is that tradebots receiving refusals during initial trade cycles have little incentive to direct their offers elsewhere in subsequent trade cycles when the magnitude of the negative refusal payoff is small. A negative refusal payoff guarantees that the continually updated expected payoff that a tradebot associates with another tradebot who repeatedly refuses him eventually falls below 0, the minimum tolerance level, at which point he ceases making offers to this other tradebot. Nevertheless, this learning process is slow when the magnitude of the negative refusal

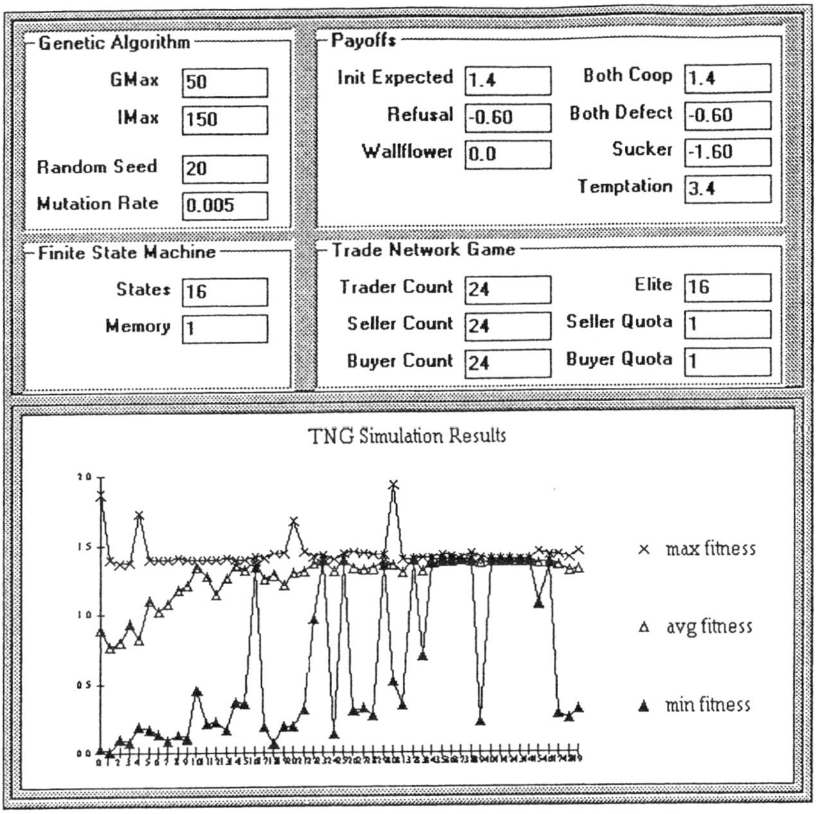

Fig. 3. Buyer-seller average fitness with DCR matching, seller quotas equal to 1, and refusal payoffs omitted from fitness scores.

payoff is small, and it is non-existent when the refusal payoff is simply set to 0.

4.2. *Two-Sided Markets*

In each two-sided market experiment, the 24 tradebots were evenly divided into 12 pure buyers (makers of trade offers) and 12 pure sellers (receivers of trade offers).

In the first batch of experiments, the acceptance quota of each seller was set to 12. Since the offer quota of each buyer was set to 1 in all of these experiments, sellers were thus effectively unconstrained regarding the number of trade offers they could have on their waiting lists at any one time. Experiments were first run with random partner matching in place of the DCR matching mechanism to obtain a benchmark for comparison. Interestingly, in contrast to buyer-seller experiments with nonbinding acceptance quotas and random

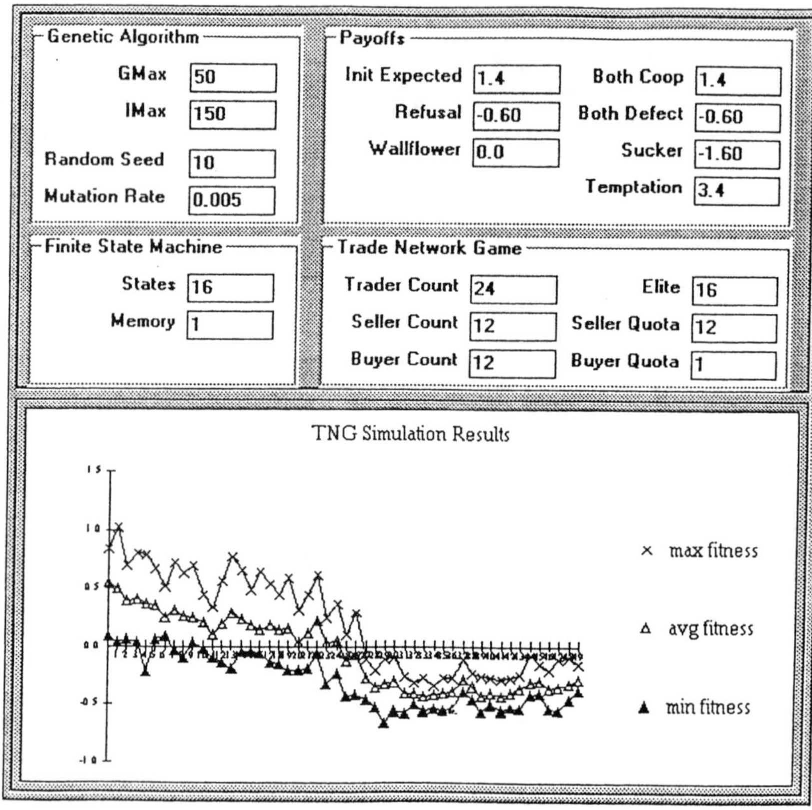

Fig. 4. Two-sided market average fitness with random matching and seller quotas equal to 12.

matching, the average fitness score attained by the tradebots tended to fall to a level between −0.4 and the wallflower payoff 0 rather than dropping all the way down to the mutual defection payoff level −0.6 (compare Figure 4 with Figure 1).

When the DCR matching mechanism was restored, the average fitness score of the tradebots typically evolved to about 1.2, a payoff level markedly below the mutual cooperation level 1.4 obtained in buyer-seller experiments with nonbinding acceptance quotas and DCR matching. Moreover, the maximum fitness score, the average fitness score, and the minimum fitness score attained by the successive tradebot generations persistently deviated from one another (compare Figure 5 with Figure 2).

As seen in Proposition 3.3, the DCR mechanism is only guaranteed to be Pareto optimal for buyers, that is, for the active makers of trade offers. The effects of this bias on average fitness scores is hidden in buyer-seller markets, where each tradebot is both a buyer and a seller. However, for two-sided

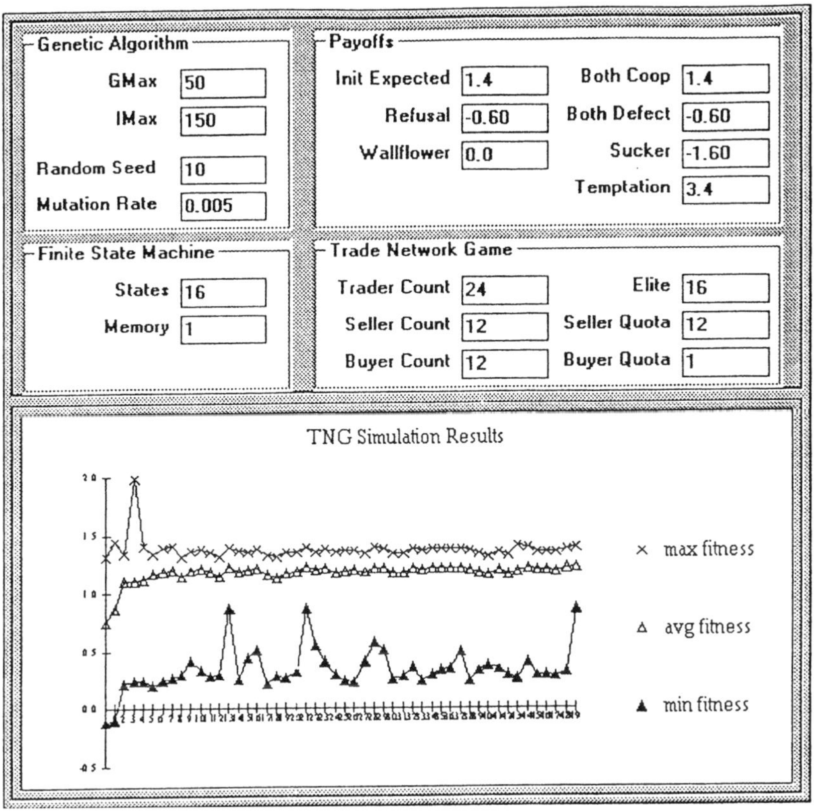

Fig. 5. Two-sided market average fitness with DCR matching and seller quotas equal to 12.

markets with buyer offer quotas set equal to 1 and with nonbinding seller acceptance quotas, the DCR mechanism appears to result in a "separating equilibrium" in which the buyers are generally achieving high fitness scores and the sellers are generally achieving low fitness scores. In particular, the extreme pickiness of buyers combined with the acceptance by sellers of all tolerable received trade offers appears to allow buyers to form long-run parasitic relations with sellers, i.e., relations characterized by successful defections within the limits permitted by the sellers' 0 minimum tolerance levels.

In the second batch of two-sided market experiments, the seller acceptance quotas were decreased from 12 to 1. Thus, instead of accepting all tolerable received trade offers, the sellers now accepted at most one received trade offer per trade cycle.

When benchmark experiments were first run with random partner matching in place of the DCR mechanism, the typical outcome was the emergence

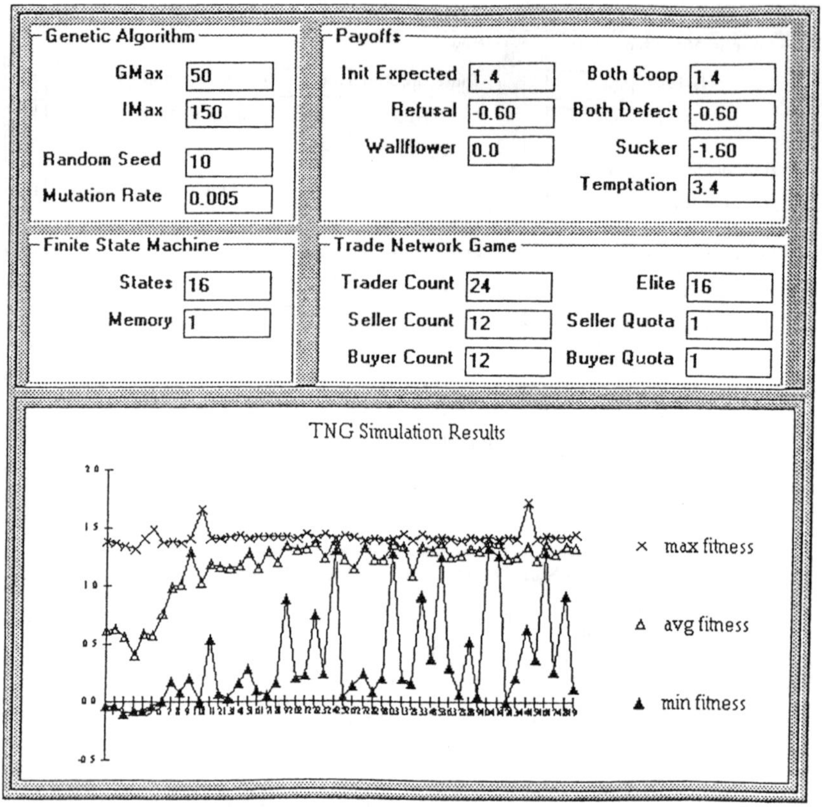

Fig. 6. Two-sided market average fitness with DCR matching, seller quotas equal to 1, and refusal payoff omitted from fitness scores.

of an average attained fitness score close to the mutual defection payoff, −0.6. This result obtained whether or not refusal payoffs were counted in the calculation of individual fitness scores. When the DCR matching mechanism was then restored, with refusal payoffs counted in the calculation of individual fitness scores, the accumulation of refusal payoffs tended to result in an average attained fitness score that was markedly below the mutual cooperation payoff level. When refusal payoffs were then omitted from the calculation of individual fitness scores, the average attained fitness score tended to evolve to the mutual cooperation level and to be close to the maximum attained fitness scores (see Figure 6).

Given the structuring of the two-sided market experiments currently under discussion, with equal numbers of buyers and sellers, common acceptance and offer quotas, and tradebots who are initially indifferent among their potential trade partners, the buyer offer quota roughly predicts the number of trade offers that each seller will receive in the initial few trade cycles.

The larger this number is, the more chance there is that mutually cooperative matches between buyers and sellers will be quickly discovered. On the other hand, if the seller acceptance quota is small relative to the buyer offer quota, then many buyers will accumulate negative refusal payoffs unrelated to the nature of their trade strategies; and if the seller acceptance quota is large relative to the buyer offer quota, opportunistic buyers have a greater chance to seek out and exploit sellers within the limits allowed by their minimum tolerance levels. Either circumstance could slow or even prevent the sustained emergence of mutually cooperative behavior.

It might therefore be conjectured that mutually cooperative behavior will best be induced in the current experimental setting when the seller acceptance quota and the buyer offer quota are equal and sufficiently large. Indeed, this turns out to be the case. In various two-sided market experiments with 12 pure buyers, 12 pure sellers, and equal seller and buyer quotas ranging from 3 to 12, the average fitness score attained by the tradebots tended to evolve to the mutual cooperation payoff level and to be close to the maximum attained fitness score even when refusal payoffs were included in the calculation of individual fitness scores.

5. Concluding Remarks

As seen in Section 3, the DCR mechanism inherits the usual static optimality properties associated with Gale–Shapley type matching mechanisms: namely, core stability, and Pareto optimality for the subset of agents who actively make offers. However, the TNG context also permits an examination of the DCR mechanism's optimality properties over evolutionary time; and the computer experiments reported in Section 4 suggest that the DCR mechanism has at least two potential problems from this evolutionary perspective.

First, if seller acceptance quotas are small relative to buyer offer quotas, the DCR mechanism tends to impose heavy transactions costs on buyers in the form of accumulated negative refusal payoffs that are unrelated to the social desirability of their trade strategies. Second, if seller acceptance quotas are large relative to buyer offer quotas, the inherent bias of the DCR mechanism in favor of buyers appears to allow buyers in two-sided markets to parasitize sellers, resulting in an average population fitness score that remains markedly below the mutually cooperative payoff level.

Systematic experimentation is needed to determine the true extent and seriousness of these problems. For example, the exogenously specified offer and acceptance quotas should more realistically be allowed to change over time to reflect both changing strategic considerations and changing budget and production relations. Also, the trade strategies for pure buyers and for pure sellers should be separately evolved since these tradebots face intrinsically asymmetric choice problems. These modifications may alleviate some of the difficulties with the DCR mechanism that arose in the Section 4 computer experiments with exogenously given quotas and pooled trade strategy evolution.

Finally, the mechanism by which trade partners are determined should itself be allowed to evolve over time along with the quotas and trade strategies. It will be interesting to see how Gale–Shapley type matching mechanisms fare in these less structured evolutionary contexts.

NOTES

1. Other game theory studies focusing on the endogenous determination of player interaction patterns, e.g., by permitting avoidance of unwanted interactions, endogenously determined probabilities of interaction, or evolution of interaction lengths, include Fogel [5], Guriev and Shakhova [7], Hirshleifer and Rasmusen [9], Kitcher [12], Mailath et al. [13], and Orbell and Dawes [17]. There is also a growing body of work by economists on multi-agent systems with endogenous interactions. See, for example, Brock and Durlauf [2], De Vany [3], Durlauf [4], Ionnides [10], and Vriend [23].
2. As previously noted, the initial population of strategies for each TNG experiment was randomly generated and each run consisted of only 50 generations with interactions between any two players limited to at most 150 separate encounters per generation. Thus, this evolution of mutual defection is not in conflict with the evolution of mutual cooperation observed for the IPD with random or round-robin matching by previous researchers when the initial strategy population was sufficiently seeded with cooperatively inclined strategies such as Tit-for-Tat or when much longer player interaction lengths were permitted.

REFERENCES

1. Ashlock, D., M.D. Smucker, E.A. Stanley, and L. Tesfatsion, 1996, 'Preferential partner selection in an evolutionary study of prisoner's dilemma', *BioSystems* 37, 99–125.
2. Brock, W.A. and S.N. Durlauf, 1995, 'Discrete choice with social interactions', Working Paper, Department of Economics, University of Wisconsin-Madison.
3. De Vany, A., 1996, 'The emergence and evolution of self-organized coalitions', in M. Gilli (Ed.), *Computational Methods in Economics and Finance*, Boston, MA: Kluwer Academic Publishers, pp. 22–50.
4. Durlauf, S.N., 1996, 'Neighborhood feedbacks, endogenous stratification, and income inequality', in W.A. Barnett, G. Gandolfo, and C. Hillinger (Eds), *Disequilibrium Dynamics: Theory and Applications*, Cambridge University Press, to appear.
5. Fogel, D.B., 1995, 'On the relationship between the duration of an encounter and the evolution of cooperation in the iterated prisoner's dilemma', *Evolutionary Computation* 3, 349–363.
6. Gale, D. and L. Shapley, 1962, 'College admissions and the stability of marriage', *American Mathematical Monthly* 69, 9–15.
7. Guriev, G. and M. Shakhova, 1995, 'Self-organization of trade networks in an economy with imperfect infrastructure', in *Proceedings of the International Workshop on Agents, Cooperation, and Communication*, San Marco di Castellabate, Italy.
8. Hauk, E., 1995, 'Leaving the prison: A discussion of the iterated prisoner's dilemma under preferential partner selection', Working Paper, European University Institute, Florence.

9. Hirshleifer, D. and E. Rasmusen, 1989, ‘Cooperation in a repeated prisoner’s dilemma with ostracism’, *Journal of Economic Behavior and Organization* 12, 87–106.
10. Ionnides, Y.M., 1995, ‘Evolution of trading structures’, Working Paper, Department of Economics, Tufts University, Boston.
11. Kirman, A., 1994, ‘Economies with interacting agents’, Working Paper No. 94-05-030, Santa Fe Institute, NM.
12. Kitcher, P., 1992, ‘Evolution of altruism in repeated optional games’, Working Paper, Department of Philosophy, UC San Diego.
13. Mailath, G., L. Samuelson, and A. Shaked, 1994, Evolution and endogenous interactions, SSRI Working Paper 9426, University of Wisconsin-Madison.
14. Lindgren, K. and M.G. Nordahl, 1994, ‘Cooperation and community structure in artificial ecosystems’, *Artificial Life* 1, 15–37.
15. McFadzean, D., 1995, ‘SimBioSys: A class framework for evolutionary simulations’, Master’s Thesis, Department of Computer Science, University of Calgary, Alberta, Canada.
16. McFadzean, D. and L. Tesfatsion, L., 1996, ‘A C++ platform for the evolution of trade networks’, *Computational Economics*, Special Issue on Programming Languages, to appear.
17. Orbell, J.M. and R.M. Dawes, 1993, ‘Social welfare, cooperators advantage, and the option of not playing the game’, *American Sociological Review* 58, 787–800.
18. Roth, A. and M.A.O. Sotomayor, 1990, *Two-Sided Matching: A Study in Game-Theoretic Modeling and Analysis*, Cambridge: Cambridge University Press.
19. Smucker, M.D., E.A. Stanley, and D. Ashlock, 1994, ‘Analyzing social network structures in the iterated prisoner’s dilemma with choice and refusal’, Department of Computer Sciences Technical Report CS-TR-94-1259, University of Wisconsin-Madison.
20. Stanley, E.A., D. Ashlock, and L. Tesfatsion, 1994, ‘Iterated prisoner’s dilemma with choice and refusal of partners’, in C. Langton (Ed.), *Artificial Life III*, Proceedings Volume 17, Santa Fe Institute Studies in the Sciences of Complexity, Reading, MA: Addison Wesley, pp. 131–175.
21. Tesfatsion, T., 1979, ‘Direct updating of intertemporal criterion functions for a class of adaptive control problems’, *IEEE Transactions on Systems, Man, and Cybernetics* SMC-9, 143–151.
22. Tesfatsion, L., 1995, ‘A trade network game with endogenous partner selection’, Economic Report No. 36, Iowa State University, Ames.
23. Vriend, N., 1995, ‘Self-organization of markets: An example of a computational approach’, *Computational Economics* 8, 205–231.

FRANCESCO LUNA

Learning in a Computable Setting. Applications of Gold's Inductive Inference Model *

ABSTRACT. The *Theory of Recursive Functions* is here employed for a rigorous formalization of the learning process. We adopt the model proposed by Gold (1967) in the context of natural language acquisition. Among the merits of this literature is that of providing a fairly articulated theoretical grammar to tackle a complex phenomenon such as learning.
The question we ask is whether a boundedly rational agent can *learn* how to form rational expectations. Our stylized learner is described as a Turing Machine in the attempt to coherently incorporate in the analysis the notion of procedural rationality. The results we present cast some serious doubts on the relevance of the Rational Expectations Hypothesis even as the reference point for an *as if* assumption.
Concentrating our attention on a "two step learning procedure" suggested by Spear (1989), on the one hand we show how hysteresis can greatly reduce the positive learning results obtained so far in the literature; on the other hand, we suggest that institutions may play an important role in the learning process thanks to the pre-processing of information they perform, the uncertainty reduction they foster, and the collective memory resources they make available.
As a by-product we also present a version of *strong nativism* in line with the concept introduced by Chomsky (1981). In particular, imposing some realistic features on the learner and assuming that the learning process converges, we obtain – following Osherson et al. (1989) – that the cardinality of the class of regimes that can be successfully learned is finite. In other words, the spectrum of economic organizations going from perfect decentralization to absolute central planification should contain only a finite number of intermediate shades.

1. Introduction

The importance of learning in a dynamical economic system is obvious. How to model the learning process is, however, not so evident. We have chosen to

* A previous version of this paper appeared as OFCE Document de travail No. 94-05. We would like to thank Professors Kumaraswamy Velupillai and Axel Leijonhufvud for their precious comments and encouragement. Any remaining errors are, as usual, the author's. A *Human Capital and Mobility* Grant is gratefully acknowledged.

H. Amman et al. (eds.), Computational Approaches to Economic Problems, 271–288.

refer to the *theory of recursive functions* as the source for a rigorous formalization. In line with a famous metaphor like Patinkin's "utility computer" and Lucas characterization of the economic agent as a collection of procedures, we will concentrate on effective learning procedures. In other words, our stylized learner will be exhaustively described by a Turing Machine (TM).

Neuropsychologists and cognitive scientists often adopt this framework in their analysis of first language acquisition by children.[1] Inside economic theory, this choice can be justified from a bounded rationality point of view since the emphasis devoted to algorithms and computable functions is essential to a coherent appraisal of procedural rationality.

Spear (1989) asks whether it is possible for a boundedly rational agent to get to know his/her environment so well as to form perfectly rational expectations. The proposed characterisation of bounded rationality is precisely the one suggested by computability theory and the learning model adopted that of inductive inference as given by Gold (1965, 1967). Spear's work has not been followed by other significant efforts in the same direction, even though the theory of recursive functions has proven an important tool of analysis for Microeconomics with Rustem and Velupillai (1990) and Lilly (1993) on the computability of preference orderings.

The present note is intended as a reconsideration of Spear's seminal paper with some amendments and generalisations. In particular, concentrating our attention on the "two step learning procedure" presented in the first part of that article, on the one hand, we show how hysteresis can greatly reduce the positive learning results obtained by Spear; on the other hand, we suggest that institutions may play an important role in making information "user friendly" hence in facilitating the learning process.

Section 2 explicitly presents Gold's model with some more recent results obtained by Osherson et al. (1986), Smith (1982), Daley (1983) and others. The purpose of this, perhaps tedious, part is that of describing rather precisely the reference framework so that the conclusions reached in the rest of this study can be put into a correct perspective. Spear's OLG model with rational expectations is given sketchily in Section 3. We refer to the original article for further details on the particular structure. In Section 4, we employ the inductive inference model in the context of the OLG framework and we point at different economic scenarios that are suitable for its application. Section 5 is devoted to institutions. We present examples and propose some analogies diverting a little from both OLG and Gold's model. We draw our conclusions in the final section.

2. An Inductive Inference Model

Gold (1967) is a reference point for most of the literature on computable models of inductive inference. The problem tackled in that paper is language acquisition, and the results therein are a generalization of those obtained by the same author in 1965 on the identifiability of computable functions. A function $f : \mathbf{N} \to \mathbf{N}$ is computable if there exists an algorithm or some mechanical rule that performs the required mapping. It is easy to show that not all functions are computable. To see this, consider the fact that an algorithm is nothing but a finite string of characters drawn from a finite alphabet. Obviously, there can be at most a countable infinity of such strings, whereas, even considering only those func- tions that are defined on the natural numbers, there is an uncountable infinity of them.

Imagine the following game: at fixed intervals, let us say for $t = 1, 2, \ldots$ a person is presented a new piece of information about an unknown object. Before receiving the following input, this player (whom we will call the *learner*) has to produce a guess of what object may account for the stream of information observed so far. The learner will win the game if, after some finite number of instances, his/her guess does not change anymore and it is indeed for the object which "inspired" the other players.

In an important variation of this game, the person who is to identify the hidden object may ask some questions about it and receive appropriate answers. It is very much what a researcher usually does in a laboratory working on some controlled experiment. The fundamental difference with the previous version is that the "answer" at each point in time may not depend on the latest question only, but may be indirectly dictated by the series of previously asked ones. In other words, the sequence of experiments may as well modify the initial investigated phenomenon.

Both "games" are examples of inductive inference analysed by Gold (1965, 1967). In the first case – originally denoted as *time-function identification* – a learner (a TM) receives at regular intervals of time an input which is the coded representation of the ordered pair $(x, f(x))$ so that $\langle x, f(x)\rangle$ is a natural number. Before the next input, the learner is required to output a guess: the Gödel number of the function whose graph contains the points observed so far. The learner will be said to have *intensionally identified* $f(x)$ if, for any possible sequence according to which the graph of $f(x)$ is presented, the guess will converge to a single index after a finite number of instances not to change again.

The second setting is called a *black box identification* problem. A learner, besides having to guess an index for the unknown black box b, will have also to decide what value x to input at each t in order to observe the output b_t. If the output depends on the latest input only, then the black box identification problem is just a reformulation of the time function one: $b_t = b(x_t)$. However, it may well be the case that $b_t = b(x_1, \ldots, x_t)$. There is some path dependence – history matters – and the learner may be able to identify (if anything at all) only some mapping (which the black box has eventually stabilised on) quite different from the "true" one. Think of the black box that will give as its only

TABLE 1

	Recursive	Primitive Recursive	Finite Automata
Time Functions	??	YES	YES
Black Boxes	NO	NO	YES

output the first input received, x_1, no matter what the subsequent inputs are. It may be identified as the constant function $f(x_t) = c$ for $c = x_1$.

It is important to note that identifiability has to be referred to a class of functions or black boxes. In fact, the identification of a single function can be trivially obtained by some learner (a machine) that always outputs the same guess: the index of that particular function. We introduce at this point some useful notation.

A *text* τ is an infinite string of natural numbers of the form $\{\langle x_1, f(x_1)\rangle, \langle x_2, f(x_2)\rangle, \ldots\}$; τ_n is the projection of the text τ on the first n elements. In other words τ_n is the sequence of points belonging to the graph of $f(\cdot)$ observed by the learner up to time n. Note that, by definition, a text contains all (with repetitions admitted) and only points in the graph of $f(\cdot)$. A learner $\lambda(\cdot)$ *converges* on a text τ to a guess γ if for any $n > n_0$ (with n_0 a finite natural number) $\lambda(\tau_n) = \gamma$. $\lambda(\cdot)$ *identifies* $f(\cdot)$ if it converges to γ on every text for $f(\cdot)$ and γ is the index (according to a well-defined Gödel numbering) for $f(\cdot)$. A class of functions Φ is *identifiable* if there exists a learner $\lambda(\cdot)$ which identifies all the elements of the class.

The learnability results obtained by Gold for functions and black boxes are summarized above in Table 1.

In words, on an *arbitrary text*, only primitive recursive time functions – and proper subsets of this class such as those functions generated by a finite automaton – can be learned (i.e. intensionally identified in the limit). Furthermore, the class of black boxes which is identifiable is smaller since it encompasses only finite automata. Very significantly, however, it is proved by Gold (1967) that a much larger class of time functions, namely all recursive ones, is identifiable if the text is ordered according to some primitive recursive function. Gold dismisses this case as highly unlikely in any real situation, however, Blum and Blum (1975) note that such a primitive recursive enumeration of the graph of a function can be easily obtained by a dove-tailing procedure. We will come back to this aspect when we deal with the role that institutions may play in a learning process.

A text is not the only possible way to present information to the learner. For example, an *informant* (in Gold's terminology) would contain both positive and negative instances along with a label attached to each one to specify whether the point belongs or not to the graph of the function to be identified. Clearly also the concept of intensional learnability can be generalized and the characteristics of the learner made more specific. For a detailed analysis of the possibilities we refer to Osherson et al. (1986). We enumerate and comment on a subset of such variations on the theme.

It is a well-known result of Recursion Theory (see, for example, Rogers 1987, p. 22) that each partial recursive function has a countable infinity of distinct indexes. This suggests the first generalization called *extensional identifiability* by Osherson et al. (1982) or *Behaviorally Correct* identifiability by Case and Smith (1983). According to this notion, a function $f(\cdot)$ will be extensionally identifiable if, for every text of $f(\cdot)$, $\lambda(\tau_n)$ will converge to a class of guessed indexes that are all for $f(\cdot)$.

Next, one may consider successful the learning process that converges to a function which is "close enough" to the "true" one. By "close enough" we mean a function $f'(\cdot)$ whose graph is different from the graph of $f(\cdot)$ only in a finite number of instances. More precisely, let $G(f)$ indicate the graph of $f(\cdot)$, then the cardinality of the set

$$[G(f) \cup G(f')] - [G(f) \cap G(f')] \tag{$*$}$$

is finite. The function $f'(\cdot)$ for which $(*)$ is true is called a *finite variant* of $f(\cdot)$. A function is *finite difference*[2] (intensionally) identifiable if $\lambda(\tau_n) = \gamma'$ for $n > n_0$ on any τ for $f(\cdot)$ and γ' is the index for $f'(\cdot)$ where $f'(\cdot)$ is a finite variant of $f(\cdot)$. As usual, the class Φ will be finite difference learnable if each of its members is finite difference identifiable.

If the previous generalizations arose from the observation that the learnability concept was perhaps too strict, one may remark that the description of the learner is too vague and that some structure should be imposed for the sake of verisimilitude. The first of these specifications is *memory limitation.* Formally, a learner $\lambda(\ )$ is said to be n memory limited if given two different texts τ and σ such that their projections τ_n and σ_n coincide for the latest n observed points, it will be true that whenever ($\lambda(\tau_{n-1}) = \lambda(\sigma_{n-1})$ this will imply $\lambda(\tau_n) = \lambda(\sigma_n)$. At time n, the learner will produce the same guess for τ_n and σ_n. It can be shown that there exists a class of functions which can be learned, but not by an n-memory limited learner no matter how big n is.[3]

Another interesting assumption that could be imposed on the learner is that of *gradualism.* According to this hypothesis, after having devised some *complexity metric*, a learner may not produce a new guess which is farther than some predetermined constant k from the previous guess as measured in the accepted metric. Remember that each guess is the index of a well-defined function, so the condition implies that the learner should improve gradually and in some cases it (the TM) will correct its mistakes only partially. This restriction on the ability of the learner may remind someone of the well-known hypothesis of adaptive expectations in economics. There is an essential difference, however; gradualism will be in terms of functional forms rather than simply in terms of a new parametrization. For example, starting from a linear conjecture, the revised formulation may be a second order polynomial rather than a modified intercept and angular coefficient. Note that the updating may, anyway, be insufficient if, for example, the unknown function is a third order polynomial or exponential and these functional forms are outside the learner's reach imposed by k.

3. A STYLIZED RATIONAL EXPECTATIONS MODEL

Let S be a set of state variables, both exogenous and lagged endogenous. We denote with the set of forecast functions from S to P: i.e. the set of spot market prices for the economy. The economy will be described by a set of functions mapping the current state and the *ex- pected* spot market prices into *realized* Temporary Equilibrium (TE) prices.

$$p^e = f(s) \tag{1}$$

$$p = h(s, p^e), \tag{2}$$

where p^e denotes a vector of expected prices, s a vector of state variables and p is a vector of realized TE prices.

Equivalently, one can assume that the economy maps admissible forecast functions $f \in \Phi$ into TE price functions $f_1 \in= \Phi_1$, that is, there exists some function $g : \Phi \to \Phi_1$. We will show below that the two formulations are almost equivalent, however, the former one allows us to point at some characteristics of the mapping that are easily overseen by adopting the latter formalization.

We now introduce the computability constraints on the functions and mappings employed so far. By this we mean that g, h, $f \in \Phi$, and $f_1 \in \Phi_1$ are all computable functions or, equivalently, functions that can be calculated by a Turing Machine. In other words, we assume that any example of procedural rationality will be captured by some algorithm; furthermore, accepting Church's Thesis in this analysis, every rule or procedure is equivalent to a TM.[4] However, if a function is shown to be uncomputable, it would be too hasty to affirm that a human being cannot somehow compute it. In this regard Gödel stated:

> [T]he results mentioned ... do not establish any bounds for the power of the human reason, but rather for the potentiality of pure formalism in mathematics.[5]

It may be remarked that if we can justify the computability assumption on the price forecast on the basis of procedural rationality, it is not evident why we should impose the same constraint on the economy map. For example, the latter may less restrictively be assumed as *semicomputable*.[6] In fact, since here the economy map could be approximated in the limit by a computable function – i.e. a forecasting rule in our case – the notion of Rational Expectations may work at least as a reference point. Giving up even this weaker assumption will deprive the RE concept of any relevance in a computable setting as the one depicted.

For consistency we also require S to be countable. Hence, we consider only functions defined on the natural numbers.[7] By applying some Gödel-numbering procedure, we can rewrite (1) and (2) as:

$$p^e = \varphi_i(s) \tag{1'}$$

$$p = \varphi_j(s, p^e), \tag{2'}$$

where i and j uniquely represent the TM for $f(\cdot)$ and $h(\cdot)$ respectively. The other formalization is:

$$p^e = \varphi_i(s) \tag{3}$$

$$p = \varphi_{g[i]}(s). \tag{4}$$

Working on (1') and (2') we obtain

$$p = \varphi_j(s, \varphi_i(s)). \tag{5}$$

By the so called *Smn* theorem of recursive function theory, there exists a total function $k(\cdot)$ such that

$$\varphi_j(s, \varphi_i(s)) = \varphi_{k[j,i]}(s).$$

The fact that $k(\cdot,\cdot)$ is computable assures us that there exists some TM with index e such that

$$k[j,i] = \varphi_e(j,i).$$

Applying once more the *Smn* theorem we see that

$$k[j,i] = \varphi_{r(e,j)}(i)$$

Call $\varphi_{r(e,j)} = \hat{g}$ and we obtain

$$p = \varphi_{\hat{g}(i)}(s). \tag{6}$$

In other words, both (4) and (6) map state variables into TE prices and both g, $\hat{g} : \Phi \to \Phi$ even though nothing assures us that $g = \hat{g}$. We now use g for simplicity, but we will come back to the difference between g and $\hat{g}$. A Rational Expectations Equilibrium (REE) is obtained in this framework when for each s

$$p^e = p = \varphi_{g(i)}(s)$$

that is an REE is a fixed point of $g(\cdot)$ (or of $\hat{g}(\cdot)$) in the following recursive function theory sense:

$$\varphi_i = \varphi_{g(i)}. \tag{7}$$

Equation (7) can be easily understood if we interpret φ_i and $\varphi_{g(i)}$ as programs. What (7) states is not that φ_i and $\varphi_{g(i)}$ are the *same* program (which would be true if $i = g(i)$), but rather that φ_i and $\varphi_{g(i)}$ have the *same effect*.

We need now to spend a few words on the set of computable functions Φ. In particular, there are two possible assumptions we can make. We may assume to be the set of *all* recursive functions (partial and total) or bind Φ to contain only *total* recursive functions. A *partial* function is not defined for every possible value of its argument; in other words the TM which represents that function will not halt for some input. To assume that the forecast price function or the economy price function is partial amounts to assume (in the interpretation offered by McAfee (1984)) that under some states of nature some markets may fail to open. This possibility does not appear completely unrealistic if we consider some notion of uninsurable risk. Another possible explanation for this scenario is given by Axel Leijonhufvud with what we will call the "Knight metaphor". The situation is similar to that faced by two chess players when suddenly (it does not really matter whether there was a small a priori probability of this occurrence) it is announced that a particular rule, notably how the knight moves, is not valid any longer, but *no alternative* is given. The experience of certain Eastern European countries is an example of such a kind of *hard* uncertainty.

The assumption Φ being the set of total recursive functions (maintained by Spear for example) is based on an analogy with the results on the existence of temporary equilibrium prices in more traditional settings (which, in particular, accept the continuity of S).

Under the former assumption, the existence of the fixed point described in (7) is warranted by the so called Recursion Theorem if the function $g(\cdot)$ is total. Note that $\hat{g}(\cdot)$, which was obtained thanks to the *Smn* theorem, is total as a by-product of the same theorem so that, in this case, the assumption of Φ being the set of all recursive functions is sufficient for the existence of a REE for the economy characterized by $\hat{g}(\cdot)$.

On the other hand, it is necessary to *assume* that $g(\cdot)$ is total *and* that is has a fixed point (in the sense of (7)) to be sure of the existence of a REE in case Φ is the set of total functions.

4. Learning Rational Expectations

To recapitulate, our stylized learner (a Turing Machine) is faced with the problem of inferring $\varphi_{g(i)}(\cdot)$ from the text composed of natural numbers of the form $(\langle s_1, p_1\rangle, \langle s_2, p_2\rangle, \ldots)$. In particular, the identification process is assumed to proceed in two steps. At first, the agent/learner will forecast p^e employing a single forecasting rule φ_i. He/she will keep doing so until the identification of the relevant $\varphi_{g(i)}$ is accomplished. In the second step, the learner will have to repeat the previous procedure for as many different forecasting rules i as necessary to identify $g(\cdot)$ itself. It is assumed that at this point some algorithm exists to determine that particular i such that $\varphi_i = \varphi_{g(i)}$, that is the REE forecasting rule.

As an example of the generality of this setting one may interpret φ_i as the production decision of a duopolist which generates the reaction function $\varphi_{g(i)}$ on part of the competitor. the possibility of identifying the reaction function itself may turn out to be an important advantage. As a matter of fact, a successful identification would be automatically translated into a Stackelberg leadership.

Employing the results summarized in Table 1, it is easy to show that the first step of the learning process will be successful if $\varphi_{g(i)}(\cdot)$ is an element of the set of primitive recursive functions. In the particular economic model considered, we obtain Proposition 3.3 in Spear (1989):

> If the Temporary Equilibrium price function is primitive recursive, agents can identify it.

Let us remember that this is only the first step of the complete learning procedure; however, the identification is guaranteed in the limit. In other words, there is no way for the learner – or for any outside observer for that matter – to know when the convergence has occurred. An analogy can be found with statistical inference techniques that are based on some version of the law of large numbers. When estimating a set of parameters, for example, only confidence intervals can be given and consistency will have the estimates converge to the "true" values only in the limit. There is, however, one further complication: in a classical-statistics parameter estimation problem the underlying model is known (or assumed) to be true and only the correct parametrization is at stake, whereas, the very functional form is also to be inferred in Gold's learning model.

As for the second step, we assume the agent knows (how to calculate) the index i of the forecasting rule he/she is adopting. By changing this rule (hence the index i) the agent can observe a sequence of numbers like $(\langle i_1, g(i_1)\rangle), \langle i_2, g(i_2), \ldots)$ where each $g(i_n)$ is the index of the TE price function related to the forecasting rule i_n. This is obviously a black box identification problem. We can proceed in two different ways. According to the first one, we consider the black box output as the image of (and only of) the latest input. As pointed out in Section 2, this is a disguised time-function identification problem, and the same learnability results hold. In particular, if $g(\cdot)$ belongs to the class of primitive recursive functions, then it will be possible to learn it. This is the approach taken by Spear and based on the model specification given by (3) and (4). However, going back to $\hat{g}(\cdot)$ we notice that it is defined as

$$\hat{g}(\cdot) = \varphi_{r(e,j)}(\cdot).$$

This suggests that the structure "hidden" behind the market pricing function is more complex than the one envisaged by (3) and (4). The forecast-rule – and the behaviour it implies – may have an impact on the institutional organization of the economic system and any change of that rule will likely trigger an institutional *modification* rather than a complete redefinition. In other words, when experimenting a new forecasting procedure, the agent will not deal with a *tabula rasa*, but with a palimpsest with many layers which are, in part at least, the result of previous forecast-behaviour. Hence, it appears plausible to interpret the observed $\hat{g}(i_n)$ as the output of a black box mapping the finite string of inputs $(i_1, i_2, \ldots, i_n)$ as summarized by the index j of $\hat{g}(\cdot) = \varphi_{r(e,j)}(\cdot)$. The particular sequence of rules adopted in the past has an effect on how the present system works, there is path dependence.

What are the consequences of this approach for the learnability results? Once more exploiting Gold's theorems summarized in Table 1 we immediately conclude that $\hat{g}(\cdot)$ will be identifiable in the limit if it belongs to the class of finite automata. It is important to remark that this is not a trivial problem. Gold (1972) proposes some effective procedures to identify an unknown FA black box which is resettable at will. In other words these algorithms need to be implemented on a certain number of identical black boxes or, equivalently, the single available black box has to be switched back to its initial state each time that the experimenting sequence requires it. This is obviously something that cannot be assumed to be possible when dealing with an economic system for the same reasons we mentioned above against the time function like identification problem. On the other hand, sequential experiments that do not need the black box re-initialization in the identification process may not exist even for fairly simple finite automata as shown, for example, by Kohavi (1970).

Going back to the general problem of function identification, we may follow a different approach. We will specify the characteristics of the learner and the concept of learnability; then assume that the learning process converges. What can be said of the class of functions that is identified? We will use here a modified version of the result obtained by Osherson et al. (1989).

Let us assume that the learner has limited-memory and adapt his guesses only gradually, that is a new guess cannot be much more complex than the previous one (where the complexity is measured according to some well-specified metric). Furthermore, assume that the text sequentially observed by the learner is *noisy*: a finite number of different points (with possibly infinite repetitions) may be from the graph of other functions. It turns out that the class of functions that can be identified has finite cardinality: there is only a finite number of different functions that can be inferred under these assumptions. Note that no constraint is imposed on the type of functions – whether primitive recursive, recursive, or recursive enumerable. It is also important to stress that the identification problem has not become a trivial one. It can be shown that the learner may not make up his/her mind, that is converge to the right index even though there are only two functions in the class.

More formally:

ASSUMPTION I. For all functions $f \in F$ and for all texts τ for f, the learner λ converges on τ.

Note that Assumption I does not state that the identification will be *necessarily* correct (the index on which the learner converges to may be for some $f' \neq f$) even though it is obviously compatible with a successful identification.

ASSUMPTION II. The learner is n-memory limited for some $n \in \mathbf{N}$.

See the formal definition on a previous page.

Let Γ be the set of guesses γ available to the learner. Γ may be infinite even though the set of functions that can be identified turns out to be finite. Following Osherson et al. (1989) we call an *Ordering* of Γ any isomorphism between Γ and $\mathbf{N}$ (or some finite subset of $\mathbf{N}$ in case Γ is finite). Let O be such an ordering and let $\gamma', \gamma \in \Gamma$. $O(\gamma)$ denotes the natural number that is assigned to γ by O. γ is called *minimal* (in O) if for every $\gamma' \in \Gamma$ such that $\varphi_\gamma = \varphi_{\gamma'}$, then $O(\gamma) \leq O(\gamma')$. In other words, γ is minimal if it is the index of the simplest function that generates the observed graph.

ASSUMPTION III. There is an ordering O of Γ and a natural number k such that for all $f \in F$ and for all finite projections (finite strings) σ.

(1) For all points $s = \langle x, f(x) \rangle$, if $s \in \text{Graph}(\lambda(\sigma))$, then

$$O(\lambda(\sigma \wedge s)) < O(\lambda(\sigma)) + k,$$

where $\lambda(\sigma)$ is the guess that the learner outputs when it has observed the finite string σ and $\sigma \wedge s$ denotes the concatenation of the finite strings σ and s.

(2) There is a finite string t such that
  (a) $rng(t) \subseteq \text{Graph}(f)$
  (b) $\lambda(\sigma \wedge s)$ is an index for $f(\cdot)$
  (c) $\lambda(\sigma \wedge s)$ is minimal in O or $O(\lambda(\sigma \wedge s)) < O(\lambda(\sigma)) + k$.

(1) asserts that the complexity of the guess will not be greatly affected by a single new piece of information (another point in the graph of the hidden function) which is, moreover, already in the graph of the currently guessed function. According to (2) the learner can eventually guess the true hidden function, no matter how misleading was the previous finite string he/she got to observe.

PROPOSITION.[8] Let λ and F satisfy Assumptions I, II, and III. Then F is finite. Note that k is left unspecified so that for large k Assumption III on gradualism is relatively weak. An interesting joint-product of the proof of the above proposition is that the cardinality of F is precisely determined and equal to $2k$.

The most immediate consequence of such a proposition is that the number of *regimes* – where with regime we refer to a political and institutional setting and the set of consistent beliefs and reliable expectations that it fosters among all economic actors – is finite. This may be considered a version of *strong nativism* on the social organisations that can be learned by an economic agent, not very much different from the theory of strong nativism in natural languages proposed by Chomsky (1981).

5. Institutions and Learning

What role can institutions play in the learning process? We maintain that they may give a positive contribution in at least three respects: memory enhancement, error reduction and data pre-processing.

We have seen that a realistic constraint to impose on the learner is that of memory limitation. It is possible to show that there exist classes of functions that can be identified, but not identified by an n-memory limited learner. This result is not really surprising. Let us consider the following example. The class of functions, F, object of the identification process is composed of the following elements

$$f_j = \{2^i : i \in \mathbf{N}\} \cup \{3^j\} \quad \text{for each } j \in \mathbf{N}$$

and

$$f'_j = \{2^i : i \in \mathbf{N} \text{ and } i \neq j\} \cup \{3^j\} \quad \text{for each } j \in \mathbf{N}.$$

τ and τ' are two texts for two elements of $F := \{\ldots, \langle k, 2k\rangle, \langle k, 3^k\rangle, \ldots\}$, $\tau' = \{\ldots, \langle k, 3^k\rangle, \ldots\}$ where $\langle k, 2^k\rangle$ appears only once in τ – and in that position – and never in τ'. For the rest τ and τ' are identical. A learner λ*1*-memory limited will converge (if anywhere) on the same index for both texts even though τ is for f_k and τ' is for f'_k. Obviously, an unlimited memory learner will not be mistaken by this kind of text; however, notice that for this particular example, also a *2*-memory limited learner would distinguish between the two languages on τ and τ'. More generally, institutions may offer some *common memory* resource. Libraries and organizations that collect data and publish or manage various data-banks are examples of this kind of institutions.

Furthermore, certain institutions may have an indirect, but nevertheless essential function. The uncertainty reduction that is obtained in a well-designed institutional organization allows the individual members to devote a greater amount of resources to some preferred activity with likely increment of productivity. In terms of memory and information processing ability, an increase in the *entropy* of the system – intended as the informational content of signals bombarding the learner – will require an augmented absorption of memory resources and, if these resources are limited, it will lead to a decrease in the performance in all activities, learning included. A very pertinent example is offered by Leijonhufvud and Heymann (1994) and concerns the high inflation experience of various Latin American countries. The ongoing disappearance of the institution *stable money* is translated into a "waste" of resources that have to be devoted to financial management. The recorded absence of the market for long term loans and the failure of certain arbitrage conditions can be explained in terms of this increased entropy. The identification of low-frequency patterns has to be forsaken in view of the need to infer high-frequency patterns that are essential for the day-by-day survival of the firm, no matter how myopic the strategies adopted may appear.

As far as the error reduction ability of institutions, Smith (1982) and Daley (1983) point at the positive correlation between the precision of the identification process result and the number of learners working in parallel on the same problem. In particular, Smith shows how the collection of functions that can be finite-difference intensionally identified with at most l mistakes employing n machines working together is a subset of the collection of the functions that can be finite-difference intensionally identified making at most $\lfloor l/m \rfloor$ mistakes using $n \cdot m$ machines. Daley obtains the equivalent result with the different concept of extensional learnability. Hence in this case, the role of the institutions is that of organizing various learners in a parallel network of research and information. Any research and development department is the most obvious real world analogy, but it is also worth remarking that any firm as such may benefit from this sort of economies of scale and its very existence may be partly explained by it.

The last aspect we consider is data pre-processing. Gold (1967) stresses that the order in which information is presented may be fundamental for a positive learning result. In particular, the most interesting one is the fact that any computable function is identifiable on a text which is a primitive recursive presentation of its graph. This result looks more like a curiosum than anything else; however, Blum and Blum (1975) show how a mechanical procedure called *dove-tailing* will have the graph of a recursive function presented precisely according to a primitive recursive text. Take any partial recursive function represented by a Turing machine $\varphi(\cdot)$. At time $t = 0$ perform the first step of the calculation of $\varphi(0)$. If this one step is enough to obtain an output from the machine, then the first element of the primitive recursive text for $\varphi(\cdot)$ will be $\langle 0, \varphi(0) \rangle$, otherwise let the first element of the text be $\langle *, * \rangle$. Perform next the second step on $\varphi(0)$ and produce the second element of the text as before (it will be either $\langle *, * \rangle$ or $\langle 0, \varphi(0) \rangle$). Next calculate the first step of $\varphi(1)$ and if this is sufficient to obtain the final

TABLE 2

	Step 1	Step 2	Step 3	Step 4
$\varphi(0)$	$t = 0$	$t = 1$	$t = 3$ Halts	–
$\varphi(1)$	$t = 2$	$t = 4$	$t = 6$	$t = 9$ Halts
$\varphi(2)$	$t = 5$	$t = 7$ Halts	–	–
$\varphi(3)$	$t = 8$	$t = 10$		

$$\tau_{11} = \{\langle *, * \rangle, \langle *, * \rangle, \langle *, * \rangle, \langle 0, \varphi(0) \rangle, \langle 0, \varphi(0) \rangle, \langle 0, \varphi(0) \rangle, \langle 0, \varphi(0) \rangle, \langle 2, \varphi(2) \rangle, \langle 2, \varphi(2) \rangle, \langle 1, \varphi(1) \rangle, \langle 1, \varphi(1) \rangle\}$$

result (that is the Turing machine halts) the third element of the text will be $\langle 1, \varphi(1) \rangle$, otherwise the third one will simply be the repetition of the second element. Table 2 and the following finite string exemplify this procedure.

This procedure may remind someone of the *time sharing* organization of a computer network composed of various users and only one CPU. The reason for adopting such a method is the fact that the function $\varphi(\cdot)$ may be partial, that is, undefined for some $n \in \mathbf{N}$. Dove-tailing will prevent the machine from being trapped into an endless calculation.

It comes natural to ask whether institutions could somehow be organizing "chaotic" signals to transform them into a well-arranged information flow. According to this approach (for which the dove-tailing procedure is an analogy rather than a metaphor) an institution works as a "problem solver" or at least as the media through which ready-made solutions are offered to the public whenever they are found. This does not imply that those solutions are the most accurate or the simplest ones; they are just the first that have been worked out. Some agents will adopt these approximate solutions benefiting from the reduced uncertainty and the saved resources they would have had to "invest" to obtain possibly inferior results; some others will try to beat the system attempting to figure out a better solution to the problem at hand, be it a product innovation, a new financial instrument, or a more effective forecasting rule.

A primitive recursive enumeration of the graph of a partial function appears as a most unlikely thing to present itself in reality, and the dove-tailing procedure requires already the knowledge of the function to produce such an enumeration. However, the possibility of information presenting itself in such a manner cannot be dismissed a priori; as a matter of fact, the Newtonian universe is primitive recursive and the laws that would govern such a system are still used to send rockets to the moon and are an extremely good local approximation of the "real" laws of nature.

We suggest one further analogy for the data pre-processing role played by an institution. This one is drawn from the neural network literature. Consider the XOR (exclusive OR) Boolean function. This logic function of two arguments (A, B let us say) is TRUE if either A or B but not both, is true. We can project the graph of such a function in a two-dimensional space as follows:

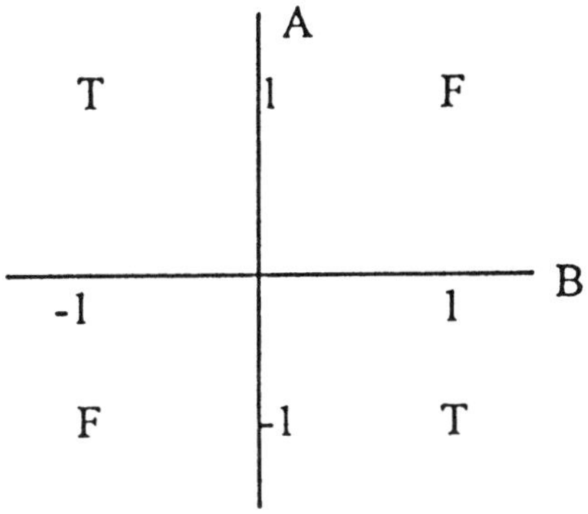

where 1 stands for TRUE and -1 for FALSE. It is immediate to conclude that the set of $\{A, B\}$ values for which XOR (A,B) is TRUE is not linearly separable from the "false set."

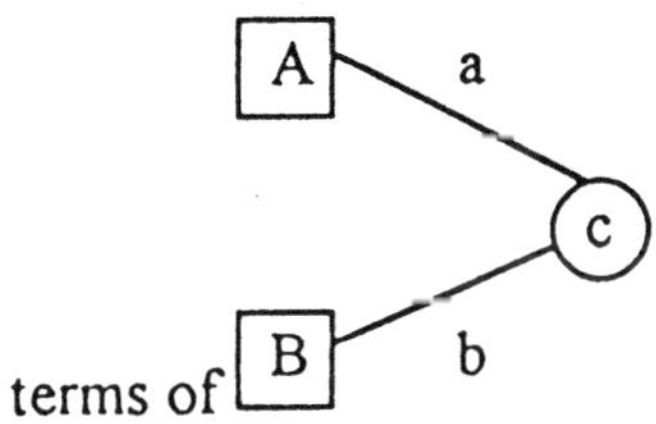

In terms of neural networks this implies that the net above – where the □'s are the input nodes (which assume the values 1 or -1 according to whether the input is true or false) a, b are the weights, c is a threshold value and the final node is the output – cannot correctly classify all possible inputs. In other words, this net cannot learn how to calculate the XOR function if it employs simple (linear) rules for its elaboration of the input.

On the other hand, the following net for particular integer values of the weights and thresholds calculates with no mistakes the XOR function. In particular, the output neurode – what we can consider the final user of the information flow, the learner – will perform just simple algebraic additions and judge whether the result is positive or negative.

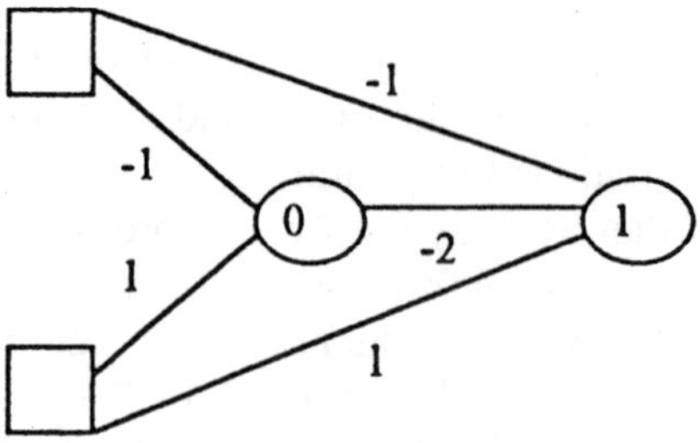

The introduction of the hidden neurode – which we would definitely indicate as an institution – makes it possible for the output cell – our stylized agent – to rely on some very simple "rules of thumb" for implementing the correct behaviour in the face of a complex environment. Note that the agent has direct access to the original information. The institution on its part reacts to the same news and does not solve the problem for the final user, rather it pre-processes the data volunteering some framework inside which the learner can be successful with relatively little effort.

6. CONCLUSIONS

Computability offers a rich and rigorous framework of analysis which can be easily applied to Economic Theory. This paper has been concerned with the dynamic interaction of agents and their environment as represented by a learning process. The sometimes vague notion of procedural rationality finds, we believe, its most appropriate description within a computable context. In this respect one of the purposes of this paper has been that of providing a suitable language to tackle a complex phenomenon such as learning.

The results stress the importance of institutions for a successful outcome of the individual's learning process thanks to the organization and pre-processing of information they bring about, the uncertainty reduction they foster, and the collective memory resources they make available.

On the other hand – as we have hinted at elsewhere and as we are currently developing in our research – the very specialization of certain institutions in the face of an abrupt change in the socio-political or technological environment may slow down the learning process itself. Therefore, the relation between individuals and institutions is not unidirectional. In fact it is interactive: the individual who, on the one hand, designs the institution, will, on the other hand, ultimately be constrained by its very existence in a sort of path dependence which moulds the evolution of society and *bounds* the exercise of the individual's rationality.

NOTES

1. See the recent volume edited by Matthews and Demopoulos (1989).
2. The same notion of learnability is referred to as *almost everywhere* identification by Blum and Blum (1975) and *subidentification* in Minicozzi (1976).
3. See Proposition 3.3 in Osherson et al. (1982).
4. The Constructivist School does not agree on this point, but we will not consider the possibility of *constructing* a procedure which is not equivalent to some TM.
5. Quoted in Davis (1965).
6. A real function f is semicomputable from below iff there exists a computable real function $g(x, k)$ non decreasing in k with $f(x) = \lim_{k\to\infty} g(x, k)$. A function f is semicomputable from above if $-f$ is semicomputable from below.
7. Actually, we could consider all rational and algebraic numbers. In other words, the functions could be defined on computable numbers for which there exists an isomorphism with the naturals.
8. Equivalent to Proposition 8 in Osherson et al. (1989) the proof will be found in the appendix of that article.

REFERENCES

Blum, L. and M. Blum, 1975, 'Toward a mathematical theory of inductive inference', *Information and Control* 28, 125–155.

Case, J. and C. Smith, 1983, 'Comparison of identification criteria for machine inductive inference', *Theoretical Computer Science* 25, 193–220.

Chomsky, N., 1981, *Lectures on Government and Binding*, The Pisa Lectures Publications, Dordrecht: Foris.

Daley, R.P., 1983, 'On the error correcting power of pluralism in BC-type inductive inference', *Theoretical Computer Science* 24, 95–104.

Davis, M. (Ed.), 1965, *The Undecidable*, New York: Raven Press.

Gold, M.E., 1965, 'Limiting recursion', *The Journal of Symbolic Logic* 30(1), 28–48.

Gold, M.E., 1967, 'Language identification in the limit', *Information and Control* 10, 447–474.

Gold, M.E., 1972, 'System identification via state characterization', *Automatica* 8, 621–636.

Kohavi, Z., 1976, *Switching and Finite Automata Theory*, New York: McGraw-Hill.

Leijonhufvud, A. and D. Heymann, 1994, *High Inflation*, Oxford: Oxford University Press.

Lilly, G., 1993, 'Recursiveness and preference orderings', *Journal of Economic Dynamics and Control* 17, 865–876.

Matthews, R.J. and W. Demopoulos (Eds), 1989, *Learnability and Linguistic Theory*, Dordrecht: Kluwer Academic Publishers.

McAfee, R.P., 1984, 'Effective computability in economic decisions', mimeo.

Minicozzi, E., 1976, 'Some natural properties of strong-identification in inductive inference', *Theoretical Computer Science* 2, 345–360.

Osherson, D.N., M. Stob, and S. Weistein, 1982, 'Learning strategies', *Information and Control* 53, 32–51.

Osherson, D.N., M. Stob, and S. Weistein, 1986, *Systems That Learn*, Cambridge, MA: MIT Press.

Osherson, D.N., M. Stob, and S. Weistein, 1989, 'Learning theory and natural language', in R.J. Matthews and W. Demopoulos (Eds), *Learnability and Linguistic Theory*, Dordrecht: Kluwer Academic Publishers.

Rogers, H., 1987, *Theory of Recursive Functions and Effective Computability*, Cambridge, MA: MIT Press.

Rustem, B. and K. Velupillai, 1990, 'Rationality, computability, and complexity', *Journal of Economic Dynamics and Control* 14, 419–432.

Smith, C., 1982, 'The power of pluralism for automatic program synthesis', *Journal of the Association for Computing Machinery* 29, 1144–1165.

Spear, S.E., 1989, 'Learning rational expectations under computability constraints', *Econometrica* 57(4), 889–910.

PART FOUR

New Computational Methods

PIERRE VALLOIS AND CHARLES S. TAPIERO

The Range Process in Random Walks: Theoretical Results and Applications

ABSTRACT. This paper summarizes and apply some known results regarding the Range Run Length (RRL) in random walks. Explicitly, the inverse of the range process in random walks is evaluated for processes such as the symmetric and asymmetric discrete random walks, the discrete "birth death range process", as well as Wiener processes with and without drift. Some of the results stated are proved elsewhere while a number of applications spanning the detection of outliers, R/S analysis and the estimation of the Hurst exponent for time series, as well as application to the control of "variability" are suggested.

1. Introduction

The study of the range process is a topic of recurrent interest. Feller as early as 1951 remarked that it is difficult to compute the range distribution in a symmetric random walk. Recently, Imhof (1985, 1992) as well as Vallois (1993) have renewed interest in this process and have derived some theoretical results regarding the generating function of the range process for some specific discrete and continuous processes (see also Dvoretzki and Erdos 1951, Jain and Orey 1968, Jain and Pruitt 1972, Troutman 1983, for related papers). For example, Imhof (1985) calculated the Laplace transform of the time needed to attain a given range in a Wiener process while Vallois (1993) has obtained the Laplace transform of the time needed to attain a given range in discrete symmetric and asymmetric random walks as well as in continuous random walks. Particular characteristics such as the mean and the variance of these processes has been calculated by Vallois and Tapiero (1995). For symmetric random walks only Daudin (1995) has also calculated higher order moments. Finally, Vallois (1995), has recently calculated the probability distribution of the run length distribution of the range process which turns out to have complicated expressions which we reproduce here as well. The purpose of this paper will be two fold. First we summarize the basic results known regarding the range process. Second, we derive the mean of an asymmetric birth-death

H. Amman et al. (eds.), Computational Approaches to Economic Problems, 291–307.

random walk and apply our results to a number of problems of particular interest in the statistical detection of outliers, in the control of quality and in the R/S analysis currently applied in finance (for the statistical specification of the Hurst exponent for time series for example, see Peter 1995). For simplicity, results are given without proofs but references are given to working papers as well as published articles where these proofs have been included.

The range process of a time series $\{x_t, t \geq 0\}$ provide additional information regarding the underlying evolution of the series x_t which can be used for estimation and test-control purposes. This information is specific in two ways, first the range has a long memory of past samples observed and second, the range process is far more sensitive to shifts and to outliers than the variance process (as estimated through ARCH or GARCH models). In this sense, the range process, combined with now classical estimation techniques for series volatility can provide efficient detection schemes for outliers or for the chaotic behavior of time series.

Traditionally, the record of such series, such as,

$$y_t = x_t \tag{1}$$

are used to estimate and/or control the underlying process. Consider the following process,

$$x_{t+1} = x_t + \varepsilon_t; \quad y_t = x_t, \tag{2}$$

where ε_t is a Bernoulli random variable with parameter p,

$$\varepsilon_t = \begin{cases} +1 & \text{with probability } p \\ -1 & \text{with probability } q. \end{cases} \tag{3}$$

An estimation of the process x_t based on the time series $\{y_0, y_1, \ldots, y_t\}$ can then be found by Bayesian recursive or other techniques, yielding the probability distribution $P(x_t/y_0, y_1, \ldots, y_t)$ or at least some of its parameters. If the parameter p is not fixed over time, it is generally much more difficult to obtain some results (although approximations based on non-linear recursive estimators – the filter equations – can be obtained). When the error term ε_t is assumed to be normally distributed, Bayesian, maximum likelihood and other techniques can be used for such and more general models. For time varying variance, ARCH and GARCH models have recently been suggested (Engle 1982, Bollerslev 1986). ARCH (AutoRegressive Conditional Heteroskedastic) models for example, provide an approach to estimate the process variability based on a series of past squares. The Engle model is defined as follows:

$$x_t = u_t + \sigma_t z, \tag{4}$$

where z is a standard normal random variable, u_t is another equation representing the mean evolution of the process while σ_t is a non-stationary standard deviation which is given by the ARCH model as follows:

$$\sigma_t^2 = a_0 + \sum_{j=1}^{p} a_j \sigma_{t-j}^2. \tag{5}$$

In order to obtain parameter estimates, the Engle model runs the following regression:

$$x_t^2 = a_0 + \sum_{j=1}^{p} a_j x_{t-j}^2 + \varepsilon_t. \tag{6}$$

In a similar vein, we might use the statistical characteristics of the range process to detect changes process variability. The range process defines a time series over the periods $(0, t)$ is given by $\{R_t, t \geq 0\}$

$$R_t = \text{Max}[x_0, x_1, x_2, \ldots, x_t] - \text{Min}[x_0, x_1, x_2, \ldots, x_t]. \tag{7}$$

Samples range defined over time intervals of length N can, of course, be defined as well. For example, such ranges will be given by:

$$\begin{aligned} R_t^N &= \text{Max}[x_{t-N}, x_{t-N+1}, x_{t-N+2}, \ldots, x_t] \\ &\quad - \text{Min}[x_{t-N}, x_{t-N+1}, x_{t-N+2}, \ldots, x_t] \end{aligned} \tag{8}$$

and exhibit an N periods memory. It is noteworthy that ARCH-GARCH models which are used to model volatility do not measure the same variation as the range process. The latter process, for example, will be much more sensitive to outliers than say the variance (ARCH) processes. In fact, we shall indicate later on that combined estimates based on the range process and ARCH estimators can provide powerful means to detect change in time series and in particular, their chaotic behavior.

Since R_t is a growing process, we can, equivalently, study its inverse process, the run length process. Explicitly, this is the first time that the range process reaches a given value a;

$$\theta(a) = \text{Inf}(t \geq 0; R_t \geq a). \tag{9}$$

Clearly, $\{R_n < a\}$ is equal to $\{\theta(a) > n\}$ and therefore the law of R_t can be studied instead through the run length $\theta(a)$. Below we consider some essential results regarding this run length $\theta(a)$ and subsequently, a number of applications are outlined.

2. The RL of Random Walks

For reference, consider process (2) with barriers defined by $(-a, b)$, $a \geq 0$, $b \geq 0$, at which we stop the process. Assuming that t is the first time the process reaches this barrier, we have:

$$t = \text{Inf}\{s \geq 0, x_s = -a, b\}. \tag{10}$$

It is well known (Chow et al. 1971) that the probability of reaching one or the other boundaries is given by

$$P(x_t = -a) = \begin{cases} \frac{1-(1/\lambda)^b}{1-(1/\lambda)^{a+b}} & \lambda \neq 1 \\ b/(a+b) & \lambda = 1 \end{cases} \tag{11}$$

$$P(x_t = b) = \begin{cases} \frac{(1/\lambda)^b-(1/\lambda)^{a+b}}{1-(1/\lambda)^{a+b}} & \lambda \neq 1 \\ \\ a/(a+b) & \lambda = 1, \end{cases} \tag{12}$$

where

$$\lambda = q/p. \tag{13}$$

Further, the average run length (ARL) of such a process is

$$\text{ARL} = E(t) = \begin{cases} \frac{b}{p-q} - \left(\frac{a+b}{p-q}\right)\left(\frac{\lambda^a(\lambda^b-1)}{\lambda^{a+b}-1}\right) & \lambda \neq 1 \\ \\ ab/2p & \lambda = 1. \end{cases} \tag{14}$$

Note that $(\lambda^{x_n}; n \geq 0)$ is a martingale. Using the stopping theorem, it is easy to check that (11) and (12) hold. We also introduce the following martingale: $(x_n - n(p-q); n \geq 0)$. Using once more the stopping theorem we obtain (14).

We turn next to the range process $\{R_t, t \geq 0\}$ and summarize essential results for a number of random walks.

2.1. *Symmetric Random Walks*

For a symmetric random walk ($p = q = 1/2$), the ARL for a range to reach an amplitude a and its variance are given by (Vallois and Tapiero 1995):

$$\begin{cases} \text{ARL} = E(\theta(a)) = \frac{a(a+1)}{2} \\ \\ \text{VRL} = \text{Var}(\theta(a)) = \frac{a(a-1)(a+1)(a+2)}{12}. \end{cases} \tag{15}$$

Daudin (1995) has extended these results by computing the four first centered moments. Of course, a time series presumed to be a symmetric random walk will have, over the "long run" a constant coefficient of variation $\mathrm{ARL}/\sqrt{\mathrm{VRL}} = \sqrt{1/3}$.

2.2. *Asymmetric and Birth-Death Random Walks*

When the process is asymmetric however, the ARL of the range process is far more difficult to compute. A birth-death random walk which includes of course the asymmetric random walk is given by:

$$\varepsilon_t = \begin{cases} +1 & \text{w.p. } p \\ 0 & \text{w.p. } r \\ -1 & \text{w.p. } q, \end{cases} \tag{16}$$

where ε_t are independent random variables with stationary growth probability $p > 0, r \geq 0, p + q + r = 1$, in the time interval $(t, t+1)$. If $r = 0$, we have as a special case the asymmetric random walk. Of course, a reflection can be used to model a simple single server discrete time queuing model where p is the probability of an arrival in the time interval $(t, t+1)$ while the probability of a unit departing the system is equal to q in $(t, t+1)$. For this process, let $\lambda = q/p$, then the amplitude's ARL is given by (Tapiero and Vallois 1996):

$$\begin{aligned} \mathrm{ARL} &= E(\theta(a)) \\ &= \frac{1}{p(\lambda-1)}\left(\frac{(a+1)^2}{\lambda^{a+1}-1} - \frac{a^2}{\lambda^a - 1} - \frac{1}{\lambda-1} + a\right) \text{ if } \lambda \neq 1. \end{aligned} \tag{17}$$

As a special case, note that when $q = p$, $\lambda = 1$, then $r = 1 - q - p$ and the ARL is reduced to

$$E(\theta(a)) = \frac{a(a+1)}{4p} . \tag{18}$$

Of course, we obtain the ARL found earlier by letting $p = 1/2$. Such a result partly confirms our analysis. When $r = 0, p + q = 1$, we fall in the special case of an asymmetric random walk. Note that in this case, the ARL has exactly the same functional form as Equation (17).

$$\begin{aligned} \mathrm{ARL} &= E(\theta(a)) \\ &= \frac{1}{(q-p)}\left(\frac{(a+1)^2}{\lambda^{a+1}-1} - \frac{a^2}{\lambda^a - 1} - \frac{1}{\lambda-1} + a\right) \\ &\quad \text{if } \lambda \neq 1, \quad q + p = 1. \end{aligned} \tag{19}$$

Further, for a biased random walk with $q = 0$ while $p + r = 1$ (and thus $\lambda = 0$), it can be easily verified that the ARL equals a/p. Note that the variance of the RL of the asymmetric random walk has not been thus far calculated. Using simulation, however, tables can be constructed providing a numerical characterization of the variance of the RL and its empirical distribution. When $p + q = 1$, the variance component is reduced to $4p(1 - p)$. When $p = 1/2$, then there is no drift and we obtain the previous symmetric random walk. We shall obtain also the equivalent results for continuous Wiener processes with drift later on. A comparison of the ARL for symmetric and asymmetric random walks will also allow the construction of non-parametric tests for testing hypotheses regarding the drift coefficient of the random walk.

In the long run, and for the case $r = 0$, Vallois (1995) has also shown that the RL converges to a normal distribution. Explicitly,

$$\frac{1}{\sqrt{n}}\left[\theta(n) - \frac{n}{|p-q|}\right] \to N\left(0, \frac{4pq}{|p-q|^3}\right) \quad \text{for} \quad p \neq q. \tag{20}$$

It is noteworthy to note that for $p \neq \theta(n)$ is of order cn where c is some constant while for $p = q$, $\theta(n)$ is of order n^2. This means that for the asymmetric case there is a drift which induces less randomness and thus the range will eventually be 'dominated' by the drift component. In the symmetric case, there is more 'randomness' and thus the range process will have far greater variability. In this case, Vallois has also shown that in distribution we have:

$$\frac{\theta(n)}{n^2} \xrightarrow{\text{dist}} \xi, \tag{21}$$

where ξ has a Laplace Transform which is given as follows

$$E(e^{-v\xi}) = \frac{1}{ch^2(\sqrt{v/2}))}, \quad ch(x) = \frac{e^x + e^{-x}}{2}. \tag{22}$$

Using our results and calculating the case $p+q = 1$ (or $r = 0$), we calculated for $a = 2$ and $a = 5$ the ARL$/a^2$ which is shown to be almost linear in $p(q)$. Explicitly, the computed figures are given by:

p	0.50	0.55	0.60	0.65	0.70	0.75	0.80	0.85	0.90	0.95	0.99	0.999
a=2	0.750	0.746	0.736	0.720	0.699	0.673	0.642	0.609	0.574	0.537	0.507	0.500
a=5	0.600	0.582	0.534	0.472	0.410	0.355	0.310	0.273	0.243	0.219	0.203	0.200

Of course, it is possible to perform such computations with great ease which we have done using MAPLEV and on which a number of plots were generated. These plots and computations are not included here for brevity's sake.

2.3. *The Range of Wiener Processes*

For Wiener processes, Imhof (1985) has calculated the probability generating function of the range process. There are a number of results which have been found by Vallois (1995) in particular regarding processes with drift and which are presented here as well. Let $\{w(t), t \geq 0\}$ be a Wiener process and let $\theta(a)$ be the first instant an amplitude a is reached. Then, the Laplace transform of this time is given by,

$$E(e^{-\lambda\theta(a)}) = \frac{1}{[ch(a\sqrt{\lambda/2})]^2}, \quad \lambda \geq 0. \tag{23}$$

As a result, the mean and the variance of this process are:

$$\text{ARL} = E(\theta(a)) = a^2, \quad \text{VRL} = \text{var}(\theta(a)) = a^4/12. \tag{24}$$

The proof of this proposition can be found in Imhof (1985).

2.4. *The Range of a Wiener Process with Drift*

A generalization to a Wiener process with drift is summarized below. Let $\alpha > 0$ be a drift parameter and let $\{B_t, t > 0\}$ be a Brownian motion whose origin is 0. The Brownian motion with drift is defined by

$$X_t = B_t + \alpha t, \qquad t \geq 0, \tag{25}$$

with range given by

$$R_t = \operatorname*{Max}_{u \leq t} X_u - \operatorname*{Min}_{u \leq t} X_u. \tag{26}$$

Then the Laplace transform of $\theta(a)$, the first instant the range reaches the amplitude a is given by:

$$E(e^{-\lambda\theta(a)}) = \frac{F(\alpha,\nu)}{[G(\alpha,\nu)]^2}, \quad \nu = -\alpha + \sqrt{\alpha^2 + 2\lambda}\,, \tag{27}$$

where

$$\begin{aligned} F(\alpha,\nu) &= \frac{2(\alpha+\nu)}{2\alpha+\nu}\Bigg[(e^{2\gamma}+1)(e^{2\gamma+\nu a}+e^{-\nu a}) \\ &\quad - 4e^{2\gamma} + 4\alpha\left(\frac{ch(\nu a)-1}{\nu}\right)e^{2\gamma}\Bigg] \end{aligned} \tag{28}$$

$$G(\alpha,\nu) = e^{2\gamma+\nu a} - e^{-\nu a}, \quad \gamma = \alpha a. \tag{29}$$

Further, this process' ARL and its VRL are given by:

$$\begin{aligned} \text{ARL} &= E(\theta(a)) = \frac{a^2}{2}\,\Phi(\gamma), \\ \Phi(\gamma) &= \frac{2}{\gamma}\left[\frac{e^{4\gamma}-1-2\gamma e^{2\gamma}}{(1-e^{2\gamma})^2}\right] - \frac{1}{\gamma^2}; \quad \frac{\partial\Phi(\gamma)}{\partial\gamma} < 0. \end{aligned} \tag{30}$$

Moreover,

$$\mathrm{VRL} = \frac{a^4}{12}\,\Lambda(\gamma) \tag{31}$$

$$\Lambda(\gamma) =$$

$$= 3\left[\frac{-4\gamma - 5 + 4e^{2\gamma}(4\gamma^3 + 6\gamma^2 + 2\gamma + 5) - 2e^{4\gamma}(8\gamma^4 + 24\gamma^2 + 15)}{\gamma^4(e^{2\gamma} - 1)^4}\right]. \tag{32}$$

For a proof see Vallois and Tapiero (1996b).

We note here the special feature which indicates that the ARL and the VRL are equal to a product of the ARLs (and the VRLs) for a Wiener process and a function of the product $\alpha a = \gamma$ only. Further, whenever the drift becomes infinitely small, the ARL and the VRL converge to the previous results of a Wiener process without drift.

2.5. *The Range Probability Distribution of a Random Walk*

Finally, we shall summarize below and without proof a most recent result calculated by Vallois (1995) which provides actually the probability distribution of the RL for an asymmetric random walk. Although it is a cumbersome expression it is treatable using numerical means and thus allows us to construct statistical tables for parametric tests of the range in random walks. Further research is required both in terms of applications yet to be devised as well as in the construction of tables based on this distribution.

Let p, be the probability of the random walk growth and let n be the test amplitude. Then the probability that the RRL(n) equals $n + k$ is given by the following:

$$P(R_a \leq n) = (2\sqrt{pq})^{a+1}(\Gamma_{n+1,a} - \Gamma_{n,a}), \tag{33}$$

where

$$\Gamma_{n,a} = \frac{1}{2n\lambda^{n/2}} \sum_{\substack{0<m<n/2 \\ \varepsilon=\pm 1}} \varepsilon^{a+1-n}\frac{2(\varepsilon\sqrt{\lambda})^n + (-1)^{m+1}(1+\lambda^n)}{(1-2\varepsilon\sqrt{pq}\,\cos(\xi_{n,m}))^2}$$

$$\times \cos^{a-1}(\xi_{n,m})\sin^2(\xi_{n,m})$$

$$\text{with } \xi_{n,m} = m\pi/n \text{ and } \lambda = q/p. \tag{34}$$

Further study of this expression and limit cases (applied to reliability of the range) can be found in Vallois and Tapiero (1996b).

3. Applications

The applications we consider are presented to augment the motivation on the range process and R/S analysis. Some of the results considered here are currently under study.

3.1. *The Hurst Exponent for Random Walks*

The Hurst exponent is currently attracting interest for the characterization of financial time series (to detect long run memory and the chaotic behavior of time series). Its origin are due to Hurst who began working on the Nile River Dam project in about 1907 and studied the random behavior of the dam's and the influx of water from rainfall. Some observations were made pointing out that if the series were random, the range would increase with the square root of time. This is confirmed by our analysis for the range of Wiener processes. In particular let a be a given range. The mean time needed to attain this range by a random (wiener process) series is $t = a^2/2$. In other words, the time needed to attain a range a will be proportional to the square root of time, that is, $a = \sqrt{2t}$. Hurst noted subsequently that most natural phenomena follow a biased random walk and sought to characterize this bias through a parameter H, which is the Hurst exponent. It is defined essentially through re-scaling the range into a dimensionless factor leading to the following observation (which has been verified in many situations and shown to be fairly robust):

$$\frac{R_T}{S_T} = (\alpha T)^H, \tag{35}$$

where T is time, H is the Hurst exponent, R is the range, S the standard deviation (both estimated using samples of length T) and finally α is a constant. In Hurst R/S analysis, the time series is subdivided in equal spans of time. The data are then transformed by eliminating any mean trend within the samples and dividing by the sample standard deviation.

A theoretical analysis of the Hurst exponent based on run length statistics of the range was developed in Tapiero and Vallois (1996). In particular, we prove that the Hurst exponent is 0.5 for a Wiener process while the exponent corresponding to finite sampling in random walks and Wiener processes with drift is also calculated. A modified exponent based on amplitude run length statistics is calculated by solving the following equation:

$$E\left[\frac{R_{\tilde{N}}}{S_{\tilde{N}}}\right] = E(\varepsilon\tilde{N})^H, \tag{36}$$

where $\tilde{N}$ is the random amount of time required to attain a range of specified size a while $R_{\tilde{N}} = a$. In order to calculate the standard deviation, note that the variance is proportional to time and therefore the standard deviation statistic is

$$\begin{aligned} S^2_{\tilde{N}} &= \text{var}\left(\sum_{i=1}^{\tilde{N}} y_i \Big/ (\tilde{N}-1)\right) \\ &= E_{\tilde{N}}\text{var}\left(\sum_{i=1}^{\tilde{N}} y_i \Big/ (\tilde{N}-1)\right) + \text{var}_{\tilde{N}} E\left(\sum_{i=1}^{\tilde{N}} y_i \Big/ (\tilde{N}-1)\right) \\ &= E_{\tilde{N}}\left(\frac{1}{(\tilde{N}-1)^2}\left(\sum_{i=1}^{\tilde{N}} i\right)\right) + \text{var}_{\tilde{N}}\left(\frac{\sum_{i=1}^{\tilde{N}} Ey_i}{\tilde{N}-1}\right) \\ &= E_{\tilde{N}}\left(\frac{\tilde{N}}{2(\tilde{N}-1)}\right) + \text{var}_{\tilde{N}}\left(\frac{\sum_{i=1}^{\tilde{N}} Ey_i}{\tilde{N}-1}\right) = \frac{1}{2}, \end{aligned} \tag{37}$$

where y_i are the ith record (taken at time i) taken from a Wiener process which has of course a zero mean and a variance of i. Therefore,

$$S_{\tilde{N}} = 1/(\sqrt{2}) \tag{38}$$

and thus we obtain the above equation.

A Taylor series approximation for the run length statistic, expanded around the Average Run Length (ARL) needed to attain the amplitude provides as well the following estimates:

$$\begin{aligned} (\tilde{N})^h &= (\text{ARL}_a)^h + h(\text{ARL}_a)^{h-1}[\tilde{N} - \text{ARL}_a] \\ &\quad + \frac{1}{2}\, h(h-1)(\text{ARL}_a)^{h-2}[\tilde{N} - \text{ARL}_a]^2. \end{aligned} \tag{39}$$

In expectation, we thus are able to show that $h = 0.5$ is the only solution of such an equality (for a Wiener process). By noting that $E(\tilde{N})^h$ is the Mellin transform of the run length distribution, its calculation (which has not to date been done) will provide an exact estimate for the Hurst exponent for random walks and for finite sampling in Wiener processes with and without drift.

3.2. *The Range Process and the Control of Quality*

The control of quality using x-bar charts for example, has emphasized primarily the control of processes based on the detection of mean process changes. CUSUM charts as well as EWMA charts provide a refinement of these schemes. Often, range charts are used to detect within samples' variation to confirm the "mean-testing" procedure. The control of variability (through sequential estimators of the variance or the range process) is not, usually, considered. The properties of the range process presented here, provide a departure point for the control of range variations. Let $\{x_n, n \geq 0\}$ be a stochastic process of the quality produced as a function of the quantity n produced on that system. For simplicity, assume that the process state increases or decreases by increments $\delta = 1$ only and $r = 0$. As a result we have a biased random walk which is defined by

$$x_{n+1} = x_n + \varepsilon_n, \qquad x_0 = 0 \tag{40}$$

with

$$\varepsilon_n = \begin{cases} +1 & \text{w.p. } p \\ -1 & \text{w.p. } q, \end{cases} \tag{41}$$

where ε_n are independent random variables with stationary growth probability p, the larger x_n the poorer the quality. We shall now make the assumption that the process cannot be observed continuously but change in the process amplitude are detected. If there is no trend (either decreasing or increasing the process, i.e. $p = q$ or $\lambda = 1$), the mean time to reach an amplitude a is of course $a(a+1)/2$. Now assume that we observe a sequence y_n of amplitudes after the production of the nth unit. Of course, if we note that the range growth is greater than expected under the hypothesis of $\lambda = 1$, then the estimated ARL $= y_n(y_n+1)/2$, will tend to be larger than n, the observed production unit. Thus we can construct a non-parameteric test based on the successive observation of y_n's. Explicitly, for a series of observations y_n define the following sign variable:

$$S_i = \begin{cases} +1 & \text{if } i < y_i(y_i+1)/2 \\ -1 & \text{if } i \geq y_i(y_i+1)/2. \end{cases} \tag{42}$$

Then we can state that if k consecutive signs are positive (meaning that the range is consistently underestimated), we can presume that the process is out of control. This implies of course that some attention will have to be given to investigate the causes of such a state. For example, say that at $n = 16$ and we observe an amplitude of 8. If the process were to be symmetric, such an amplitude would in the mean be observed at the $(8)(9)/2 = 36$th observation. While, in the mean, it corresponds to a process with λ equalling some values of between 0.3 and 0.35. As a result, we might be induced to believe that the process is out of control, or behaving unexpectedly. Generally, we can define the following statistic:

$$\tau(a) = \frac{t(a)}{\text{ARL}(a)}\,;$$

$$\text{ARL}(a) = \frac{1}{p(\lambda-1)}\left(\frac{(a+1)^2}{\lambda^{a+1}-1} - \frac{a^2}{\lambda^a-1} - \frac{1}{\lambda-1} + a\right) \text{ if } \lambda \neq 1, \tag{43}$$

where $\tau(a)$ is the amplitude (range) observed at time t and ARL(a) is equal to the expected time for such an amplitude to be observed under the assumption that the process has parameters (p, r, q). We construct the sign test:

$$S_t = \begin{cases} +1 \text{ if } \tau(a) < 1 \\ -1 \text{ if } \tau(a) \geq 1. \end{cases} \tag{44}$$

The sequence $(S_1, S_2, \ldots, S_t)$ can then be used to construct non-parametric (detection) test. These tests can be made parametric if we use directly the probability distribution of the range process however. For example, if "k" subsequent tests are equal to 1, then we can presume that the observed process has larger range than the presumed process with parameters (p, r, q). Such practice is commonly used in statistical control charts to detect mean changes. In such charts $k = 5$, meaning that the probability of such a sequence is $(0.5)^5$ is too small to be considered a regular sequence and thus may justify some further investigation. In our case, the distribution of the run length is not symmetric and thus the calculation of the probability of a sequence with k subsequent identical values (whether positive or negative) cannot be calculated as it is done usually. Additional tests can be constructed, based on the run length sequence probability. In the same manner, we can use the record of the standardized range $(\tau(a))$ and observe the evolution of observed and the expected run length required to attain a given amplitude. Such a test would be useful when the state of the random variable cannot be observed directly but its range (for some physical reasons) is observable. For example, if we consider the standardized random variable

$$\Delta(t, a) = \frac{[\tau(a) - \text{ARL}(a)]}{\sqrt{\text{VRL}(a)}} \tag{45}$$

and assume that this random variable is approximately normal, the sum of squares observed along a time series can be presumed to have a chi-square distribution which can be used for test and estimation purposes. Namely, the statistic

$$\sum_{i=1}^{T} \Delta^2(i, a_i) = \sum_{i=1}^{T} \frac{[i - \text{ARL}(a_i)]^2}{\text{VRL}(a_i)}, \tag{46}$$

where i is the time index and a_i is the amplitude observed at time i whose theoretical ARL and VRL are given by ARL(a_i) and VRL(a_i). For example, for a standard Wiener process, we will have:

$$\sum_{i=1}^{T} \Delta^2(i, a_i) = \sum_{i=1}^{T} \frac{[i - (a_i^2/2)]^2}{(a_i^4/12)} \approx \int_0^T \frac{1}{\sqrt{3}} [2(t/a^2(t) - 1)]^2 dt, \tag{47}$$

where $a(t)$ is the range sample path.

3.3. *Detection of Outliers*

The range process provide also a statistical foundation for testing outliers. If at a given time t the recorded amplitude a is larger than expected (i.e. at time t and amplitude a, $\tau_a < \text{ARL}(a)$ and remains the same for a certain number of time periods, we can presume that the first time which led to growth of the range is an outlier. If, however, the range keeps increasing over time while the signs are consistently positive, we can presume that there is no outlier and that the process has become increasingly unstable (i.e. with larger variations). To confirm that such a point was an outlier, we can proceed by eliminating the observation that led to the jump in the range at the candidate point and observe the behavior of the process without that point. Evidently, if the "deleted" series has a theoretically predictable range process, then the deleted value will indeed be the outlier. Although such an approach is intuitive, our theoretical results provide a statistical foundation for such claims. For example, by noting that the range and the standard deviation statistics (R_t^N, S_t^N) vary at different speed and with

$$S_t^N = \frac{\sqrt{\sum_{i=1}^{N}(x_{t-i} - \hat{x}_{t-i})^2}}{N-1}, \qquad \hat{x}_t = \frac{\sum_{i=1}^{N} x_{t-i}}{N}, \tag{48}$$

it is possible to devise detection schemes for outliers based on the samples ratios R_t^N / S_t^N. Of course, since the range process is far more sensitive to an outlier than the standard deviation process, as soon as the R/S ratio will be greater than a given test value calculated using the theoretical statistical properties of the range and standard deviation processes, we will be able to infer that the current value recorded is an outlier, or potentially a warning that the process has changed. Further study of such outliers and various detection schemes based on R/S analysis can be found in Vallois and Tapiero (1996b).

3.4. *Tests of Hypotheses Based on the Range Process*

Consider a process whose normal operation is characterized by a parameter set $\lambda = \lambda_0$ while a process out of control is characterized by the parameter set $\lambda \neq \lambda_0$. Assuming that is a statement of the ith hypothesis

$$\begin{cases} H_0 : \lambda = \lambda_0 \\ H_1 : \lambda \neq \lambda_1. \end{cases} \tag{49}$$

We can construct a test based on the specification of average run lengths under both the Null and the Alternative hypotheses and the sequence of ranges observed over time. Let α be the type I error of the hypothesis, then the amplitude test value n which will specify that the hypothesis is rejected with an error α is found by a solution of the following equation:

$$P(R_a \geq n) = 1 - P(R_a \leq n) = \alpha, \tag{50}$$

where the cumulative range distribution has a known functional form (as stated previously). Of course, following the standard procedures of Neyman–Pearson theory, we can construct a number of test on the amplitude

4. Conclusion

This paper has summarized basic and known results regarding the range process, some of which have been found by the authors. This field of study is particularly important in light of the increased interest given to the study of series volatility and is therefore complementary to the study of ARCH and GARCH models which emphasize standard deviation (or variance) estimators in non-stationary time series. A number of applications have also been indicated to provide further motivation for the study of such a process.

Acknowledgements

The authors are grateful to support from the CERESSEC and EU Contract ERB 4050PL930200 on Decision Support for Maintenance Management and Quality Control (Human Mobility Program, 1993–1995).

Appendix 1: Proof of Equation (17)

First, observe that $\theta(a)$ is a stopping time. Moreover, on $\{x_{\theta(a)} > 0\}$

$$\theta(a+1) - \theta(a) = \inf\{n \geq 0, x_{n+\theta(a)} - x_{\theta(a)} = 1 \text{ or } -a-1\}.$$

Using the fact that $\{x_n; 0 \leq n \leq \theta(a)\}$ is independent of $\{x_{n+\theta(a)} - x_{\theta(a)}; n \geq 0\}$, we have

$$E\left[(\theta(a+1) - \theta(a))1_{\{x_{\theta(a)}>0\}}\right] = P(x_{\theta(a)} > 0)E[T(-a-1,1)]$$

$$P(x_{\theta(a+1)} > 0, x_{\theta(a)} > 0) = P(x_{\theta(a)} > 0)P(x_{T(-a-1,1)} = 1).$$

By symmetry, on $\{x_{\theta(a)} < 0\}$,

$$\theta(a+1) - \theta(a) = \inf\{n \geq 0, x_{n+\theta(a)} - x_{\theta(a)} = -1 \text{ or } a+1\}.$$

Consequently,

$$E\left[(\theta(a+1) - \theta(a))1_{\{x_{\theta(a)}<0\}}\right] = P(x_{\theta(a)} < 0)E[T(-1,a+1)]$$

$$P(x_{\theta(a+1)} > 0, x_{\theta(a)} < 0) = P(x_{\theta(a)} < 0)P(x_{T(-1,a+1)} = a+1),$$

where

$$T(\alpha, \beta) = \inf\{n \geq 0, x_n = \alpha \text{ or } \beta\}$$

with $-\alpha$ and β being positive integers.

LEMMA 1. Let $a \geq 1$, then

$$P(x_{\theta(a)} > 0) = \begin{cases} \frac{\lambda-1}{(\lambda^a-1)(\lambda^{a+1}-1)} \left(a\lambda^a - \frac{\lambda^a-1}{\lambda-1}\right) & \text{if } \lambda \neq 1 \\ 1/2 & \text{if } \lambda = 1 \end{cases}$$

Proof. It is obvious that if $\lambda = 1$, $P(x_{\theta(a)} > 0) = 1/2$. We now assume that $\lambda \neq 1$. We check Lemma 1 by induction on $a \geq 1$. If $a = 1$, simple calculation shows that

$$P(x_{\theta(a)} > 0) = \sum_{n=1}^{\infty} r^{n-1} p = \frac{1}{\lambda + 1}.$$

By induction, we verify that this holds as well for the case of $a + 1$. We set $\gamma_a = P(x_{\theta(a)} > 0)$. Using successively these equations, we obtain:

$$\begin{aligned} P(x_{\theta(a+1)} > 0) &= P(x_{\theta(a)} > 0)P(x_{T(-a-1,1)} = 1) \\ &\quad + P(x_{\theta(a)} < 0)P(x_{T(-1,a+1)} = a + 1) \end{aligned}$$

$$\gamma_{a+1} = \frac{\lambda(\lambda^a - 1)}{\lambda^{a+2} - 1}\gamma_a + \frac{\lambda - 1}{\lambda^{a+2} - 1}.$$

Applying simple calculations, we prove the required formula. ∎

LEMMA 2. Assume that $a \geq 0$, then

$$E[\theta(a+1) - \theta(a)] = \frac{1}{p(\lambda - 1)}\left(\frac{(a+2)^2}{\lambda^{a+2} - 1} - \frac{2(a+1)^2}{\lambda^{a+1} - 1} + \frac{a^2}{\lambda^a - 1} + 1\right).$$

Proof. Using the previous relations and Lemma 1, we have:

$$\begin{aligned} &E[\theta(a+1) - \theta(a)] \\ &= \frac{1}{p(1-\lambda)}\left((1 - \rho_1)\left(a + 1 - (a+2)\frac{\lambda(\lambda^{a+1} - 1)}{\lambda^{a+2} - 1}\right)\right. \\ &\left.+ \rho_1\left(1 - \frac{(a+2)(\lambda - 1)\lambda^{a+1}}{\lambda^{a+2} - 1}\right)\right) = \frac{1}{p(\lambda - 1)}(\rho_2 + \rho_1\rho_3), \end{aligned}$$

where the parameters ρ_1, ρ_2, ρ_3 are given by the following:

$$\begin{aligned}
\rho_1 &= \gamma_a = \frac{\lambda - 1}{(\lambda^a - 1)(\lambda^{a+1} - 1)} \left(a\lambda^a - \frac{\lambda^a - 1}{\lambda - 1} \right) \\
&= \frac{a}{\lambda^a - 1} - \frac{a+1}{\lambda^{a+1} - 1} \\
\rho_2 &= a + 1 - \frac{(a+2)\lambda(\lambda^{a+1} - 1)}{\lambda^{a+2} - 1} = -1 + \frac{(a+2)(\lambda - 1)}{\lambda^{a+2} - 1} \\
\rho_3 &= -a + \frac{(a+2)\lambda(\lambda^a - 1)}{\lambda^{a+2} - 1} .
\end{aligned}$$

Moreover,

$$\begin{aligned}
\rho_1\rho_3 &= -\frac{a^2}{\lambda^a - 1} + \frac{a(a+1)}{\lambda^{a+1} - 1} + \frac{a(a+2)\lambda}{\lambda^{a+2} - 1} - (a+1)(a+2)\rho_4 \\
\rho_4 &= \frac{\lambda(\lambda^a - 1)}{(\lambda^{a+1} - 1)(\lambda^{a+2} - 1)} = -\frac{1}{\lambda^{a+1} - 1} + \frac{1 + \lambda}{(\lambda^{a+2} - 1)} .
\end{aligned}$$

The results follows immediately. ■

It is now easy to check the proposition by induction (where we have $\theta(0) = 0$).

References

Bollerslev, T., 1986, 'Generalized autoregresive conditional heteroskedasticity', *Journal of Econometrics*, 307–327.

Chow Y.S., H. Robbins, and D. Siegmund, 1971, *The Theory of Optimal Stopping*, New York: Dover Publications.

Daudin, J.J., 1995, 'Etude de l'amplitude d'une marche aléatoire de Bernoulli', *Recherche Opérationelle/Operations Research (RAIRO)*, forthcoming.

Dvoretzky, A. and P. Erdos, 1951, 'Some problems on random walk in space', *Second Berkeley Symp. Mth. Stat. and Prob.*, pp. 353–368.

Engle, R., 1987, 'Autoregressive conditional heteroskedasticity with estimates of the variance of U.K. inflation', *Econometrica* 55, 987–1008.

Feller, W., 1951, 'The asymptotic distribution of the range of sums of independent random variables', *Annals of Math. Stat.* 22, 427-432

Hurst, H.E., 1951, 'Long terms storage of reservoirs', *Transaction of the American Society of Civil Engineers* 770–808.

Imhoff, J.P., 1985, 'On the range of brownian motion and its inverse process', *Ann. Prob.* 13(3), 1011–1017.

Imhoff, J.P., 1992, 'A construction of the brownian motion path from BES (3) pieces', *Stochastic Processes and Applications* 43, 345–353.

Jain, N.C. and S. Orey, 1968, 'On the range of random walk', *Israel Journal of Mathematics* 6, 373–380.

Jain, N.C. and W.E. Pruitt, 1972, 'The range of random walk', *Sixth Berkeley Symp. Math. Stat. Prob.* 3, 31–50.

Burnside, C., M. Eichenbaum, and S. Rebelo, 1993, 'Labor hoarding and the business cycle', *Journal of Political Economy* 101, 245–273.

Chow, G.C., 1991, 'Dynamic optimization without dynamic programming', Econometric Research Program, Research Memorandum, No. 361, Princeton: Princeton University.

Chow, G.C., 1993a, 'Statistical estimation and testing of a real business cycle model', Econometric Research Program, Research Memorandum, No. 365, Princeton: Princeton University.

Chow, G.C., 1993b, 'Optimum control without solving the Bellman equation', *Journal of Economic Dynamics and Control* 17, 621–630.

Christiano, L.J., 1987, 'Dynamic properties of two approximate solutions to a particular growth model', Research Department Working Papers, No. 338, Federal Reserve Bank of Minneapolis.

Christiano, L.J., 1988, 'Why does inventory fluctuate so much?', *Journal of Monetary Economics* 21, 247–280.

Christiano, L.J. and M. Eichenbaum, 1992, 'Current real business cycle theories and aggregate labor market fluctuation', *American Economic Review* 82, 431–472.

Corana, A., M.C. Martini, and S. Ridella, 1987, 'Minimizing multimodal functions of continuous variables with the simulating annealing algorithm', *ACM Transactions on Mathematical Software* 13, 262–280.

Eichenbaum, M., 1991, 'Real business cycle theory: Wisdom or whimsy?', *Journal of Economic Dynamics and Control* 15, 607–626.

Goffe, W.L., G. Ferrier, and J. Rogers, 1991, 'Global optimization of statistical functions', in H.M. Amman, D.A. Belsley, and L.F. Pau (Eds), *Computational Economics and Econometrics*, Vol. 1, Dordrecht: Kluwer.

Hansen, G.H., 1985, 'Indivisible labor and business cycle', *Journal of Monetary Economics* 16, 309–327.

Hansen, L.P., 1982, 'Large sample properties of generalized methods of moments estimators', *Econometrica* 50, 1029–1054.

Hansen, L.P. and K.J. Singleton, 1982, 'Generalized instrument variables estimation of nonlinear rational expectations models', *Econometrica* 50, 1268–1286.

Newey, W.K. and K.D. West, 1987, 'A simple, positive semi-definite, heteroskedastcity and autocorrelation consistent covariance matrix', *Econometric* 55, 703–708.

King, R.G., C.I. Plosser, and S.T. Rebelo, 1988, 'Production, growth and business cycles I: The basic neo-classical model', *Journal of Monetary Economics* 21, 195–232.

Metropolis, N., Rosenbluth, A.W., Rosenbluth, M.N., Teller, A.M., and Teller, E., 1953, 'Equation of state calculation by fast computing machines', *The Journal of Chemical Physics* 21, 1087–1092.

Semmler, W., 1995, 'Solving nonlinear dynamic models by interative dynamic programming', *Computational Economics* 8, 127–154.

Semmler, W. and G. Gong, 1994, 'Estimating and evaluating equilibrium business cycle models', Working Papers Series, No. 56, Department of Economics, New School for Social Research.

Semmler, W. and G. Gong, 1996a, 'Estimating parameters of real business cycle models', *Journal of Economic Behavior and Organization*, 30.

Semmler, W. and G. Gong, 1996b, 'Estimating stochastic growth models: A comparison of different data sets', New School for Social Research, Memeo.

Singleton, K., 1988, 'Econometric issues in the analysis of equilibrium business cycle models', *Journal of Monetary Economics* 21, 361–386.

Taylor, J.B. and H. Uhlig, 1990, 'Solving nonlinear stochastic growth models: A comparison of alternative solution methods', *Journal of Business and Economic Statistics* 8(1), 1–17.

PART FIVE

Computational Methods
NETWORKING AND SOFTWARE

ALOK GUPTA, DALE O. STAHL, AND ANDREW B. WHINSTON

The Internet: A Future Tragedy of the Commons?*

ABSTRACT. In the future, data communication networks' interoperability will become critical from both technological and business strategy perspective. Significance of interoperability has to be evaluated in terms of the overall economic performance of the system. In this paper we present our view of the future of data communication networks, challenges in interoperability, and the economic challenges that will arise in this "real-time" economy. We provide insights derived from applying economic general equilibrium approach to these networks, e.g., the impact of competition and interoperability on the competing entities that own different parts of the network. We believe that potential excessive congestion is the single largest obstacle in the feasibility of a global, interoperable network. We discuss simulation experiments we have carried out to determine approximate priority prices in real-time and discuss the potential benefits in managing congestion through such a pricing scheme. We define a framework for policy research for an interoperable network which may facilitate electronic commerce. We also discuss the issues related to market structures such as monopoly, duopoly, and more competitive ownership of the parts of public data communication networks.

1. Introduction

A "tragedy of the commons" arises when a common resource is degraded by over use. Well-known examples are ocean fisheries, urban roads, air and water. Whenever a public good (or "bad" as in the case of road congestion) does not belong to some legal entity empowered to manage the resource through usage restrictions and/or fees, there are inadequate incentives for individual users to restrict usage to the socially optimal level. Consequently, the public good deteriorates (or the public bad swells), and the public suffers a loss relative to the potential social benefits of the commons.

Congestion on the Internet is a present and potentially paralyzing public bad. Today, Internet services include email, FTP, Telnet, IRC, Gopher, WWW,

* This research was funded in part by National Science Foundation grant #IRI-9005969 and #IRI-9225010, but does not necessarily reflect the views of the NSF. Partial support was also provided by the Texas Advanced Research Program.

H. Amman et al. (eds.), Computational Approaches to Economic Problems, 347–361.

and limited real-time audio/video services such as MBONE. The evolution of these services indicates a desire for a perfectly interoperable communication network where any kind of information can be digitized and then shared, transmitted, or stored. To some extent rapid and easier access tools that provide technical interoperability have been the key players in the growth rate of the Internet usage, which has been estimated to be at an approximate annual rate of 100%. With the advent of WWW access to information on the Internet has become easier and more user friendly – not to mention highly data intensive. The result of increased availability of user friendly interfaces and high speed of access coupled with higher awareness about these services has started creating serious congestion problems on the Internet. Consequently, the debate has started on the viability of a multi-service class, interoperable, data communication network in the long run. Several experts believe that there will be separate networks providing different services with little interoperability – even though the infrastructure elements, such as communication lines, may be the same. We believe that an interoperable network can indeed be supported and designed; however, it will require a substantially different network management perspective. In this paper we discuss the issues related to the very subsistence of a multi-service class, interoperable, network via a priority pricing scheme.

Let us first define the objective of a multi-service class network and our definition of interoperability – since there seems to be little consensus on that. The objective of an interoperable network is not simply to provide access to different forms of communication via a single interface, but also to provide the ability to customize a communication session according to need at any given time. The common definition of an interoperable network is a network which provides several services without any perceived deterioration in quality of any service, however, such a network may not ever be possible or even needed. In contrast, we define an interoperable network as a network providing several services with acceptable deterioration in service quality, for example, if at any given time full screen video conferencing is not available, users may choose to use smaller screen, audio only, or they may even delay their conference for an acceptable amount of time. We think the benefits of providing interoperability may far outweigh the degradation in service quality – if it is managed properly. In this paper, we use the words service quality and service requirement to mean the response time delivered or required for a particular service since once the data is digitized response time can cover practically all the aspects of service quality, for example video quality, audio clarity, and lag.

To deliver an appropriate service quality the most important factor is the bandwidth available to transmit and/or receive data. At present the Internet backbone is comprised of T1 and T3 lines with the data transmission speeds of 1.5 and 45 Mbps, respectively; this is orders of magnitude greater compared to a decade ago when almost the entire backbone was running at 56 kbps. In the next 5 years this increase in capacity may be increased to gigabit ranges. However, the number of servers and users both have increased enormously in the last 3 years and, as mentioned earlier, the services provided on the network have become much more data intensive. Therefore, congestion will be a growing problem; in fact, congestion is the main culprit which may foil the emergence of a global, interoperable, data communication network.

We are focusing on the issue of negative externalities in this paper in contrast to the much touted positive externalities. An interoperable network, by definition, has positive externalities. The users of this network have opportunities to use several different services in conjunction to customize their work environment. In many instances the value of usage is derived from the very fact that the users have access to other users of this network. However, overuse of the network to such an extent that it deteriorates service quality will generate offsetting negative externalities, since just being connected is of little value unless it can be used in a productive manner. A network with sufficient interconnectivity to exhaust all the potential positive externalities will still be susceptible to a tragedy of the commons due to negative externalities. In our modeling of the Internet the positive externalities are embedded in the value of the services; we then look at the effect of congestion.

The instinctive economic solution to a tragedy of the commons is to assign property rights. Hence, it might appear to some observers that the transfer of the NSF backbone to the private sector, being an assignment of property rights over network hardware, is the solution to the problem of congestion. However, this assignment of property rights falls short of solving the problem. Each owner of network infrastructure will seek a pricing structure that maximizes its profits subject to the pricing structure of competing network owners and the price-sensitive demands of users. The resulting non-cooperative pricing structures will not necessarily be (and generally will not be) socially optimal (Scotchmer 1985a, 1985b). This gives rise to an interoperability problem of a different kind, i.e., the problem of providing incentives to different entities to provide hardware/protocol interoperability. Note that this is not simply the question of standards but of economic incentives to design and implement standards.

An alternative approach to resolving congestion problems when private markets fail is price regulation or Pigouvian taxes. If a public entity has the necessary data on traffic and congestion, it could compute approximately optimal congestion tolls, and then impose them or levy a corresponding tax. Either way, this approach amounts to a restriction on the property rights of the network owners which must be given a legal grounding.

In Section 2 we present evidence that the Internet congestion problem is not merely theoretical nit-picking, but instead poses significant economic efficiency losses relative to the Gross Domestic Product. In Section 3, we survey our existing understanding of how a privately-owned and operated Internet might function and perform relative to the benchmark of a social optimum. In Section 4, we recommend a simulation modeling approach for policy research. Finally, in Section 5, we outline a recommendation for NSF's involvement in the continual growth of the Internet.

2. Magnitude of the Problem

Gupta et al. (1996b, 1996c) conducted a simulation study of the Internet to compare its performance under the current free-access policy and under optimal pricing. The model presented there is based on general equilibrium theory in economics, but departs from the Arrow–Debreu framework in a manner that makes the results computationally practical, it employs the concept of a "stochastic equilibrium" in which (i) average stochastic flow rates of price-sensitive service requests are optimal for each user given the prices and anticipated delay, and (ii) the anticipated delays are the correct ex-ante expected delays given the average flow rates. An optimal stochastic equilibrium is one which maximizes the net social benefits. We derive a formula that characterizes the priority prices that support an optimal stochastic equilibrium. These prices are optimal congestion tolls.[1]

This equilibrium concept and associated results have significant informational and computational advantages. First, it allows the decentralization of the resource allocation process to the user level and reduces the information required for the user's decision problem to current rental prices and current expected delays. The administrative and communication costs of distributing this information pales in comparison to the associated costs of billions of Arrow–Debreu contingency markets (or even spot auction markets). Secondly, prices can be adjusted in real-time such that they remain in a neighborhood of the theoretically optimal prices, furthermore this process can be decentralized. Again the computational and communication costs of this mechanism pales in comparison to that of fixed-point algorithms for Arrow–Debreu equilibrium prices. Although, it might be impossible to achieve exact optimal pricing in practice for a volatile environment such as the Internet, we have demonstrated that it is possible to compute near-optimal prices in real-time. As a result of this near-optimal pricing, users with different values for the same service will choose different ways or time to obtain the service. This, in turn, can provide substantial reduction in peak loads and will achieve better distribution of the load over time.

Computation of the optimal prices requires accurate information on the arrival rates and expected waiting times. We used an iterative approach where the current estimates of the prices are computed given the historical information on flow rates and waiting times. This iterative approach is implemented and analyzed by using simulation techniques where we estimate the prices using the transient information to guide the system towards a stochastic equilibrium. In the next subsection we present the simulation model which we used to estimate the prices and calculate the benefits.[2]

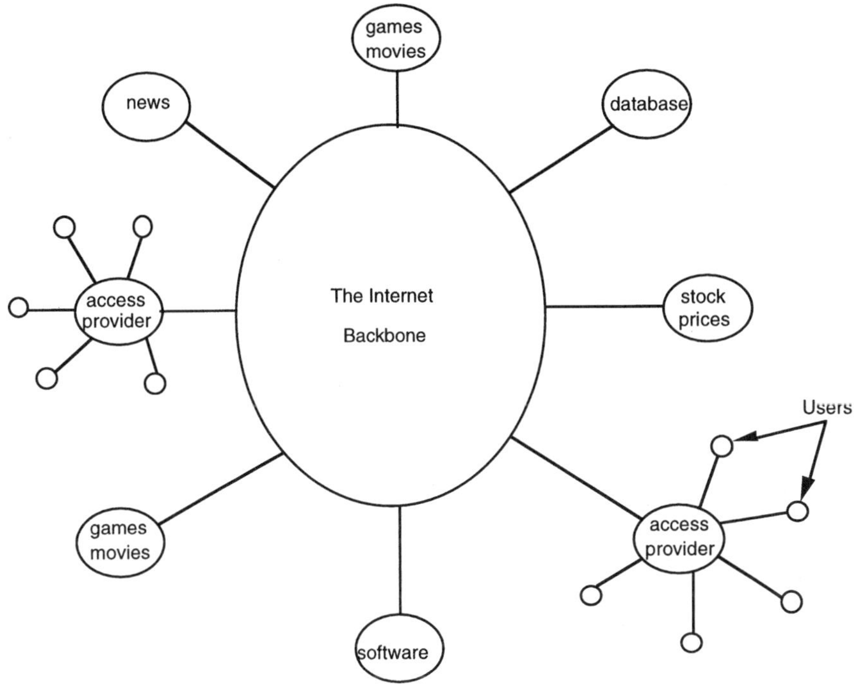

Fig. 1. A conceptual model of the Internet.

2.1. *The Simulation Model*

Figure 1 presents a conceptual model of the Internet. Essentially, we model the Internet infrastructure as a black-box, i.e., we aggregate the total delay at the server such that it appears that delay is only suffered at the server.[3] The users are connected to the Internet through some access providers (which can also be considered a service). The access providers and the service providers, e.g., news, movies, video-conferencing, databases, etc., are "directly" connected to the Internet through a data-pipeline of a certain capacity. In this model, the capacity of the data-pipeline is essentially the bottleneck for the service providers.[4] In the absence of any pricing mechanism as more users demand a service, the quality of the service (in terms of data transfer rates) suffers.[5] Furthermore, as congestion increases at the data-pipeline, the backbone also experiences more due to the resending of lost packets. The network service providers are able to monitor the loads at different servers, and they impose prices according to the load imposed by the servers on the backbone due to the congestion at their gateways. Since these prices are not estimated at the equilibrium conditions, they are approximate at any given time.[6]

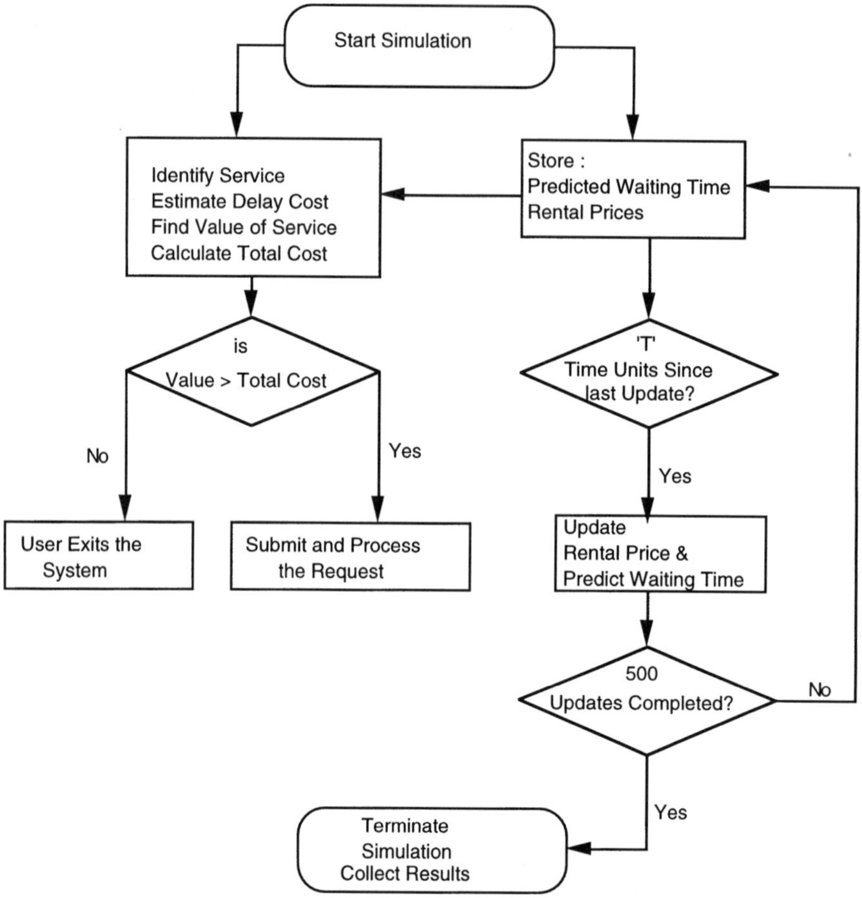

Fig. 2. Flow chart of the simulation model.

Figure 2 provides a flow diagram of the simulation model. The arrival rates to the system are price/cost sensitive; to explore the effect of demand scaling (from exogenous growth trends), we vary a parameter X_0. We can also interpret X_0 as the arrival rate to the system that would occur if there were free access and zero expected waiting times (i.e., the hypothetical uncongested arrival rate or the demand for network services). Note that realized arrivals into the system, being price and delay-sensitive, are always less than X_0.

Upon the arrival of a potential service request the type of service required is identified; a service is characterized by the amount of computational cycles required at a server. Then, the current estimates of prices and predicted waiting times are obtained for all the servers offering the particular service (and updated every T units of time). We generate user values and delay costs from normal distributions. The mean delay costs are set to be less than 1% of the mean job value. The user evaluates the total expected cost of this service in terms of her delay cost and the service cost against her value of the service. If the total cost of the service is higher than her value for the service the user quits the system; otherwise, she submits the request for obtaining the service.[7]

A user's request is sent to the server which was chosen as the least cost server. If the server queue is empty, the request is immediately processed; however, if some job requests exist in the server queue, then the requests are handled in a FIFO manner.

The results presented here are based on a model which has 50 servers and 100 services. A server can provide several of the 100 services, and a service can be provided on up to 25 servers. A service "directory" was determined randomly and fixed throughout the simulation run. The capacity of the data pipelines at the servers are generated through a random process to be among the following: (i) 128 kbps (kilobits per second), (ii) 256 kbps, (iii) 384 kbps, (iv) 1.544 Mbps (megabits per second), (v) 4.0 Mbps, and (vi) 10.0 Mbps. The first three choices here represent 2, 4, or 6 multiplexed ISDN (Integrated Services Digital Network) data channels respectively, the fourth choice is the capacity of a T1 line, and fifth and sixth choices are typical of those achieved via Framerelay or SMDS (Switched Multimegabit Data Services) connections. The size of each service is also randomly generated to be in the range of 10 Kb–15 Mb (or, 1.22 kilobytes–1.8 megabytes); the distribution is chosen such that there are higher number of smaller services to simulate a more realistic service request distribution. The mean size of service is 2.4 Mb. The service directory and the network configuration, in terms or service sizes and server capacities, were kept constant for all the results reported here.

We examine this system under a free access policy and optimal priority pricing. We compare these two pricing policies under different sets of load conditions by increasing the scaling parameter X_0. A higher X_0 induces more load on the system and helps in understanding the behavior of a network with fixed capacity under increasing load. Note that we consider fixed monthly charges as free access since there are no usage based charges. A misconception is that the time based connection charges are usage based charges, in data communication networks time based charges are poor indicator of actual network usage and have practically no "optimal" allocation capability. In fact, it can be argued that time based charges are a flat-rate pricing scheme where it does not matter how much actual network usage has taken place, for example charges would be the same whether 5 bytes are transferred in an hour or 15 megabytes.

2.2. *Simulation Results*

The results presented below involve two different information conditions.[8] First, the results for the free-access policy is based on perfect information regarding the waiting times.[9] However, providing perfect information in a realistic situation is not practical because of excessive cost involved in computing new information for every new request; furthermore, several requests can be submitted virtually at the same time making this waiting time information invalid even if it was financially possible to provide perfect information.

In the more realistic condition of imperfect condition, users would need to generate (or access) estimates of expected waiting times during the current period. Because stochastic queues have the property that the variance is at least as large as the mean, the task of generating accurate estimates from a finite amount of data in real-time is non-trivial. We have experimented with many statistical methods, and have had good results under the optimal pricing policy; however, the predictions under free-access at higher loads are sufficiently poor to result in negative net benefits. Therefore, to provide a conservative estimate of the cost of congestion, the reported net benefits from a free-access policy are based on perfect information.

The results for the optimal pricing policy are based on predicted waiting times instead of perfect information. In this case both prices and predicted waiting times are updated at the same time whereas in the former case only prices are updated after a fixed interval of time.

Table 1 displays net benefits and delay costs in dollars per month per server; these computations are based on calibrating the capacity cost according to the average cost of a T1 connection as follows. The current rental cost of a T1 line is about $1500 per month, which implies that the cost of a 2.45 megabit/second capacity (the average capacity of servers in our simulation) is about $2000 per month, or $0.00077 per second. The average job size in our simulation program was 2.4 Mb, so an average server would handle one job/sec. Thus, it is reasonable to assume that the mean value of a job is at least the cost of processing: i.e. $0.00077. In our simulation, the mean cost of delay was set to 0.008 times the mean value of a job (or only $0.022 per hour).[10] Table 1 compares the performance of a periodic update pricing case where delay information is not perfect with performance of free access with perfect information. This is an extremely conservative comparison, still pricing does significantly better than free access resulting in substantial gains. If we use the same information assumptions for free-access and optimal pricing, then the estimated Internet benefits of optimal pricing over free-access double.

To scale these per-server estimates to the U.S. Internet (last column), we multiplied by 250,000, as a conservative estimate of the number of servers on the Internet having an average capacity of an average server in our simulation.[11] Thus, we arrive at a conservative estimate of the potential efficiency loss in the order of $10 billion annually. Given the historical growth rate of the Internet (100%), the potential loss will exceed $100 billion annually by the year 1999 or sooner.

The results presented here are suggestive of the benefits of applying a near-optimal pricing scheme on the Internet. Essentially, without a pricing

TABLE 1

Estimated dollar benefits per month with perfect information for free access and periodic updates for pricing

Arrival Rate (X_0)	Benefits with prices (in $)	Benefits free access (in $)	Delay Cost with prices (in $)	Delay Cost free access (in $)	Internet Benefits (in $)
50	1749.3276	1338.9921	123.9569	639.0016	103 Million
100	2776.1812	630.6611	266.6029	1732.0273	536 Million
250	3881.9087	515.7304	1629.5195	2041.7187	842 Million
500	4401.1711	483.7473	3261.6245	2145.9051	979 Million

mechanism users with zero or low delay cost have nothing to discourage them from over utilizing the services; however, with a pricing mechanism they are forced to obtain only the services for which their value is higher than the cost. In addition they choose the appropriate service class dependent upon their service requirements. Service providers, on the other hand have incentives to provide multiple service classes because they can generate higher revenues and provide better service overall.

2.3. *Capacity Expansion*

An alternative to optimal congestion tolls is to increase the capacity of the Internet so no one experiences congestion. We believe that the arguments in favor of simply over-providing the capacity on the Internet are in error. There are physical and cost limitation of providing capacity, whereas on the application level the desire for additional capacity seems boundless. Furthermore, the future applications on the Internet will have inherently different quality of service requirements. Thus, it is essential that appropriate resource management techniques be developed and tested for a multi-service class network.

To explore the cost of this capacity-expansion approach within our simulation model, we set $X_0 = 250$ and incrementally increased the capacity of every server in proportion to the aggregate delay costs experienced at that server until the aggregate net benefits rose to the level obtainable with optimal pricing and the original capacity. The required increase in capacity was 4.274 times the original capacity. The current monthly rental cost of this capacity expansion is \$6550 compared with a benefit increase of \$3184 per server. Thus, it would be uneconomical to increase capacity enough to achieve the same net benefits that could be obtained from optimal pricing.

3. Private Market Outcomes and Policy Research

In the presence of externalities (such as congestion) it is well known that non-cooperative private market outcomes are not socially optimal. Further, given the interoperability requirements of the Internet, the number of network competitors will be finite and of non-negligible size. In other words, the classic assumption of many small price-taking suppliers will be far from holding. Instead, the Internet market will be better described as a game with a small number of strategic players. Further, the game has some characteristics of a Prisoners' Dilemma, which implies that the tragedy of the commons is not likely to be avoided by the non-cooperative outcome.

We know very little about how a privately owned Internet might function. The bulk of the theoretical results are confined to the unrealistic case of identical users, in which case two-part tariffs can support the social optimum. Intuitively, a monopolist who charges an access fee and a usage fee, since he can extract all the user surplus with the access fee, has the incentive to maximize that surplus by charging a usage fee equal to the optimal congestion toll (Oi 1971). Further, even if there are several (identical) network providers (and identical consumers), they will choose a usage fee equal to the optimal congestion toll (Scotchmer 1985b).

Unfortunately, these results vanish in the realistic case with heterogeneous users. For example, if users differ in how they value delays, then the social optimum will involve segregation of users by delay cost into subnetworks, but some of the subnetwork owners have incentives to upset this optimal segregation. It is not hard to construct simple examples for which there does not exist a "pure-strategy" non-cooperative equilibrium.[12]

To illustrate this point, we have formally studied a very similar model with two independent identical privately owned networks A and B, and two types of users that differ only by their delay cost. We assume that expected waiting times depend on aggregate demand according to the standard Poisson formula. The social optimum calls for segregation of the consumers: one type uses network A exclusively, while the other type uses B exclusively. Each network owner chooses an access fee and a usage fee. It turns out that the social optimum cannot be supported by a non-cooperative equilibrium. Even a constrained social optimum in which users are indifferent between A and B cannot be sustained as a non-cooperative equilibrium. Indeed, there exists no pure-strategy non-cooperative equilibrium.

For this overly-simple model, we can prove that there exists a stationary non-cooperative equilibrium in mixed (i.e. probabilistic) strategies. However, we are skeptical about the relevance of that game-theoretic "solution" in the real-world, especially since it is beyond our ability to compute this solution even without real-time constraints. Furthermore, in a more realistic dynamic setting, there are potentially countless other game-theoretic solutions that involve complex inter temporal strategies.

To understand the complexity of this game, consider what is involved in forecasting the network outcome given some fixed pricing structure. Taking a hypothetical assignment of users to various components of the network, what are the expected waiting times throughout the network? The expected waiting times are a function of the demand for services, which in turn depend on the expected waiting times. Thus, forecasting the expected waiting times involves the solution of a fixed point problem for each component of the network. But then given these expected waiting times, the users will choose the least cost alternative, so the tentatively assumed assignment of users is likely to be inconsistent with cost minimization. We need to solve another fixed point problem with the waiting time fixed point problem nested within just to solve for the network outcome at some fixed pricing structure.

Now the owners of the components need to consider alternative pricing structures, and for each alternative they need to solve the above two-level nested fixed point problem. A non-cooperative pricing equilibrium entails solving a higher level fixed point problem. Recognizing the rapid dynamic changing nature of the Internet, it is not clear that the players will converge to an equilibrium of the game before the game itself changes.

Formal game theory assumes that the payoff function that maps players' strategies to outcomes is given. But as we have just argued, the process that implicitly defines the payoff functions entails a two-level fixed point problem for each potential configuration of players' strategies. Thus, the real players will likely face considerable uncertainty about the payoff function, and will need to adopt statistical methods for revising their assessments.

On top of these problems, the organizational structure of the private Internet is complex. At the ground level, we have the phone lines, fiber optic cable, routers and servers. At the next level, we have service providers (data bases, shopping services, finances, etc.), and above this level, we have information brokers (such as AOL, Prodigy, and Microsoft). It is likely that the higher level brokerages will severely limit the ability of network entities to use access fees to extract surplus, in which case they will lack effective incentives to charge optimal congestion tolls.

In this environment, we may need an active public policy involving price regulation or Pigouvian taxes to avoid a tragedy of the commons. In the classic common resource situation, the imposition of a public fee (or tax) equaling the marginal social cost of use will avoid the tragedy. Such a fee is equivalent to optimal congestion tolls. The simulation results of Gupta, Stahl and Whinston strongly suggest that the computation of optimal taxes is feasible.

However, since the environment is so complex, the optimal policy is not obvious. We need to develop a model of the Internet that contains the essential and important characteristics of the Internet, which can serve as a test bed for conducting policy studies. Figure 3 graphically presents this model

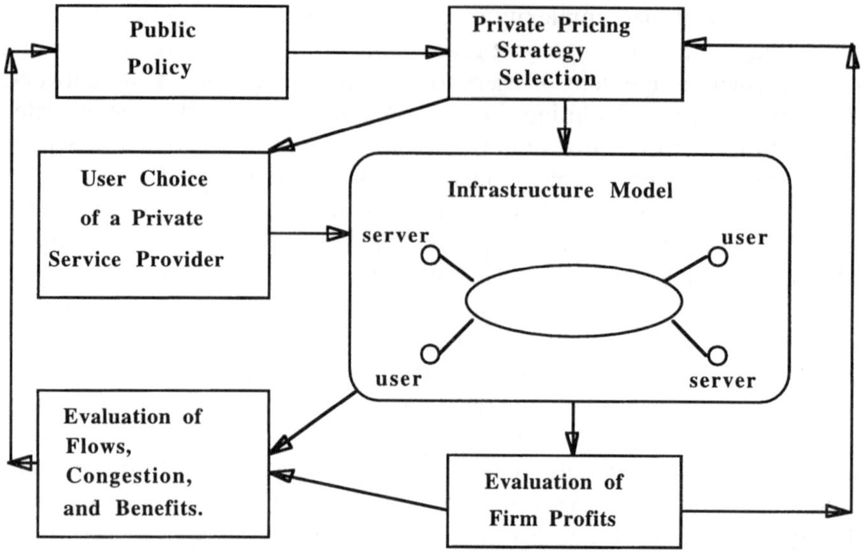

Fig. 3. A model of policy research.

and depicts the interaction among different entities involved in facilitating (debilitating) commercial Internet.

We will use this model to explore/analyze several key questions, for example: How will alternative regulations or taxes affect the industry structure, the pricing schemes, the pattern of use across service and user classes, congestion, social benefits, and investment incentives? Will the Internet become dominated by a few powerful players and if so will that favor efficiency? Will there be incentives for or against interconnection agreements? How desirable is a multi-service class, platform independent, interoperable network is, as compared to specialized networks for specialized services? What impact will competition have on potential service quality?

The economic stakes are sufficiently high so we can safely predict that considerable private research will be devoted to devising profitable strategies for the real game. As academics, we are interested in anticipating how the real players might behave, and what public policies should be adopted to protect the common resource aspect of the Internet. A central research agenda item would be to determine what (if any) dynamically stable strategies arise. Simulation is the only practical way to pursue this question.

During such simulation runs, profits, delay costs, net benefits and efficiency losses can be measured. Alternative public policies concerning price regulation, taxation, vertical and horizontal mergers can be incorporated into the model and simulation runs can be used to determine the impacts. Does the policy tend to stabilize or destabilize the system? Who are the winners and losers? Are capital investment incentives distorted or corrected?

A further promising methodological approach that would build on these simulation studies would be laboratory experimentation with human players. For example, a simulation program could be modified to take pricing decisions from a human subject for a specified subnetwork, and use boundedly rational strategies for the remainder of the network. Perhaps we would learn from the human behavior how to improve the performance of the simulated players, or perhaps the human subjects would learn more about the behavior of the system and the consequences of their actions. In the latter case, such a simulation/experimental platform could be valuable in the education and training of the players in the real game. Alternative experimental paradigms would include several human players, teams of players, and tournaments in which participants across the Internet could be invited to submit programmable strategies that would be entered in a multi-round tournament to see which strategies would emerge as winners.

4. SUMMARY

In this paper we summarize our earlier research which indicates that priority pricing can be effectively used to manage the traffic on the Internet. However, with rapid commercialization of the Internet several additional concerns and challenges are facing the researchers in management and economics. In particular, different parts of the public networks will be owned by different entities and there will be competing service providers providing similar services to users. Clearly, it is unlikely that all of them will use same pricing scheme; in fact, competition may force providers to not charge congestion tolls or subsidize them. It is a very complex task to evaluate the possibilities analytically. We tried to analyze a simple game with two providers with two types of customers to see if there is a solution to this game, however, there seems to be no analytic equilibrium to this game. In reality, there may be many big service providers (electronic departmental stores), and the possible pricing strategies may be complex, continuously evolving, and inherently dynamic. We propose a model which will incorporate learning models of pricing strategies and embed them with our simulation models to explore the possible pricing dynamics among competition.

Finally, if left unregulated, the pricing strategies which may emerge from above mentioned competition may force monopolistic market or a single multi-service class network may practically be not feasible. However, hastily drawn legislation with little understanding of its impact may end up providing the same results. Thus, it is imperative that public policies and regulations be tested for their impact before they are enforced. We plan to look at public policy issues with evolving pricing strategies to guide and shape the future regulatory policies to design, maintain, and sustain a public data communication network for electronic commerce.

Since we have little historical experience to go on, it is vitally important that we build as quickly as possible a knowledge base concerning ownership structure, strategic pricing, and policy effectiveness. The structural changes already unleashed by the privatization of the NSF backbone will create repercussions that we may forever be reacting to. Future policy decisions should be based on sound analysis and testing prior to implementation.

NOTES

1. Some other derivations of congestion tolls are provided by Mendelson and Whang (1990), MacKie-Mason and Varian (1995), and Shenker (1995).
2. The theoretical model and analytical results are presented in Gupta et al. (1996c), the simulation model is also discussed in detail there.
3. Delay within the backbone can be easily modeled as in Gupta et al. (1996a).
4. From the users' perspective, in reality, the bottleneck is either the server's pipeline or the slowest data communication link in their path to the server.
5. Note that some users might decide not to get the service because of excessive delays, however, users with negligible delay costs will try to obtain the service regardless of the delays. Thus, with no pricing mechanism the services can potentially be accessed by only the users who value it the least.
6. Very little is known about the performance and/or design of feedback mechanisms to control the processes in real-time. To our knowledge, our effort is the first systematic, theoretically supported, approach to such real-time problem solving. We have gained valuable insights and have developed several mechanisms for consistent predictions in real-time. The details of these approaches are beyond the scope of this paper and will be presented elsewhere.
7. Realistically, this work would be done by a smart agent executing on the user's machine.
8. More detailed results of this simulation study are presented in Gupta et al. (1996c).
9. Note that the perfect waiting time information scenario case is the "best-case" scenario for our implementation of the free access policy because users first check where can they get the fastest service and the information they get is exact.
10. Note that this figure for delay cost is probably too low by an order of magnitude. However, recalibrating delay cost to 10% of the mean value of a job (or $0.277 per hour) leaves the net benefits and reported in Table 1 essentially unchanged. On the other hand, a uniform rescaling of the value of a job and the delay cost would, of course, simply rescale all the numbers in Table 1 proportionally. Thus, Table 1 is conservative.
11. Conservatively, as of October 1994, there were 2.5 million servers on the Internet (source: MATRIX News); it is safe to assume that collectively 10% of those servers have a capacity equivalent to our server capacity.
12. Witness the phone company wars.

REFERENCES

Bohn, R., H.-W. Braun, and S. Wolff, 1994, 'Mitigating the coming Internet crunch: Multiple service levels via precedence', Technical Report, San Diego, Supercomputer Center, University of California at San Diego, ftp://ftp.sdsc.edu/pub/sdsc/anr/papers/precedence.ps.Z.

Gupta, A., D.O. Stahl, and A.B. Whinston, 1996a, 'An economic approach to network computing with priority classes', *Journal of Organizational Computing and Electronic Commerce* 6(1), 71–95.

Gupta, A., D.O. Stahl, and A.B. Whinston, 1996b, 'Pricing of services on The Internet', in W.W. Cooper, D. Gibson, F. Phillips, and S. Thore (Eds), *IMPACT: How IC2 Research Affects Public Policy and Business Markets*, Westport: Quorum Books, forthcoming.

Gupta, A., D.O. Stahl, and A.B. Whinston, 1996c, 'A stochastic equilibrium model of Internet pricing', *Journal of Economic Dynamics and Control*, forthcoming.

MacKie-Mason, J. and H. Varian, 1995, 'Pricing congestible network resources', *IEEE Journal of Selected Areas in Communications* 3, 32–51. Available from ftp://gopher.econ.lsa.umich.edu/pub/Papers/pricing-congestible.ps.Z.

Mendelson, H. and S. Whang, 1990, 'Optimal incentive-compatible priority pricing in the M/M/1 queue', *Operations Research* 38, 870–883.

Oi, W., 1971, 'A Disneyland dilemma: Two-part tariffs for a Mickey Mouse monopoly', *Quarterly J. of Econ.* 85, 79–96.

Scotchmer, S., 1985a, 'Profit-maximizing clubs', *J. of Public Economics* 27, 25–45.

Scotchmer, S., 1985b, 'Two-tier pricing of shared facilities in a free-entry equilibrium', *Rand J. of Econ.* 16, 456–472.

Shenker, S., 1995, 'Service models and pricing policies for an integrated services Internet', in B. Kahin and J. Keller (Eds), *Public Access to the Internet*, Cambridge, MA: MIT Press, forthcoming.

Stahl, D., 1992, 'Evolution of smart players', *Games and Economic Behavior* 5, 604–617.

HANS M. AMMAN AND DAVID A. KENDRICK

The DUALI/DUALPC Software for Optimal Control Models

ABSTRACT. The DUALI/DUALPC software is a system for solving quadratic-linear optimal control models. DUALI (which is pronounced "dual I") provides a graphical interface for both deterministic and stochastic models as well as solvers for deterministic models and for passive learning stochastic models. DUALPC provides a personal computer version of the DUAL software, which solves both deterministic and stochastic control models including adaptive (dual) stochastic control models. DUALI/DUALPC runs under Windows 95 and Windows NT.

1. Introduction

The DUALI/DUALPC software is a system for solving quadratic-linear optimal control models. DUALI (which is pronounced "dual I") provides a graphical interface for both deterministic and stochastic models as well as the solvers for deterministic models and for passive learning stochastic models. DUALPC provides a personal computer version of the DUAL software, which solves both deterministic and stochastic control models including adaptive (dual) stochastic control models. DUALI/DUALPC runs under Windows 95 and Windows NT on personal computers.

In this paper we introduce the DUALI/DUALPC system by providing a short history of past versions, a description of the present state of the software and a wish list for the future.

2. Past Software

The original DUAL software was a product of a research project which involved two electrical engineers (Edison Tse and Yaakov Bar-Shalom) and two economists (Alfred Norman and David Kendrick) in an effort to apply

H. Amman et al. (eds.), Computational Approaches to Economic Problems, 363–372.

engineering stochastic control methods to the modeling of dynamic stochastic economic systems. As one part of that project Norman and Kendrick separately coded in Fortran an adaptive control algorithm so that the two codes could be checked against one another for errors. Kendrick's version of the software which was completed around 1980 and given the name "DUAL" is the predecessor of the DUALI/DUALPC software which is discussed in this paper.

The DUAL software was developed on a CDC 6600 machine and was designed to solve deterministic as well as stochastic quadratic-linear optimal control models. The heart of the code was a set of procedures to solve certainty equivalence, passive learning and active learning control models using Kalman filter methods for updating state and parameter estimates. These procedures were embedded in a Monte Carlo procedure so that the three methods could be compared. The code included allowance for uncertainty in (1) initial conditions, (2) additive noises, (3) parameter uncertainty and (4) measurement noise.

The first substantial update of the DUAL code was done by Paul Coomes in 1984 when he ported the code to Fortran on the IBM 3081D mainframe. This was followed by a major rewriting of the code by Hans Amman in 1990 for the faster Fortran compilers of the day which also included provision for parallel processing on mainframes (Amman and Kendrick 1992).

Subsequently, the code was ported to Sun workstations and later to IBM and compatible personal computers. The personal computer version was given the name DUALPC and made available to users around 1992. This personal computer version of the DUAL code was limited to small models because of the fixed dimension in the Fortran code and the limited memory available in the personal computers of the time.

In parallel to Amman's efforts with DUALPC Kendrick began work on a C language version of the deterministic part of the code. This code slowly but surely evolved to provide a windows-based interface for the DUALPC code. Thus the new code was given the name DUALI for it role as an interface. Over time a number of the solution procedures from DUAL were ported from Fortran to C and added to DUALI until it contained deterministic procedures and passive learning stochastic control procedures complete with the Kalman filter and Monte Carlo methods. Memory management in the C language code and larger personal computer memory sizes meant that problems of substantial size could be solved with this code.

Meanwhile, Amman was updating the DUALPC code for the 32-bit environment of Windows 95 and Windows NT with virtual memory capabilities so that large active learning models could be solved on personal computers. Thus the DUAL software of the present now consists of Fortran versions for mainframes and workstations as well as personal computer versions with a windows interface.

3. PRESENT SOFTWARE

The present DUALI/DUALPC software moves the DUAL software a half-step forward by providing in DUALI a Windows-style interface and the deterministic and passive learning portions of the code written in the C language with internal memory management. Also, the adaptive learning portion of the code in DUALPC has been modified to run under the 32 bit version of Windows and to make use of virtual memory so that problems with substantial dimensions can be solved. In addition DUALPC has been ported to OS/2.

The software will be described here by first discussing the algorithms which are embodied in it. This will be followed by a description of the computer codes and the interface. Finally, there will be a discussion of the link between the DUALI and DUALPC components.

3.1. *Algorithms*

The DUALI/DUALPC software is designed to solve quadratic-linear deterministic and stochastic control models as discussed in Kendrick (1981) and as extended to problems with forward looking variables in Amman and Kendrick (1993, 1996b). Here we consider first the alternate functional forms for the criterion function and the system equations and then we discuss the treatment of forward-looking variables.

3.1.1. *Criterion Function*

The software supports two forms of the criterion function, namely the quadratic tracking function and the quadratic form. The quadratic tracking criterion contains desired paths for both state and control variables while the quadratic form does not explicitly contain these terms but does contain linear as well as quadratic terms and a cross term for states and controls. The quadratic tracking criterion is written

$$J = \frac{1}{2}(x_N - \tilde{x}_N)' W_N (x_N - \tilde{x}_N) + \frac{1}{2}\sum_{k=0}^{N-1}\{(x_k - \tilde{x}_k)' W_k (x_k - \tilde{x}_k) + (u_k - \tilde{u}_k)' \Lambda_k (u_k - \tilde{u}_k)\} \qquad (1)$$

and the quadratic form is written

$$J = \frac{1}{2} x_N' W_N x_N + x_N' x_n + \sum_{k=0}^{N-1}\left\{\frac{1}{2} x_k' W_k x_k + w_k' x_k + x_k' F_k u_k + \frac{1}{2} u_k' \Lambda_k u_k + \lambda_k' u_k\right\}, \qquad (2)$$

where x_k = state vector – an n vector; x_k = desired state vector – an n vector; u_k = control vector – an m vector; $\tilde{u}_k$ = desired control vector – an m vector; W_N = symmetric state variable penalty matrix at terminal period, N; W_k = symmetric state variable penalty matrix for period k ($k = 0$ thru $N-1$); w_N = linear state coefficient vector for period N; w_k = linear state coefficient vector for period k ($k = 0$ thru $N - 1$); Λ_k = symmetric control variable penalty matrix for period k ($k = 0$ thru $N-1$); λ_k = linear control coefficient vector for period k ($k = 0$ thru $N - 1$); F_k = coefficient matrix for the x–u cross term (the ability to input the F_k matrix has not yet been implemented as of 9/16/95).

DUALI supports both of these forms but DUALPC presently supports only the quadratic tracking function.

3.1.2. *System Equations*

The software supports two different forms for the system equations – the regular form which groups all variables for period $k+1$ on the left hand side of the systems equations and the "Pindyck" form which place some of the $k+1$ variables on each side of the systems equations.

The regular (or "I") form is normally written as

$$x_{k+1} = Ax_k + Bu_k + c_k, \quad k = 0, \ldots, N-1, \tag{3}$$

where A = state vector coefficient matrix ($n \times n$); B = control vector coefficient matrix ($n \times m$); c_k = exogenous vector for period k ($n \times 1$).

A slightly different version of the usual system equations (3) is used in DUALI. The modification is made to explicitly accommodate exogenous variables. This is done by replacing the exogenous vector c_k with a coefficient matrix C and a vector z_k of exogenous variables. Thus the system equations become

$$x_{k+1} = Ax_k + Bu_k + Cz_k, \quad k = 0, \ldots, N-1. \tag{4}$$

The typical structure of the C matrix is a first column which contains the constant terms from the system equations with the remainder of the matrix containing coefficients which multiply exogenous variables in the systems equations. Consistent with this structure, the z_k vector usually has a one in the first position followed by a column of the exogenous variables. Moreover, these exogenous variables are time-varying in most cases so the vector z_k is time-varying.

The Pindyck (or "I–A") form of the system equations used by Pindyck (1973) is more like a structural than a reduced form. It is written

$$x_{k+1} = A_0 x_{k+1} + A_1 x_k + B_1 u + k + C_1 z_k, \quad k = 0, \ldots, N-1. \tag{5}$$

These equations can be converted to the form (4) by inverting the $I - A_0$ matrix to obtain

$$A = (I - A_0)^{-1} A_1$$

$$B = (I - A_0)^{-1}B_1$$
$$C = (I - A_0)^{-1}C_1. \tag{6}$$

Thus the name I–A for the Pindyck form of the system equations. Note that this form requires that the matrix $I - A_0$ be invertible.

3.1.3. *Forward-Looking Variables*

The rational expectations models, viz. Sargent and Wallace (1975), make use of forward looking variables. This specification can be accommodated to a substantial extent in DUALI and DUALPC. Systems equation in the regular or I form with forward looking variables are written

$$x_{k+1} = Ax_k + Bu_k + Cz_k + D_1 x^e_{k+1|k} + D_2 x^e_{k+2|k}, \tag{7}$$

where $x^e_{k+1|k}$ = the expected value of the state variable at period $k + 1$ as projected from period k; D_1 = forward looking variable parameter matrix for the $k + 1 \mid k$ variables; D_2 = forward looking variables parameter matrix for $k + 2 \mid k$ variables.

In this example the maximum lead for the forward variables is two periods. If one is solving a deterministic model in DUALI the maximum lead can be set. Forward-looking variable capabilities are not yet implemented in the DUALPC code; however, the DUAL code which runs on workstations and mainframes permits specification of a lead of two periods.

System equations in the Pindyck or I–A form with forward variables are written

$$x_t = A_0 x_t + A_1 x_{t-1} + B_1 u_{t-1} + C_1 z_{t-1} + \hat{D}_1 x^e_{t|t-1} + \hat{D}_2 x^e_{t+1|t-1}. \tag{8}$$

This specification can be used in the DUALI code with deterministic models.

3.2. *Codes*

3.2.1. *DUALI*

DUALI Version 0.31 is compiled under Windows NT using Microsoft Visual C++ Version 4.0. The Microsoft Development Studio is used and the code is restricted to the C language. The C++ language is not used in the present version nor is the Microsoft Foundation Class employed. The version number of the DUALI code at 0.31 is still well short of 1.00. The code is in a state where it runs well enough to be used under rather close supervision by the authors. It can be used for student exercises and to do research work; but is not yet robust. The manual for DUALI is Amman and Kendrick (1996a).

In its present stage of development the DUALI software is a useful tool for

1. Developing small models with a few state and control variables and solving these models as deterministic models or as passive learning stochastic control models.

2. Obtaining repeated solutions to large models such as the Pindyck (1973) twenty-eight state variable model or the Fair (1984) small linear twenty-four state variable model. Penalty weights can be altered with facility and solutions obtained which can be cut and pasted into spreadsheets and plotted. The interface is sufficiently easy to use that it is practical to have classes of graduate students or perhaps upper level undergraduates do stabilization experiments with the models.
3. Creating small models with a variety of specifications such as models with system equations in different forms and models which do or do not have forward variables.

In contrast the present version of the DUALI software is not as useful a tool for

1. Inputting and then modifying the structure of a large models. Structural modification means changes such as altering the set of variables and equations which are in a model. Each time the model is altered it is necessary to re-enter the data since there are as yet no commands in DUALI such as “Add a Variable” or “Delete an Equation”. With small models re-entering the data is not such a task, but with large models it can be a time consuming chore. So if one wants to use DUALI for this purpose it is probably best to modify the model outside of DUALI. The matrices can be created in a spreadsheet and then transferred to an ascii file or can be created directly in an ascii file with an editor. This file in turn can be imported in DUALI using its import capabilities.
2. Solving adaptive stochastic control problems. This cannot be done in DUALI alone but can be done by using DUALI in combination with DUALPC as will be described below.

3.2.2. *DUALPC*

DUALPC Version 1.1 is written in Fortran and compiled with Microsoft Fortran Power Station 4.0 under Windows NT. It includes virtual memory management and can be used to solve adaptive control models with state, control and time period dimensions in the tens. The code also runs under OS/2. DUALPC and its predecessors have been in use for many year so it is robust and has been used to solve a substantial variety of stochastic control models. There is not a separate manual for DUALPC rather the DUAL manual for the workstation and mainframe version can be employed, i.e. Amman and Kendrick (1992).

3.3. *Interfaces*

The DUALI code employs a windows-style interface to facilitate the use of the code by both beginners and seasoned users. The user is asked to specify the dimensions of the model and then to provide acronyms for the variables. Also, a dialog box is used to elicit from the user the specification of the criterion function, systems equations and forward variables. This information is then used to request from the user only the particular matrices and vectors which are required for the specified model structure. Also, when a matrix input is requested a spreadsheet form appears with columns and rows labeled with the acronyms. This facilitates correct entry of the matrices and vectors.

One of our goals for the DUALI/DUALPC software has been to slowly but surely lower the entry cost for students and researchers to make use of quadratic-linear economic optimal control models. A step in this direction in taken in the DUALI software by asking the user to specify the model type as well as the functional forms. Thus if the user specifies that the model is deterministic with a tracking criterion function and regular system equations then only the data for (i) the W and Λ matrices in the criterion function, (ii) the A, B and C matrices in the systems equations and (iii) the vectors for the desired paths for the states and controls is requested. The user does not have to understand anything about stochastic specifications, measurement equations or forward variables in order to make effective use of the software. The aim is to hide as much as possible of the complexity of stochastic control models from novices user while making it fully available to seasoned users.

3.4. *DUALI to DUALPC Link*

The DUALPC software can be used either in conjunction with DUALI or in a stand-alone capacity. If DUALPC is used with DUALI the user can exploit the visual interface to enter the matrix data and/or to make changes in parameters on in penalty function weights. DUALI can then be used to write an ascii input file for DUALPC. Following this the problem can be solved by using the DUALPC software.

The experienced DUALPC user may want to by-pass DUALI altogether and use DUALPC directly to solve deterministic, passive learning and active learning versions of their models. In contrast, the newcomer to DUALPC may find it best to use DUALI first to solve some deterministic and then passive learning versions of the model before progressing to adaptive learning with DUALPC.

4. Future Software

4.1. *Near Term*

Our first priority for the DUALI/DUALPC software is to integrate DUALI and DUALPC so that DUALPC can be called directly as a solver from within the DUALI code. Thus it would not be necessary to write an ascii file from DUALI, exit from DUALI and then run DUALPC. Since DUALI and DUALPC are both in 32 bit code and run under Windows, we are hopeful that this integration of the C code in DUALI and the Fortran code in DUALPC can be accomplished in a relatively small amount of time.

Also, a number of changes are planned for the DUALI code in the near term. First among these is the development of a system for providing easy access to a number of example models such as those of Abel (1975), Pindyck (1973), Fair (1984), Sargent and Wallace (1975) and MacRae (1972). This system of examples is designed to lower entry cost for new users by enabling them to see how a variety of types of control theory models are specified in DUALI.

The next project for DUALI is to add the capability to do certainty equivalence (CE) solutions inside the Monte Carlo loop. Since OLF solutions are already programmed into this loop and since the Kalman filter code is already in place, this task should not take too much programming time. Once the CE capability is in place the user will be able to do Monte Carlo runs to compare the performance of CE and OLF solutions in DUALI before progressing to DUALPC in order to compare CE, OLF and adaptive learning (DUAL) solutions.

Another project is to develop the capability to add or delete a variable or an equation. This would enable users to make structural changes to large models within the code rather than having to make these modifications outside of DUALI and then re-import the model.

4.2. *Further in the Future*

Even in this day of integrated development environments for programmers, one can think of more improvements in thirty minutes than one can program in 300 days. However, we want to indicate a few of the things we are thinking about in order to have feedback from present and future users about which of our ideas should be given highest priority and what other ideas should be added to our list.

One of the problems with the present version of DUALI is that inputting large matrices is somewhat difficult. A relatively easy fix will help matters greatly. This is to change the scrolling so that the row and column labels remained fixed as the spreadsheet is scrolled. A more difficult fix is to speed up the scrolling speed. As has been demonstrated by Adam Anderson in his spreadsheet software component, this can be accomplished at a small cost by having only the active matrix element window in the spreadsheet be an edit window rather than having all of the matrix elements be edit windows.

If the integration of the C language code from DUALI and the Fortran language code from DUALPC does not go well then we might consider adding code for active learning into DUALI in the C language. This decision can be made after we have gained some experience with the integrated DUALI/DUALPC code.

We have also considered the possibility of adding export capabilities so that models in DUALI can be written as ascii files for importation into GAUSS or GAMS. Each of these software systems has some comparative advantages for certain types of research on optimal control models so it would be nice to be able to export to them.

5. Conclusions

The DUAL software which started life as Fortran code with fixed input formats on mainframes is now coming available on workstations and personal computers. In particular the personal computer version in the form of the DUALI/DUALPC software runs under Windows 95 and Windows NT. The DUALI component exploits the windows interface to lower somewhat the entry cost for new users and increase the efficiency of seasoned users. Also, it provides deterministic and passive learning solution methods within the DUALI code. The DUALPC code has been improved to include virtual memory. This combined with the high speed processors and large disk of modern PCs running Windows 95 or Windows NT enables users to solve adaptive control models of substantial size on personal computers.

References

Abel, Andrew B., 1975, 'A comparison of three control algorithms to the monetarist-fiscalist debate', *Annals of Economic and Social Measurement* 4(2), 239–252.

Amman, Hans M. and David A. Kendrick, 1992, 'A user's guide for DUAL, a program for quadratic-linear stochastic control problems', Technical Paper 90-4 (Revised August 1992, Center for Economic Research, The University of Texas, Austin, Texas 78712.

Amman, Hans M. and David A. Kendrick, 1993, 'Forward looking behavior and learning in stochastic Control', *The International Journal of Supercomputer Applications* 7(3), 201–211.

Amman, Hans M. and David A. Kendrick, 1996a, 'The DUALI/DUALPC software for optimal control models: User's guide', TP-92-03, Center for Applied Research in Economics, The University of Texas, Austin, Texas, September 1992, revised February 1996.

Amman, Hans M. and David A. Kendrick, 1996b, 'Forward looking variables in deterministic control', *Annals of Operations Research* 68, 141–160.

Fair, Ray C., 1984, *Specification, Estimation, and Analysis of Macroeconometric Models*, Cambridge, MA: Harvard University Press.

Kendrick, David A., 1981, *Stochastic Control for Economic Models*, New York: McGraw-Hill.

MacRae, Elizabeth Chase, 1972, 'Linear decision with experimentation', *Annals of Economic and Social Measurement* 1, 437–447.

Pindyck, Robert S., 1973, *Optimal Planning for Economic Stabilization*, Amsterdam: North-Holland.

Sargent, Thomas J. and Neil Wallace, 1975, "Rational' expectations, the optimal monetary instruments, and the optimal money supply rule', *Journal of Political Economy* 83(2), 241–254.

Advances in Computational Economics

1. A. Nagurney: *Network Economics.* A Variational Inequality Approach. 1993
ISBN 0-7923-9293-0
2. A.K. Duraiappah: *Global Warming and Economic Development.* A Holistic Approach to International Policy Co-operation and Co-ordination. 1993
ISBN 0-7923-2149-9
3. D.A. Belsley (ed.): *Computational Techniques for Econometrics and Economic Analysis.* 1993 ISBN 0-7923-2356-4
4. W.W. Cooper and A.B. Whinston (eds.): *New Directions in Computational Economics.* 1994 ISBN 0-7923-2539-7
5. M. Gilli (ed.): *Computational Economic Systems.* Models, Methods & Econometrics. 1996 ISBN 0-7923-3869-3
6. H. Amman, B. Rustem, A. Whinston (eds.): *Computational Approaches to Economic Problems.* 1997 ISBN 0-7923-4397-2

KLUWER ACADEMIC PUBLISHERS – DORDRECHT / BOSTON / LONDON